THE
TURBULENT
DECADE

———

THE
TURBULENT
DECADE

CONFRONTING
THE REFUGEE CRISES
OF THE 1990S

Sadako Ogata

FOREWORD BY KOFI ANNAN

W. W. NORTON & COMPANY
NEW YORK · LONDON

Source for all maps: UNHCR-Geographic Information and Mapping Unit.
Geographic Data from: Global Insight Digital Mapping © 1998 Europa Technologies
Ltd. Maps on pages 105, 133, 205, and 279 reprinted by permission of Oxford
University Press.
Disclaimer: The maps in this document do not imply the expression of any opinion
on the part of UNHCR concerning the legal status of any country, territory, city, or
area of its authorities or the delimitation of frontiers or boundaries.

For information about permission to reproduce selections from this book,
write to Permissions, W. W. Norton & Company, Inc., 500 Fifth Avenue,
New York, NY 10110

Manufacturing by R. R. Donnelley, Harrisonburg
Book design by Dana Sloan
Cartography by John McAusland
Production manager: Amanda Morrison

Library of Congress Cataloging-in-Publication Data

Ogata, Sadako N.
The turbulent decade : confronting the refugee crises of the 1990s / Sadako Ogata ;
foreword by Kofi Annan.— 1st ed.
p. cm.
Includes index.
ISBN 0-393-05773-9 (hardcover)
1. Office of the United Nations High Commissioner for Refugees. 2. Refugees.
3. Refugees—Services for. 4. Refugees—International cooperation. I. Title.
HV640.3.O45 2005
362.87′09′049—dc22
2004026998

W. W. Norton & Company, Inc.
500 Fifth Avenue, New York, N.Y. 10110
www.wwnorton.com

W. W. Norton & Company Ltd.
Castle House, 75/76 Wells Street, London W1T 3QT

2 3 4 5 6 7 8 9 0

To refugees and colleagues
who work with refugees

CONTENTS

MAPS

FOREWORD

BY KOFI A. ANNAN

S adako Ogata served as United Nations high commissioner for refugees during one of the most challenging periods in the history of the organization. The end of the cold war brought political change and an end to long-standing international conflicts, paving the way for the return of hundreds of thousands of refugees. At the same time, ethnic, tribal, and religious conflicts proliferated, in which population displacement was no longer a mere consequence of war, but often its very purpose. The result was massive disorder, from the disintegration of the former Yugoslavia to the genocide in Rwanda. The unprecedented challenges for the Office of UNHCR were compounded by the limited humanitarian and political means available to respond.

Against this backdrop, the provision of humanitarian assistance and the presence of aid workers on the ground quickly became a means of protecting communities ravaged by war. Increasingly, humanitarian workers had to carry out relief operations in the midst of internal conflict. Under Sadako Ogata's leadership, UNHCR developed a standby emergency response capacity and, for the first time in its history, conducted large-scale airlifts of food and other relief items, with the support of interested governments.

At the same time, determined not to allow relief efforts to become a humanitarian fig leaf or a substitute for meaningful political action, Sadako Ogata made strenuous efforts to engage member states in the search for lasting solutions to conflicts. She understood that what was required was a convergence of humanitarian, political, and security action among major international and regional powers. Those efforts

helped ensure recognition by member states of the link between finding solutions to population displacement and building a climate of
international peace and security.

This compelling memoir recounts the successes and failures of the
international community in responding to human catastrophe. It
illustrates the courage of refugees, the dedication of humanitarian aid
workers and the vision of a determined leader. It tells us that Sadako
Ogata left no stone unturned in her efforts to protect the world's dis-
possessed. At the same time, it reminds us that the challenges and
dilemmas of "the turbulent decade" still confront us today. May this
memoir serve as an enriching guide to our responses in the future.

ACKNOWLEDGMENTS

I am indebted to my UNHCR colleagues who worked with refugees during the turbulent decade of the 1990s. With a dedicated staff and a clear mandate to protect refugees, the organization operated at the front lines of humanitarian catastrophes. As the world moved from a tight bipolar order to a loose and fractured structure, interethnic, tribal, and separatist armed conflicts dominated the scene. This book is an eyewitness account of the global transition, with a focus on the very high human cost

I first wish to thank the Ford Foundation for inviting me to spend two years as scholar in residence after my retirement in order to assess and write my account of the preceding decade. Without the support and encouragement of Susan Beresford and her Ford colleagues, I would not have had the freedom to concentrate on research and writing. They were generous in providing both space and assistance. I am grateful to Jubin Goodarzi, who as research assistant, went through all my papers that had been entrusted to the UNHCR archives in Geneva and brought relevant materials to my attention, and to Kelly Greenhill, who prepared annotated bibliographies on publications that covered the subject matter under examination.

My close collaborators at UNHCR should be given special acknowledgment: Gerald Walzer (deputy high commissioner during a substantial period of my tenure), Francois Fouinat, Karen Abu Zayd, Kolude Doherty, Irene Khan, Wilbert van Hovell, Johan Cels, Chikako Saito, Shoko Shimozawa, Michelene Saunders-Gallemand, and all others in the High Commissioner's Executive Office. Special tribute goes to Sergio Vieira de Mello, Assistant High Commissioner, who inspired us all by his friendship and leadership and whose loss is sorely missed. I also wish to recognize several others—Ivan Sturm, Joel Boutroue, Kallu Kalumiya, and Eric Morris—for sharing with me their insights into the operations with which they were involved.

My deepest appreciation goes to Soren Jessen-Petersen, Nicholas Morris, and Filippo Grandi, not only for their outstanding contributions at headquarters and in field operations but also for reviewing the entire manuscript and providing useful comments both on facts and interpretations. Michael Doyle also reviewed the manuscript and gave me critical insights. Nik Gowing shared his valuable studies.

Thanks are extended to Jean-Yves Bouchardy for the maps, Ron Redmond and his colleagues for the photos, and Claudia Fletcher and Maki Shinohara for a range of administrative assistance.

Many at Norton have assisted me in putting my thoughts and materials into these pages. They followed me with patience as I meandered through restructuring and rewriting. I am especially grateful to Roby Harrington and Aaron Javsicas.

Last but not least, I wish to thank my husband, Shijuro, and my children, Atsushi and Akiko, for their understanding and encouragement. They remained supportive throughout my absence from home while I moved all over the world, assisting refugees.

Needless to say, none of the above-mentioned institutions or individuals bears responsibility for what I have written, but all of them helped develop the stories and improve them.

THE
TURBULENT
DECADE

	IRAQI KURDS	BALKANS
1988	Ali Hasan al-Majid ("Chemical Ali") leads military operation aimed at eliminating Iraqi Kurds.	
1989		
1990	Led by Saddam Hussein, the Iraqi government invades Kuwait.	
1991	U.S.-led coalition forces drive Iraqi forces out of Kuwait. The Iraqi forces' operation to suppress the uprising of Kurds in the north and Shiites in the south leads some 1.8 million Kurds to flee to Turkey and Iran. Coalition launches Operation Provide Comfort, establishing security zone in northern Iraq. UNHCR launches rehabilitation program for Kurds return to the north.	Fighting erupts in Croatia as Slovenia and Croatia declare independence from Yugoslavia. UNHCR begins humanitarian relief operation.
1992	Elections are held in Kurdish safe haven, but two main political parties, the Kurdish Democratic Party (KDP) and the Patriotic Union of Kurdistan (PUK), come out even. As a result, tensions emerge among the Kurds.	European Community recognizes the independence of Croatia, Slovenia, and Macedonia. Bosnia and Herzegovina proclaims independence. Serbia and Montenegro form Federal Republic of Yugoslavia, with Slobodan Milosevic as head of state. UNPROFOR deploys to Croatia and later to Bosnia and Herzegovina. Sarajevo airlift begins.
1993		Vance and Owen peace talks begin in Geneva. Airdrop operation expands to other besieged enclaves. Security Council declares Srebrenica, Sarajevo, Tuzla, Zepa, Gorazde, and Bihac safe areas.
1994	The two main Kurdish factions, the KDP and the PUK, begin battling each other.	Framework agreement signed for the establishment of federation between Bosnian Croats and Muslims.

GREAT LAKES REGION	AFGHANISTAN
Tutsi exiles, many of whom fled during the crisis in Rwanda leading up to its independence in 1962, form the RPF (Rwandan Patriotic Front) and attack Rwanda. Civil war ensues.	Soviet forces depart the year before, but the number of Afghan refugees reaches 6.2 million.
	Mohammed Najibullah government falls. Return of 1.6 million refugees.
Hutus and Tutsis in Rwanda sign power-sharing agreement in Arusha. UN forces (UNAMIR) are deployed to oversee the agreement. Assassination of Hutu president of Burundi in October prompts revenge killing of Tutsis in Rwanda, and refugee exodus begins.	Factions form coalition government, headed by President Burhanuddin Rabbani, but fighting continues.
Plane crash kills presidents of Rwanda and Burundi. Genocide starts with Hutu extremists in Rwanda attacking Tutsis and moderate Hutus. Within twenty-four hours, 250,000 Hutu refugees flee to Tanzania. More than 1 million Rwandans flood into Goma, eastern Zaire, in four days. Operation Turquoise launched, with French troops deployed to Rwanda and Zaire. Security rapidly deteriorates in eastern Zaire.	Taliban forces capture Kandahar.

	IRAQI KURDS	BALKANS
1995	The United States mediates a fragile cease-fire between the two Kurdish groups.	Srebrenica falls to Serb forces. Croatia launches Operation Storm, retakes Krajinas from the Serbs. Dayton Agreement ends the war in Bosnia.
1996	UNICEF reports that 4,500 children under the age of five are dying per month in Iraq as a result of hunger and disease. United States launches missiles against Iraqi posts in southern Iraq after Iraqi military crosses into Kurdish security zone.	NATO-led Implementation Force (IFOR) carries out demilitarization of Bosnia and Herzegovina. UNHCR is charged with repatriation of refugees and displaced persons.
1997	Local rebels invade "security zone" in northern Iraq. U.S., British, and French troops withdraw support. Flight of 75,000 Iraqis to Iran.	
1998	Iraqi officials expel UN arms inspectors, and the Security Council condemns Iraq. Voluntary repatriation of 10,000 Iraqis with UNHCR assistance, all returning to Kurdish-controlled northern Iraq.	UN Transitional Administration (UNTAES) leaves eastern Slavonia and the region returns to Croatian sovereignty. Fighting erupts in Kosovo between Yugoslav forces and Albanian separatists. The OSCE sends observers to Kosovo.
1999	The international community maintains economic sanctions against Iraq for the tenth year.	Talks collapse in Rambouillet, France. NATO launches air strikes on Yugoslavia, Major refugee outflow to Macedonia and Albania. Yugoslav security forces withdraw, and Kosovo Albanians return with NATO entering the province, but Serbs are displaced in turn. UNMIK administration established.

GREAT LAKES REGION	AFGHANISTAN
In the absence of deployment of international troops to separate the former soldiers, Zairean security forces are deployed to refugee camps in Zaire. Security Council adopts a resolution to investigate reports of military training and arms support to the former Rwandese armed forces (FAR) in Zaire.	Taliban capture Herat and advance to Kabul.
Security deteriorates in Masisi region, and thousands of Tutsis flee toward Goma. Refugees on the move, from Uvira to Bukavu and from Kibumba to Mugunga, fleeing attacks on camps. Security Council approves dispatch of multinational forces to eastern Zaire. Corridor opens during fighting in Goma, allowing 450,000 refugees to return to Rwanda while others flee southwest.	Taliban capture Jalalabad and Kabul. Najibullah captured and hanged. Fighting between Taliban and mujahideen in western and central Afghanistan.
Zairean rebel forces (AFDL) take Kinshasa. Mobutu Sese Seko overthrown. Humanitarian agencies pursue fleeing refugees into the Zaire rain forests. Refugees airlifted home from Tingi Tingi and other settlements.	Fighting continues in western, central, and northern Afghanistan. Taliban briefly capture northern city of Mazar-i-Sharif.
Civil war erupts in the neighboring Congo Republic. Civil war opens in Democratic Republic of the Congo with heavy involvement of neighboring countries. Burundi refugees flee to Tanzania. Tension grows between Burundi and Tanzania. Nelson Mandela appointed mediator.	
	Taliban take Mazar-i-Sharif. Number of internally displaced reaches 500,000.

	IRAQI KURDS	BALKANS
2000	The government attempts to "Arabize" Kurdish districts through "nationality correction," and thousands of Kurds who refuse to sign a form changing their nationality are expelled to northern Iraq.	Slobodan Milosevic ousted. Kostunica becomes president of FRY.
2001		Yugoslav forces enter the Kosovo buffer zone as NATO leaves the area. Conflict erupts in Macedonia. Former President Milosevic arrested and extradited to The Hague.
2002		
2003	U.S.-led Coalition forces take military action against Iraq. Saddam Hussein is overthrown, but the battle between Iraqi insurgents and coalition forces continues.	Serbian Prime Minister Zoran Djindjic killed in Belgrade.

GREAT LAKES REGION	AFGHANISTAN
	Worst drought hits Afghanistan, affecting millions as civil war continues.
	September 11 attacks prompt U.S.-led coalition forces to launch air strikes against Taliban and Al Qaeda. Taliban regime collapses, and Afghan exiles begin to return home. Bonn Agreement establishes an interim authority headed by Hamid Karzai. The ISAF deploys to Kabul.
Agreement reached to establish Democratic Republic of the Congo transitional government. Rwandan and Ugandan troops withdraw.	Coalition war continues in southeastern Afghanistan in an attempt to capture Osama Bin Laden. UNHCR launches a massive repatriation operation, assisting 1.8 million refugees and 400,000 internally displaced people to return home. Ethnic Pashtuns continue to flee the north, and drought-affected population remains displaced in large camps by the border with Pakistan. Karzai appointed by loya jirga as head of the Transitional Authority.
	Refugees continue to return, and much of the country normalized, but security deteriorates in parts of Afghanistan, with insurgent activities. The ICRC and UNHCR staff killed in the south. NATO takes over the ISAF.

1991	The Paris Agreements of October end twelve years of war in Cambodia; UNHCR begins assistance for repatriation. Apartheid ends in South Africa; UNCHR opens office in Johannesburg to help the return of South African exiles. Economic and social downturn prompts Albanian outflow to Italy.
1992	Following the collapse of the Soviet Union, ethnic tensions rise in the newly independent states. Ethnic and religious violence erupts in Georgia, Tajikistan, and North Caucasus (Nagorno-Karabakh).
1993	UNHCR completes the voluntary repatriation of 370,000 Cambodians.
1994	Russian requests UNHCR to assist the Chechen populations displaced as a result of conflict between the Russian forces and the separatist republic.
1995	UNHCR assists the return of 1.7 million Mozambican refugees from six neighboring countries following the peace agreement in 1992.
1996	UNHCR holds CIS conference to address the population movements in the former Soviet republics.
1997	A military coup in Sierra Leone forces more than 400,000 Sierra Leoneans to flee.
1999	A peace accord was signed to end the nearly decade-long civil war in Sierra Leone. More than 800,000 people flee violence in East Timor following the vote for independence from Indonesia. UNHCR completes repatriation of 42,000 Guatemalan refugees from Mexico, while 22,000 are given permanent settlement.
2000	War erupts again between Ethiopia and Eritrea. UNHCR expands program to assist Colombia with nearly two million internally displaced people resulting from internal conflict since 1985.

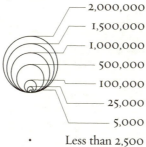

Populations of Concern
to UNHCR, 1999*
by Country of Asylum or Residence

Population size

2,000,000
1,500,000
1,000,000
500,000
100,000
25,000
5,000

· Less than 2,500

*Includes refugees, asylum-seekers, recently returned refugees, internally displaced persons (IDPs), recently returned IDPs and others of concern. Figures as of 31 December 1999.

Europe

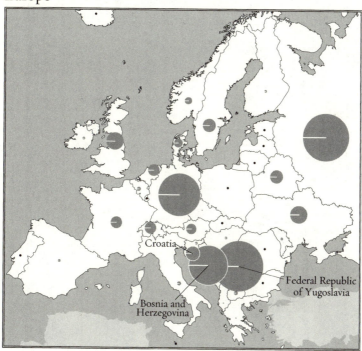

Croatia

Bosnia and
Herzegovina

Federal Republic
of Yugoslavia

Americas

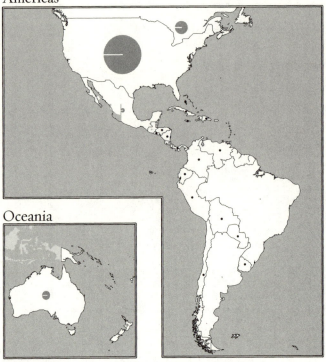

Oceania

Africa

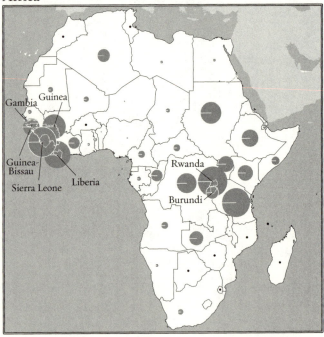

Gambia
Guinea
Guinea-Bissau
Sierra Leone
Liberia
Rwanda
Burundi

Georgia

Armenia

Azerbaijan

INTRODUCTION

I arrived in Geneva on February 17, 1991, to start my work as the United Nations high commissioner for refugees (UNHCR). It was the fortieth anniversary year of UNHCR. I was elected by the General Assembly to be the eighth high commissioner: the first woman, the first Japanese, and the first academic. I left the office ten years later, after observing the fiftieth anniversary of the office on December 14, 2000. In that half century the world had undergone enormous changes, and so had UNHCR. Those ten years were particularly marked by wars and massive outflows of refugees. At the same time, the end of the cold war brought numerous displaced people home. I had the privilege of steering the organization that stood on the humanitarian front lines with courageous and dedicated colleagues, day and night and through war and peace.

What led me to the post was a series of coincidences. I was a scholar of diplomatic history and political science who had specialized in analyzing foreign policy decision making. In this connection I had done some studies on the League of Nations at the time of Japan's military action in Manchuria, undertaken a comparative examination of the Japanese and United States normalization process with China, and written articles on various aspects of the United Nations. My direct participation in the deliberations of the UN General Assembly began in 1968, when I was invited to serve on the Japanese delegation. An alliance of women's organizations had negotiated with the Foreign Ministry an agreement to include a woman on the delegation at the time of Japan's entry into the United Nations in 1956. Senior lawyers and academics had served when suddenly there was an opening in

1968. I was tapped. With two small children, assuming this post was difficult from a family point of view, but my husband and parents encouraged me to go. They knew of my interest in international affairs and were confident that I could make a contribution. This marked the beginning of my involvement with the United Nations. Later I served as minister plenipotentiary at the Permanent Mission of Japan to the United Nations in New York for three and a half years. The whole family moved to New York. As a delegate I gained considerable experience in multilateral diplomacy.

The one direct exposure I had had to refugees was in 1979, when I led the Japanese government mission to plan and provide assistance to Cambodian refugees. I recall the shock and sympathy I felt for the refugees as I walked through the Thai-Cambodian border and visited UNHCR's Khao-i-Dang holding center. I also served on the UNICEF Executive Board for several years and on a few field trips in Asia learned the realities of children-based social development. Participating in the work of the Special Committee on Peacekeeping Operations of the General Assembly, I learned about the legal and operational problems relating to the work of the United Nations on peace and security, and I was privileged to have occasions to visit the peacekeeping forces deployed in the Golan Heights and in Cyprus. From 1982 to 1985 I was Japan's representative on the United Nations Commission on Human Rights, where I was exposed to the horrors of human rights violations. At the same time, I became familiar with the politics of human rights as played out in intergovernmental bodies. Through my varied involvement in the United Nations, I learned to look at the UN from two perspectives: the theater of the much-exposed conference diplomacy, by which delegates met to discuss common directions, and the operational activities that impacted on the real world of security and poverty. I valued the operations as meaningful contributions by UN organizations that actually made a large difference to people worldwide.

The occasion that led me to UNHCR was the sudden resignation of High Commissioner Thorvald Stoltenberg. At the time I was in Yangon, the capital of Myanmar, as the special rapporteur of the

Commission on Human Rights. The announcement surprised me because Stoltenberg had been in office for only ten months; he was leaving to become the foreign minister of Norway. Upon my return to Japan, another surprise was waiting for me. Many governments were vying to identify candidates. The Japanese government asked about my availability. I had never applied for any UN posts. I had a satisfying academic job and a family to enjoy. Although I had gone abroad on many short missions, I had never aspired to leave home. After considerable prodding, however, I agreed that if I became a serious candidate, I would consider it.

At the start there were more than fifteen or sixteen candidates who were lobbying fiercely. A little later I learned that the number was down to six. Still later I heard that I was among the two or three finalists. Then I received word from New York that Secretary-General Javier Pérez de Cúellar wished to meet me. By then I wanted the post. My banker husband traveled to Europe constantly, and our children were grown up. I had served for two years as the dean of the Department of Foreign Studies at Sophia University in Tokyo and felt ready to move. It was near Christmas 1990 when the secretary-general phoned to tell me he wished to present me to the General Assembly for election. With the endorsement of the General Assembly, life turned very hectic, as I quickly had to prepare myself for departure. It was toward the end of the academic year 1990, and I had to grade exams and papers and approve theses. I could not abandon students just because I was moving to another assignment. I finally left for Geneva in late February 1991, intending to serve the three-year remainder of my predecessor's term.

I found myself starting my tenure in the midst of the Gulf War. Large numbers of foreign workers had been evacuated out of the region, but no refugee outflow had taken place. While I was conscious that UNHCR might be facing an emergency, my first task was to deal with the protocol requirements of meeting officials inside and outside the office, the chairman of the UNHCR Executive Committee and the Geneva city authorities. In the second week after my arrival the secretary-general called the heads of UN agencies to New York to consult and coordinate the UN humanitarian operation in the gulf. I then spent a few weeks going through internal briefings by the five regional bureaus and the three functional departments of legal, personnel, and financial affairs. I must have asked a lot of questions because much of the content was new to me. I learned later that my reputation in the field was that UNHCR now had a new high commissioner who asked a lot of questions.

Soon I was to realize, however, that no amount of briefing could compensate for my direct exposure to outbreaks of refugee emergencies. In the fourth week, in mid-March, I faced three emergency situations. The first was a sudden increase in the number of Kurdish refugees fleeing to Iran and Turkey. Our task was to help prepare for their reception in Iran, by mobilizing goods and personnel for the establishment of large-scale camps. Soon I would have to become personally involved, but the immediate step was to make sure that the staff was getting into place quickly and that necessary resources would be mobilized.

The second emergency was the ever-deteriorating situation in Ethiopia. The signs of approaching famine had been prevalent for some time. Triggered by the spreading internal conflict in Somalia, people suddenly began to move. Some 200,000 Ethiopians who had previously taken refuge in Somalia began to repatriate, while 150,000 Somalis moved into Ethiopia to escape from the lack of security in their country. We had to make preparations to receive these inflows of people. We arranged for food, shelter, and transportation, then quickly assessed the financial needs and presented an $18 million emergency appeal to donors, asking for an immediate response. The Japanese government expressed its readiness to contribute $8.4 million. I felt encouraged by Japan's ready support. The Ethiopian situation was to move through series of emergencies with the fall of the oppressive leftist Mengistu regime, followed, however, by the successful victory of the liberation forces.

The third emergency grew when large numbers of Albanians on boats crossed the sea to Italy. The developments in and around Albania were indicative of the types of problems that confronted Europe and UNHCR. We had to take initiatives on two fronts: We had to convince the Italian government to abide by the principle of extending protection to asylum seekers and to help save these people, and we had to send a mission to the Albania government to persuade it to receive back those who volunteered to return without subjecting them to harsh punishment. The Albanian situation had worsened with acute economic and social downturns. We had to send emergency supplies by planes to Tirana and deploy staff to cover the situation. I learned later that some of the Albanians had decided to go to Italy because of what they had seen on television. They had been impressed with stories that dogs and cats were fed on silver plates and thought that human beings would certainly be treated better if they only went across the sea. The power of information, especially television images, was creating a dangerous pull. We recalled how information had brought down the iron curtain and eventually the Berlin Wall. The Albanian problem lingered, and the Italian government sent large-scale food aid for some time. Again, years later at the time of the Kosovo crisis, Italy became involved from a very early phase, reflecting its determination to prevent the problems that continued to exist between the two countries from getting out of hand.

After coping with those three emergency situations within a week, I wondered what lay ahead of me and my office. Douglas Stafford, the American deputy high commissioner, tried to encourage me. He told me, "You will face many emergencies from now on. But I can assure you that you will not have to deal with three new emergencies in the same week!" I might not have to deal with three new emergencies every week, but I certainly had to confront critical situations daily. I had to give attention and take action almost simultaneously on widely diverse issues. The world was undergoing enormous geopolitical changes without effective and up-to-date means to counteract them. The refugee problems symbolized the gap between the emerging challenges of the coming decade and the limited political and humanitarian mechanisms to respond. I realized that UNHCR had to be extra-resourceful to meet the challenges ahead.

The demise of the cold war, which started with the fall of the

Berlin Wall and the breakdown of the Communist regimes in the
Soviet Union and Eastern European states, accelerated political
changes and brought solutions to long-standing international confrontations. At the same time, the loosening grip of superpower domination resulted in the proliferation of civil and community-based
conflicts. Adventurous regional hegemons and longtime ethnic, tribal,
and religious rivalries began to hold sway. No effective formulas to
deal with uprisings dominated by nationalism and localism were yet
in view.

In December 1950 the Office of the United Nations High Commissioner for Refugees was created by the UN General Assembly as a
subsidiary body. UNHCR's core mandate was the protection and
assistance of refugees and the search for solutions to the problems of
refugees. The following year the United Nations Convention Relating to the Status of Refugees was adopted. Two of its most important
provisions were the definition of the term *refugee* (Article 1) and the
prohibition of expulsion or return (Article 33).[1] The establishment of
UNHCR and the adoption of the UN Refugee Convention in 1950
and 1951 provided a formal global structure to respond to the needs of
refugees and standards for their protection under international law.
While neither UNHCR's core mandate nor the principles upheld in
the convention underwent any revision, the environment in which
UNHCR worked and the activities it undertook changed significantly over the years.

The changes were noted first of all in the geographical coverage of
UNHCR's activity. From concentrating on the solution of the European refugee problem in the early years, UNHCR shifted its focus to
Africa, with assistance provided to the victims of the wars of national
liberation that engulfed the continent through the 1960s. Its role further expanded when refugee problems arose in the newly independent states in Asia, particularly on the Indian subcontinent, where
communal violence led to the partition and creation of two separate
states, causing the displacement of fourteen million people. In addition, the refugee flight from Indochina caused by anticolonial wars
and East-West confrontation had an impact far beyond Southeast

Asia as large numbers of refugees were resettled in Europe and the United States. The 1980s were characterized by heightened cold war and proxy wars in developing countries, notably in Mozambique, Afghanistan, and Central America, each of which produced many refugees. In addition to war, famine aggravated the human displacement in the Horn of Africa.

The world that I faced at the beginning of 1991 had just moved away from the rigidly controlled cold war structure. There were signs of new globalizing trends, with increasing movements of goods and people across borders. The loosening structure brought to the surface interethnic and separatist armed conflicts at regional and national levels. At the same time, the decade offered fresh opportunities for the return and reintegration of refugees. Improvements in the East-West climate created possibilities to bring long-standing conflicts to an end in the Horn and southern Africa, Cambodia, Central America, and Afghanistan. UNHCR had to grapple with two simultaneous challenges, one to protect refugees in the midst of internal wars and communal conflicts and the other to carry out the large-scale repatriation of refugees to still-insecure and unstable home countries. Moreover, it had to expand its operational coverage not only over refugees but also over a wide range of displaced and affected victims. From a humanitarian organization of the UN system with a clear focus on refugees, it had to lead and coordinate ever-growing humanitarian activities with a growing number of partners.

The breakup of the Soviet Union unleashed massive population movements in the countries that organized themselves to form the new Commonwealth of Independent States. The erection of new national boundaries left many Russians and others of diverse nationalities outside their homelands. Many of them tried to repatriate themselves to their original homes. In the course of the 1990s more than three million people were estimated to have arrived in the Russian Federation. UNHCR, in response to a Russian request, opened the first UN agency office in Moscow in September 1991 to extend legal and operational assistance to deal with the massive population movement. The predominant solution for refugees, migrants, and formerly deported people, all of whom the Russians labeled "forced migrants," was repatriation. Other CIS countries also faced large-scale population displacement and the migration of such people as the Crimean Tatars, Kazakhs, and Tajiks.

Interethnic and separatist conflicts grew in the southern Caucasus over Nagorno-Karabakh and the Georgian autonomous territories of Abkhazia and South Ossetia. In the northern Caucasus, Chechnya's declaration of independence in November 1991 led to a heavy Russian military offensive, resulting in the flowing out of 250,000 refugees to neighboring Russian republics. The Russian government requested UNHCR to provide humanitarian assistance to the displaced population. My travels took me to ten republics of the former Soviet Union and repeatedly to the Russian Federation.

UNHCR launched its first emergency operation in the Russian Federation in volatile Chechnya. Vincent Cochetel, a UNHCR staff member who was in charge of cross-border assistance to Chechnya, was kidnapped for eleven long months. We discreetly worked for his safe release, while providing assistance to all those displaced within Chechnya as well as in the neighboring republics. It was an excruciating ordeal for his family and his friends as well as my office. In November 1999, I went to Moscow and to Ingushetia and Chechnya to express our readiness to provide humanitarian assistance, while underscoring Secretary-General Kofi Annan's message to Prime Minister Vladimir Putin urging him to exercise restraint in the use of force toward civilians. With regard to the victims of the civil conflicts in Russia and the CIS countries, UNHCR faced continuous difficulties in trying to solve their problems through return and resettlement.

At the global level, however, successful repatriations of refugees were carried out, particularly in southern Africa, Asia, and Central America. The heightened cold war tensions and proxy wars had caused a massive displacement of populations in these continents. The climate of détente had a direct bearing on the solution of the problem of many refugees who had endured long exiles. In southern Africa, a major breakthrough followed the independence of Namibia in 1990. UNHCR's involvement in Namibian repatriation allowed us to help return South African political exiles from abroad. UNHCR opened what became the first UN office in Johannesburg in September 1991. On behalf of Secretary-General Pérez de Cuéllar, who was stepping down, I went to South Africa at the end of 1991 to head the UN delegation to the first multiparty conference known as Codessa. It was a momentous occasion, symbolizing change in South Africa.

A relationship of mutual confidence developed with the South African leaders and particularly with Nelson Mandela, strengthening the base of UNHCR's activities in southern Africa. It opened the way for the repatriation of South African refugees and political exiles from several neighboring countries. These developments in turn impacted favorably on Mozambique, where the return of 1.7 million refugees from six neighboring countries took place in 1994–1995. In the Horn of Africa, the fall of the Communist Mengistu regime in 1991 resulted in the repatriation of Ethiopian refugees from Eritrea and Somalia. But the long years of war and famine marred the return. There were enormous relief and rehabilitation needs while available assistance, whether short or long term, remained very limited.

In Indochina—Vietnam, Laos, and Cambodia—where wars of liberation had resulted in the victory of Communist forces, more than 3 million people had fled to neighboring countries. A complex and comprehensive solution to cope with the settlement of refugees had to be devised. The repatriation of Cambodian refugees from Thailand was carried out as an integral part of the 1991 Paris Peace Accord and the creation of the UN Transitional Authority in Cambodia (UNTAC) to oversee the process. UNHCR was responsible for coordinating the repatriation of more than 360,000 people from March 1992 to May 1993 in time for them to register and vote in May elections to set up the Cambodian government. I attended the closing of border camps in Thailand, waved off the refugees returning home on trucks and trains, and visited Cambodia to support the operations. Led and coordinated by Sergio Vieira de Mello, the UNHCR special envoy, Cambodia provided the testing ground for a comprehensive repatriation and reintegration operation under the overall responsibility of the United Nations. I thought of the refugees I had seen in 1979 at the Thai border and wondered where they were, back home or somewhere overseas.

As for the settlement of the Vietnamese boat people who had flooded the Southeast Asian countries, an international consensus had been reached at the 1989 Geneva Conference to seek a solution by linking asylum with legal migration in what was known as the Comprehensive Plan of Action. UNHCR was tasked to implement the process but faced enormous difficulties. The process that determined refugee status did not function properly in many Southeast Asian countries, and the voluntary return of rejected cases made no progress. We faced tensions in the Vietnamese camps and frequent outbreaks of violence in the Hong Kong camps. The key to the solution proved to be the country of origin, Vietnam, which made efforts to halt illegal departures and allowed the exits of those with proper claims. A combination of establishing legal migration and providing assistance to the returnees contributed to bringing to an end the saga of Indochina's refugees.

In Central America the end of the cold war brought new opportunities for solving the refugee problems. Central America in the 1980s was the scene of mass human displacement resulting from three separate civil wars in Nicaragua, El Salvador, and Guatemala. Two million people were uprooted and displaced in neighboring countries in Central or North American countries. The conflicts had been caused by violent struggles between the landless poor, demanding social and agrarian reform, and the landowning elites, supported by right-wing governments and the military. The rebel movements were influenced and supported by the Communist regime in Cuba. The United States, on the other hand, supported right-wing governments in order to prevent the spread of communism and to safeguard their economic interests.

UNHCR faced two major obstacles in its effort to protect and assist people in Central America affected by heightened cold war tensions and proxy wars. The first was the situation of the displaced population. Of the many who had fled their countries, only a limited number were recognized as refugees by the receiving countries in the region, while the majority either did not have the opportunity to apply for refugee status or did not seek it in fear of deportation. UNHCR was therefore deprived of access to a large number of people in need. The second obstacle was the mixture of refugees with the armed opposition guerrillas in the camps in Honduras and Mexico. UNHCR's efforts to maintain a clear division between the refugee communities and the armed groups were thwarted, especially when the host Honduras government was in support of the contras or the Salvadoran military regime.

However, reflecting the changed post–cold war environment, peace agreements were reached in Central America in the early 1990s. UNHCR's main operations in the region then turned to repatriation. The United Nations played an active role not only in mediating peace between the conflicting parties but also in establishing observer missions to ensure the process. The UN Observer Mission in El Salvador (ONUSAL) and the UN Verification Mission in Guatemala (MINUGUA) addressed issues of promoting justice and human rights as well as questions of land distribution and strengthened local institutions. The return and reintegration of refugees and displaced persons contributed to the peace and nation-building process of the region.

As for me, I was particularly pleased with the occasion to attend a refugee camp–closing event in Mexico in 1999. Between 1984 and 1999 some forty-two thousand refugees had been repatriated to Guatemala. President Ernesto Zedillo of Mexico and President Alvaro Arzú of Guatemala decided to observe jointly a special event of closing the camp in Santa Domingo Kaste, Mexico, and sending the last group of refugees home. Those who decided to stay in Mexico were given citizenship and welcomed to continue their productive lives of farming. Rarely could such a satisfactory solution be reached for all concerned. In the case of the Guatemala refugees, the situation back home had improved considerably, and the government expressed its commitment to honor their rights. Mexico had favorable citizenship laws and had vast territory to give to the new citizens. I wished that there were more occasions when UNHCR could give options from which to choose their future to refugees.

Problems of asylum were also rampant in the 1990s. Particularly in the Caribbean region, the movement of migrants and asylum seekers from Haiti and Cuba faced diverse responses from the United States. For several decades the interdiction of Haitians at sea had been a source of grave contention between the U.S. government and UNHCR, humanitarian organizations, and advocacy groups. Haitians were viewed as economic migrants fleeing a harsh but non-Communist government in contrast with Cubans, who were recognized as refugees under persecution. The number of Haitian boat people shot up again in 1994, and the top of the agenda at my first meeting with President Bill Clinton on May 12, 1994, was their treatment. The president asked UNHCR's cooperation in devising an internationally credible system of refugee treatment. Both sides nominated special representatives to deal with the solution of the problem. The *Washington Post* headlined the consultation as UN ASSISTS US. A new and full refugee determination procedure on board the USS *Comfort* was proposed. This arrangement resulted in some Haitians' being granted asylum and resettled in the United States. However, it did not last long because the numbers awaiting interviews grew too rapidly, and many wound up being taken to Guantanamo. Because of continuing political instability in Haiti and the proximity of affluent America across the sea, the mixed Haitian migration and asylum-seeking issue persisted through the decade and even beyond.

There were numerous humanitarian situations that deserve careful description and analyses. There were many instances of hope and despair that flash back in my mind. In writing this book, however, I have decided to concentrate on four critical situations. Northern Iraq, the Balkans, the African Great Lakes region, and Afghanistan have been selected not only because of the scale of the refugee outflow and the complexity of the population movement but also because of the strategic interests of the international and regional governments.

Above all, these cases reveal the complex interplay between political, military, and humanitarian actors in the ongoing refugee crises of the 1990s.

I have been often quoted as having stated, "there are no humanitarian solutions to humanitarian problems." What I wanted to emphasize was that refugee problems are essentially political in origin and therefore have to be addressed through political action. Humanitarian action may create space for political action but on its own can never substitute for it. However, since most refugees in the 1990s were caught in internal conflicts of ethnic cleansing, genocide, and militarized camps and settlements, solutions to their problem required decisive intervention by leading international and regional states or by the UN Security Council. The intervening states were rarely willing, if not afraid, to become parties to the internal conflicts. Refugee crises alone did not evoke military involvement. I made strenuous efforts to urge the more involved states and the political organs of the United Nations to become more engaged in settling humanitarian crises. Following the painful lessons of the African Great Lakes region, UNHCR introduced the ladder of options concept as a means of addressing the different types and degree of lack of security that arise in refugee populated areas.

UNHCR activities turned more proactive and holistic as the refugee outflows became massive and mixed with sizable numbers of internally displaced persons and affected civilians. UNHCR coordinated large-scale relief operations. The provision of relief was an important means of protecting the people and had to be carried out in accordance with the humanitarian principles of neutrality and impartiality to all victims in need. On the basis of the experiences of the Balkan conflicts, UNHCR also focused on developing better means of coping with the repatriation of refugees after mass atrocities and called on the development agencies to join forces to fill the assistance gap that usually followed emergency operations. We sought as well ways to rebuild communities through cultivating coexistence among returning populations.

Humanitarian assistance ameliorated suffering or served to bridge the victims over periods of time but on its own could not reach solutions. Occasionally humanitarian activities were accused of prolonging conflicts, yet it was unrealistic to believe that the assistance to tens of thousands of people could be terminated without the arrival of peace and political settlements. My "no humanitarian solutions to humanitarian problems" statement was an expression of frustration, never meant to be a call for no action.

1.

THE KURDISH
REFUGEE CRISIS:
SETTING THE STAGE

The Gulf War of 1991 was a major watershed in the development of multilateral diplomacy and humanitarian action that set the stage for the post–cold war period of the 1990s. Around 4 million people were displaced in the twelve months following Iraq's invasion of Kuwait in August 1990. In the next few months more than 1 million migrant workers and other foreign nationals were evacuated from Iraq and Kuwait to Jordan and other neighboring countries and eventually helped back to their countries. Some 850,000 Yemenis living in Saudi Arabia also streamed back to their homeland. The United Nations Security Council demanded Iraqi withdrawal from Kuwait, but failing to obtain compliance, the council authorized the use of force to end the Iraqi occupation. Led by the United States, Operation Desert Storm liberated Kuwait. It was, however, in the aftermath of the Gulf War that revolts broke out in the Shia and Kurdish areas of Iraq, and refugee outflows came to dominate the Middle East scene.

The Shia rebellion in the south was crushed by the Iraqi forces that had quickly recovered from the defeat in Kuwait. Some 70,000 refugees fled to Iran, and another 30,000 went to the southern tip of Iraq and sought protection from the coalition forces. In the north the

Kurdish uprising was suppressed by strong Iraqi military inroads and provoked one of the largest and fastest refugee outflows. By mid-May 1.3 million Kurds had fled to Iran, and more than 450,000 toward Turkey. In this period 500 to 2,000 Kurds were reported to have perished daily.

During the 1991 uprisings and suppression in Iraq the coalition forces did not intervene. With regard to the Shia rebellion, they remained ambivalent to any idea of establishing a safe haven, as proposed by some Iraqi opposition groups. Even afterward, during the winter of 1991–1992, when there was evidence that the southern marshes were being drained by the Iraqi authorities to flush out the opposition, no action was taken by the coalition forces. Their approach stayed minimalist, limited to adopting the policy of imposing a no-fly zone for Iraqi aircraft over the south. The United States was disinclined to overthrow Saddam Hussein because it feared the emergence of a pro-Iran Shia government in Baghdad.

In the Kurdish north, however, the massive refugee outflow had serious humanitarian consequences and prompted strong political response. The Security Council on April 5, 1991, adopted Resolution 688, which condemned the consequences of the repression of the Iraqi civilian population as threatening international peace and security and insisted that Iraq "allow immediate access by international humanitarian organizations to all those in need of assistance in all parts of Iraq and make available all necessary facilities for their operations." The secretary-general was to use all the resources at his disposal to address urgently the critical needs of the refugees and displaced Iraqi people.[1] In short, the resolution drew a distinction between the Iraqi government and the people and called for humanitarian intervention.

The assistance required by Iran for receiving the Kurdish refugees was massive, but with concerted international support the situation was brought under control. Along the Turkish border the fate of the refugees turned catastrophic because the Turkish government, which itself faced a significant Kurdish insurrection, attempted to block their entry at the border. The coalition member states, committed to maintain the use of Turkish air bases for NATO, were mute in response to

Turkey's refusal to grant asylum. The televised images of desperate Kurds trapped in the Iraqi-Turkish mountain range pressed the U.S.-led forces to intervene in northern Iraq to establish a security zone. To them the solution was to prompt a quick return home of the Kurds.

UNHCR Operations in Iraq, through November 1991

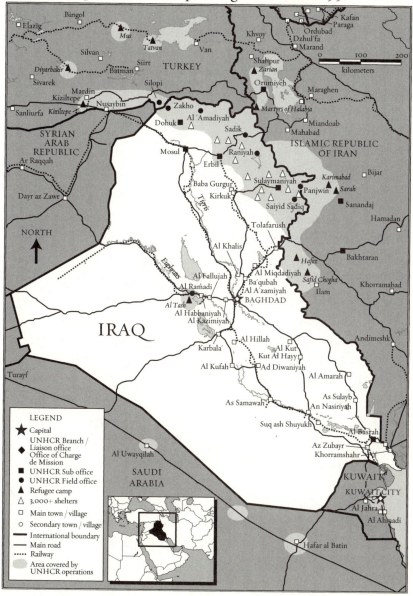

The Kurdish crisis opened up the beginning of international intervention in internal wars to protect refugees and displaced persons. It occasioned the start of military involvement in humanitarian emergencies, with varying implications that required careful scrutiny. It also influenced the humanitarian community to explore new methods for the protection of refugees and displaced persons. The setting up of safe havens in their own countries to return those who had been in fact *refoulé* had serious implications both in law and in security. Starting with the Kurdish crisis, the convergence and divergence of humanitarian and military imperatives became more and more significant for UNHCR operations in the 1990s.

EMERGENCY RESPONSE

Televised images of desperate Kurds trapped in the Iraqi-Turkish mountain range rallied international public opinion and pressed coalition governments for quick action. Backed by the action authorized by the Security Council Resolution 688, U.S. President George Bush announced on April 16, 1991, the launching of Operation Provide Comfort to establish a security zone in northern Iraq, to bring back the Kurdish refugees, and to build refugee camps. A no-fly zone was also declared in northern Iraq. The coalition forces organized and carried out the distribution of emergency relief supplies. In spite of all the available military hardware and personnel, there were serious logistical problems because of the harsh mountain terrain. With the humanitarian situation more and more centered on refugees, UNHCR was expected to become fully involved and to expand its operational responsibilities quickly.

I had been in office for a little more than a month when the refugees started to flee in unprecedented speed and scale to Iran and Turkey. We made intense efforts to prepare and cope with the looming emergency. There were, however, other related problems that were varied and complex. First were the special problems developing in Kuwait, where an estimated 170,000 resident Palestinians confronted possible deportation. Historically, some 400,000 Palestinians had led normal prosperous lives in Kuwait. During the Gulf War, part of the Palestinian population collaborated with Saddam Hussein, and some were suspected of having engaged in killings and atrocities. When the war was over, many Kuwaitis turned their anger against the Palestinians, canceling their residence permits and calling for their deportation. Many of the Palestinians held Egyptian and Syrian travel documents, but these countries refused to issue visas. The Palestinians in Kuwait faced the danger of not having any place to stay or to go. The representative of the Palestine Liberation Authority approached UNHCR and appealed for its intervention. I called on the ambassador of Kuwait in Geneva and then sent a high-level mission to Kuwait to discuss the Palestinian issue. We contacted neighboring governments and asked for humanitarian considerations. Within the UN system, there are divisions of responsibilities that are guarded carefully. Palestinians are under the mandate of the United Nations Relief and Works Agency in the Middle East (UNRWA), within specific geographical areas of operation. Since Kuwait fell outside the UNRWA boundaries, and since the protection needs were acute, UNHCR took action. We had to move with caution, as the issue was delicate and required confidence building on all sides. Altogether, our efforts bought time and led to easing the pressure for immediate action and to finding a solution.

The second related problem involved some thirty thousand Iraqis who had gone to the southern tip of Iraq and sought protection from the coalition forces, which also held some fifteen thousand or more prisoners of war. The issue was the protection and assistance of these groups of people after the withdrawal of the coalition forces. To cope with a unique situation, UNHCR dispatched another high-level mission to Kuwait and Saudi Arabia, led by Nicholas Morris, to consult the authorities, the coalition command, and the International Committee of the Red Cross (ICRC). Morris was to serve as my special envoy for the overall Kurdish crisis. For the boundary between Iraq and Kuwait, the Security Council established a demilitarized zone, ten kilometers into Iraq and five kilometers into Kuwait, and requested the secretary-general to deploy immediately a UN observer unit to monitor the zone for violations of the boundary and for any hostile action mounted from one side against the other. The secretary-general asked UNHCR to protect and seek solutions for refugees and displaced persons in the zone under the United Nations Iraq-Kuwait Observation Mission (UNIKOM).

Saudi Arabia offered to provide asylum and assistance for these others, to be fully financed by the government. Its generosity was appreciated, but the process was bound to be difficult. Processing and verifying the prisoners of war would be done by the ICRC, but how UNHCR would deal with those who were not recognized as prisoners was not agreed on, especially those who refused to return to Iraq. There were already disturbances among some civilians who were to be moved to Saudi Arabia. UNHCR and the ICRC worked out an understanding of their respective roles and cooperated with the Saudi authorities to set up camps housing some thirty-three thousand in Rafha. In the several years that followed, some went back to Iraq, and twenty-five thousand were resettled in other countries, including the United States. The effects of the human displacements of the Gulf War took a long time to heal. I visited the very well-managed Rafha camp in 1993 and realized then the long-lasting aftereffects of displacement that followed the Gulf War. When I left office in 2000, there were still more than five thousand Iraqis at Rafha.

World attention, however, focused on the Kurdish refugees who fled in massive numbers to Iran and to Turkey. The movement was rapid. In five days the number of refugees fleeing to Iran jumped from fifty thousand to one million. They benefited from what we lauded as an "exemplary" response by the government, which kept open its borders and provided emergency assistance from its own resources. UNHCR quickly supplemented the assistance with pre-positioned supplies. Iran had long-term experience of dealing with emergencies and inflows of refugees from Afghanistan and now from Iraq.

For Turkey, large numbers faced difficulties crossing the border. Turkey had serious internal problems with its own Kurdish minorities and was not ready to receive a large inflow of Kurds. I wrote to President Turgut Ozal on April 3, 1991, referring to the large number of Iraqis on the border between Turkey and Iraq, many of them women and children. I requested that the government allow these asylum seekers to cross the border so that they could be afforded safety and shelter, while assuring UNHCR cooperation to mobilize international support.[2]

The situation turned critical as the refugee population swelled, with 1.3 million moving into Iran and another half million scattered across the isolated and inhospitable mountain range bordering Iraq and Turkey. The Iranian government asked me to come on an emergency mission. It was unusual for a government like Iran, capable and self-assured, to ask for help. The massive refugee inflow was causing a genuine crisis. I left for a mission to Iran and Turkey on April 14, 1991. It was my first field visit as high commissioner and my very first call on postrevolution Iran. The authorities welcomed me cordially. I had an audience with President Hashemi Rafsanjani and held numerous consultations with ministry officials, diplomats, UN agency colleagues, and the press.

We flew to visit refugee camps in Bakhtaran and West Azerbaijan. As I boarded the huge battered military helicopter, it dawned on me what an unusual job I had undertaken. I had never been in a helicopter in my life. Besides, the local culture of wearing long black clothes and hiding my hair with a scarf was also uncomfortable. But I had to try. Standing at the hilltop and watching the long queue of people and vehicles—cars, buses, tractors, trucks—trying desperately to cross over to Iran, I could feel the pain of the people fleeing danger and seeking safety. There was a fifty-kilometer wait on the mountain road leading to Bakhtaran and an eighty-five-kilometer wait to West Azerbaijan. We also stopped our cars along the road. Refugees circled us and told horrendous stories of their flight. Many of them had arrived with serious wounds caused by mines and bullets. We were told by Iranian refugee officials and UNHCR staff members that our relief efforts lacked nearly all essentials, that there were too few tents. Four planes laden with blankets, medical supplies, and tents had just arrived. (They were the start of what became more than 240 UNHCR flights to transport emergency relief.) However, they were obviously not enough. A massive mobilization of resources was needed to avert a human catastrophe. Because of political considerations, however, the coalition countries were loath to assist Iran by providing relief assistance. It therefore fell on UNHCR to shoulder the responsibility of delivering relief supplies to Iran, which had received 70 percent of the Kurds who fled Iraq.

The visit to Turkey and the border areas was more complicated. We flew from Tehran to the Turkish town of Diyarbakir, where we immediately boarded a helicopter for a tour of the border areas. A UNHCR emergency team reported from those areas that the situation was critical, that up to eight sites on all Turkish borders were holding four hundred thousand refugees or more. Hundreds and thousands were reported arriving on the Iraqi side, but the situation was impossible to confirm. Purified water and sanitation were the absolute priority. Turkish authorities and the Red Crescent Society, international nongovernmental organizations (NGOs), and local Kurds were making great efforts. The team expressed concern over the forced returns apparently taking place at the border. Conditions were very harsh for the refugees as temperatures dropped below zero at night, and the mountain paths were rocky and steep. Many refugees were suffering from hunger, disease, exposure, and wounds.[3] The government of Turkey accepted the coalition's offer to provide humanitarian assistance. American, British, and French planes began dropping meals ready to eat (MREs). They started a trucking operation of bulk food, potable water, blankets, and tents from their bases to the border towns of Silopi and Diyarbakir. The Turkish strategy was to move the refugees from the mountain sites to the lowlands inside Iraq, where medical and distribution centers would be set up and where relief supplies from donor governments and NGOs would be concentrated.

After the helicopter survey, we went to Silopi to meet with the local government officials. We also talked with a few of the twenty thousand refugees who had been brought down from the mountain and were received in quickly set-up tent sites. They were barely recovering from their harsh flight, obviously relieved as they tried to dry their clothing and cook meals. I felt the need to seek sanctuary outside Iraq for those displaced by the recent hostilities. After an overnight stay in Ankara, I flew to the southern town of Antalya for discussions with President Ozal. I reminded him that my main request had been to allow the entry of the Kurdish asylum seekers, as I'd conveyed to him in my earlier letter. He received me cordially and rolled out maps to show me and my staff the various population locations in Turkey. He portrayed the position and problem of the Kurds, referred to his Kurdish lineage from his mother's side, and expressed his genuine sympathy for their plight. A few weeks before, he had broached the idea of a safe haven for the Kurds inside northern Iraq. Thereafter he wanted the United Nations to assume responsibility for the displaced Iraqis and help return them ultimately to their homes.

I followed up the audience with President Ozal with an intense consultation with the undersecretary of foreign affairs on April 17, and we established an accord on the steps to be followed. We agreed that a humanitarian solution had to be found for those Iraqis presently on the Iraqi-Turkish border. They had to be moved "from the remote and exposed mountain locations to flat areas where humanitarian assistance could be provided for them." The government of Turkey, together with the governments of the United States, the United Kingdom, and France, would "establish encampments in suitable locations in the border area," after which the "United Nations should assume responsibility for the care and maintenance of the displaced Iraqis, and the ultimate goal is their successful and safe return to areas of origin in Iraq." It was also understood that UNHCR would be "the focal point for operational coordination of the United Nations system."[4] The central issue was to agree on where the suitable locations would be. To me, the big question was whether the refugees would accept being moved to a safe haven inside Iraq, from which they had fled.

SAFE HAVEN AND RETURN OF KURDS

On April 16, 1991, U.S. President George Bush announced that the coalition forces would move into northern Iraq to establish camps for the Kurds. On April 5, the Security Council had adopted the historic Resolution 688, which condemned the repression of the Iraqi civilian population and demanded Iraq remove the threat to international peace and security and allow immediate access by international humanitarian organizations. The immediate aim was to protect the Kurds in danger and misery as well as to realize a quick refugee return. The objective of the operation, however, went beyond humanitarian concerns. While accommodating Turkey's concern for internal stability, it also aimed at transferring the overall security responsibilities as quickly as possible to the United Nations. The coalition governments were not inclined to recommit their troops to northern Iraq, nor did they entertain any support for Kurdish independence. They were ready for decisive action and wanted a quick handover to the United Nations. For the UN, however, the plan was double-edged. It might have the immediate advantage of relieving the sufferings of the refugees, but could the UN assure the security of the Kurds, and for how long? Some fifteen thousand Iraqi soldiers were in northern Iraq.

From a humanitarian perspective, there were advantages in bringing down refugees from the Iraqi-Turkish border in order to provide them with immediately needed assistance. The central issue for the United Nations and UNHCR was how to assure the security of the refugees in northern Iraq. Several aspects had to be covered. The first was the legal question of obtaining the Iraqi government's agreement to the United Nations' operational presence. The second aspect was ensuring coordinated action with the coalition forces. The third was protecting the interest and will of the refugees.

The United Nations had been attending to the humanitarian needs of people from Iraq and Kuwait since 1990. A regional humanitarian plan of action relating to the crisis between Iraq and Kuwait had been presented in October 1990 to solicit support for international assistance covering the entire region. The secretary-general followed up on the humanitarian situation after the war in the spring of 1991 and sent missions to assess the expanding needs. The latest interagency mission headed by Undersecretary-General Martti Ahtisaari in mid-March observed that the recent conflict "had wrought near-apocalyptic results" upon the economic infrastructure of Iraq, and it recommended urgent action to confront the impending crises.

The secretary-general sent two other envoys to Baghdad. First was Eric Suy, the head of the UN office in Geneva, as his personal representative with a political mandate to insist that Iraq allow immediate access to international humanitarian organizations to all parts of the country. The second was Sadruddin Aga Khan, as executive delegate to lead the UN interagency humanitarian program in Iraq, Kuwait, and the border areas between Iran and Turkey.

Sadruddin Aga Khan, a highly experienced former high commissioner for refugees, succeeded in concluding a memorandum of understanding between the United Nations and the Iraqi minister of foreign affairs. Both sides recognized the urgent need to alleviate the suffering of the Iraqi civilian population and to promote the return home of Iraqi displaced persons. They agreed to take measures for the benefit of the displaced, primarily based on their personal safety and provision of assistance to them. The Iraqi government agreed to cooperate with the United Nations and to include a humanitarian presence wherever necessary, at UN suboffices and humanitarian centers (UNHUCs) staffed with UN civilian personnel. The government would assist in the prompt establishment of UN structures and activities, for a period ending December 31, 1991. The agreement provided a legal base for UN agencies to operate inside Iraq.

As a newcomer I was a bit perplexed by the complex setup of the UN operational structure. Where would I belong, and with whom would I coordinate on what? For UNHCR, there was the additional task of fine-tuning with the coalition forces the movement of refugees to the safe haven. Besides, I should have to obtain resources to carry out an emergency operation that had not been foreseen to assist Iraqi refugees not only in Turkey and Iran but also inside Iraq. On April 12 the UN agencies issued an appeal of $400 million for a period of three months. The UNHCR portion was $238 million. In one month we received $130.5 million, but the contributions were rapidly depleted and we were in constant need of funds.

Within our office there were serious concerns over extending protection to refugees inside hostile Iraq territory from which they had fled. Some strongly opposed the establishment of a safe haven as a substitute for asylum. Our very presence inside Iraq could be used by neighboring countries as a pretext for denying asylum to refugees. Such precedent setting would be detrimental to our basic mandate of refugee protection. Yet to object to the emergency measures adopted by the coalition states might result in the denial of protection and assistance to refugees for whom UNHCR was established.

UNHCR was mandated to protect and assist people who were outside their own countries and unable to return as the result of well-founded fears or persecution on grounds of race, religion, nationality, political opinion, or membership in a social group. This meant that people displaced within their own borders did not come under the legally defined international refugee protection regime. While states were obliged not to return people to situations where they might be persecuted, they could not be forced to provide them asylum. The Kurdish issue severely tested UNHCR's protection mandate. Should we follow the legal dictate of not exercising our mandate inside the border and thereby refrain from helping those prevented from crossing, or should we stand more on realistic humanitarian grounds and extend whatever support we could?

I decided to take the realistic humanitarian course. I believed that the question of our mandate should be understood in the context of the fundamental principle to protect refugee lives. The Kurdish refugees were people of primary concern to UNHCR. If the access was from the Turkish side, we would have to cross over from Turkey and bring them to flat areas, provided we adopted measures to ensure their security. Topographically the flat areas were on the Iraqi side of the mountain range. The concept of safe haven in northern Iraq established a precedent for intervening in conflict situations on behalf of ethnically specific groups of victimized civilians.

The secretary-general's meeting with the U.S. delegation in Paris on April 20 helped clarify the overall operational setting. Sadruddin Aga Khan and I were invited to participate. General James P. McCarthy, deputy commander of the U.S. European Command, briefed us on the activities undertaken by the U.S. Army at the Turkish-Iraqi border. He indicated that the army had already delivered eighteen hundred metric tons of food for the refugees and were exploring ways of delivering more. He thought two hundred thousand refugees could be put initially in the Zakho Valley in northern Iraq, where twenty thousand had originated. The Iraqi Army in the area had agreed to withdraw to thirty kilometers from Zakho and would not intervene. General McCarthy emphasized that the coalition forces would not allow the Kurds to return to this area before being sure of their safety. He insisted on the need for the U.S. forces to have a refugee expert work with them, stating, "We know how to deal with logistics but not how to deal with refugees." The U.S. Army would set up camps but wanted to hand them over to the United Nations as soon as possible. It would help from the outside whenever it was needed. I asked about the Turkish position in connection with the U.S. plans. General McCarthy confirmed that the Turkish authorities wanted all operations to take place inside Iraq.[5]

U.S. Ambassador to the UN Morris Abrams, who was present at the meeting, was interested in knowing how the secretary-general intended to dovetail the UN activities with those of the coalition forces. He understood that the executive delegate and I were being asked to do something "most unusual": to settle refugees in areas that might not be entirely safe. The secretary-general indicated that the UN staff to operate in Zakho should come from Baghdad, as covered in the memorandum of understanding, but that additional personnel coming from the Turkish border should be approved by Iraq. He insisted that UN coordination with the coalition forces be discreet and not formal and that the UN take over the management of the camps as soon as possible. He reminded us all that the UN flag should not be raised wherever there was any other flag. In a private meeting after the departure of the U.S. delegation, the secretary-general confirmed that UNHCR would take over the management of the camps in northern Iraq and that he would so inform the Iraqi authorities.[6]

Now the speed of implementing the operation in northern Iraq was turning into an issue. The Iraqi government informed the secretary-general that the U.S. Army had already entered the Zakho region on April 20 to establish centers for assisting displaced Iraqis in Iraqi territory. Although the Iraqi government was opposed to the steps taken by the U.S. Army, it did not hinder the operations because it did not oppose the provision of humanitarian assistance to Iraqi citizens. It was also very keen to have the United Nations assume immediate responsibility. The coalition forces as well were in a great hurry to move the Iraqis back into Iraq and exerted enormous pressure on UNHCR. On the question of quick action and handover to the UN, their interests and those of Baghdad converged. The office of the UN executive delegate also got onto the operational bandwagon and started convoys to Zakho, one from Baghdad and another from Silopi in Turkey. They were trying to open up routes where returning refugees would receive food, water, and medical care at way stations to be set up. Teams from UN agencies, including UNHCR, UNICEF, and the World Food Program (WFP), were to move along these routes, monitoring the movement and bringing in supplies.

The coalition forces embarked on a massive repatriation operation referred to as Operation Provide Comfort. The one constant imperative was that the Kurds should move out of the mountains and return to Iraq. The U.S. officials contended that the refugee encampments in the mountains could not be sustained in the summer because of diminishing water resources. They recognized that the tent camps in the Zakho Valley could not accommodate thousands of people, so they expanded the safe haven area southeast to Dohuk. UNHCR believed that the refugees should be encouraged to go all the way back to their homes and won the agreement of the coalition forces. The repatriation program gained considerable momentum. Some two hundred thousand were estimated to have left the mountains. The pressure brought on the Kurds to return was immense.

The U.S. Army wanted UNHCR to assume full responsibility for the repatriation and became impatient with what it perceived as our inadequate response. We were increasing our field staff presence rapidly. We had taken over the control of the Zakho camps by mid-May, opened up suboffices in three northern Iraq towns, and coordinated the relief activities of nongovernmental organizations. In Iraq alone, no fewer than seventy-five UNHCR international staff workers were deployed. In addition, we were running a massive refugee operation in Iran. To the military, however, UNHCR's presence was thin, and our deployment slow. General John Shalikashvili was said to have remarked that he was "sitting there with great anticipation to hear that the UNHCR teams have fanned out." The general's impression colored the reaction of the coalition states that later shaped the G7 initiative to establish a strong coordinating office within the United Nations structure.

Another factor that tended to delay UNHCR's operation was its commitment to ensure voluntary repatriation. The refugees were rapidly returning back. What worried them most was the assurance of security. They were leaving the mountains because the conditions were untenable but also because they knew that the coalition forces would be present in northern Iraq. Many refugees assumed there would be a prolonged coalition presence in northern Iraq. They were told that the coalition forces would not abandon them. UNHCR tried to establish a voluntary repatriation procedure that would provide the refugees correct and realistic information on which they could make their choice. The Turkish government interpreted UNHCR's attempt to verify the voluntary character of returns as an impediment, if not even a delaying tactic. I had to send a note on UNHCR's activities to the Turkish ambassador in defense of voluntary repatriation.

The question of how security would be provided in northern Iraq after the departure of the coalition forces remained uncertain. The United Nations looked for various security options. Some coalition states proposed a police force to monitor a cease-fire agreement between the Iraqi Kurds and the central government. The executive delegate negotiated an agreement with the Iraqi government to deploy a United Nations contingent of up to five hundred guards. The contingent's mandate did not cover the security needs of the Iraqi returnees but was "to protect UN personnel, assets and operations." The guards were to "be deployed to wherever there is a UN presence (transit camps, UNHUCS, relay stations, transit centers)."[7] However, it was in the interests of the coalition forces to present the guards as helping provide security for the returnees, and this impression was not dispelled clearly by the executive delegate and his staff. Many refugees and returnees expected the guards to protect them, and my staff in Iraq was even asked, "Where are your tanks?" The guards were first assigned to the Zakho/Dohuk area and thereafter to other transit centers that were set up.

The repatriation movement, however, depended on the effectiveness of security currently provided by the coalition forces. I wrote to the secretary-general on May 17, 1991, that in my opinion, "nothing short of a negotiated settlement accompanied by some form of international guarantees can offer a lasting solution to this human tragedy, one of the most dramatic of our times."

In late June 1991, on my first visit to the White House, I appealed to President George Bush that American forces stay longer in northern Iraq. I explained to him that the refugees had returned with the expectation of international coverage of their security but that UNHCR could not provide them such assurance. The president understood my concerns, but he said that American forces had to leave lest they be accused of having imperialist designs. I was also received by Secretary of Defense Dick Cheney and Chairman of the Joint Chiefs of Staff Colin Powell. I thanked them for the cooperation of the military. Secretary Cheney informed me that he had just spoken to the president, who had taken note of my comments on the security question. The president had confirmed that he was eager to pull the troops out of the gulf but that the withdrawal would take place in a gradual and responsible way. Cheney added that the military had learned a lot from their involvement in the humanitarian operation, and General Powell commented that the experience was both rewarding and useful training. They were eager to know about the deployment of the UN guards and UNHCR's operations, including funding, staffing, and logistical capacity.

My visits to the Oval Office and the Pentagon were unprecedented. It was the extraordinary context of the Gulf War, especially the developments in northern Iraq, that led the high commissioner for refugees to seek security support by the military. In the following years I had to make similar requests for refugees in conflict situations in the Balkans and the African Great Lakes region. Usually the military were eager to exit quickly, earlier than humanitarians believed was opportune. In the gulf context, the United States maintained five thousand troops in Turkey, and coalition aircraft continued to patrol the no-fly zone over northern Iraq.

By June the last of the mountain camps in the Iraqi-Turkish border had been closed. The movement back that started in late April was virtually over in early June. Large-scale returns from Iran also began in April. During this period more than twenty thousand military personnel were involved in the operation in northern Iraq, using two hundred aircraft for transporting logistical and emergency supplies. More than fifty international humanitarian organizations participated in the emergency relief efforts. The operation broke new grounds in civil and military collaboration. Many lessons were learned, as both sides accommodated each other's different modes of operations and assumptions. However, with the emergency phasing down, UNHCR and the humanitarian agencies had to continue attending to the massive assistance of feeding and sheltering the returnees.

The refugees returned, but to a devastated land. Many wished to return to villages that had been razed when they were moved away from the border years earlier. The repatriation moved rapidly. By the end of May 1991, 95 percent of Dohuk's four hundred thousand and 75 percent of Erbil's one million populations had come back. The return to Kirkuk was slow because the Iraqi government did not allow the UN to set up a suboffice in the governorate, which had been the scene of the Kurdish uprising.

The rapid return of Iraqi refugees meant an equally rapid need for rehabilitation. The fact that they returned did not mean that they could move back to their homes. While some decided to settle in the ruins of their original villages, others looked for further assurances of safety. With the harsh winter a few months ahead, UNHCR decided to launch a comprehensive winterization program in September to prepare for the needs of up to 62,000 families (372,000 people). The program had a dual objective: one to address the basic shelter needs of individual families by providing building materials; the other to establish throughout the western provinces a minimum infrastructure that would restore the health services and water supply systems. The call for winterization mobilized people and goods. The program created a storm of activity involving sixteen hundred trucks that carried tons of building materials from Turkey. Hundreds of international and local workers helped distribute and assist thousands of families. The people themselves worked hard to waterproof and insulate their roofs. In less than six weeks the program attained its objective of forty thousand single-room shelters. Families living in tents were reduced to a limited number in Kirkuk that were still hesitant to return. Food was supplied by WFP, and essential nonfood supplies, such as blankets and kerosene stoves, were provided to families in need.

The winterization program stood out as a legendary precedent for UNHCR's emergency rehabilitation operation. Aside from the immediate benefit profiting the returnees, it had a positive impact on the local residents by encouraging them to become engaged in joint efforts to restore normal village lives. In June 1992, with the end of the Kurdish refugee crisis and with most of the victims' having returned to northern Iraq, UNHCR handed over the relief operation to UN agency colleagues, led by UNICEF. The economic conditions remained difficult, however, inasmuch as northern Iraq suffered from a double economic embargo: UN sanctions against Iraq, imposed since 1990, and an internal embargo by the Iraqi government. The need for food, fuel, and other basic subsistence items persisted.

Kurdish leaders valued the degree of autonomy that developed out of the safe haven and took steps to establish their own government. Elections were held on May 19, 1992, but the two main political parties, the Kurdish Democratic Party (KDP), led by Mustafa Barzani, and the Patriotic Union of Kurdistan (PUK), headed by Jalal Talabani, came out even. The coalition governments took the position that they would not recognize an independent Kurdish political entity. UN agencies and NGOs also refrained from assisting the Kurdish government to avoid giving the impression that they were giving it de facto recognition and sanctioning the political fragmentation of Iraq. The two Kurdish parties clashed in early 1994, and fighting broke out intermittently over the next several years.

The Kurdish population continued to live in poverty and uncertainty. Inter-Kurdish fighting, internal sanctions brought about by Baghdad, and UN sanctions and international indifference altogether virtually doomed the Iraqi Kurdish people to lives of deprivation and hardship.

Concluding Observation

The Kurdish refugee crisis set the stage for refugee protection operations in the succeeding decade. First, the scale and speed of refugee flight were unprecedented. Within one week 1.75 million Kurds fled northern Iraq, causing a humanitarian catastrophe in the neighboring countries and along the Iraqi-Turkish border. Second, the pace of the return was equally rapid, requiring emergency rehabilitation. Third, the military involvement under humanitarian auspices broke new ground in civil-military collaboration.

Backed up by Security Council Resolution 688, the coalition forces intervened to set up a safe haven in northern Iraq and bring back the Kurdish refugees. The fact that the coalition forces had been deployed in the gulf region facilitated the triggering of early military action. In the decisions leading to the intervention, however, intense diplomatic negotiations developed among the main actors: the U.S. government, the United Nations, and Iraq. The United States pushed for quick action to bring back the refugees but pressed for an equally fast handover to the United Nations. The UN negotiated an agreement with the Iraqi government to ensure the legal basis for UN humanitarian operations on Iraqi territory. It also concluded with the Iraqi government a memorandum of understanding that favored a UN humanitarian presence to the continuing deployment of coalition forces. The overall objective of all the parties converged as they concentrated on meeting the immediate humanitarian needs of the Iraqi Kurds.

The dilemma faced by UNHCR to implement the intervention initiated by the military was complex. There was the legal issue of accommodating to Turkey's de facto denial of asylum to Kurds and of helping return them to their places of origin. There was also the practical challenge of physically ensuring the security of the returning Kurds. The presence and support of the coalition forces in the area of return influenced many refugees to opt for return. But for UNHCR, with its limited civilian capacity, the responsibility to extend security coverage after the departure of the coalition forces loomed very large. I pressed President Bush and other high U.S. authorities for a continuing military presence. The United Nations negotiated the deployment of UN guards with the Iraqi government. The guards were formally responsible for protecting UN personnel and premises, but their presence, however limited, filled the security gap faced by the people in a hostile environment after the departure of external intervening forces.

The Iraqi operation changed the forms of relief assistance. The coalition forces introduced enhanced logistic capabilities by resorting to massive airlifts, land transport, and troop contingents. UNHCR, on its part, had to gear up its emergency preparedness and response capacity. We increased the emergency fund of ten million to twenty million dollars with a greater degree of flexibility for its use. We installed specially trained emergency preparedness and response officers (EPRO) and teams and built stockpiles of emergency relief supplies. Through arrangements for the priority access of goods and people with governments and nongovernment sources, we equipped ourselves with a surge capacity to meet future contingencies.[8] I personally took interest in developing UNHCR's emergency capacity. In the kind of world we faced in the 1990s, a refugee-related emergency could take place any time in any part of the world. I believed that UNHCR's credibility would be determined by its performance at the first instance of the emergency.

The coalition member states took a host of initiatives to strengthen the overall operational capacity of UN agencies. The British prime minister was ready to propose at the London G7 summit the setting up of "a powerful UN agency, with advanced modern equipment" under the command of a senior military figure or logistics expert.[9] The political declaration of the London Economic Summit, 1991, reiterated the central role of the United Nations in reinforcing a multilateral approach to the solution of common problems. The summit states committed themselves "to making the UN stronger, more efficient and more effective." In order to strengthen coordination, they proposed "the designation of a high level official, answerable only to the United Nations Secretary-General, who would be responsible for directing a prompt and well-integrated international response to emergencies, and for coordinating the relevant UN appeals."[10]

UNHCR was certainly ready to join in, but I believed that certain fundamental problems in advancing efficiency and effectiveness had to be recognized. First of all, the separate stances of the United Nations and the coalition forces had to be understood. The United Nations did not force its entry into northern Iraq but negotiated its presence by concluding an agreement with Iraq for the operation of international humanitarian organizations on Iraqi territory. Second, civilian organizations are not command-structured; they differ from military organizations, which are headed by generals and followed by large contingents of foot soldiers. Third, humanitarian organizations work with the victims and find solutions with them. The needs of the victims are varied, and UNHCR must reflect the voluntary compliance of refugees in reaching solutions.

The coalition states presented the issue of strengthening the UN's emergency capacity to the General Assembly. After lengthy debate, the assembly adopted the resolution requesting that the secretary-general appoint an emergency relief coordinator and establish a Department of Humanitarian Affairs (DHA). As the world was moving toward a succession of conflicts with vast human displacements, it was fortunate that the UN system would include an office dedicated to the coordination of emergency operations. Humanitarian agencies would have to strengthen their field presence and emergency preparedness to contribute to a well-coordinated overall UN mission.

In the months following the return of refugees to northern Iraq, the humanitarian agencies were engaged in a large rehabilitation operation to prepare the population for the coming winter. UNHCR launched a massive shelter program, purchasing building materials and distributing them to the population. The people themselves worked hard and succeeded in completing the reconstruction before the arrival of severe weather. The rehabilitation operation proved that humanitarian emergencies had to span the entire process from massive flight to return and rehabilitation and that resources had to be made available to cover the entire cycle.

Politically the Kurdish desire to move from safe haven to autonomy following international military intervention was not supported by the coalition governments, which refrained from endorsing the political fragmentation of Iraq for fear of regional instability or the emergence of a pro-Iranian regime. The two leading Kurdish parties were unable to form a partnership and even fought intermittently. Economically the situation remained precarious. Humanitarian aid provided by UN agencies sustained about one-third of the population. The fact that the Kurds were not allowed to embark on their own nation building meant that they were structurally linked to the fate of the Iraqis in the rest of the country. The Iraqi society as a whole suffered from both the repressive policies adopted by the regime of Saddam Hussein and the punitive economic sanctions levied by the international community. The consequences of the international humanitarian intervention did not extend beyond alleviating the immediate humanitarian crisis of the Kurds in the aftermath of their 1991 uprising.

2.
PROTECTING
REFUGEES
IN THE
BALKAN WARS

In terms of massiveness of population displacement and scale of international relief operations, the Balkan conflict from 1991 to 1999 was unprecedented. That the conflict developed on the southern flank of Europe added to the exceptional geopolitical impact of the situation. The images of atrocities were portrayed daily on television screens to all parts of the world. United Nations peacekeeping forces acting alongside civilian humanitarian workers attracted intense political and public attention.

The breakup of the Socialist Federal Republic of Yugoslavia brought to the fore the power struggle among the three main ethnic constituent groups of Serbs, Croats, and Muslims. It started in June 1991 with the declaration of independence by Slovenia. The small and ethnically homogeneous Slovenia won its independence with relative ease, but when Croatia followed, the result was totally different. The Yugoslav Army (JNA) and Serb paramilitaries rapidly moved to seize control of Croatian territory. Croats were expelled from areas that fell under Serb control, while Serbs were forced out of their homes by Croatian forces. The pernicious feature of what became known as ethnic cleansing manifested itself early in the Croatian breakup. The European Community (EC) combined efforts with the United Nations to achieve a cease-fire and the political settlement of the Yugoslavia conflict. However, the European governments failed to prevent the siege of Vukovar and the massacre that followed, nor could they stop the Serb shelling of historic Dubrovnik.

Cyrus Vance, representing the secretary-general of the United Nations, negotiated an agreement with the Croatian government and the JNA to deploy UN troops and police monitors to Serb-held areas. Eastern Slavonia, western Slavonia, and the Krajina were designated United Nations protected areas, where twelve thousand peace-keepers were deployed. The United Nations Protection Force (UNPROFOR) was established on March 13, with headquarters in Sarajevo. At the time Sarajevo was seen as a neutral location, and UNPROFOR's presence was expected to provide a stabilizing factor against increasing tensions throughout Bosnia and Herzegovina.

The optimism created by the deployment of UNPROFOR did not last for long. The European Community recognized Slovenia and Croatia as independent states on January 15, 1992, and called on the Bosnian government to hold a referendum on independence. Bosnia and Herzegovina was the most ethnically mixed of all the republics. According to the 1991 population census, the three main groups in the republic were Muslims (44 percent), Serbs (31 percent), and Croats (17 percent). When Bosnia and Herzegovina declared independence in March 1992, against the opposition mostly of the Serb population, Serbian paramilitary forces moved into the eastern part of the republic and began killing and expelling Muslims and Croat residents. The European Community recognized Bosnia and Herzegovina on April 6, 1992, while violence spread throughout the republic. Serb forces from the Yugoslav Army took to the hills surrounding the capital, Sarajevo, and began attacking it with artillery. By mid-June Serb forces were controlling two-thirds of Bosnia and Herzegovina, and approximately one million people had been forced out of their homes.

UNHCR began its operation in Yugoslavia in November 1991, in response to the request of the Yugoslav delegation to the Executive

Committee meeting of UNHCR for assistance for the population displaced in Croatia. At the time preceding independence, the displaced persons were not legally refugees. I therefore consulted the United Nations Secretary-General Javier Pérez de Cuéllar, who formally requested me, "on the basis of your related humanitarian expertise and extensive experience, to assist in bringing relief to needy internally displaced persons affected by the conflict." He thought that my action might have a "welcome preventive impact in helping to avoid the further displacement of population, as well as contributing to the creation of conditions that would ultimately permit refugees and displaced persons to return to their places of origin."[1]

At the time UNHCR was just coming out of the massive operation involving the exodus of 1.7 million Kurds in northern Iraq. To many of us at UNHCR, Yugoslavia appeared a no-win situation. European arbitration and cease-fire efforts were proving ineffective. However, with the prospect of the federal republic's breaking up into independent states, internally displaced people were bound to turn into refugees crossing international borders in need of UNHCR protection. I foresaw the increase of both refugees and the internally displaced and judged that the wisest course might be to become engaged ahead of time and take whatever preventive measures possible. We started the assistance operation in Croatia at the end of 1991.

In the following five years UNHCR operated in the expanding war zones of Croatia and Bosnia and Herzegovina. The conflict was characterized by the objective shared by the three ethnic groups to displace and uproot people in order to establish ethnically pure, if not dominant, republics. It was indeed a war of "ethnic cleansing." It broadened the mission of UNHCR, which could no longer limit its protection coverage to refugees but had to extend it also to internally displaced persons and even affected civilians. Massive relief assistance was provided to some 2.7 million victims. UNHCR played the lead role for all humanitarian agencies in confronting the crises, which were political in objective and military in context. It developed partnerships with the international political negotiators representing the United Nations and the European Community, as well as the UNPROFOR forces.

The Balkan conflict expanded in 1998 to Kosovo, the autonomous province of Serbia. A long-simmering unrest between the majority Kosovo Albanians and the administering Serbs intensified with the Serbian security forces' resorting to strong military action against the Kosovo Liberation Army (KLA) and their supporters seeking independence. People were forced to leave their homes. UNHCR led the assistance operation throughout Kosovo. When NATO took decisive military action to make Serb Security forces withdraw, Serbia resorted to the massive expulsion of Kosovars to neighboring Albania and Macedonia. Heavy NATO bombing, together with active U.S. diplomatic maneuvers, resulted in the Serb forces leaving Kosovo. The refugees returned home at an unprecedented speed. The United Nations was tasked to administer an interim administration while NATO forces maintained security. UNHCR led the repatriation and reintegration. In the short run, the international response to the Kosovo crisis brought success. However, the ethnic problem remained now with the Serb minority facing insecurity in the liberated Kosovo and with the future status of Kosovo unsettled.

While humanitarian operations contributed greatly to alleviating misery and extending security to the victims, they could not solve the political problems that underlay the wars in the Balkans. The causes ranged from memories of historical injustices, aspirations for ethnic domination, unheeded exercises of force and violence, and obsessions over greater power and political independence. The political and diplomatic measures taken by the Security Council and by Western governments were neither effective nor sufficient to settle the conflict. The United States was late in taking up a leading role. The ethnic character of the displacement conditioned the peace-building process after the conclusion of the Dayton Peace Agreement. The repatriation of refugees and internally displaced persons proved slow and difficult, particularly in Bosnia and Herzegovina, for minority returns. Reversing ethnic cleansing remained a formidable challenge that required new efforts at community rebuilding. The lessons learned from the Balkan conflict were, on the one hand, the enormous contributions of humanitarian operations in the process of war and peace and, on the other, the clear limitations in seeking solutions to the underlying problems.

Croatia and Bosnia and Herzegovina

OPERATING IN WAR: AIRLIFTS AND CONVOYS

UNHCR started assistance operation in Croatia. On December 17, 1991, the first UNHCR convoy distributed relief to Zagreb and Belgrade. I appointed a relatively junior Spanish colleague, Jose Maria Mendiluce, as my special envoy to lead the humanitarian operation. He was resourceful and had a record of active involvement in conflict situations. The original purpose of our work was to supplement the International Committee of the Red Cross's assistance of goods to be distributed by the local Red Cross. In no time UNHCR's assistance programs increased tremendously in response to the rapidly rising needs of the displaced population in Bosnia and Herzegovina. UNHCR found itself taking the lead role after the withdrawal of ICRC delegates from Bosnia in late May 1992. An attack on a Red Cross convoy in Sarajevo took the life of the head of its delegation, and the ICRC considered the act directed against its emblem. UNHCR found itself operating in the middle of the ongoing "ethnic cleansing," in which the most important need became the protection of people on the spot or getting them to relative safety.

The challenges ahead of UNHCR in the Balkan operation were multiple. First, it had to ensure that refugees would be generously received. Refugees went to European countries in search of asylum. They needed quick acceptance without being subjected to lengthy procedures to determine their refugee status with the possibility of being rejected. In fact what characterized the conflict was the political objective of displacing and uprooting people in order to establish ethnically pure zones. "Ethnic cleansing" was a policy that forced people to turn into refugees. UNHCR was caught in a scandalous twist. Although its basic mandate was international protection, it had to insist on the right of people to remain in their homes in safety and dignity regardless of their ethnic, national, or religious origins. Colleagues from the field reported numerous incidents in which they were faced with requests by people to help them leave their homes because of mounting threats of killing, intimidation, and detention. To help their departure would be lending themselves to "ethnic cleansing." To advise them to stay might be condemning them to death.

An equally important mission was the protection of internally displaced persons. In the absence of adequate legal principles or effective enforcement mechanisms that covered internally displaced persons, international presence proved to be the only available tool for their protection. UNHCR's presence would also respond to the concerns of those who had not yet moved from their homes but feared they might be removed. UNHCR had to place colleagues in conflict zones instead of evacuating them out from insecure situations. We posted large contingents of field protection officers throughout Bosnia and Herzegovina and opened as many as twenty-seven suboffices. Their functions ranged from responding to the safety and assistance needs of the fleeing people to negotiating with the local authorities to counteract displacement and to publicly denouncing abuses as a last resort.

In addition, measures had to be taken to ensure the security of the staff. Being close to victims meant sharing their dangers. In many instances, protection became the active hands-on physical coverage of security on behalf of victims. Our colleagues were directly exposed to life-threatening situations. UNHCR management had to be doubly attentive to the security needs of the staff: to provide them with flak jackets and bulletproof vehicles and to incorporate coverage for stress as well as mandatory leave systems.

Above all, UNHCR had to strengthen its logistical capacity to meet the needs of the victims because relief assistance played a central role in the protection of victims. As the operation expanded in Bosnia and Herzegovina, world attention focused more and more on the plight of citizens under siege in the capital of Sarajevo. The Serb forces had taken position in the surrounding hills and resorted daily and nightly to heavy shelling. The city hardly functioned, with no public transport, deserted streets, and economic life at standstill. There were debates in the Western capitals and in the Security Council in New York over how to save the citizens of the city. Strong pressure was exerted to open the Sarajevo airport to allow delivery of humanitarian relief.

The United States organized a relief airlift in the middle of April 1992 that brought in ninety thousand prepared meals, forty thousand blankets, and thirty metric tons of medical supplies. Turkey also arranged an airlift of supplies. UNHCR faced increasing difficulties in procuring and delivering relief goods to Sarajevo. Threats, theft, and intimidation not only affected the deliveries but also endangered the security of the staff. It was not exceptional for UNHCR to negotiate its way through ninety roadblocks to get relief goods from Zagreb to Sarajevo.

In preparation for an airlift operation, John Bolton, assistant secretary of state for international organization affairs, came to see me on June 27, 1992, to discuss relief planning for Sarajevo. He told me at the outset of the meeting that the United States had offered support for an airlift under UN auspices but that the secretary-general had rejected it, citing political sensitivity. Bolton said that the United States was disappointed by that reaction but that the offer remained on the table. Eric Morris, director of our Division of Programs and Operational Support, gave him detailed information on UNHCR's state of preparedness. He had just returned from Belgrade, where he set up a planning cell. A group of professional staff and teams of drivers, radio operators, and interpreters who had gained experience in northern Iraq had been identified for the Balkan operation. Two staff members, including a logistician, were at the Sarajevo airport, assessing its capacity for reception and distribution. Morris stated that one major issue remained unsettled: where to draw the line of minimal security conditions for the staff to operate. Deputy High Commissioner Douglas Stafford noted that UNHCR had just obtained thirty-two flak jackets for staff destined for Sarajevo and that we were now encroaching into operations in Third Geneva Convention territory—i.e., war zones—which are normally the province of the ICRC. We all agreed that while a Sarajevo airlift was important symbolically, land convoys were crucial for the large number of people throughout the country who were in desperate need of assistance.[2]

On June 29, 1992, President François Mitterrand of France flew into Sarajevo with emergency supplies. UNHCR had received no specific information on the Mitterrand mission, but our staff helped with the unloading. There was no one else at the tarmac to give a hand. His visit marked a breakthrough. On the same day, the Security Council adopted a resolution to open the Sarajevo airport, and a French infantry company arrived with air traffic control elements. The Canadian battalion traveled from Croatia to take up position at the airport. The UNHCR staff worked with the local population to set up a distribution system to deal with relief supplies to be flown in. Offers of help quickly poured in. More than twenty governments and nongovernmental organizations expressed their readiness to provide aircraft, experienced personnel, and humanitarian supplies. The airlift began on July 3, and eleven flights landed the first day. Within the first week, more than one hundred flights carried twelve hundred metric tons of much-wanted humanitarian supplies.

For UNHCR, the Sarajevo airlift was a novel experience that required adjustments on many fronts. In Geneva an airlift operations center was set up with seconded air force officers from the United States, the United Kingdom, France, Canada, and Germany. They were situated in a small room with computers and fax machines to plan flight schedules. Traditionally, civilian humanitarian workers kept their distance from military activities. The arrival of the military on the UNHCR premises sent out internal shock waves. An airlift information center was installed in the adjacent room to collect and distribute relevant documentations. An emergency task force for the

Sarajevo airlift was also organized to coordinate the activities within UNHCR headquarters as well as with field offices and with governments providing planes and supplies. François Fouinat was called back from Cambodia to serve as coordinator for the Yugoslavia operation at headquarters; the Cambodian operation had just reached the phase of regular repatriation. The duration of the airlift was of course unknown, but at the time we estimated a few weeks' duration, after which we would review the situation. Nobody at the time ever dreamed that it would turn out to be the longest-running humanitarian airlift in history, surpassing the Berlin airlift, and would continue until January 9, 1996.

Of particular concern was the status of the aircrews engaged in humanitarian assistance. The legal advisers of the United Nations and the crew-contributing governments consulted and agreed to designate them "expert on missions for the UN." In fact the crews considered themselves to be serving under the high commissioner's command and left me with the nicest citation when they ended their service.

An equally difficult part of the operation was the establishment of the land route to carry relief goods from the airport to the city. The route became known as snipers' alley, where convoys faced numerous attacks on the way. Exposed to an entirely novel and dangerous challenge, UNHCR ordered ten bulletproof four-wheel-drive cars, in addition to thirty-two flak jackets. Protecting the staff from constant and unforeseen danger remained the highest-priority consideration.

On the sixth day of the airlift I flew on the UNHCR flight to Sarajevo from Zagreb in a British C-130 Hercules. It was a beautiful flight, following the Dalmatian coastal line and then flying over the high mountain range. I had a seat in the back of the cockpit, a position I was to be given on many flights to Sarajevo in the next few years. As we approached the airport, the plane made a sharp dip while landing in order to avoid any shooting from the ground, a practice to which I also became accustomed. At the airport I was met by UNPROFOR's Sarajevo commander, General Lewis Mackenzie, and the UNHCR staff. Our staff was living in a makeshift accommodation in the hangar. I was given a flak jacket and then driven to the city in a military personnel carrier. These cars had no windows, so I could not see anything outside. Only a few colleagues could accompany me to the city because of the high security precautions. Some journalists who came on the flight were unhappy about this restriction, but they had been warned ahead of time. I was later told that a few made it to Sarajevo anyway, hiding in the cargo of relief goods.

I wanted to go to the city to assess the situation of the people first-hand and to examine the distribution system that had been set up. After being unloaded at the airport, supplies were transported by UNHCR to five distribution centers around the city. Three local nongovernmental organizations, representing the three ethnic communities, helped with the actual distribution. We went to a building that housed displaced people who were receiving relief supplies flown in by the airlift. My colleagues who had visited various parts of the city described to me scenes of devastation and hunger. They told me of women, children, and elderly people living in "dungeonlike" boiler rooms with little water, food, or electricity. Children looked undernourished. A local doctor reported that many families had been living on little more than carbohydrates: macaroni, rice, or bread. Sarajevo had been under siege for three months.

We went for a fifteen-minute walk through the bomb-scarred streets of the old city. There were welcoming smiles and hand waving from the streets and from all the windows. Mendiluce was recognized by the citizens, and some came forward for a warm hug. They seemed to feel that peace and normality were returning to Sarajevo, that the world was no longer abandoning them. Waving back, I shared their optimism and a determination to make things work. We laid flowers, just plucked from a neighborhood garden, at the site of the May 27, 1992, mortar attack that had killed sixteen people lined up for bread outside a bakery. We heard mortar fire from the surrounding hills, reminding all of us that Sarajevo was still a very dangerous place. My five-hour visit there was one of my most memorable experiences as high commissioner, one that I recall vividly even today.

We returned to Zagreb again on the UNHCR airlift flight to

travel by land to Belgrade through some of the worst-hit regions of
the war: UN Protected Areas West and East and Vukovar. Judith
Kumin, UNHCR chief of mission, and our Belgrade colleagues met
us at the crossing, and we had a picnic lunch out in the woods. Kumin
had learned the language and gave us an insightful analysis of the Serbian scene. In some villages all the houses had been destroyed. In others the burning and shooting had been very selective, proving that
specific ethnic groups had been targeted to be either killed or expelled
from the area. Traveling through the devastation, we immediately
realized the difficulty of returning the refugees home. The destruction of Vukovar was total. Only frames of large buildings remained.
Muslims from Bosnia were continuing to cross over to Croatia. In
some areas we heard heavy artillery, and the convoy route had to
be changed.

Wherever possible, we visited refugees in reception centers. In
Djakovo I talked to a twelve-year-old girl, Amra, and her mother,
who asked us to find Amra's father and six-year-old sister. She spoke
good English and told me how they had been forced to flee Bosnia
three months before and how she had learned English watching Hol-
lywood films on her video player. In Belgrade we went to the Red
Cross–run reception center and met several families who had taken
refugees under their wings. A Serb woman from Bosnia, with several
children, was staying with a Serb working family also with many children. Her husband had stayed behind, presumably to fight. She was
grateful for the hospitality, and she asked me to tell the Americans
that Serbs were generous people. Asking around, I noted that poor
people tended to be more generous in sharing misery. In Belgrade,
invitations to stay in people's homes were extended more by lower-
income families than by the upper classes.

Upon returning from my first field visit to the Balkans, I concluded first that the Sarajevo airlift was moving well, thanks to the
widespread support of governments and particularly the large relief
supply promised by the European Commission; second, that the
attention on Sarajevo was vital, but that there were "many Sarajevos"
all over the country, the needs of which also had to be met; third, that

the airlift was important, but that the real challenge would be in running land convoys, thus necessitating getting more trucks and more international drivers; fourth, that given the ethnic dimension of displacement and war, the return of people to their homes would be extremely difficult, and other solutions might have to be explored; and fifth, that an international conference on the humanitarian aspects of the crisis had to be organized to deal with the massive human displacement and mobilization of assistance, as well as to urge political solutions to their plight.

The Sarajevo airlift operation during the next three years delivered lifesaving food, medicine, and other humanitarian aid. By mid-March 1995 it had flown more than 12,100 sorties and delivered more than 150,500 metric tons of food and 14,500 metric tons of medical supplies. Two other significant but complicated functions of the airlift were medical evacuation and passage for officials and journalists. Since UNHCR was in charge of coordinating the airlift, it came under pressure from all those who asked for access. Needless to say, medical evacuation was a high-priority humanitarian action that prompted support from all concerned. The first patient out of Sarajevo was a baby girl born with a hole in her heart who had to be evacuated with her mother. At the time there were up to two hundred critically ill patients in Sarajevo hospitals who required evacuation. For each patient, necessary security and in-transit medical care had to be set up, travel documents obtained, and receiving governments and hospitals confirmed. The Serb side insisted on numerically matching the evacuation of Serb patients with Bosnian patients. There was constant politicization of the medical evacuation activities and criticism of the evacuation setup. Nevertheless, in the end, nearly eleven hundred patients and fourteen hundred accompanying relatives left Sarajevo by air.

The question of airlifting Bosnian government officials out of Sarajevo was a complicated issue that worsened in time. To begin with, these officials were not authorized to use air transport in and out of the capital because of security concerns. A clearly identified flight carrying them might become the immediate target of enemy

action. However, there was a recognized need for some Bosnian officials to have access to air transport out of Sarajevo in order to undertake political and humanitarian negotiations. The burden of selection
fell on UNHCR. A list of official delegation members was drawn up.
But with time and the acceleration of the peace negotiations, the list
also expanded. Abuses increased as passengers turned up at the Sarajevo airport with manifestly false reasons. Even the official delegations brought along large quantities of baggage that had to be left off
the flights, causing political problems between the military operators
and the Bosnian government. The military operators of the airlift
became concerned that these abuses might endanger the safety of the
flights. At one time, when security incidents involving the transport of
Bosnians increased, the three operators of airlifting Bosnian delegations—France, Canada, and the United Kingdom—decided to restrict
access. They faced strong Bosnian political criticism.

Carrying Bosnian delegations or not, the Sarajevo airlift had acute
security problems. Many of the conditions that the Security Council
laid down to ensure the security of the airport and its approaches had
not been met. Nevertheless, the airlift operation was undertaken and
carried out because of the dire humanitarian needs of the people of
Sarajevo. The loss of an Italian G222 with four crew members on September 3, 1992, came as a shocking reminder of the risks involved.
The airlift had to be suspended immediately. A preliminary investigation suggested that the aircraft "had been struck at least by one mis-
sile that had been provided with infra-red guidance."[3]

A small portion of the wreckage was brought to my office, and it
lay on top of a torn piece of blanket intended for Sarajevo. It was later
made into a wall piece and hung at the entrance of the UNHCR
headquarters building in Geneva. At the time I had to decide what
recommendation to make on resumption of the airlift, and to find
ways to supplement the goods that were not reaching Sarajevo by air.
While waiting for detailed reports from technical investigation, I
requested that UNPROFOR obtain reconfirmation of security
arrangements locally from all the Yugoslav parties.

After the suspension of the airlift UNHCR increased the number of road convoys to Sarajevo, as well as the daily tonnage. Routes were opened from Split to Sarajevo. Trucking into Sarajevo steadily increased, but convoys carrying supplies were stopped and harassed continuously at checkpoints. There were incidents involving weapons drawn on convoy drivers as well as shelling from neighboring hills. One convoy that was forced to take a dangerous mountain road lost a truck that slipped from the muddy track into a ravine. The driver escaped injury, but tons of precious relief supplies were lost. These incidents took place as I met the leaders of various warring factions in Geneva, to urge better security assurances for the humanitarian relief operation. Finally, on October 3, 1992, the airlift to Sarajevo resumed. I was conscious of the risks involved but grateful that the United States had decided to take the lead in resuming the flights. In the course of three and a half years, the airlift had to be suspended many times. The humanitarian air bridge was vital for the survival of the citizens of Sarajevo.

The airlift carried essential relief supplies to the population. In time it grew from supplying food, plastic sheeting, and blankets to providing a wide range of amenities for the life of the city: transport of mail, import of newsprint, passage of officials, and evacuation of the sick and wounded. The land convoys also carried fuel in the form of diesel, wood, and coal. The people of Sarajevo looked to UNHCR, and particularly to the airlift, as a symbolic message from the international community that they had not been forgotten or abandoned.

However, my special envoy, Mendiluce, warned me about the intrinsic difficulties that we faced. "UNHCR should be very clear, and public, about our inability to administer the capital of BH [Bosnia and Herzegovina]. . . . The problem of keeping Sarajevo alive is more than a relief problem. The reality is that one party prevents us from bringing in anything which they do not want to see brought in; another party harasses and shells convoys and blows up bridges; and the government itself mutilates its own facilities and diverts relief for its own purposes. UNHCR is trying to assist civilians in the face of obstruction from all parties. This is unsustainable. . . . Instead of continuing to assume tasks we cannot perform, we must state that without an end to the war, people will continue to die, and in greater numbers."[4]

Eventually the land convoys through various parts of Bosnia and Herzegovina expanded enormously. Between 1992 and 1995 UNHCR coordinated a massive logistical operation in which some 950,000 metric tons of humanitarian relief supplies were delivered to various destinations. The largest portion consisted of food provided by the World Food Programme (WFP). Other UN agencies, such as UNICEF, the World Health Organization (WHO), and the Food and Agriculture Organization (FAO), along with international non-government organizations, participated under the UNHCR umbrella. Most of these organizations relied on UNHCR for assurances of security and official accreditation. At the height of our effort there were over three thousand humanitarian personnel from over 250 organizations carrying UNHCR identification cards and over 2,000 vehicles in Bosnia and Herzegovina with UNHCR registration plates. The UNHCR convoy operation consisted of 250 trucks, with teams provided through governments, among them Denmark, Norway, Sweden, the United Kingdom, Germany, and the Russian Federation. The logistics centers were Belgrade (for Yugoslavia and eastern Bosnia), Zagreb (for Sarajevo and central Bosnia), and Split (for Sarajevo). By air and by land, the humanitarian relief operation in Bosnia and Herzegovina was unprecedented in scale and scope. Altogether it was extraordinarily complex as the operation was carried out against the background of war. Respective ethnic groups vied for the supplies, obstructing others from receiving benefits. I came to understand fully how the war in Bosnia and Herzegovina was fought, not only on the battlefield but also in the political and humanitarian arenas.

MULTIPLE PARTNERS: ICFY AND UNPROFOR

We continued our humanitarian operations by air and by land, but there was no end to misery. We knew that the war had to end and a political settlement had to come. How could we mobilize assistance to cover the needs of the ever-expanding displaced population? How could we entice the political will of the world leaders to intervene quickly and effectively? The idea of an international conference had been on my mind for some time. I had broached the subject with Secretary-General Boutros Boutros-Ghali in June 1992, when I saw him in Rio de Janeiro at the occasion of the UN Conference on Environment and Development. He responded favorably to the idea but thought I should take the initiative with his support rather than have himself take the lead. There were precedents for UNHCR's calling for international meetings on refugees to arouse support and seek solutions: the International Conference on Assistance to Refugees in Africa (ICARA); the Comprehensive Plan of Action (CPA) on Indochinese Refugees; the International Conference on Central American Refugees (CIREFCA). As we examined what steps to take, Thorvald Stoltenberg, foreign minister of Norway, called to tell me that the idea of a Balkan humanitarian conference was floating among the Nordic governments and suggested that I take the lead. After preliminary consultations with several European governments, I approached British Prime Minister John Major, who was the EC president, at 10 Downing Street. He warmly welcomed the initiative. He offered to contact key countries personally, so that a high-level ministerial meeting could be realized. The meeting proved to be the beginning of a close collaboration with the British government that grew in the course of the Balkan wars.

At UNHCR we immediately set to work. Soren Jessen-Petersen, my superbly able chef de cabinet, was to coordinate the meeting, in terms of both substantive input and conference preparation. The date had to be almost immediate, because ministers were already leaving capitals for the summer holidays. The one problem I faced was my own availability. I had been scheduled to make my first official visit to China, a major Asian country providing important support for Indochinese refugees. To postpone or to change an official visit because of developments in Europe would not be diplomatically correct. My colleagues urged me to go to China, and they assured me they would be fully responsible for good preparation. I left for China as planned and came back on July 25, just in time for the meeting.

The International Meeting on Humanitarian Aid for Victims of the Conflict in the Former Yugoslavia took place on July 29, 1992, in Geneva. Eighty-six states attended, including delegates from all the states of the former Yugoslavia and the neighboring countries most affected by the crisis. Twelve international agencies and two consortia of nongovernmental organizations also participated. The delegations were headed by senior officials. Although it was not intended to be a pledging conference, the meeting generated an additional $43.8 million for the UNHCR program. Offers of support that covered planes, trucks and drivers, and medical equipment and expert personnel were announced. The meeting proved encouraging and rewarding.

I opened the meeting by stressing the "urgent and compelling need to reinforce humanitarian action." At the same time, I emphasized that "humanitarian action cannot be sustained for long without an effective political solution." I recalled that UNHCR had been established originally to help World War II refugees in Europe. For the last thirty years we had been active elsewhere in the world, but now we had to return to a prosperous Europe haunted by death and the misery of refugees. I described the realities of "ethnic cleansing," which was at the heart of the conflict. Referring to my recent visits to Yugoslavia, I spoke of an incident that had just taken place in a town called Bosanski Brod. In most cases people were forcefully displaced by brutal force, but in Bosanski Brod the mayor had organized a convoy of buses and cars to expel four thousand Muslims and had provided them with documents to show that they had given up their properties as "gifts" and were leaving "voluntarily." What sinister bureaucratic violence!

I outlined the problems confronting UNHCR, from massive assistance to meet immediate needs for the winter to the eventual requirements for the return of refugees and reconstruction. I introduced two aspects of refugee protection in the ongoing Balkan context: preventive protection and temporary protection. UNHCR traditionally understood *protection* to mean first of all the right to seek asylum and the right to return for all those who desired it. We realized that in the current Balkan context, *protection* should be defined above all as "the right to be allowed to remain in one's home in safety and dignity, regardless of one's ethnic, national or religious origin." If the policy of ethnic cleansing were to be defeated, protection must include the notion of prevention.[5]

There was widespread agreement among the participants that preventive measures must be taken to reduce factors that compelled displacement. However, in discussing how to prevent and contain population movements, many emphasized the need to encourage people to stay in the safe areas nearest their homes. A number of them proposed the creation of safety areas or safety zones to make eventual return much easier. Slovenia and Croatia favored the creation of these areas in Bosnia and Herzegovina. France supported the idea but cautioned that these areas or zones would require military protection. A number of other states warned that these arrangements might unwittingly support the process of ethnic cleansing.[6] It had not been UNHCR's intention in presenting the idea of preventive protection to move on to the creation of safe areas or safety zones. We had been thinking in terms of strengthening our presence by monitoring the treatment of minority groups, mediating at the local level, and exposing practices of forced relocation. We were aware that for prevention to be fully effective, it had to be backed up by political action. Obviously, the primary concern of the Western European states was the arrival of large numbers of refugees crossing their borders from the former Yugoslavia states.

The second aspect of protection I presented to the meeting was a request to all states to provide temporary protection to those fleeing the former Yugoslavia. I emphasized that keeping borders open for those who need protection is an important act of solidarity. What was most needed in the current crisis was a flexible system of temporary protection that would respond to the emergency need for asylum as well as encourage return. Delegates were generally positive in their response, inasmuch as they could provide protection to those fleeing the war zones without subjecting them to an expensive and time-consuming procedure for determining refugee status. Burden sharing had already become a hotly debated issue among European governments. Some had offered to accept or were considering accepting refugees on a quota basis from other refugee-receiving countries. I took the position that whatever mechanisms for burden sharing were adopted, they should not limit the refugees' right to seek asylum. While countries that were receiving large numbers of refugees, such as Germany, stressed burden sharing on the basis of those refugees, others, such as the United Kingdom, argued on behalf of overall contributions that included peacekeeping and financial and other resources. The application of temporary protection remained a high priority. Such questions as "How temporary is temporary protection?" or "How do you terminate?" were seriously debated. UNHCR set up working groups among concerned governments to examine the application of temporary protection.

The meeting closed with an agreement to set up a follow-up committee. One of the points at issue was the coordination mechanism to mobilize the enormous material and financial resources necessary. The meeting recommended that UNHCR continue as the lead agency in partnership with UNICEF, WHO, the International Organization for Migration (IOM), the International Federation of Red Cross and Red Crescent Societies (IFRC), and the International Council of Voluntary Agencies (ICVA) and cooperate closely with the ICRC. These were the agencies that had been in the former Yugoslavia. The UNHCR lead role received unanimous but somewhat nuanced agreement. Sweden, for example, found it necessary to underline the importance of the interagency coordination mechanism that had been set up by the establishment of the UN Department of Humanitarian Affairs, while others stressed that UNHCR's lead operational role should be reinforced by overall strategic coordination and fund-raising by DHA.

The secretary-general had asked Undersecretary for Humanitarian Affairs Jan Eliasson, the former Swedish ambassador to the UN, to represent him at the meeting. I was very pleased to welcome him.

I was fully in favor of soliciting support from the undersecretary to mobilize UN expertise and political support. However, I thought that the kind of operation UNHCR had been assigned to lead had to be coordinated in the field. We were already facing enormous difficulties raising funds, negotiating access, and running airlifts and land convoys through war zones. To me, humanitarian coordination is not a bureaucratic management issue but a hands-on daily sharing of planning, information, and risks among experienced staffs in the field.

As the situation on the ground deteriorated, the need for coordination intensified. UNHCR was ready to provide necessary human and material resources, we had set up fourteen warehouses and opened twenty-seven field offices. To meet the needs of over 2.7 million people throughout the six republics in the summer of 1992, the UN agencies appealed for funds at the level of $282 million. Since nearly half the population in need were in Bosnia and Herzegovina, special consideration had to be given there. There were three points where supplies arrived: Zagreb, Belgrade, and Split. All three developed into enormous logistics hubs with arriving supplies and departing fleets of trucks. Road convoys had to follow carefully selected routes to chosen destinations. A great deal of negotiation was required with the parties in actual control to go through checkpoints. Humanitarian operations had to abide by the principles of neutrality and impartiality if they were to gain the trust of all parties, and relief assistance had to be given in accordance with needs. Pressure came from all parties demanding better share. The convoys faced constant threats and obstructions.

Following up on the momentum of the Geneva meeting on July 29, the United Kingdom in its capacity as head of the EC held the International Conference for the Former Yugoslavia (ICFY) in London on August 26–27, 1992. Cochaired by EC president John Major and UN Secretary-General Boutros Boutros-Ghali, it was to be a conference in continuous session, carrying out negotiations with the Yugoslavia parties. Lord David Owen and Cyrus Vance were nominated to cochair the steering committee. Six working groups were set up to probe into issues of concern to reach settlements on issues that rose following the breakup of the former Yugoslavia.[7] Regional organizations, such as the Organization of Islamic States (OIS) and the Organization of Security and Cooperation in Europe (OSCE), were also invited.[8]

I was appointed to chair the Humanitarian Issues Working Group. The decision came directly from Boutros-Ghali. The secretary-general expected peace negotiations to be carried out by the European Community, while peacekeeping would be the UN's responsibility. He also wanted UNHCR to continue to lead the humanitarian operations. Within the United Nations, there were moves to give this role to others, such as the undersecretary in charge of humanitarian affairs. I was a bit apprehensive about whether I could carry the dual role of heading the lead UN humanitarian operations and chairing a working group under the London Conference. However, I saw merit in directly dealing with the political and diplomatic participants in the conference because I could serve as the medium through which to bring the humanitarian realities to the political leadership. I could also solicit their support to weigh in against the obstructions of the peoples and groups involved. Besides, I had been long convinced that the humanitarian problems would not be solved without an overall political settlement for Yugoslavia. The ICFY came as a challenge to seek and promote solutions to the conflict.

Involvement in the ICFY structure certainly gave me additional work and responsibilities. As the steering committee cochairs, Owen and Vance, set up their headquarters in Geneva, I participated in their meetings almost weekly, together with Martti Ahtisaari, the chairman of the Bosnia and Herzegovina Working Group, which was charged with the mapping of the future republic. He closely followed the negotiations of the cochairs with the involved groups and people and examined the existing constitutional framework of the republics in order to come up with a final peace plan.

There were three main tasks assigned to my Humanitarian Issues Working Group: to seek ways to deliver humanitarian assistance effectively, to realize the progressive return of refugees, and to dismantle the detention centers. The first two tasks fell directly under my mandated mission as high commissioner for refugees. For the third, I invited the participation of the ICRC. Much of the substantial work assigned to the working group had to be carried out through our field operations. As for conferences, I decided to hold two kinds of meetings. The first kind was of the whole to which all concerned states as well as operationally involved international organizations would be invited. This formula made possible the attendance of delegations of the Federal Republic of Yugoslavia—Serbia and Montenegro—which had been under economic sanctions by Security Council Resolution 757 of May 20, 1992, and been excluded from all UN conferences. Both republics, however, hosted refugees. To hold meetings on refugees in the Balkans without their presence would have been meaningless. The large and well-attended meetings of the working group of the whole certainly helped keep together international support and commitments. The follow-up issues agreed upon by the Geneva meeting of July 1992 were gradually subsumed under the ICFY Humanitarian Issues Working Group.

The second type of the working group meeting was small and limited. It usually consisted of Yugoslavian parties and specifically interested humanitarian organizations. In one of the early talks in Geneva the cochairmen addressed the future constitutional arrangements for Bosnia and Herzegovina with the three Bosnian parties. I used the occasion to hold Humanitarian Issues Working Group meetings on September 18 and 19, to gain assurance of access and safety of airlifts and land convoys. All three Bosnian parties guaranteed the safety of the airlift operations. Radovan Karadzic, the Bosnian Serb leader, was generally forthcoming in expressing assurances, while Mate Boban, the Croat party leader, tended to be reserved. He categorically denied responsibility for the downing of the Italian plane. The Bosnian Muslim side emphasized the serious need for additional assistance and repeatedly asked for the opening of the Tuzla airport. The Serbs resisted this request, and the airport was never opened. On the land convoys, we spent a considerable amount of time discussing routes envisaged by UNHCR with different comments and proposals from all sides. The Serbs and the Croats argued that too little assistance reached their respective populations. I insisted that assistance would be distributed in accordance with the needs of the populations, not on the basis of equality among the parties. Karadzic stated that more attention should be given to eastern Bosnia and mentioned a large concentration of destitute displaced persons near Ozren. I promised to bring his request to the attention of the convoy planners. At the London meeting the three parties had agreed to designate local representatives at all locations to facilitate the passage of the convoys. I had to remind them to implement the process and notify us by the deadline of September 24.

At the second meeting of the Humanitarian Issues Working Group with the parties on October 5 and 16, 1992, I brought to their attention several problems that our UNHCR colleagues were facing in spite of the assurances by the party leaders. For example, the Bosnian local commander in Tarcin was not prepared to demine the section of the road to Sarajevo, causing problems to supplying aid by land. I had several serious complaints against the Serbs, who stopped and shelled the convoys at checkpoints on the Mostar road. There were two serious issues for UNHCR: the supply route to eastern Bosnia and the ongoing persecution in the Banja Luka region. The Bosnian delegation emphasized the need to prioritize assistance to Sarajevo and three enclaves in Serbian-held territory in eastern Bosnia: Srebrenica, Zepa, and Gorazde. The Bosnian stated their appreciation of UNHCR's efforts, but they cautioned against establishing any supply lines into Bosnia directly from Serbia and proposed alternative routes. One of the delegates declared that no food from Belgrade would ever reach the people, "You are trying to make agreements with killers and barbarians. They want to starve our people. You are too soft with them. We need military means." We had to make them understand that the convoys had to follow the easiest routes and not cross many dangerous front lines.

The situation in the Banja Luka region was extremely worrying. I had asked the cochairs to visit the area in order to prevent the situation from deteriorating for the local Croat and Muslim populations. In the past few weeks at least thirty thousand non-Serbs had fled to central Bosnia, where they were not accepted, and some died at the front lines. An experienced UNHCR fieldworker, Michael Petersen, reported on what he had witnessed. In his travels he came to the confrontation line between Banja Luka and Travnik and from a small hill saw a bus from Prijedor draw up off the road. He watched as the passengers were herded out and made to walk with bags holding the few possessions they were able to collect. The Serbs started to fire small arms over their heads. Then, as they moved out of range, shell fire started while they struggled on, stumbling and running. Some fell wounded while others died. Unable to help, Petersen was transfixed. Citing the incident, I insisted to Karadzic that there could be no excuse for the ongoing persecution in the region and urged him to make a public statement calling on all authorities and civilians to respect human rights and to live peacefully together. He agreed that something had to be done and would act immediately upon return. The working group setup provided opportunities to place humanitarian concerns on the political agenda and to present to the cochairs problems that required solutions while peace negotiations were going on.

The Bosnian parties tried to be on their best behavior at the working group meetings in Geneva. They issued statements of good intent most of the time but never put them into action. At times they protested and made myriad demands. When agreements were reached, they placed their signatures on documents binding them to cooperate. I collected many signatures of Yugoslav presidents and Bosnian party leaders. My Balkan expert colleagues, François Fouinat and Wilbert van Hovell, who accompanied me to the meetings, did their best to bring reason and mutual interest to the negotiating table. The solemn conference rooms in the Palais des Nations turned into smoke-filled Balkan cafés. At least I got to know these people. I talked to them bluntly and made demands. But I had no illusions. The war continued on the ground, with no solution in sight.

The Humanitarian Issues Working Group also dealt with the problem of dismantling the detention centers, with representatives of the ICRC joining the small negotiating meetings. The photos of emaciated inmates taken through barbed wire had hit the world press. The ICRC was able to reach agreement for the simultaneous release of five thousand detainees by all three sides from ten different locations. Croatia was ready to free six hundred prisoners from the Mostar prison. This was good news. Some thousand detained persons were released on October 19. The rest remained subject to continued pressure and negotiations. There were further problems. Those released had no place to go. Their homes had been destroyed. Even if they were freed and the Bosnian Serb guards were withdrawn, the hostility of local civilian Serbs to the inmates was more violent than that of the captors. In the end the ICRC and UNHCR decided to seek the escort of UNPROFOR from Manjaca, in northern Bosnia, to Croatia. UNHCR would set up a reception center in Croatia and negotiate departure for settlement to third countries. It was another dilemma of lending a hand to the process of ethnic cleansing, but we concurred that saving lives was the encompassing humanitarian principle that overrode all other concerns.

As we dealt with the Bosnian parties to gain assurance of better and safer access for humanitarian operations, the cochairmen were invited to address the UN Security Council. I was also asked to brief the council on humanitarian issues in the former Yugoslavia. To me, it was like crossing the humanitarian Rubicon. The long-upheld principles of neutrality and impartiality were generally interpreted by the humanitarian community to mean keeping a clear distance from political involvement. No head of a humanitarian agency had ever addressed the Security Council. I decided to take advantage of the opportunity in order to gain the council's understanding and political support. The refugees expected the council to support and shield them from all threats and obstacles. I also wanted to plead for quicker deployment of UN peacekeepers.

On November 13, 1992, I addressed the council. While insisting that the presence of the international organizations on the ground made a big difference, I said that they were not enough to confront the systematic uprooting of people. I concluded by stating that "UNHCR alone cannot prevent massive suffering and deaths during the winter" and that we needed a "renewed commitment by the parties to respect safe passage of relief goods and non-disruption of public utilities"; "immediate deployment of UNPROFOR and flexibility in application of their mandate to provide extensive support in logistics"; "massive bilateral and multilateral provision of resources"; and "pressure on all concerned—inside and outside the region—to keep borders open for those fleeing to survive, and urgently to receive all detainees being released."[9]

From January 24 to 27, 1993, I traveled to Zagreb, Belgrade, and Sarajevo with two objectives in mind: to meet with the political leaders and to consult with UNPROFOR. Security incidents were on the rise, and I needed renewed pledges for the safety of all those engaged in relief efforts. I also had to work out new modalities for collaboration with UNPROFOR in light of the passage of Resolution 770 on August 13, 1992. The secretary-general had recommended an expansion of UNPROFOR's mandate to support UNHCR's efforts to deliver humanitarian relief throughout Bosnia and Herzegovina and particularly to provide protection at UNHCR's request. An additional six thousand soldiers were to be deployed from Britain, France, Canada, and Spain. However, the deployment of the troops took time, and I had to appeal to the troop-contributing countries for quicker action.

I arrived in Sarajevo on a day of particularly heavy shelling and was warmly received by President Alija Izetbegovic and members of his administration. I was shocked by the ongoing destruction of the city. Security incidents were rising rapidly and affecting the relief operation. A Bosnian staff member of UNHCR who had greeted me on my arrival was shot at the airport ten minutes later and taken to the French field hospital. He was then evacuated to Paris. His life was saved, but the threatening reality of the war was brought very directly to me. Driving through the city, we saw window after window sealed with UNHCR-marked plastic sheeting; Mendiluce had distributed to the citizens transparent plastic materials together with window frames and simple tools to cover their windows. All over the city we saw UNHCR-marked windows, including the presidency building and other public buildings. One of our Sarajevo colleagues, Tony Land, told me that a visiting U.S. delegation asked him why UNHCR had so many offices throughout Sarajevo! The plastic sheets combined with a relatively mild winter helped prevent the citizens from freezing to death. We discussed ways to improve the distribution of supplies in Sarajevo. The government officials kept reminding me of the importance of getting relief supplies to the Muslim enclaves in eastern Bosnia.

The meetings in Zagreb concentrated on the refugee situation in Croatia. Fresh fighting in the Krajina was producing new refugee outflows of Serbs from Croatia. On the one hand, persecution in the Banja Luka region was creating hundreds of new Croat and Muslim refugees. Vice-President Mate Granic, who was in charge of refugees, while expressing Croatia's strong commitment to the protection of refugees, asked for international support. Both he and President Tudjman emphasized the need for further financial assistance. We agreed on a new formula of assistance by extending financial support to Croatian host families and to the national health insurance system to cover the refugees. On the other hand, I asked Croatia to do everything possible to restrain the Bosnian Croat forces (HVO). The increase in the security incidents in Bosnia was attributed largely to the HVO, which was responsible for blocking relief convoys from the Dalmatian coast. Granic confirmed that Tudjman would contact the Bosnian Croats to urge the safe passage of relief convoys. The heart of the matter was, however, that fresh heavy fighting was brewing between the HVO and the Bosnian government forces. The two armed forces, which had been restrained in their common stance against the Serbs, were now in conflict to maintain and expand their respective areas of control. Central Bosnia was turning into a main battlefield in 1993.

The visit with President Dobrica Cosic in Belgrade was an interesting experience of exposure to Serb nationalism. Milosevic had installed Cosic, a distinguished novelist, as president of the rump state of Yugoslavia in 1992 to buttress the respectability of Serb nationalism. Cosic thanked me for the assistance given to refugees and assured me that Yugoslavia would keep an open-door policy for refugees irrespective of their religious or ethnic origin. I appealed to him to use his moral authority to stop the psychological spiral of violence that was rampant in Bosnia. He said he "would not stop asking the Bosnian Serbs to leave innocent civilians in peace," but he worried "as a Yugoslav and a Serb that the forces of evil had been awakened in the Serbian people too." He was deeply suspicious that ethnic cleansing continued to take place in Croatia and that the Serbs in the Krajina would face a "second genocide."

I urged Serb republic President Milosevic to use his influence to stop the Bosnian Serbs from shelling Sarajevo, fighting in eastern Bosnia, and in particular persecuting the non-Serbs in the Banja Luka area. He expressed his support of UNHCR's mission but in turn requested the provision of oil and medicine. He accused the world of "Satanizing" the Serbian people. He was also extremely critical of the Croatian "aggression" in the Krajina. One point of agreement that resulted from this meeting was over Kosovo. I expressed my concern that an estimated three hundred thousand Kosovo Albanians had left the region for Western Europe. UNHCR wanted to report on the situation in a balanced way but had not obtained agreement to the opening of an office in Pristina. Milosevic denied that the Albanians had been pressured to go but assured me that the opening of a UNHCR office was "no problem." He delivered on his agreement, and UNHCR was able to open a suboffice soon thereafter. At the time the Western European countries were not prepared to recognize the asylum needs of Kosovo Albanians and were trying to gain reliable information from UNHCR. Our familiarity with Kosovo was to help us operate there in later years.

My consultations with UNPROFOR marked the beginning of a new relationship of collaboration between the military and the humanitarian agencies. Until then UNHCR had had only limited contact with UNPROFOR, with the exception of Sarajevo and the airlift. Initially, UNPROFOR had not been mandated by the Security Council to support UNHCR, which had some misgivings at being closely identified with the military force. Our preference even after the adoption of Resolution 776 would have been to move relief convoys without a military escort. However, because we operated in war zones, we realized the need for protection to safeguard not only our staff but also our supplies. Still, there was no field structure that linked the humanitarian and military wings of the United Nations. General Satish Nambiar, the UNPROFOR commander, reported to New York, while UNHCR's special envoy reported to Geneva. The device of the special envoy had the advantage of managing UNHCR operations coherently in the entire region, and it gave me a direct link with the field. Only in May 1993, when Thorvald Stoltenberg was appointed the special representative of the secretary-general, were the two UN functions brought together at the field level. The UNHCR special envoy was then given a dual reporting line, to Stoltenberg in Zagreb and to me in Geneva.

Under the then-existing circumstances, UNPROFOR and UNHCR clearly saw the need for better coordination and communication. UNPROFOR recognized that it had to enhance its protective coverage of relief convoys. There had been instances in which it had failed to dispatch armored personnel carriers (APCs) to rescue UNHCR staff and drivers or had retreated under fire. There had been cases of attacks on and shelling of UN civilian premises without any support. We decided to establish a joint planning and coordination cell in Zagreb to plan the delivery schedule in advance and to agree on routes where escort would be provided. However, the operational collaboration between UNPROFOR and UNHCR was to undergo changes as UNPROFOR took a more combative role with the intensification of the war and as NATO forces veered toward more and more air strikes and bombardment.

Better coordination or not, there was one fundamental condition that limited UNPROFOR's relations with UNHCR: The Serbs did not allow UNPROFOR deployment in territories under their control. In other words, much of eastern Bosnia and the Banja Luka region were out of bounds to UNPROFOR. UNHCR had to operate without UNPROFOR protection in 70 percent of Bosnian territory. On the other hand, throughout central Bosnia, UNPROFOR and UNHCR collaborated effectively to their mutual benefit.

In 1993 central Bosnia became the main battlefield between the HVO and the Muslim government forces. Growing tensions exploded into full fighting in the spring. The conflict was triggered by the attempts on the part of the HVO and Muslims to enlarge their respective territorial claims in preparation for the forthcoming peace settlement. The ICFY cochairs had been fully engaged in preparing peace plans and drawing up divisional maps. At a plenary session of the Bosnian parties and presidents of Croatia and Yugoslavia on January 2, 1993, the cochairmen introduced a three-part package plan comprising ten constitutional principles, a detailed cessation of hostilities agreement, and a map. Bosnia and Herzegovina was envisaged as a decentralized state that would give substantial autonomy to the provinces. The delineated ten-province structure had serious territorial implications. The Serbs, who militarily controlled 70 percent of the land territory of Bosnia, would have to withdraw from 38.6 percent of that territory. The Bosnian Serbs opposed the plan. The Bosnian Croats accepted the three-part package in full. President Izetbegovic on behalf of the Bosnian Muslims accepted the constitutional principles but not the map, which he claimed recognized the results of ethnic cleansing, an argument that won support not only among the Muslims but also abroad, particularly in the United States. Negotiations over the map continued over the following few months. In March, Karadzic signed a revised text on the condition that the Serb National Assembly gave final approval. The National Assembly rejected the agreement on May 5–6.

Faced with rebuff, the Vance-Owen plan had to be further revised and negotiated. I recognized the complexity of the negotiating process when the challenge was to work out a legal document with territorial demarcations. The parties were ready to fight out their claims. It was partly the mapping that caused the intensification of military action. Could an internationally mediated plan be imposed on parties that were ready to fight still more? How far could the Serb forces be made to withdraw from territories that they had occupied without being confronted by brute force?

In the meantime fighting spread farther in central Bosnia, particularly in the Mostar-Jablanica region. Tens of thousands of civilians either fled or were trapped in besieged pockets. Distributing humanitarian relief under the circumstances was a high-risk operation. On June 1 an attack occurred on a twelve-truck convoy, escorted by Canadian UNPROFOR troops and headed for Maglaj, where thirty-two thousand Muslims were desperately in need of relief supplies. The convoy had taken the precautionary measure of staying inside a tunnel while sending one truck at a time into town to unload. A huge explosion at the mouth of the tunnel killed two Danish truck drivers and one Bosnian interpreter. Five others were injured; one of them was listed in serious condition. Four days before, a two-truck convoy led by an Italian nongovernmental organization had been hijacked on its way to Zavidovici. Five Italians were beaten, robbed, and then shot. Two escaped, but the others were missing and feared dead. One month later on August 15, a UNHCR staff member was shot and killed in Vitez, while driving an unmistakable UNHCR armored vehicle. In spite of the great help given by UNPROFOR soldiers, there was a limit to the protection they could provide when convoys and relief staff were deliberately targeted.

The succession of grave security incidents against humanitarian convoys and staff grieved and angered me. I recall a note from a colleague that reflected clearly the sentiment of the staff: "I have a personal and philosophical unrest in my mind, when we neither can protect the people nor agree to inhumane policies. All I try to remember every day is that we are here to save as many lives as possible and to alleviate the suffering." Indeed, we all wanted to carry on, but we faced parties that were making our work more and more impossible in many areas. In fact all parties seemed to believe that our humanitarian assistance fed their "enemy."

In view of the deteriorating situation on the ground, I called for the Humanitarian Issues Working Group meeting in Geneva to meet the political and military leaders of the Bosnian parties. President Cornelio Sommaruga of the ICRC also participated. I tried to impress on them that the primary responsibility for averting further disaster was theirs. After serious negotiations, they agreed to suspend fighting along the major supply routes for the passage of humanitarian convoys, to ensure complete and secure freedom of movement for the United Nations and international humanitarian organizations, to prevent the diversion of humanitarian assistance to the military, and to release all civilian detainees in accordance with the arrangements already set up with the ICRC. We had won some concessions, but for how long?

Some media speculated that the United Nations was using the threat to withdraw from Bosnia and Herzegovina as a bargaining chip to demand concessions from the Bosnian parties. I denied such intentions. However, I reiterated at the July 16, 1993, meeting of the Humanitarian Issues Working Group with all government representatives that "humanitarian action cannot and must not be a substitute for decisive political action." I expressed my commitment to continue, but if the United Nations were to retreat, it would only be because of those who rendered the mission impossible.[10] Later that year, on October 25, immediately after the killing of a UNHCR driver and the wounding of nine UNPROFOR soldiers, UNHCR suspended all convoy operations in central Bosnia. We judged that we had to suspend our activities in areas where the minimum operating conditions no longer existed.

SREBRENICA AND THE SAFE AREAS

In eastern Bosnia, UNHCR concentrated its efforts to keep the besieged capital, Sarajevo, and the Muslim enclaves alive. The land convoys to supply eastern Bosnia came from Belgrade and Split. The HVO blocked and threatened the operation as supplies went through central Bosnia, and the Bosnian Serb Army tried to prevent relief assistance from reaching the enclaves.

The enclaves in eastern Bosnia were municipalities and villages— namely, Srebrenica and the surrounding areas, the Zepa area, Gorazde, and Cerska-Kamenica area. The people in these enclaves were mostly Muslims and were facing population increases resulting from the arrival of those who had fled the fighting in other areas. The Serbs attacked the enclaves to counter the Muslim attacks from the enclaves, and they believed that the composition of the population of the enclaves would determine the future map of the country. The civilians in the enclaves were surrounded by Serb military forces and lived in appalling conditions, often without the most basic needs and services. The entire population was totally dependent on external assistance.

In Srebrenica the besieged population was estimated at approximately fifty thousand. At the time of the 1991 census, it had had a population of thirty-seven thousand of whom 73 percent were Muslims and 25 percent Serbs. When the conflict broke out, the Serb paramilitaries from Srebrenica, reinforced by Serbs from other parts of eastern Bosnia, held the municipality for several weeks but were driven out by the Muslim forces. Then the Serbs fought back and brought the area largely under their control. UNHCR was aware of the critical conditions of the enclave population, but our convoys were denied clearance by the Serb forces that controlled the roads. The conditions under which the land convoys operated in eastern Bosnia were becoming increasingly difficult. I reported to the secretary-general: "Verbal and physical intimidation, arbitrary arrests of UNHCR staff, theft of vehicles, targeted shelling and shooting, harassment at check points, and unfounded and politically motivated press campaigns are not incidental, but have become a daily risk."[11]

Against this critical backdrop I learned that the City Council of Sarajevo was instituting a boycott of the delivery and distribution of UNHCR supplies in protest of the terrible humanitarian conditions of the Muslim enclaves in eastern Bosnia. I was upset and angered by what to me seemed the politicization of humanitarian assistance by the Muslims. I telephoned Mendiluce and instructed him to warn President Izetbegovic that the humanitarian supplies were for the suffering victims of Sarajevo, and the political leaders should not refuse the distribution of our assistance to the victims.

At the time I was on a mission to Africa to visit the countries in the Great Lakes region. In Nairobi I saw on television images of the

Sarajevo airport, with piles of supplies and lines of trucks suspended from delivery and felt the urge to take immediate action. I was traveling from Nairobi to Bujumbura to visit the Rwandan refugees who had been hosted by Burundi for more than thirty years. I had never been there before and was uncertain of its access to international communication. I knew that Nairobi had the best press center in Africa and that a press conference was planned for the next day. I decided to announce my decision to suspend assistance to Sarajevo. In the meanwhile, Jessen-Petersen, my chef de cabinet, frantically contacted Mendiluce, in Bosnia and Stafford, my deputy high commissioner in Geneva, to inform them of my decision and instruct them to take appropriate action.

Citing all the odds against which UNHCR and other humanitarian staffs had been pursuing their mission, and specifically referring to the Bosnian government's refusal to allow the distribution of relief to those in dire need, I announced on February 17, 1993, that I was taking four steps: "Move UNHCR blocked convoys back to their bases and immediately suspend all relief activities in Serbian-controlled Bosnia. Suspend all UNHCR activities in Sarajevo and withdraw most staff, leaving only a skeleton UNHCR presence in the besieged city of 380,000. Suspend land convoys and the airlift to Sarajevo. Maintain at a reduced level UNHCR relief operations in areas of Bosnia where UNHCR can still operate." I used very harsh words and accused the political leaders on all sides for "making a mockery of our efforts" but assured them that "when they request me to resume our operations, I will do it immediately provided they guarantee to keep the promises . . . concerning unhindered passage for humanitarian assistance."[12]

No decision that I took in my ten years as high commissioner caused as much havoc. That night the Security Council president made a statement "condemning the blocking of convoys and impeding of relief supplies in Bosnia-Herzegovina" and demanded that the parties concerned "give the United Nations High Commissioner for Refugees the guarantees she has sought . . . and thus facilitate the resumption of the full humanitarian relief program." However, New

York was reported to have been taken by surprise. The secretary-general was on a mission in Japan, and the secretariat had not been informed ahead of time. I wrote to the secretary-general on February 17 from Nairobi that "I felt compelled to suspend part of the assistance activities" and that "this operational decision had been made after consultation with your Special Representative, Mr. Vance," whom I had called the night before. In this letter I also expressed my hope that "this partial suspension will allow the leaders to reflect on their obligations towards their people and that they will provide guarantees for a quick resumption of the suspended UNHCR activities."[13] I thought I had cleared my lines, but the media reports that reached me in Bujumbura reflected a critical view among some diplomats and UN staffers that I should have consulted the secretary-general ahead of my decision.

A strong note of reprimand was relayed from the secretary-general through his chef de cabinet that he was "concerned about your announcement yesterday (17 February), without prior consultation with him, that aid operations in Bosnia were being suspended on 'operational' grounds." He argued that no decision over suspension should be regarded as purely operational in view of the great political sensitivity involved. He reminded me that political negotiations were being carried out in New York and that member states were expressing "forceful criticism of the decision."[14] In New York I was perceived as having overstepped my mandate. While everyone was appreciative of the frustration and extreme difficulty I faced, UNHCR was expected to carry on its relief work without ever questioning any threshold to politicization that I would refuse to cross. As I flew out of Bujumbura, I was amazed that my decision had made worldwide headlines. I was also surprised to read in the newspapers that I was contemplating resignation. "Never," I told Jessen-Petersen, "not over something like this."

Anxious faces greeted me at the Geneva airport. We went to the office and immediately tried to collect information from various parts of Bosnia as well as to contact the secretary-general. On the morning of the twenty-first, Vice-President Ejup Ganic of Bosnia came to the UNHCR office in Zagreb to thank us for the temporary suspension of the airlift. He said that the action had brought global attention to the fate of the Muslims in the eastern enclaves. He brought a message from President Izetbegovic to the effect that he had recommended an end to the boycott of relief supplies in Sarajevo and now requested the resumption of the airlift as soon as possible.[15] The media reported that the secretary-general sent a message to me "asking to resume the humanitarian aid." It portrayed the development as one in which the strong-willed Boutros Boutros-Ghali had won a row with Sadako Ogata and implied that I had been overruled. The secretary-general was also reported to have added, "I am supposed to direct this operation."[16]

Speaking directly to the secretary-general by phone on the twenty-first, I found him much more sympathetic. He said that he fully understood my reasons for suspending assistance and emphasized that I should not hesitate to contact him for consultations at any hour of the day or night. Of course I expressed my regret for having caused any controversy. On February 22, only five days after the suspension, the airlift was resumed with sixteen sorties. I never thought the Bosnian government could afford a long suspension, but it was a bit short even from my calculation.

I received a lot of support from the staff and media. My governing board, the Executive Committee, convened a special session and expressed its strong support for my action. A number of world leaders, including three former high commissioners, wrote me that the decision signified a gesture that emphasized the priority of humanitarian principles. Nevertheless, I recognized that there had been a serious failure in internal communications. I requested that Irene Khan, my able lawyer executive assistant, investigate the reasons for "the discrepancy between the decision announced by HC and that implemented by the field" and for "the failure to notify the UN Secretariat of the decision before they [sic] heard from the media."[17] I felt confident that my decision was justified but regretted that the com-

munication failure had been costly. For an agency responsible for dealing with humanitarian catastrophes, there was no room for inadequate consultations to back up clear instructions.

The airlift resumed, and convoys moved to Sarajevo, but the
attempts to reach the enclaves were still obstructed. Conditions in
Cerska and Srebrenica were rapidly deteriorating. Reports from our
field officers based on eyewitnesses and radio operators in the area
spoke of massacres and atrocities against local villagers, including
women and children. Survivors were trying to flee and appealing for
help. The UNPROFOR commander in Sarajevo, General Philippe
Morillon, felt prompted to take action on his own and traveled to Srebrenica with a small group. Arriving on March 11, he found the municipality under virtual siege, overflooded with displaced persons, and in
a panic. Initially, he was even prevented from leaving but was allowed
to do so two days later after addressing a public gathering. He tried to
assure the people that they were under the protection of the United
Nations and that he would not abandon them.

All through February and March our convoys were blocked for
weeks. Road conditions, fighting on the ground, and obstructions by
Serb forces as well as communities altogether made access to these
enclaves impossible. While my special envoy shuttled among the
headquarters of the Bosnian political leaders to gain their support and
commitment toward unimpeded access, we began to look for other
means of delivery, including airdrops. The U.S. government informed
me that it was ready to airdrop relief supplies from high altitudes.
President Clinton, in a meeting with the secretary-general on February 25, 1993, shared his plan to parachute food and medicine to
remote areas. He assured the secretary-general that the operation
would be carried out in coordination with the United Nations and
UNHCR and characterized it as an "extension of the airlift currently
under way into Sarajevo." He emphasized that the purpose was to
supplement the land convoys, that it was "a temporary measure,
designed to address the immediate needs of isolated areas." He added
that the priority for airdrops would be strictly humanitarian, "without
regard to ethnic or religious affiliation."

When General Morillon and his team arrived in Srebrenica, they reported on the impact of the airdrops. They had observed a continuous stream of arrivals throughout the day and night with very meager supplies of food or places to stay. People just huddled around little fires in the main streets. A stream of thousands of people would hurry up the mountainside to pick up the assistance coming in through the air, but usually those who were in the greatest need—women, children, recent arrivals—did not succeed in getting hold of the packs of ready-to-eat rations. The drops had unfortunately resulted in some deaths when people were either directly hit or crushed by those who rushed to the site.[18]

Airdrops were helpful as the means of last resort for the delivery of food, medicine, and other needs to besieged communities in eastern and central Bosnia. The modalities of delivery improved with time. Information sheets were dropped in advance to prepare the population for more orderly receipt. From packs of ready-to-eat army meals, the food became large bulks that could be cooked by women and reach families in need. Later I visited the air base in Germany to observe what developed into a multinational airdrop operation. I remember being amused by coming across Bosnians wearing pairs of shoes made out of parachute canvas and cord.

In the meanwhile, UNHCR faced new difficulties as it managed to bring in three convoys to Srebrenica in March 1993. The Serbs allowed us to bring in food and medicine but not shelter materials. When the trucks, after unloading the supplies, turned around to depart, they were stampeded by people desperate to flee Srebrenica. In the process, several people were crushed to death. Altogether more than 5,560 persons, including women, children, elderly, and wounded, forced themselves onto the trucks. The UNHCR staff operating the convoys faced determined parents intent on saving their children. The staffers had to help get children on the trucks and take them to Tuzla, and they told me stories of painful family separations and horrifying accidents. The issue of evacuation became a central policy issue that I had to raise with the secretary-general. I proposed two options to him: "immediately enhance international presence, including that of UNPROFOR, in order to turn the enclave into an area protected by the UN, and inject life-sustaining assistance" or "organize a large-scale evacuation of the endangered population in Srebrenica."[19] To ensure safety, the evacuation option required the cooperation of all parties, in particular of the Bosnian authorities.

Those authorities in Tuzla as well as in Srebrenica opposed the evacuation of the Muslim population lest the enclaves turn empty of women and children and facilitate a Serb offensive. For similar reasons, the Bosnian government opposed evacuations to safety throughout the war. The Serbs, on the other hand, were intent on blocking aid coming in but supported UNHCR to carry on the evacuation. UNHCR, on the other hand, could neither adequately meet the needs of the people nor evacuate all those who wished to leave. I asked the secretary-general to seek the support of the Security Council for humanitarian access to the victims in the besieged cities and for the granting of safe passage out of the areas of combat.

At the time the Security Council was engaged in debating the situation in eastern Bosnia. The secretary-general presented my letter to the Council, after which extended consultations took place among the members. The nonaligned caucus, represented principally by Pakistan and Venezuela, was strongly in support of the Bosnian government and proposed firm action to reverse Serb attacks and to lift the arms embargo, which had been established under Resolution 713[20] as it applied to Bosnia and Herzegovina. The nonaligneds argued that the embargo hampered the right to self-defense of Bosnia and Herzegovina. Resolution 819, tabled by the caucus, was adopted on April 16, 1993. It declared Srebrenica and its surroundings a safe area that should be free from any attacks by the Bosnian Serb forces. Yugoslavia should cease to supply arms, equipment, and services to the Bosnian Serb forces. The council requested the secretary-general to monitor the humanitarian situation in the safe area and to take immediate steps to increase the presence of UNPROFOR in Srebrenica and its surroundings. However, it did not provide any clear mandate or resources to carry on the additional tasks. By adopting this resolution, the Security Council in fact ruled out my evacuation option. It condemned the Serb action for forcing the evacuation of the civilian population but gave no direction to how to prevent further humanitarian calamities.

I recognized more than ever the limits of the Security Council. Its concern was primarily political, with limited heed to humanitarian consequences. It could condemn the Bosnian Serb action, but UNPROFOR, UNHCR, and humanitarian agencies had to cope with the effects of increasingly dominant Serb power. My special envoy, Mendiluce, conveyed to me the determination of our field staffers. They urged me to continue sending convoys into Srebrenica with the anticipated result of evacuating people out of the enclaves. While the proper steps might be to press the Security Council for more decisive action, they believed that they could not afford to wait for such a move. There were risks involved in delivering assistance that would be inevitably connected with evacuation of people. Mendiluce informed me that "if Headquarters does not instruct me otherwise," he would go ahead with the convoy. He also believed that a massive evacuation should be planned, with serious consequences for the UN. It was important to recognize that despite all the problems faced by the previous convoys, more than seven thousand people had been saved and taken into Tuzla.[21]

Srebrenica became the first safe area declared by the Security Council. The idea of establishing a safe area in Bosnia and Herzegovina had been simmering for some time. It had been first raised at the London Conference of August 26 to 27, 1992, by delegates searching for ways to protect populations against forced displacements, arrests, and killings. Cornelio Sommaruga, the president of the ICRC, proposed the consideration of a safe haven for some ten thousand detainees in northern and eastern Bosnia. Also in the fall of 1992, Tadeusz Mazowiecki, who was appointed by the UN Commission on Human Rights special rapporteur on the situation of human rights in the former Yugoslavia, concluded in his report that a large number of displaced persons would not have to seek refuge abroad if the possibility of establishing security zones could be explored to guarantee security and provide food and medical care.[22]

At the government level, Foreign Minister Alois Mock of Austria, then serving as a nonpermanent member of the Security Council, led in pursuit of the possibility of establishing safety zones in various parts of Bosnia and Herzegovina. He argued that the number of refugees seeking protection would continue to rise and that recipient countries would no longer have the capacity to provide protection. The establishment of safety zones would be the only way to keep them within the country. Moreover, refugees staying outside Bosnia and Herzegovina might decide to return to their homes in safe zones. The permanent members of the Security Council were not necessarily supportive of the Austrian proposal. There were divisions, for example, between the militarily capable countries that would be expected to provide forces and other resources in the event of establishing safe areas and others that were more interested in limiting the flow of refugees into their countries. The Security Council simply invited the secretary-general to study the possibility of and requirement for the promotion of safe areas for humanitarian purposes, in consultation with UNHCR. Thereafter the term *safe areas* was used rather than *safe zones* or *safe havens* or any other such expression.

Within UNHCR, the Working Group on International Protection examined our basic position on safe areas to respond to the invitation by the council. It concluded that "the overriding principle in Bosnia and Herzegovina should be to bring safety to the people, rather than to bring people to safety." In other words, the first policy priority was to improve the level of safety and to provide assistance in the place where people were. Since suffering and displacement were caused by armed conflict, a genuine and durable cessation of hostilities should be the goal. UNHCR would be against establishment of safe areas that might distract from the necessity to bring all fighting to an end. Where displacement in Bosnia and Herzegovina was caused by ethnic persecution, special measures should be taken to improve the conditions of the remaining minority groups through three means: deployment of peacekeeping forces, human rights monitoring, and humanitarian assistance. Failing the cessation of hostilities so that admission to safety became necessary, UNHCR's priority was to seek

entry to neighboring countries or to relatively secure regions of
Bosnia and Herzegovina. To UNHCR, the establishment of one or
more clearly delineated safe areas under military protection should be
only a last option.[23]

The devastating experiences in Srebrenica in March 1993 and the
declaration of Srebrenica and its surrounding as the first safe area by
Resolution 819, followed by similar designations of Sarajevo, Tuzla,
Zepa, Gorazde, and Bihac and their surroundings as safe areas by
Resolution 824, May 6, 1993, were to change the role of the United
Nations in the war in Bosnia and Herzegovina. The safe area policy
brought some improvements to the situations in Srebrenica and Zepa.
A meeting was held in Sarajevo between the Bosnian Serb and Muslim military leaders on April 17, 1993. The UNPROFOR commander, General Lars Eric Wahlgren, acted as mediator. The two
parties agreed, effective on April 18, to a total cease-fire, the deployment of UNPROFOR, and the opening of an air corridor for the
evacuation of the seriously wounded and ill. The demilitarization of
Srebrenica was to be completed within seventy-two hours of the
arrival of UNPROFOR. All weapons, ammunition, mines, explosives, and combat supplies were to be submitted to UNPROFOR,
and no armed persons or units were to remain within the city.[24] Two
companies of the Canadian battalion and a UNHCR staff were
deployed in the safe area of Srebrenica, and medical evacuation
took place.

In May 1993 I decided to release Mendiluce from his heavy role as
special envoy and appointed Nicholas Morris to succeed him. For
nearly two years Mendiluce had carried on his mission with extraordinary courage and good judgment. He exposed himself directly to
many dangers as he operated in Sarajevo and in eastern and central
Bosnia at the height of ethnic cleansing. It was a miracle that he survived with only one traffic accident, but he was exhausted, and I could
not ask him to stay on any longer. Morris was a known leader in field
operations. He was the first one I had assigned as my special envoy for
northern Iraq in 1991, when he impressed me by his quick action and
cool command. Then he served as the UNHCR representative in

Pakistan, managing several million Afghans in border camps. I asked him to serve again in a war zone and coordinate a large humanitarian operation with diplomats and soldiers in an increasingly structured United Nations setup.

The adoption of Resolution 836 by the Security Council on June 4, 1993, marked a threshold. In addition to a mandate to provide protective support for the delivery of humanitarian relief, it extended its mission in the safe areas "to deter attacks against the safe areas, to monitor the cease-fire, to promote the withdrawal of military or paramilitary units other than those of the government of Bosnia and Herzegovina, and to occupy some key points on the ground." The resolution did not specifically request UNPROFOR to protect or defend the safe areas but essentially to be present. It authorized UNPROFOR "to take the necessary measures, including the use of force, acting in self defense." It also decided that the member states may take "all necessary measures, through the use of air power, in and around the safe areas" to support UNPROFOR.[25] The adoption of Resolution 836 had sweeping consequences, which the participating member states were aware of. However, Pakistan and Venezuela abstained on grounds that the nonaligned caucus did not consider the resolution strong enough to deter Serb aggression. The representative of the government of Bosnia and Herzegovina noted a continuing lack of will by the United Nations to confront Serb attacks on the Muslim enclaves.

The secretary-general asked the council for additional thirty-four thousand troops to carry out UNPROFOR's extended mission. He proposed a light option of seventy-six hundred for an initial reinforcement. However, the member states did not agree to provide additional forces and were not even ready to have their troops redeployed to the safe areas. It was only in January 1994 that the Canadian troops deployed to Srebrenica were able to rotate out with the arrival of elements of a Dutch battalion. In the short run, however, the safe area policy proved effective in Srebrenica and Zepa. In those two areas the warring parties agreed upon a cease-fire on the confrontation line and recognized the deployment of UNPROFOR. Limited medical evacuation was allowed, and the inhabitants could enjoy some freedom of movement.

The situation in Srebrenica, however, kept deteriorating. Limited access was granted for convoys, but the people were far from receiving adequate food and medical supplies. Infrastructure for the population was severely damaged, and the entire population was considered at risk. The water problem was particularly crucial, but permission from the Bosnian Serbs for repair of the water installation was slow to come. The UNHCR staff reported from the enclave that although it was quiet in the demilitarized zone, fighting continued on the front lines, particularly in the southeast. It was likely that more displaced persons would move into Srebrenica. Moreover, the convoys never met their planned goals.

UNHCR was uneasy by the establishment of the safe areas. If Resolution 836 were to be fully implemented, especially if UNPROFOR were to resort to the use of force, the humanitarian bond that had kept UNHCR and UNPROFOR in collaboration might be undermined. The safe area concept established by Security Council resolutions 824 and 836 was clearly anti-Serb in its orientation. UNPROFOR feared that Bosnian Serbs would impose restrictions on the freedom of movement of the United Nations, and that consequently it would be "forced to balance safe area tasks and those related to the military-humanitarian bond."[26] If the member states and NATO were to resort to the use of air power, the incompatibility between the humanitarian operation and military action over the safe areas would turn even more drastic. I foresaw that under these circumstances there would be "little or no role left to unarmed civilians engaged in humanitarian relief activities."[27] I noted an increasing gap between the Security Council and the secretary-general in New York and UNHCR in the field on the understanding of the needs of these areas. The reality was that we could carry on humanitarian action only within the range allowed by the war situation.

To begin with, Srebrenica and Zepa were remarkably different enclaves. The Srebrenica area was dominated by the town and a number of smaller villages, and the town's population had swollen enor-

mously. In the Zepa area there was no town, and most of the population was spread over ten relatively small villages. The local authorities
had kept the area in order with a limited number of displaced persons
entering it. How did one ensure the future of Srebrenica and the
other safe areas beyond the immediate need to bring in food and
medicine by convoys? Were the enclaves to turn into refugee camps
totally dependent on international relief?

Since the majority of the people in Srebrenica were those displaced from other areas ethnically cleansed by the Serbs, the social
tension between the majority refugee population and the newly
turned minority locals mounted daily. The UNHCR staff reported
that violence, theft, prostitution, and black-market activities were
becoming the dominant life pattern. Incidents were the norm of life.
Our staff members seriously questioned that Srebrenica could be run
like a closed refugee camp. They envisaged the building of viable societies with freedom of movement in and out of the enclaves. They
believed that the people should be allowed to work in the fields and
engage in productive lives. Seeds could be brought in by the relief convoys. The staffers also urged the reestablishment of local civil administration, rehabilitating utilities, reopening schools, training local
police to keep order, and reestablishing postal and other services.
They argued that the viability of the safe areas rested much more on
the functioning of the civil society and that the international community should not remain focused on the military alone.[28]

When the safe area story hit the media in the United States, I was
in Washington on my yearly visit. I called on the administration and
the Congress to update them on the refugee situation in the world
and to seek their continued support. I was received by Vice President
Al Gore, Secretary of Defense Les Aspen, Attorney General Janet
Reno, Senators Bob Dole, Ted Kennedy, and Patrick Leahy and Representatives Tom Foley and Lee Hamilton among others. I briefed
them on the situation in the Balkans and shared my concern over the
safe areas in eastern Bosnia.

On the *McNeil/Lehrer NewsHour* on May 24, 1993, Madeleine
Albright and I were asked about our respective views on the safe areas

in Bosnia. An active member of the Security Council, Ambassador Albright emphasized that the six safe havens were designated to defend the Bosnian Muslims by the UN peacekeeping forces. It was important to keep strong sanctions on the Bosnian Serbs and Serbia to make sure that areas seized through fighting and aggression would not stand. What surprised me most was her reference to the safe areas as the territorial base for the Bosnian state: "You cannot have a state without any territory, and what we're trying to do through these safe havens is to establish these as areas that represent what might at some point be a Bosnian state." Having been immersed in the humanitarian implications of the Bosnian War, I had not looked at the safe areas in such terms. I understood that territorial issues were important for peace settlements. But what about human lives? Viability of people and communities should be the top-priority items at the negotiating table. I responded to Mr. Lehrer that I expected the safe areas to assure security to the population in the enclaves, not only in military terms but also in the full sense of maintaining viable civil societies. I expressed my reservation over the safe area policy as it stood.

The safe area policy was a product of conflicting political interests as well as operational positions. As a humanitarian tool to protect victims, it was subject to political and military calculations and decisions. To the Bosnian government and its supporters, these areas were pawns for the political settlement that centered on the eventual territorial division of the Bosnian state. Operationally, they provided places where their troops could rest, train, and equip themselves as well as fire at Serb positions. The Serbs thought of the safe areas as targets of military offensives, to be overrun in order to bring eastern Bosnia under their control. The UNPROFOR presence was a complicating factor but containable so long as the scale was limited and access routes were under Serb control. However, air support by UN member states to protect UN forces, if actively implemented, would obstruct Serb war aims. The Serbs engaged in the shelling and bombing of safe areas to test the UN reaction.

UNPROFOR, for its part, found itself powerless in the enclaves. Its resources were meager, and air support by NATO was likely to endanger it and its humanitarian mission. The UN commanders in the field were generally opposed to widespread and generalized air strikes, while NATO was more ready for robust action. Our colleagues in the field were extremely critical of the Serbs' aggressive and inhumane action and were definitely in sympathy with the Muslims, although critical of the leadership that did not refrain from exposing the people to misery for political gains. They found the Croats self-centered and least trustworthy in most dealings. Balkan politics molded attitudes and behavior in all the ethnic groups that at times alienated even those with the deepest humanitarian commitments.

AIR STRIKES:
SHRINKING HUMANITARIAN SPACE

In Srebrenica, the cease-fire and demilitarization agreement by the Bosnians and Serbs brought a lull in the fighting, but the humanitarian situation continued to deteriorate. The UNPROFOR presence consisted of a Dutch battalion of approximately 780. Now, in the spring of 1994, the besieged safe area of Gorazde became the target of an intense Serb offensive. Casualties were high and in Gorazde's thirty-five-bed hospital a team of two local surgeons and a Médecins sans Frontières (MSF) anesthetist performed an average of ten major and thirty minor operations per day. Some two thousand civilians fled across destroyed surrounding villages, seeking safety. The UN faced a shortage of troops available to UNPROFOR and had only eight observers in Gorazde when the Serb offensive started. The UN asked NATO for close air support on April 10. Two strikes took place against Bosnian Serb positions south/southeast of Gorazde, and Serb military activity in the area ceased. It was a great relief that all the UNHCR staff in Gorazde and the ICRC and MSF staffs in Gorazde were reported safe and well.

Now UNHCR found itself facing a new situation, one in which NATO air strikes could take place without warning. Already our convoy operations through Bosnian Serb–controlled territory had faced security risks. Several times international staff members had had to be evacuated from their locations. We could not expose international convoy teams to the risks of air strikes on their way to or from missions. Inflammatory statements in the media identified UNHCR and the humanitarian assistance operations with war efforts against the Serbs. We took the pragmatic decision to maintain our presence in Gorazde under close review, while running convoys from Belgrade to the safe areas on a convoy-by-convoy basis. We also explored the possibility of UNPROFOR's taking over the delivery of humanitarian assistance to the enclaves. In fact, a few months earlier, UNHCR had participated in a series of policy reviews by UNPROFOR at which the question was raised of how long a civilian humanitarian assistance program should continue. There were two options for consideration: transfer responsibility for relief assistance to the parties, or "further militarize the operation where possible, and stop it where it cannot be militarized."[29]

Following the air strikes against the Serb positions south of Gorazde, relative calm returned for several months, only to be broken by Serb attacks on the safe area of Bihac. The relative stability in Srebrenica deteriorated, and UNHCR faced increasing difficulties in delivering assistance. The situation in Sarajevo turned critical as the Serbs initiated all-out war with heavy weapons. In response to NATO's rounds of air strikes, the Serbs resorted to taking UNPROFOR personnel as hostages, using them as human shields against further attack, and exposing the handcuffed images on Serb television. After a series of international interventions, including one by President Milosevic with ICFY cochairs, the hostages were released in groups. The question of UNPROFOR's resorting to the use of force was debated at the Security Council. The secretary-general noted that "when UNPROFOR used force against the Serbs other than in self defense, the Serbs quickly realized they had the capacity to make UNPROFOR pay an unacceptably high price, particularly by taking hostages." He argued in favor of an arrangement under which UNPROFOR "would abandon any actual or implied commitment to the use of force to deter attacks against the safe areas, and under which force, including air power, would be used only in self defense."[30] The

Security Council was divided on the secretary-general's assessment and proposal and would not respond. The steady deterioration and targeting of UN personnel made UN operations very difficult. The Serbs began attacks on Srebrenica on July 6, 1995, and overran one by one the eight observation points (ops) manned by the Dutch battalion.

The secretary-general had scheduled a meeting on July 8 in Geneva with civilian and military senior officials actively involved in the former Yugoslavia. Its purpose was to provide him with a strategic stocktaking of the situation on the ground and the prospects for the future. He opened the meeting stating that we had reached a turning point in Bosnia. General Bernard Janvier, the commander of the UN forces in the former Yugoslavia (UNPF), stated that in Srebrenica, ops were being manned with difficulty, but that in Gorazde no ops were manned. The UN deployment in the enclaves stood for nine hundred potential hostages, and UNPROFOR could not do much in eastern Bosnia. Janvier thought UNPROFOR should have left the enclaves. He drew a gloomy picture. The Serbs held all the cards. They controlled 70 percent of the territory, including the enclaves and part of Sarajevo. General Rupert Smith, the commander of UNPROFOR, portrayed an even more pessimistic prospect. He believed that the Bosnian government and the Bosnian Serbs were determined to achieve their aims through fighting. He added to the potential UN hostages twelve hundred UN troops in Bihac and Sarajevo. Both generals cautioned against robust approaches in order to minimize the risk of escalation of the war.

I presented a bleak assessment of the humanitarian situation. I said that UNHCR would persevere and try to protect the vulnerable groups wherever feasible, but that we were blocked in all besieged areas. During June we could meet only 20 percent of the needs in Bosnia and only 8 percent of the requirements in Sarajevo. The airlift to Sarajevo had remained suspended since April 8, and soldiers were driving our trucks over Mount Igman because it had become too dangerous for civilian drivers. I stressed the need for greater logistical support from the military in providing humanitarian assistance. The

BSA general Ratko Mladic was demanding a fifty-fifty divide of assistance, while UNHCR's policy was to provide assistance on the basis of need. A fifty-fifty division could mean starvation for the people in the enclaves. General Janvier thought that the military could take over if UNHCR were to withdraw. While the military might help in relation to Sarajevo, it could not operate in the eastern enclaves because UNPROFOR was regarded as the enemy.

The secretary-general concluded that while UNPROFOR was willing to help UNHCR, such service would require a change of mandate by the Security Council. We understood that under the circumstances of a divided Security Council, we would be left to muddle through. There was only one hope, the success of the peace negotiations being carried out at the time by the European Community (now officially the European Union) negotiator Carl Bildt. In fact we all placed large hope on Bildt's success.

Around six o'clock in the morning of July 11, Srebrenica fell to the Serbs. BSA troops attacked the protected safe area of Srebrenica. The Dutch battalion was unable to halt the Serb advance. The panicked population crowded around the Dutch compound while the Dutch commander negotiated an immediate cease-fire with the BSA. In the meanwhile as many as fifteen thousand Bosnian men began to move out of the enclave into surrounding Serb territory. As for the crowd of displaced persons, the BSA separated the women, children, and elderly from the men and put them on vehicles to be deported out of Srebrenica. Some five thousand arrived in Tuzla on the twelfth and were left at the airport. UNHCR set up emergency reception centers in Tuzla and its vicinity, but the Bosnian government insisted that the people be kept at the airstrip. The government wanted to dramatize the UN failure to the world and even asked us to designate them as "UN refugees," to be protected and assisted by the UN.

The first UNHCR team, which had left Belgrade on the twelfth, was stopped at the border but was able to reach the enclave the next day. It witnessed the UNPROFOR and Serb soldiers bringing the last group of Muslims to the Serb buses. On the way the team heard from local Serbs that large numbers were being held at the nearby football field in Bratunac and heard sporadic shooting from that direction. On the same day the BSA launched an offensive on Zepa, which it captured a few days later. Its population was expelled largely to Zenica.

On July 17 UNPROFOR provided a plane for me to visit Tuzla. Diplomats from the United States and France and officials from other humanitarian agencies joined me. We found the Tuzla airport a tented refugee village. I visited the people in the tents to hear their stories. Concerned about the fate of the males in their families, they were hysterical. We were informed of the departure of the men through the woods, but neither their safety nor their whereabouts were established. The women, while appreciating my visit, accused me. "Why could you not come before?" "Why could you not prevent the calamity!" All I could say was that we had been blocked and could not come. The sorrow and suffering of the abandoned families at the airstrip were overwhelming. I had very few words to console them. I stopped over at schools and cinemas that had been converted to emergency reception centers. I held consultations with Hasan Mura-tovic, the Bosnian government minister in charge of refugees, and promised assistance. I did insist, however, that the people had to be evacuated from the airstrip. They could not be left there as a monu-ment of international failure. I also conveyed my appreciation to Mayor Selim Beslagic of Tuzla, who had always been generous to receiving refugees. I laid flowers at the city center; the city had recently suffered a heavy toll of more than seventy young victims of Serb shelling.

Only in the aftermath of the fall of Srebrenica was the world forced to face the brutal realities of the Balkan conflict centered on the safe areas in eastern Bosnia. At Lancaster House on July 21 Prime Minister Major called a crisis meeting of foreign and defense minis-ters. From Washington, Secretaries Warren Christopher and William Perry attended together with General John Shalikashvili, now the chairman of the Joint Chiefs of Staff, members of the Security Council, the European Union, NATO, and the UN Secretariat all were lined up. Together with the secretary-general and Thorvald

Stoltenberg, I was invited to the meeting and was asked to brief the delegations on the humanitarian situation in Bosnia and Herzegovina. The chairman read out a statement in which he emphasized that the current Bosnian Serb offensive had to be met with a firm and rapid response, including the use of air power. Two important policy agreements emerged out of the meeting: NATO would draw a line around the enclave of Gorazde, and the decision on whether and how much air power to use at Gorazde would be made by NATO. The Srebrenica debacle exposed the limitations and contradictions inherent in the safe area policy. The time to take decisive action was approaching.

On the diplomatic front, new efforts were developing outside the ICFY-led negotiations. The United States had begun to involve itself in the search for a negotiated settlement. It focused on the Bosnian Croats and the Bosnian Muslims, with some backing from the government of the republic of Croatia. On March 1, 1994, the Americans successfully produced a Framework Agreement for the Federation, and an Outline of a Preliminary Agreement on the Principles and Foundations for the Establishment of a Confederation between the Republic of Croatia and the Federation. President Tudjman made it clear that the agreement that ended the hostilities between the Bosnian Croat and the Muslim forces was not directed against Bosnian Serbs. President Milosevic also took the position that the Croat-Muslim agreement was not a matter for the Serbs so long as their interests were not affected.

The United States together with the Russians also began to broker a cease-fire between the Croatian government and the Croatian Serbs. EU and UN cooperation was proving inadequate for the settlement of the Bosnian conflict. The American-led process resulted in the establishment of a contact group comprised of France, the United Kingdom, and Germany, in which the United States and Russia joined. Thereafter the peacemaking over Bosnia and Herzegovina moved away from the ICFY and the cochairmen and essentially became intergovernmental negotiations. Geneva was no longer the venue for peace talks. The main stage of the negotiations moved to

New York, while the United Nations carried on the peacekeeping and humanitarian mission in the field. There was some hope that a peace plan by the Contact Group might end the conflict.

The Contact Group unveiled its peace plan on July 4, 1994. The territorial arrangements provided 51 percent of the country for administration by the Croat-Bosnian Federation and the remaining 49 percent by the Serb authorities. The Serbs' rejection of this plan again led to intensified military action between them and the Croatian government forces. More and more, the United Nations had to face the question of how forcefully to seek NATO support and how far to pursue the humanitarian mission.

In mid-1995 several events dramatically affected the dynamics of the war in the Balkans. In August the Croatian Army launched a massive military offensive, Operation Storm, and overran all Serb-controlled areas in the western and southern Krajina region of Croatia. Some two hundred thousand Serb civilians fled east, the majority to the Federal Republic of Yugoslavia. Smaller numbers stayed in Serb-controlled parts of Bosnia and Herzegovina. At the time I was on leave in Japan, and Deputy High Commissioner Gerald Walzer, the most senior UNHCR professional with excellent management ability, immediately went to Croatia and Bosnia and oversaw the exodus. He made sure that those in flight were given necessary assistance of fuel, water, and food as they headed east. He observed that to judge from the tractors and household goods that the Serbs were transporting, they were leaving Croatia for good. The Serb exodus marked the final phase of the saga of Balkan ethnic politics. After the Serb departure, the Croatian government issued an edict authorizing the people to take over all abandoned property. The Krajina Serbs were left without property rights and had virtually no means to return. They were accepted by the Federal Republic of Yugoslavia. Milosevic made it evident to me, when I visited him a few years later over the issue of Kosovo, that he would provide them citizenship if they wished.

Another decisive incident that turned the mainstay of the war toward intensive air action was the shelling of the Sarajevo marketplace on August 28, 1995. At least thirty-eight people were killed and more than eighty-five injured. NATO was ready for a major military response. With the backing of the United States, Operation Deliberate Force began its air campaign on August 30. More than sixty aircraft pounded Serb positions around Sarajevo. It was the largest military action by NATO. UNHCR found itself unable to deliver assistance to Sarajevo. UNPROFOR volunteers drove over the dangerous Mount Igman pass. As NATO air action continued, Croatian forces advanced to Bosnia and, with the Bosnian Army, made rapid gains until their offensive was halted on September 19 as a result of pressure from the United States and other Western governments. Many Bosnian Serbs were now displaced.

A flurry of negotiations began in August. Largely led by the United States, the diplomatic team, headed by Assistant U.S. Secretary of State Richard Holbrooke, shuttled through the capitals of the former Yugoslavia. It had just lost three members in an accident on the Mount Igman pass: Robert Frasure, Nelson Drew, and Joseph Kruzel. Finally it succeeded in brokering a cease-fire. On October 5, President Clinton announced that "the governments of Bosnia, Croatia and Serbia have agreed to proximity peace talks in the United States, beginning about 25 October, aimed at bringing them close to a peace agreement." The talks were to be assisted by the negotiating team led by Ambassador Holbrooke and by the contact group partners and to continue at an international peace conference in Paris.[31] On October 12 UNPROFOR confirmed that all military action in Bosnia had ceased. A new phase of peace was opening up in the Balkans.

DAYTON AND THE BEGINNING OF PEACE

The possibility of cease-fire and peace in the Balkans brought hope and the impetus for future planning. A transition period for peace building was in the wake. UNHCR had just moved into a new headquarters building, open and functional with a large atrium. The building promised enhanced efficiency and communality. The tape-cutting ceremony, attended by Swiss authorities together with international

Main Displaced Populations from the Former Yugoslavia, December 1995

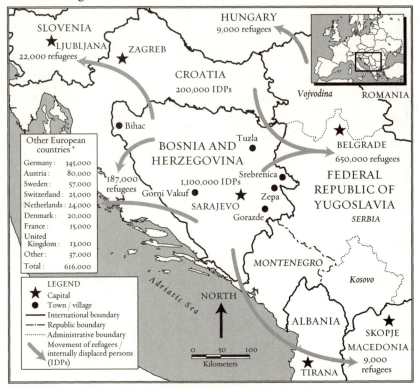

SLOVENIA

★LJUBLJANA
22,000 refugees

ZAGREB

HUNGARY
9,000 refugees

CROATIA
200,000 IDPs

Vojvodina

ROMANIA

● Bihac

BOSNIA AND
HERZEGOVINA

Tuzla
●

BELGRADE
650,000 refugees

Other European
countries*

Germany :	345,000
Austria :	80,000
Sweden :	57,000
Switzerland :	25,000
Netherlands :	24,000
Denmark :	20,000
France :	15,000
United Kingdom :	13,000
Other :	37,000
Total :	616,000

187,000
refugees   Gorni Vakuf ●

1,100,000 IDPs

Srebrenica ●

FEDERAL
REPUBLIC OF
YUGOSLAVIA

SERBIA

SARAJEVO
Gorazde ●

★
Zepa ●

MONTENEGRO

Kosovo

LEGEND
★   Capital
●   Town / village
———   International boundary
—·—·—   Republic boundary
··········   Administrative boundary
Movement of refugees /
internally displaced persons
(IDPs)

Adriatic Sea

NORTH

0   50   100
Kilometers

ALBANIA

SKOPJE
MACEDONIA
9,000
refugees

★
TIRANA

organization representatives, took place on September 28, 1995.

At the Humanitarian Issues Working Group meeting on October 10 I shared my thoughts on the prospects for peace in the Balkans and paid special tribute to the brave colleagues who had given their lives in the line of duty. I also expressed my appreciation to dedicated UN and other partners for their collaboration throughout the war years. While reiterating the importance of helping victims, I reminded the participants that providing humanitarian assistance was never the end in itself. "Our ultimate goal was and has been to solve the problems of the victims through returning them safely to their homes. UNHCR is, therefore, fully prepared to carry out its responsibility in the post-peace settlement, together with our agencies' colleagues."[32]

Though it was still very preliminary, I outlined my general think-

The 1995 Dayton Agreement for Bosnia and Herzegovina

ing concerning return. First of all, it must be voluntary, and second, it must take place in an organized and phased manner. For example, we had to ensure that adequate accommodations and basic essential services were available at the places of return. I saw the repatriation process taking place in three broad phases: first, the return of displaced persons within Bosnia and Herzegovina and Croatia; second, the repatriation of those from other republics in the former Yugoslavia; third, the return of the refugees from European countries that had given them temporary protection or resettlement. In this connection, I appealed to the refugee-hosting states to continue to provide temporary protection until UNHCR was ready to encourage return. This appeal faced increasing resistance in the course of 1996.

The prospect for peace, however, required considerable adjustment at the operational and management levels. Secretary-General

Boutros Boutros-Ghali on October 10 announced the appointment of Kofi Annan to serve as his special envoy to the former Yugoslavia and to NATO. He was to cover the transitional period and make necessary adjustments in both the military and civilian fields. With major changes foreseen for UNHCR operations, I decided to ask Soren Jessen-Petersen, at the time in charge of UNHCR's liaison office in New York, to be the special envoy to the former Yugoslavia. I considered him the best qualified to work under a rapidly evolving political and operational environment.

On November 4 we received the unexpected visit of General George Joulwan, the supreme allied commander in Europe, at UNHCR headquarters. He was accompanied by an entourage of some twenty-five persons, flanked by U.S. Ambassador Daniel Spiegel and the U.S. Mission staff. General Joulwan had one issue to address: the cooperation between the military and the civilian participants in the former Yugoslavia. He stated that extensive planning was under way on the military deployment of NATO forces following the signing of a peace agreement, but that not much was happening on the civilian side. Inasmuch as UNHCR was the predominant humanitarian agency in the former Yugoslavia, he offered us close cooperation and exchanges of information on how to proceed.

Joulwan gave us the military deployment picture under way on the bases of preliminary preparations. After the signing of the peace agreement, a transfer of authority would take place between UNPROFOR and NATO, after which NATO, organized as the implementation force (IFOR), would start its deployment through a variety of entry points: sea, air, and land. The present British and French UNPROFOR troops would be absorbed into the NATO structure. The United States would establish its headquarter in Tuzla, the French in Mostar, and the British in Gornji Vakuf. The overall headquarters would move from Zagreb to Sarajevo. Within thirty days the warring parties should withdraw two kilometers on each side of the confrontation line. The military operation must be completed within twelve months, during which time a gradual transfer of responsibility from military to civilian authorities should take place.

Those civilians would include an appointed high representative, who would be responsible for the coordination of all civilian activities and rehabilitation efforts. General Joulwan pointed out that specific information was required about UNHCR's field presence so that it would not be caught in the middle when the separation lines were set. He asked that a "map" of civilian agencies be drawn up and shared with his office. He also suggested establishing a civilian and military command group in Stuttgart. I agreed to meet the requests made by the general and shared with him my thoughts on the phased repatriation scheme. I emphasized how important it was for the military to understand the norms and practices of refugee protection. Throughout the meeting General Joulwan expressed his appreciation for the work of UNHCR and his respect for the staff, which he viewed as having "discipline." I was pleased by his comments and the recognition that he gave.

General Joulwan's visit started a flurry of activities on our part. My colleagues in Zagreb shared the information with the main aid agencies operating in Bosnia and Herzegovina and met with a mission of NATO officials to exchange views on their expected roles. On November 13 Annan met with UN agency representatives at UNHCR headquarters. He had visited several capitals to discuss the role of the UN and the UN agencies. He made it known that UNHCR would handle the humanitarian field, that the Organization for Security and Cooperation in Europe (OSCE) had been selected for elections and possibly human rights, and that the World Bank and the European Community were to be given reconstruction responsibilities. There were a host of other areas where no assignments had been made or had been overlooked, but he urged those given assignments to start planning. He did not see how at the end of the twelve months of deployment of the implementation force, the civilian side could take over. The United Nations had no replacement forces. The agencies present expressed their readiness to continue with their current work.

When I met with the secretary-general and Annan the next day, I found Boutros-Ghali pessimistic. At most he thought the United

Nations might be able to continue the civilian police or the political affairs services. The high commissioner for human rights was anxious to coordinate the human rights activities, which were expected to grow in importance, but the secretary-general seemed skeptical of expanding any UN function in view of the financial crisis that he faced.

The news of the signing of the peace agreement in Dayton came on November 21. I was at the Security Council, giving a briefing on the developments in Bosnia and Herzegovina and Rwanda, when Ambassador Albright arrived. She apologized for her lateness and announced that the agreement had been signed. That night I received the Freedom Award from the International Rescue Committee at its annual dinner in New York. Ambassador Holbrooke made a dramatic appearance straight from Dayton to the dinner and received a standing ovation. He explained that the process had been difficult and had nearly broken down toward the end but had been completed. It was a special day for all of us.

The United Kingdom decided to call for a conference on December 8 to discuss how to handle the nonmilitary parts of the Dayton Agreement. I decided to make a quick visit to the republics of the former Yugoslavia, to be ready for the conference as well as to prepare for UNHCR's repatriation operation. The Dayton Agreement preserved the unity of Bosnia and Herzegovina as a single sovereign state but split it in two: the Muslim-Croat Federation, comprising 51 percent of the territory, and a Serb Republika Srpska, comprising 49 percent of the territory. The provisions for the return of refugees and displaced persons to their homes were in Annex 7 of the agreement. The "right of all refugees and displaced persons to return freely to their homes of origin" was prominently installed at the head of the annex. UNHCR was assigned the lead role. The agreement endorsed the political objectives of ethnic separation and autonomy of both the Bosnian Serbs and the Bosnian Croats, while the formal status of Bosnia and Herzegovina as a single sovereign state ensured the political survival of the Bosnian Muslims. The provisions on the return of refugees and displaced persons to their homes of origin served as the key to the survival of an integrated state.

When I called on President Izetbegovic on December 4, he commented that following internal discussion in his government, he had decided that UNHCR should take the initiative in organizing returns. He felt confident that the cooperation with UNHCR in the peace process would continue to be productive. I was encouraged by this decision to give us the lead on returns and shared with him my preliminary thoughts on voluntary and phased returns. He made two comments: first, that the government should be given some place to have bilateral discussions with refugee-hosting governments; second, that a pilot return project for Sarajevo should be devised to set the whole process in motion. He indicated that in Sarajevo there was the chance for Bosnia and Herzegovina to remain a multiethnic society. I responded that the project was interesting but problematic, because Sarajevo was in fact a divided city. I also referred to the importance of housing, which was linked to return. UNHCR was thinking of investing in the repair of houses that were less than 30 percent destroyed; more substantial reconstruction work would be carried out by others, such as the World Bank, once they came on the scene. Prime Minister Haris Silajdzic welcomed my visit and pledged to work closely with UNHCR. He emphasized, however, that in his view, repatriation should begin with the Bosnian refugees in Western countries since they had been expelled from their homes and therefore suffered the most. The minister for refugees Muharem Cero echoed Silajdzic's line. He thought much of the return would be spontaneous and said that the government had already signed a bilateral agreement on repatriation with Austria and that others might be following. I emphasized that bilateral agreements should follow the spirit of Annex 7 and that UNHCR should be involved in order to avoid problems or complications.

The commissioner for refugees of Republika Srpska Ljubisa Vladusic was frank in expressing his difficulties and concerns. While appreciating the assistance from UNHCR, he had found the last few months extremely difficult because of the arrival of an estimated five hundred thousand people from the Krajina and western Bosnia. He was concerned that some of the required changes in the map agreed upon at Dayton could result in population movements. Serbs living in a town that was transferred to the Muslim-Croat Federation might very well wish to leave. He found the situation in Serb-held Sarajevo by far the most worrying. He said that people were very anxious and scared, and emotions were running high. He believed that an exodus of one hundred twenty thousand Serbs could happen, although the official position of the Republika Srpska authorities was that people should remain there. I pointed out that we were aware of these concerns and that we had just opened offices in the Serb areas of Sarajevo, Ilidza, and Grbavica, in order to install confidence. We had some intimation of the disturbances ahead but were hardly predicting the kind of grave crises that lay a few months ahead.[33]

The discussion with President Tudjman in Croatia focused on the plight of the refugees in Vojnic who required special aid. He proceeded to say that the country had spent millions of dollars to help refugees but that help from the international community had been inadequate. I referred to the forthcoming EU–World Bank conference in Brussels on long-term reconstruction and said that UNHCR would be ready to support the government's proposals, especially those linked to refugee return. We talked with Foreign Minister Granic about the projected return of Serbs to the Krajina and concentrated on the situation in the UN-protected sector of eastern Slavonia. The Erdut Agreement had been brokered by Stoltenberg for a transitional administration under the United Nations of one year, after which Croatian Serbs would hand over the last remaining territory under their control to the government of Croatia. In the transition period, UNHCR was to help plan and implement the return of Croat refugees and displaced persons. While some Serbs would have the right to remain in eastern Slavonia, the Croatian government did not seem ready to accept the long-term presence of a Serb majority in the area. A difficult process was foreseen. We were to hold many meetings with the Croatian authorities and the UN administrator in the coming years.[34]

In Belgrade, President Milosevic appeared generally confident over the implementation of the Dayton Agreement. He commented on the "big job" for UNHCR, inasmuch as he did not think returns would take place quickly. I asked his views on the situation of the Serbs in Sarajevo, Krajina, and eastern Slavonia. He was very concerned about Sarajevo. He referred to what he described as public inflammatory statements made by President Izetbegovic. Moreover, he thought the implementation period of forty-five days for the military withdrawals and establishment of zones of separation was not long enough and hoped the IFOR commander would extend it. People needed more time to assess the situation and make their choices. The president was encouraged to learn that some twelve thousand Serbs from the Krajina had registered to return in spite of still uncertain and fragile conditions. As for the reversion of eastern Slavonia, he believed that strict implementation of the November 12 Erdut Agreement, coupled with the parallel normalization of relations between the Federal Republic of Yugoslavia and Croatia, would prevent any flare-up. He had discussed the matter with President Tudjman. I expressed my serious concerns and wanted to be in a position to alert Milosevic in case of impending crisis. He responded positively. On the whole, he thought the situation would settle down in the Republika Srpska but expected the Federation to face many uncertainties. He insisted on the critical importance of UNHCR and urged me to enlarge its presence not only to assist in refugee return but also to give confidence and moral support to the people.[35]

At a meeting of the EU, U.S., and UN representatives in charge of the nonmilitary parts of the Dayton Agreement, held at Lancaster House, London, on December 9, I reported on UNHCR's preliminary plans to implement the return of refugees and displaced persons. I stated that my recent travel to the region had impressed me with the immensity and complexity of our task. Accurate planning was difficult because the wishes of the returning people had yet to be ascertained, the evolution of the security situation following the deployment of IFOR was uncertain, and adequate shelter for the returnees had to become available. I focused on the primary importance of creating the overall security situation and of establishing confidence-building measures. We would hope for a widespread deployment of IFOR and count on its readiness to respond to any violent interference with returns. The parties would have to establish measures to protect minorities and proclaim a genuine amnesty except for war criminals. A major housing repair and reconstruction effort would have to be undertaken in the Muslim-Croat Federation and the Republika Srpska. I warned against any attempt to engage in ethnic repopulation when the people were barely emerging from the brutal war of ethnic depopulation.

At the time of the Dayton Agreement, UNHCR estimated that there were 1,297,000 displaced persons inside Bosnia-Herzegovina. Another 820,000 displaced persons and refugees were thought to be in other republics of the former Yugoslavia. Approximately 700,000 people were under temporary protection elsewhere in Europe, half of them in Germany. In implementing the Dayton Agreement, UNHCR foresaw the need of humanitarian assistance for some 3 million displaced and war-affected people. We would have to carry on our coordination of large relief operations. At the same time, our activities would have to focus on promoting the orderly and phased returns of refugees and displaced persons and help their reintegration. We prepared a plan of operations and a two-hundred-million-dollar program, to support the return and relocation of the uprooted people in consultation with the Bosnian parties. Our initial assumption was that up to 500,000 displaced persons would return and 370,000 refugees would repatriate during 1996. We considered these, however, to be absolute maximum figures, not likely to be reached.

To carry out a formidable task, we had to count on close coopera-tion with all other implementing partners under the Dayton Agree-ment. In a way, UNHCR had never found itself so dependent on others to assume its responsibilities. First of all, the Bosnian parties had to abide by the commitments they had made to create the right conditions for return. Secondly, the international community had to make enormous strides to meet its entrusted tasks. IFOR's role was crucial. It had to implement the military provisions of the agreement to oversee the military withdrawal of the respective parties and to establish the zones of separation between them. It was also expected to increase its support for civilian implementation, including return, by stabilizing the security on the ground. The activities of the United Nations–led International Police Task Force (IPTF) to train and monitor the local police were also important to enhance security in particularly sensitive areas of return. Its deployment was, however, still very limited. The appointment of the high representative, Carl Bildt, was to provide overall guidance to the civilian aspects of the implementation and much-needed leadership to the different civilian organizations that had been brought together for the postwar reconstruction of Bosnia and Herzegovina. The wartime International Conference on the Former Yugoslavia as the main peace-negotiating structure was dissolved, and gave way to the establishment of the Peace Implementation Council (PIC). I continued to chair the Humanitarian Issues Working Group under the new umbrella.

The first challenge that severely tested all the international agencies present in post-Dayton Bosnia surfaced over the establishment of zones of separation, which differed from the original cease-fire lines. In the Mrkonjic Grad, Sipovo, and the surrounding area in central Bosnia, the transfer of authority from the Muslim-Croat Federation to the Republika Srpska was to be carried out by February 4. The HVO totally destroyed the towns as it withdrew and severely damaged communities that had survived the war. In Sarajevo, the implementation date for transfer of Serb-administered suburbs to the Federation jurisdiction was March 19. Tens of thousands of Serb families had lived for generations in the once-cosmopolitan city. UNHCR estimated that some seventy thousand Serbs were in Sarajevo, and at least thirty thousand would be willing to stay.

Unfortunately the situation turned dramatic. Some elements in Pale decided to resort to intimidation tactics to remove all Serbs from Muslim-Croat control. The Serb coordinator went on Pale television and told all Serbs to leave within three days. The announcement created panic. At the same time, the Bosnian government did little to reassure the Serbs, and extremists encouraged their flight. The transfer of Vogosca, the first suburb to go to the Federation, was scheduled to be completed on February 23. In the preceding days there was a sharp increase of trucks and vehicles transporting everything—furniture, windows, even doors. People carried their belongings in their hands or in wheelbarrows. Most Serbs departed, and the few left were mostly old and frail. Serb thugs went around intimidating people and setting fire to the houses.

The frontline suburb of Grbavica saw some of the worst violence, as Serb gangs roamed the area, setting property on fire and harassing the few Serbs still remaining there. Thick plumes of smoke billowed above the now almost deserted and eerily empty neighborhood. Morgan Morris of our field staff thought of setting up a safe house for those forced to flee the violence. The staffers came across instances of multiple rape by Serb soldiers of an eighty-five-year-old woman in her own house and the murder of the elderly mother of a famous Bosnian pianist, and they heard screams of torture all night long. UNHCR field staff received an offer from Serb women who lived above their office to turn over several apartments. As violence increased with the approach of the handover date, the field staff persuaded those most at risk to come to the "safe house," where UNHCR would try to protect them.

At first, despite the fear and violence, many people, usually elderly and alone, were reluctant to leave the only homes they had known. However, after the disappearance of another old woman from her home, local people at risk began to move to the safe house. Both Serbs and Bosnian Muslims were given safety in the safe house. Particularly sad was the story of a young Serb woman who was supposed to come to the safe house with her baby but was found dead; she had blown herself up with a grenade in the basement of her house. The safe house staff kept the baby for some nights. They finally tracked down the grandparents in the Republika Srpska, and sent the baby to their care. A couple of our staff spent the night there. They requested that the IPTF post a monitor in the safe house and IFOR station an APC outside. After considerable pleas and pressure, IFOR responded and placed an APC in front of the building. Jessen-Petersen reported that UNHCR staff in the safe house were "taking risks far beyond what is acceptable, but we have no choice as we cannot let down the civilians taking even greater risks to stay."[36]

The catastrophe triggered by the transfer of authority in the Sarajevo suburbs revealed the stark realities that impacted on implementation of the Dayton Agreement. The orchestrated campaign that resulted in the exodus of sixty thousand Serbs from the suburbs demonstrated the prevalence of the forces of ethnic division. The Bosnian Serbs and Bosnian Croats pursued their separatist policies. As for the international parties, the collaboration between the civilian and the military components responsible for implementing the agreement also proved inadequate. At the time of the Vogosca transfer, the international agency representatives, joined by Admiral Leighton Smith, commander of NATO's southern forces, met with the concerned local residents who asked for assistance to leave. Speaker of the Republika Srpska parliament Momcilo Krajisnic requested that UNHCR provide transport. Jessen-Petersen declined, repeating the position that UNHCR was doing everything possible to make it safe for the people to stay. Surprisingly, Admiral Smith suggested to Krajisnic that if he used Serb military trucks, driven by unarmed Serb soldiers, IFOR would escort them out.[37]

There was a definite lack of understanding between the civilian and military components concerning the steps necessary to prevent further ethnic division. Moreover, IFOR's reluctance to become involved in maintaining law and order and providing desperately needed security to the new minorities derived from its belief that it was not a police or fire brigade to protect individual civilians from thugs or arsonists. Mission creep was to be avoided by all means. Article VI of the Agreement on the Military Aspect of the Peace Settlement authorized IFOR "to observe and prevent interference with the movement of civilian populations, refugees, and displaced persons, and to respond appropriately to deliberate violence to life and per-

son," but defined this as only one of several supporting tasks, to be ful-
filled "within the limits of its assigned principal tasks and available
resources." The low priority assigned to this and the lack of a robust
IFOR response to violence against minorities illustrated the gap
between the promise of Annex 7 and the actual readiness to do
what was necessary to help re-create a multiethnic society. Thus the
extent of the challenge to be faced with the return of minorities was
unforseeable.

The major problem that had not been foreseen was the collapse of
local administrative functions and services. The Serb municipal
authorities left the suburbs before the transfer dates and brought
about a dangerous vacuum. Shops were closed. Telephones were not
working; medical services were gone. The residents looked for their
mayor, who had disappeared. They were hardly ready to turn to the
incoming Federation functionaries. At first the Sarajevo government
had dispatched fire trucks into Grbavica to extinguish blazes but
stopped the operation, arguing that IFOR had failed to offer the fire-
fighters adequate protection. Under the circumstances, both the
international civilian and military components that had been assigned
to implement the agreement had to meet all unforeseen risks. They
were still at a very preliminary stage of learning how to work with
each other when new challenges began.

Repatriation of Balkan Refugees: Reversing Ethnic Cleansing

UNHCR had a clear repatriation mission under the Dayton Agreement. Its success depended greatly on the overall peace process to be
carried out by all implementing partners. Most fundamental were the
Bosnian parties, which had to abide by their commitments and create
the conditions for successful returns. As for the international com-

munity, IFOR's role was crucial, for it had to implement the military provisions as well as stabilize the security conditions on the ground.

In preparation for the implementation of the peace agreement, some planning had been done. I stressed the importance of voluntary and organized returns in three phases: first, return of displaced persons within Bosnia and Herzegovina and Croatia; second, repatriation of displaced persons from other republics in the former Yugoslavia; third, repatriation of refugees from European countries that had given them temporary protection or resettlement. The availability of accommodations and essential services were important in determining the pace and process of returns. We did foresee, however, that the prospect for peace required considerable adjustment at the operational and management levels. In particular, UNHCR would have to change gear drastically from a wartime emergency-led operation to a peacetime orderly rehabilitation-centered action. As it turned out, however, the repatriation process had many characteristics of an emergency operation. UNHCR took the mission statement under Annex 7 to be sacrosanct. Repatriation was to realize "the right of all refugees and displaced persons to their homes." We interpreted our role to be one of undoing ethnic cleansing. In reality, however, the ethnic factor dominated all postwar developments.

In the first five months after the signing of the Dayton Agreement, about seventy thousand people came back, but they all were majority returns—that is, people returning to the areas in which they belong to the majority ethnic group. The record of return of minorities was dismal. The wall that divided the ethnic communities was immovable. Returnees felt confident going back to where the majority of the inhabitants were of the same ethnicity. On the other hand, people would not go to their original homes if the ethnic composition of the area had changed in a way that made them a minority. The war had changed the population composition of many areas, and the Dayton Agreement had drawn new lines separating the Republika Srpska and the Federation. UNHCR had to resort to new means to remove the ethnic wall. For returnees from the majority, the destruction or occupation of apartments and houses rather than the lack of security was the main problem. We had to devise programs to increase rapidly the capacity to absorb the returnees on the ground. We added a shelter component to our assistance program and identified target areas where the problem of accommodations was not too acute. We focused our activity on the return of minorities, but our attempts failed mostly because of the lack of security. Returnees were met by intense harassment and obstructions. No minority returns were recorded to the Republika Srpska or to Croat-controlled areas in the Federation. The result in Muslim-controlled areas was somewhat better but mixed. New confidence-building measures had to be devised to promote freedom of movements. Our UNHCR colleagues started running interentity bus lines and organized visits by displaced persons to their home areas.

In May 1996 I took an extensive six-day field trip to eastern Slavonia and Bosnia and Herzegovina because I wanted a firsthand impression of the situation. I had to review our program priorities in consultation with the authorities, international organizations, and our staff. The visit turned out to be an exceptional experience, still vivid in my memory. For the first time I could travel by road throughout the country without a flak jacket, without a military escort, and without once hearing the sound of firing. Life seemed to be coming back to the war-torn country. There was food in the markets. The streets were full of people. Cafés were opening. People came out of their houses to offer branches of lilacs. Some electricity and water were becoming available in many places. Some displaced persons were starting to go back home. I talked to returnees in several places. They were relieved that their painful exile was over and they could finally begin to rebuild their lives. These were encouraging signs. At the same time, I was reminded of the complexity of the road to lasting peace, not just of the absence of war.

I started my visit at the strategic northern town of Brcko and moved on to Tuzla, Banja Luka, Zenica, Mostar, Gorazde, and Sarajevo. As I drove through the towns and villages, the scenes of destruction remained the same as they had been since the beginning of the war in 1992. The new sight of devastated Mrkonjic Grad stood out as testimony to the severe damage caused by the withdrawing HVO, but in the half-destroyed town hospital, doctors and nurses were already hard at work. They recounted the stories of fighting and killing that had gone on after the signing of the Dayton Agreement with the changes in the entity division lines. I stopped at collective centers in many places as we drove along. In the Bosnian town of Zenica, I visited one center that housed around two hundred displaced persons from the eastern enclave of Zepa. To my surprise, I met an elderly woman who said she was a hundred and two years old. I was surprised that she could travel all across Bosnia even with help from friends and families. She told me that she had lived through more wars in the Balkans than she cared to remember. She added that as the Serbs set fire to her house, they laughed and told her not to worry, that she was too old for them to bother killing. I wondered what peace would mean to her, as well as to many others in the centers who seemed lost and abandoned.

In Tuzla, I visited Mayor Selim Beslagic, with whom I had close contact during the war. He seemed overwhelmed by the sixty thousand displaced persons from Srebrenica and other eastern enclaves still under his care. He asked for help in returning refugees and displaced persons to their homes. He seemed a bit dubious over the future political settlement of the country, as he observed that elections were bound to consolidate ethnic divisions. In Banja Luka, I met with refugee representatives from the Krajina and central Bosnia, the prime minister of the Republika Srpska, and religious leaders. The city was relatively untouched by the war, but the housing issue was extremely complicated. Serb refugees from various parts of Croatia and Bosnia had filled the houses of Bosnians and Croats who had left. For the refugees and displaced persons to return to their original homes, the Serbs would have to be forced out of their accommodations although their own houses had been taken over by other refugees and displaced persons. One solution would be to build buffer housing, but that required resources and funds.

In the scenic city of Mostar the Muslims now lived on the east and the Croats the west side of the Neretva River. The serious division between the two ethnic groups showed no change in spite of the two-year administration by the European Union. The historic Mostar Bridge no longer spanned the river. I visited a group of displaced citizens living in containers on the hill in East Mostar. They could see their houses in West Mostar, to which they could not return, not even to visit. They were older people and endured their daily lives with pain and sorrow. I raised the question of their plight when I saw the city authorities of the Croat-controlled west bank. I pressed for reconsideration. What harm could these elderly citizens bring by returning home? The issue was, however, territory and political control. In fact my colleagues shared with me their observation that the Croats were envious of the Serbs, who had been given a Serb entity, and were not about to loosen their grip over Croat-led areas.

I went to Sarajevo after a short stop in Gorazde, the enclave town that had suffered isolation and severe shelling. UNHCR staff member Eddie O'Dwyer, who had ensured a UNHCR presence in Gorazde during key periods of the war, was still there, now somewhat encouraged by the new arrival of NGO workers bringing in relief goods and shelter materials. Arriving in Sarajevo late evening, I could hardly believe my eyes. There were street and traffic lights. Lights shone from some of the half-destroyed apartment windows. The next morning we drove around the city and stopped in places that we used to visit. UNHCR had made a special effort to replace with glass the plastic sheeting that had covered a good number of the windows throughout the city. We thought that the citizens were entitled to enjoy peacetime glazing. We contracted with the Sarajevo City Development Institute to employ sixteen local companies to deliver 370,000 square meters of glass over six months that would benefit 180,000 people. I dropped by the glazing workshop to watch people come by with their window frames. The frames were then repaired, and the glass was installed. Many of the workers were demobilized soldiers, who were employed as glass cutters, installers, and carpenters. UNHCR's plastic sheeting had served for four long years. It was good that it now disappeared. We decided to publish a book of photographs to commemorate the widespread and long usage of UNHCR plastic sheeting in Sarajevo.

The tour around the Serb suburbs brought back painful recent memories. In Grbavica, I visited the safe house. I was able to meet the Serb women who had refused to accept the city's division and made their apartments available to those in need. Sitting on the sofa in the one time safe house, I was deeply moved by their stories of bravery. I also visited a Serb camp outside the city limits that was full of displaced Serbs who had fled the Sarajevo suburbs. They were Bosnia's most recently displaced people and perhaps the angriest. Many of them said that they would not return even if they got their houses back. They stated that they could never live with the Muslims again.

The May visit to Bosnia and Herzegovina underlined the importance of UNHCR to move quickly on two fronts. Our colleagues had been already grappling with the question of freedom of movement and emergency housing reconstruction. Top UN officials like me could move as they pleased in post-Dayton Bosnia and Herzegovina. But freedom of movement for ordinary Bosnian citizens was a theoretical dream. Their freedom of movement within the Croat-Bosnian Federation was difficult. As for minorities, freedom of movement between the federation and the Serb republic for them was virtually nonexistent. Rare individuals crossed the IFOR-patrolled interentity boundary line (IEBL) to visit their old homes, but very few had the courage to move back. UNHCR had been working on the idea of running interentity bus lines. During the trip I announced the start of UNHCR's bus service to connect the Serb-held village of Lukavica, south of the capital, with the western Sarajevo suburb of Ilidza. Several more key routes throughout Bosnia and Herzegovina were to follow. They would link Banja Luka with Glamoc, Zenica, Tuzla, and Bijeljina. The buses would be painted white. During the war we had run convoys of white trucks to distribute relief supplies. Now we were running white buses to transport civilians across political and military boundaries. We also entered extensive negotiations to organize groups of refugees wanting to visit their homes and family graveyards across the boundaries, trying to prevent the repeated exercise of violence that had met some of those who tried. We were not requesting IFOR to escort the buses, but we were expecting support for security. Admiral Smith, whom I met in Sarajevo, pledged cooperation by covering the security of the transport route. I visited the headquarters of the respective IFOR contingents in the course of my May visit: Americans in Tuzla, French in Mostar, and British in Gornji Vakuf. Each pledged close collaboration. The military and the civilians were beginning more and more to see commonality in their missions.

The other issue of great urgency was the acceleration of reconstruction, particularly of housing. Four years of war had caused widespread destruction of land and life. The damage to housing was extensive, affecting more than half of the housing units. The first priority was to increase the stock of usable housing through repair to accommodate some one and a half million displaced persons who lived outside their own houses and refugees who were in centers. In addition, the occupation of houses by these people blocked other returns. The obstacles of destruction and occupation had to be removed if we were to tackle the challenge of return. While the World Bank and the European Bank for Reconstruction and Development were assigned the lead role for the post-Dayton reconstruction work, UNHCR decided to take the initiative for the quick repair and reconstruction of housing linked with return. We launched a thirty million-dollar shelter trust fund early in 1996 to cover emergency shelter repairs. This program would focus on repairing houses that were less than 30 percent damaged in areas where needs were high. It would obtain such materials as doors, windows, roofs and outside walls, and electrical and heating facilities. The labor was expected to come from the recipients. We also foresaw the possibility of increasing the fund should donor governments wish to contribute. While contracting NGOs and Bosnians to implement the program, UNHCR would continue to rehabilitate collective centers, schools, and health facilities. UNHCR identified thirty-nine target areas for housing reconstruction. These were the areas to which 70 percent of the returnees were expected to settle. We worked closely with the office of the high representative to solicit its support. In early 1997 we set up the Return and Reconstruction Task Force to promote more systematic and comprehensive plans linking return with reconstruction.

UNHCR could move quickly on housing projects thanks to the support of the International Management Group, which we had established with the European Community in 1993. The group consisted of specialists in the fields of infrastructure, including energy and public utilities, and of shelter and housing. Its work was closely integrated with the activities of UNHCR. It had assisted us on infrastructure repair and construction covering water, transport, roads, and mines during the war. The IMG surveyed damage to housing caused by shells, bullets, explosives, and grenades in a large number of municipalities and provided a rough assessment of required costs. Having assisted UNHCR and humanitarian agencies during the war, the IMG contributed to the early planning for the World Bank and other reconstruction and development agencies as they entered the postconflict scene. I favorably recall the service of the IMG and of its general manager, Paul Monnory, when we confronted reconstruction challenges in many parts of the world. The arrival of reconstruction and development agencies are usually slow, and the planning period extends indefinitely as they seem to take forever to cope with preliminary surveys and assessments.

At the end of 1996 UNHCR estimated that close to 250,000 had returned to Bosnia and Herzegovina, but all of them to majority areas. Many were refugees from Western European countries. UNHCR was eager to promote return but was not ready to follow schemes that would result only in that of majorities. However, the pressure was heavy, particularly from Germany, where around 330,000 Bosnian refugees were residing. As soon as the peace accord was in place, vigorous public debate took place in Germany on the timing of the returns, the categories of persons to be compelled to return, and the types and amount of aid to be given. In short, the Germans were ready to revoke the temporary protection measures that UNHCR had requested as a crucial component of the comprehensive response to the humanitarian crisis in July 1992 and to compel returns even where these could not be to the refugees' original homes. We carried on complicated consultations with the German authorities, particularly Federal Minister of the Interior Manfred Kanther.

UNHCR recognized that temporary protection had to be lifted at some point. However, we were aware that the changes in the political terrain of Bosnia and Herzegovina would not simply allow people to return to their places of origin. Besides, many of the Bosnian refugees were from the Republika Srpska, now under Serb control, with no assurances of safety for the minority returnees. The overall reconstruction picture was grim, and houses were occupied by those who had been displaced. There was strong opposition within my office to the lifting of temporary protection lest such action result in the large-scale relocation of people. Already many were returning to the urban areas of Sarajevo and Tuzla as well as to the Una-Sana Canton, from which they had not originated. After intense internal debate, I announced at the December 16, 1996, PIC meeting that "the need for an across the board special regime of protection . . . has ceased to exist." But I also emphasized that "this does not mean that those still benefiting from this regime can now be expelled. Rather, it should differentiate based on specific situation of each particular group." Our position was that while many should be going back to rebuild their lives, there were others whose returns would depend on the removal of many political and security barriers that still existed.[38]

The big challenge for UNHCR in the coming months and years was to realize the return of minorities, which throughout 1996 was negligible and consisted mostly of older persons. UNHCR's white buses of peace, the interentity bus lines, were heavily in demand. Twelve lines of service transported five thousand passengers every week. People were beginning to make fairly spontaneous "go see visits" to their houses across the interentity lines. But return as such remained blocked. The level of reluctance and obstruction by local authorities was high, and the suspicion among the people was deep. An incident that I came across near the zone of separation just outside Brcko revealed the reality of the situation. A year before when I visited this village, the area was rubble. Now houses were being repaired everywhere. One returnee told me that he had lost his house a second time after his return. It was blown up. I expressed my sympathy to the man and told the community and the local authorities how badly such senseless acts would be taken by the international community. Donors, however generous, would not continue to fund houses that would then be blown up.

UNHCR was pressed to achieve a breakthrough on the return of minorities. New means had to be explored to encourage more minority returns. The activities of the Commission for Real Property Claims, which had been set up to deal with property settlements, had to be strengthened and supported. Carrol Faubert, who had led the operation in the African Great Lakes region, was assigned to serve as special envoy, taking over from Jessen-Petersen, who left to head the office in New York. A resourceful thinker, he came up with an idea of a program that put positive conditionality to assistance. In March 1997 we launched the open cities initiative, which promised accelerated material assistance to those local communities and municipalities coming forward with concrete steps to welcome back former residents. We invited cities and municipalities to declare publicly that they would allow minorities to return to their former homes, and we prepared a set of criteria for them to demonstrate their commitment. The authorities would be expected to take measures to reintegrate minorities into the normal life of the community; to provide equal rights and opportunities for employment, education, and appointment to public office; to practice freedom of movement, including assessment visits by minorities; and to prevent abuses, discrimination, criminality, and security incidents. The UNHCR staffers and members of other international organizations were to monitor progress. As soon as the authorities proved their willingness with actual returns, they would be immediately rewarded and supported with international assistance.

In the one year since the first municipality of Konjic was recognized in 1997, eleven cities were declared open cities. International response to the initiative was very favorable. However, the actual number of minority returns in one year was much lower than we had hoped, just over nine thousand. UNHCR was determined to carry through this initiative. We believed that if Sarajevo and Banja Luka, two major cities with long traditions of multiethnicity and cultural tolerance, would declare themselves open cities, the impact throughout the country would be strong. President Izetbegovic expressed his willingness to see Sarajevo an open city. The United States proposed a Sarajevo return initiative with precise targets and deadlines for the return of all minorities to the city and its surrounding areas. However, the return of minorities in practice remained limited. In Banja Luka too, President Biljana Plavsic of the Republika Srpska indicated that all original inhabitants of the city would be welcome to return. But she noted that a solution had to be found for refugees and the displaced, a difficult request to fulfill. At least her declared willingness to open up communities seemed encouraging. The vexing property questions, however, prevented people from moving freely back to where they had originated.

A meeting with a returnee near Knin, Croatia, opened my eyes to the stark reality. He belonged to the Serb minority. Before fleeing, he had had three houses. One had been destroyed during the war. Another had been occupied by a Croatian family that had turned it into a shop, an unlawful act, but he had no means to pursue the case legally. His third house had been assigned to a Bosnian refugee family who could not return home, because their house in Bosnia was occupied by displaced people. He possessed three houses, but he was homeless. His story showed the depth of the complicated property issues that had to be addressed regionally.

The most serious and complex set of obstacles, however, existed in people's hearts and minds. A displaced woman I met in the collective center in Trebinje in the Republika Srpska taught me what psychological barriers meant. The room she lived in was crammed, with no privacy, and poor hygienic conditions. I asked her why she did not go home. She said she had tried but decided to come back to the collective center. Returning home was the worst experience she had since she became a refugee. She had been sneered at and threatened, but much worse, she found that her neighbor, a friend with whom she had grown up, would not speak to her anymore. Her story stuck in my mind.

Fully utilizing the opportunities presented by the open cities, UNHCR continued to pursue the return of minorities. But progress came much more slowly than anticipated. Substantial numbers of people returned but to areas where they had never lived before and where they were now among the majority. The principal reasons were twofold. In the early days of peace, lack of security was the main factor discouraging returns. Some very serious incidents did occur and reinforced the conviction of many refugees and displaced people that return as a minority would expose them to intolerable risks. The other obstacle was the unresolved property issues. Emergency housing repair and reconstruction could meet limited needs, but they were far from sufficient to overcome the inadequacies of legal provisions that restituted property rights. The chains of displacement were linked to chains of houses occupied by people whose rightful properties were in turn occupied by others displaced from other places.

A particularly difficult problem centered on the return of Croatian Serb refugees and displaced persons to the Krajina and eastern Slavonia. The majority of them had gone to the Republika Srpska and to the Serb Republic of the Federal Republic of Yugoslavia. In fact the Serb Republic hosted 550,000 refugees, mostly of Serb origin, from Croatia and Bosnia and Herzegovina. Solutions for their return had to be found. Their repatriation had to be negotiated with the Croatian authorities. As for returns to Eastern Slavonia, special procedures had to be followed because the region was under the authority of the UN Transitional Administration of Eastern Slavonia (UNTAES). The issue of the return of the displaced persons and refugees to their places of origin was central to the successful implementation of the Erdut Agreement, concluded separately from the Dayton Agreement between the United Nations and Croatia. UNHCR served as the chair of the Joint Implementation Committee on Refugees and Displaced Persons and actively negotiated for satisfactory arrangements with all the parties until Croatia reestablished full authority over eastern Slavonia.

The committee came up with proposals to reach satisfactory goals for returns through pilot projects dealing with so-called two-way returns. The thrust of the project was to link the return of Croat displaced persons to eastern Slavonia with that of the Serb displaced persons to Krajina and other parts of Croatia. Though at a slow pace, an estimated 40,000 people left the UNTAES region between 1996 and 1998. There remained some 11,500 displaced people generally comprised of unaccompanied elderly persons and other very vulnerable groups. Our own assessment was that a large number of the Croatian Serb displaced persons were likely to leave for Serbia. Serious efforts had to be made to avoid the departure of Croatian Serbs who were long-term residents in their places of origin. When I discussed the Serb repatriation issue with President Milosevic in April 1998, he agreed that a good number of the Croatian Serb displaced persons in eastern Slavonia could come to Serbia. Moreover, he stated that the major part of the Croatian Serbs who fled to Serbia would stay there and would become citizens. The authorities were already looking for land.[39] A large-scale ethnic relocation was in progress while UNHCR kept working for return and for the restoration of multiple ethnicity.

Little by little, the general situation showed signs of settling down. Within Bosnia and Herzegovina there were some signs of improvement. The perception of insecurity was somewhat receding. The sixty-thousand-strong IFOR, though scaled down, continued its presence as the Stabilization Force (SFOR). The Multinational Specialized Unit of SFOR was deployed in 1998, with the mission to step in to prevent violence and build confidence within communities. The high representative exercised his authority to remove obstructionist officials and implement property laws. The IPTF played important parts in strengthening the local police capacity.

However, only in the first months of 2000 was a substantial increase in the number of minority returns noted in Bosnia and Herzegovina. A major rise also began in Croatia after the change of government in December 1999, following the death of President Tudjman. In fact, during my trip to Bosnia and Herzegovina in the spring of 2000, I sensed the beginning of a real change in the environment. There were positive signs. I went to witness the first joint meeting of the mayors of Prijedor in the Republika Srpska and of Sanski Most in the Federation. The mayors were there to consult on administrative measures for the mutual support of returning minorities. These were towns from which many people had been totally "cleansed" at a very early period of the war. But even there people were beginning to come back on their own, to clear the rubble and start repairing their houses. There was a group of women who had returned but were living in a transit accommodation. They complained bitterly about the lack of support and asked us to do more. If minorities were returning to Prijedor and Sanski Most, I thought surely there was hope for the future. In the town of Dvrar in the federation, on the other hand, the prewar Serbian majority had left in 1995 and been replaced by Bosnian Croat displaced people from central Bosnia. The town was politically and economically under the control of extremist HVO elements, and SFOR had been unable to prevent serious outbreaks of violence against Serbs. Now Bosnian Serbs were returning in fairly large numbers but were compelled to live away from the city center. There were tensions and harassments. UNHCR staffers were keeping contact with both ethnic groups and even trying to develop interethnic women's group activities. I was uncertain of the future of the town.

Everywhere I went, I noted that economic problems were becoming predominant. Unemployment, caused by both war and the transition to a market economy was high all over. The lack of jobs was a major deterrent to the return of refugees, especially of younger people. All people were weighing their options, taking into careful consideration what might be the economic consequences of staying where they were, returning to their original homes, or moving elsewhere. With joblessness becoming a major reason for the failure to accelerate returns, we had to look at job-creating possibilities to bring back communities that had broken up because of the war. Visiting the communities in Bosnia and Herzegovina, I frequently noticed that returning residents were complaining that there were no more factories to go to work in. Before the war there had been a shoe factory, or a brick factory, or even a mill, where jobs were shared among people of different ethnic groups. We decided to try out an initiative that we might call Jobs for Coexistence, combining job creation with community building. In short, workplaces or industrial sites would be restored if there was communal participation. To launch such an initiative, the private sector had to be brought in. I talked about this idea to representatives of the business community and received encouraging responses. Businesspeople understood such projects to be a seed for the promotion of peace building and refugee return, ultimately leading to the development of an economically viable environment.

UNHCR already had some experience with community building through the Bosnian Women's Initiative, which we launched in 1996. We had always had special programs to try to protect women and children in war, but after Dayton we began to focus on the empowerment of women in our community programs. The war produced many single-headed households, with women in care of children, the elderly, and the disabled. They needed help for shelter repair and legal measures to cope with contentious property rights problems. They required university education, skills training, access to microcredits to start business enterprises. The U.S. government took an interest in the program, and President Clinton announced an initial contribution of five million dollars to formalize the establishment of the Bosnian Women's Initiative. UNHCR worked with a host of international NGOs to prepare projects and implement them throughout the country. Out of these projects, networks of women were gradually developing and ready to join in the community-building efforts that were becoming central.

Nearly five years after Dayton and concentrating on returning refugees and displaced persons, we began to search for broader solutions to deal with displacement problems. From emergency lifesaving rescue operations in Vogosca, interentity bus lines, emergency shelter repair, open cities, and Bosnian Women's Initiative to Jobs for Coexistence, our field offices did good work and came up with new methods of approaching problems. The idea of using coexistence as an operational tool whipped my thinking. In Bosnia and Herzegovina and Croatia, we had to help return people to communities still unhealed after mass violence and still unprepared to receive partici-pants, either victims or perpetrators, home. The situation was unset-tling for everyone. Communities that were strained emotionally and economically had little generosity to offer. The returning people found others living in their houses or no houses at all. Very often they found themselves living next to those who had acted as enemies. If houses were blown up, if killings were repeated, the cycle of violence would be repeated in communities that had not healed.

The international community sought solutions by strengthening justice and human rights. The International Criminal Tribunal for Yugoslavia was set up. Human rights groups were actively promot-ing mechanisms for protecting human rights and the rule of law. UNHCR recognized the importance of legal and judicial institutions and was ready to contribute to developing justice systems. But my own observation was that formal legal institutions and measures were neither sufficient to cope with the large number of people returning to divided communities nor able to help them learn to coexist again. We had to devise small-scale, nonjudicial, and community-based activities through which people would recognize common interests, work together, learn together, think together, and eventually live together.

Our exposure to the realities of people returning to war-torn divided communities in post-Dayton Bosnia and Herzegovina and Croatia led us to embark on a project called Imagine Coexistence. We found a partnership in the Program on Negotiation at Harvard Law School, under the leadership of Professor Martha Minow, who had just begun to address the sources and solutions to group conflicts.[40] The project aimed at developing skills and criteria to design coexis-tence projects and at helping members of divided communities and humanitarian workers move toward solutions through "imagining" coexistence in the course of their activities. Led by the UNHCR staff in Banja Luka, together with local NGOs organizing workshops for potential and selected participants from different ethnic groups, including local authorities, pilot projects begain in Dvrar and Prijedor. They brought the Serbs, Muslims, and Croats closer by opening venues for dialogue and shared work experiences. A coffee and cake shop, a drying chamber for fruits and vegetables, a communal strawberry farm, and other small projects were installed to provide common workplaces for residents from different ethnic groups. Women's associations, youth recreation groups for folk dancing, and sports also brought people together. Cohabitation did not necessarily produce immediate reconciliation, but large numbers of returnees from all ethnic groups began to live together again, not only in the same country but often in the same neighborhood. Grassroots small-scale community-based activities take time to produce results and have to be complemented by developments in other areas—for example, education, health, media, sports, and recreation. Above all, they have to be reinforced by a national program of reconciliation coupled with better job opportunities and fairer legal and social institutions.

Kosovo

As UNHCR grappled with promoting minority return of refugees and internally displaced persons in Bosnia and Herzegovina, a new conflict broke out in Kosovo. Long-simmering unrest was growing between the majority Kosovo Albanians and the administering Serbs. It took on a new dimension in February 1998, when the Serbian security forces intensified operations against the emerging Kosovo Liberation Army (KLA) and its supporters.

Historically Kosovo was a fully autonomous province until its status was abolished on the initiative of the then Serbian Republican Party head Slobodan Milosevic in 1989. The Kosovo Albanians, constituting 90 percent of the population, boycotted the Serbian state authorities and set up parallel systems for almost every aspect of daily life, including employment, health, and education. The international community was concerned over the growing political confrontation in

Displaced Populations from Kosovo in Neighboring Countries/Territories, through Mid-June 1999

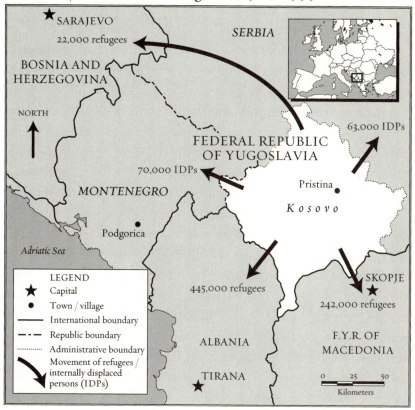

Kosovo. The International Conference on the Former Yugoslavia (ICFY) assigned the Working Group on Minorities to examine and propose solutions to the ethnic and cultural divide in Kosovo. However, the relations between Serbian authorities and Kosovo Albanians continued to worsen. It should be pointed out that the issue of Kosovo was not included in the Dayton negotiations. It had been deliberately sidelined in the attempt to stop the war in Bosnia and Herzegovina, and it remained outside the international Balkan agenda. The Albanian demand for independence grew, but Ibrahim Rugova, the president of the self-declared Republic of Kosovo, who headed the League for Democratic Kosovo (LDK), advocated peaceful resistance to achieve that objective. With no progress in sight, the more radical Kosovo Liberation Army emerged in 1997 and, in response to constant provocation by Serb forces, resorted to violence, attacking police and security forces.

UNHCR had run a suboffice in Pristina since 1993. I had obtained President Milosevic's agreement for UNHCR's presence in order to collect firsthand information on the situation in Kosovo. At the time an estimated three hundred thousand Kosovo Albanians had left the region for Western Europe to obtain work. Some sought asylum, but Western European countries were not prepared to recognize their claim and constantly turned to UNHCR for more information. Our report to the Western governments was that our findings substantiated the existence of tension and confrontation in Kosovo but not necessarily of violence and persecution that required across-the-board protection. We asked that asylum claims be individually examined and that the applicants not be expelled especially during the harsh winter months, when they would have trouble meeting their daily needs.

We were also brought to the Kosovo situation by the presence of refugees. When half a million Serbs were expelled from Croatia in the summer of 1995, a large number had fled to Serbia. Some fourteen thousand had been transferred to Kosovo and accommodated in collective centers. These were schools and public buildings and were generally in very poor condition. We intervened repeatedly and asked for improvements. Besides, we did not want the refugees to be housed in schools because they might be perceived as "occupying" educational facilities when education was a contentious issue between the Albanians and the Serbs. When conflict intensified, especially in the region of Drenica, the Serb refugees were worried and expressed their desire to be relocated. I asked the administrative authorities in Kosovo to move them to safer places.[41] Thus, through direct exposure to the widespread dissatisfaction of the people and involvement with refugees, UNHCR was concerned over the growing tension in Kosovo.

In the spring of 1998, during my extended tour of the five countries in the former Yugoslavia, I made a short visit to Kosovo. Then I brought the deteriorating situation in Kosovo to the attention of the Security Council and reported that the fighting and violence in the Drenica area had caused the displacement of more than twenty thousand Kosovars. Unless the opposing sides developed a meaningful dialogue that could contain the demands of the extremists, I foresaw a growing crisis, with the possibility of further internal displacements and refugee outflows. Governments in the region, especially of the former Yugoslav republic of Macedonia and the republic of Montenegro, were justifiably worried by the prospect. On purely humanitarian grounds, I felt obliged to echo their concerns and to relay the negative effects of sanctions on their fragile economies and the most vulnerable people. I urged that "suitable pressure be exerted on the Government of the Federal Republic of Yugoslavia to establish constructive dialogue with the Albanian leadership."[42]

Violence escalated throughout the spring and summer. The Serb security forces intensified attacks against Kosovo Albanians suspected of involvement with the KLA. In the middle of August I sent Jessen-Petersen to Kosovo on an extensive field visit and warned against the impending humanitarian crisis. The displacement of people increased, with some 20,000 fleeing across the mountains to Albania. Many others made their way to Montenegro and various other parts of Europe. By September there were an estimated 175,000 internally displaced people, living with friends and families or camping out in the woods and fields. The UNHCR and ICRC field staffs jointly delivered humanitarian assistance. The large presence of displaced persons out in the open troubled the international policy makers, but they remained inactive. They were cautious lest any action to stop these abuses strengthen the KLA. President Milosevic made some concessions when he met Russian President Boris Yeltsin on June 16, 1998, and expressed his readiness to control the activities of his security forces. He agreed to provide the Belgrade diplomatic corps access to the region and to ensure UNHCR and ICRC operations for immediate relief and to help return refugees and the internally displaced persons. UNHCR expanded its operational capacity to respond to the assistance requirements. It opened additional field offices in Kosovo to cover the entire province. It tried to culti-vate close liaison with the Kosovo Diplomatic Observer Mission (KDOM) inasmuch as we needed better and more reliable informa-tion to help all those involved in the humanitarian operation. We were fully aware that one of the important functions of a lead agency was accurate and timely information sharing, especially in conflict sit-uations such as Kosovo.

At the time the Serb security operation appeared to have two objectives. The first was to establish full control over Kosovo, espe-cially over border zones with Albania and Macedonia, as well as areas where the KLA had gained dominance or had a high-profile presence. The second was to force people to flee their homes or the places where they had sought refuge and thereby separate the KLA fighters from local civilians. The terror tactics followed a set pattern. Forces would come to villages and demand the surrender of weapons. They would disrupt electricity and other services. Then they would shell, detain, or threaten the residents and give them short notice to leave. The return home of the forcibly displaced population outside the bor-der zone and other sensitive areas was publicly encouraged by the authorities. The people hesitated to return since nothing was done to allay the fears of those who had fled in terror. In these circumstances, the ability of the humanitarian organizations to fill the immediate material needs of the people was very limited and still less for con-taining the violence and addressing the political and security threats in the province.

From September 24 to 29, 1998, I made another mission to the Federal Republic of Yugoslavia and Albania, to get a better grip on the situation. The humanitarian organizations were alone and exposed, and I felt obliged to communicate my observations to the interna-tional community. From my first talk with President Milosevic, I real-ized that our assessments of the situation were far apart. He started by saying in effect that there was no longer a problem since the KLA had been defeated and people were going home. He accused UNHCR for passing out exaggerated reports and numbers that had been used as propaganda by the international community. I argued, however, that his security forces were resorting to disproportionate use of force in order to terrorize and subjugate the population. Without an immediate and fundamental change in the Serbian approach, the cycle of violence and repression would only lead to large-scale population displacement. My special envoy, Nicholas Morris, and those who accompanied me, who had personally witnessed scenes of atrocities, substantiated my views. In spite of serious differences, we agreed that we would continue to work together for the protection and return of the displaced people. Milosevic expressed his appreciation of UNHCR's work over the years and repeated his commitment to cooperate over Kosovo. UNHCR was to be assured full and free access anywhere to carry out its humanitarian mission. This promise was, however, seriously tested upon our arrival in Kosovo the next day.

Early in the morning of September 26, 1998, in Pristina we received word that a large group of newly displaced persons was congregating near a mosque in Rasnik. We decided to change our scheduled course and go immediately to that village. President Milosevic had assured us full access. It was a good way to test the government's commitment. After more than an hour's ride we reached an open ground by a mosque where several thousand displaced persons had arrived by cars, trucks, and tractors. Most had been expelled from their village weeks ago, had wandered through the mountains, and had moved several times in search of a place where they felt less insecure. I went inside the mosque and sat on the floor to talk with several exhausted women. Their stories were horrifying. The Serbian police had come to their village and demanded the surrender of weapons. Then they had cut off the electricity and ordered them to leave. The Serbs had looted, burned, or destroyed everything the villagers left. Animals had been burned in the barns or shot in the fields. There were children lying around the mosque in a state of shock and exhaustion, unable to talk. The ICRC staff had just taken those with shrapnel wounds to the local hospital.

After leaving the mosque with a heavy heart, I shared my observations with the international press, which had kept up with our changed schedule and followed us. I immediately wrote about what I had seen to President Milosevic. Reiterating my position that the scenes that confronted me were not isolated events, I insisted that they "reflect an established pattern of actions and disproportionate use of force by the security forces." I reminded him that we at UNHCR had "demonstrated our objectivity over years of close cooperation: our concern is for victims without distinction, and for the respect of basic humanitarian principles." I concluded that "I am deeply concerned by the evidence of my own eyes of what is happening in Kosovo and Metohija. Your Excellency has both the responsibility and the power to stop it."[43] Then we drove across the mountain to Montenegro.

At the capital, Podgorica, I appealed to President Milo Djukanovic to keep the borders open in spite of the heavy refugee load the Montenegrins were suffering. The mayor of the border town, Rozaj, where we had spent the night, said that it could no longer cope with the arriving refugees. The town was really facing a catastrophe. I promised to respond to its generosity and try to mobilize more support through advocating its need for assistance. In Podgorica we received a surprise visit from the Serb refugee commissioner, Bratislava Morina, who had come from Belgrade in a presidential aircraft. She thanked me for my encounter with the displaced persons in Rasnik, then told me that there were no more displaced persons in the area. What she tried to convince me of was that those people were all villagers who had been collected and transported to stage a "displacement show" to impress me. I realized that I was facing a Serb propaganda counteroffensive to the international TV coverage of my visit. I had to tell her that I had had long experience with refugees and could not be so easily tricked. She had most likely been sent personally by the president upon receipt of my letter.

My first trip to Albania was also full of unexpected events. As soon as we arrived at the hotel in Tiranë, we were surprised by gunshots; we learned that a soldier guarding the prime minister's office, which was next to our hotel, had shot a passerby and killed her. In Tiranë we learned that as yet the number of refugees from Kosovo was limited to some twenty thousand. However, the poor infrastructure and ram-

pant lawlessness in some parts of the country seemed sure to compli-
cate any smooth reception of refugees. UNHCR warehouses had
already been looted three times, and supplies completely lost. In looking for refugee reception sites, we faced the issue of uncertain property rights. I had to request a quick decision on the allocation of land
and buildings for the collective accommodation for refugees. I called
on Prime Minister Fatos Nano, only to find he had suddenly been
called by the president and asked to resign. This was the Albanian setting in which in six months' time we had to carry out a major refugee
operation.

I returned from my mission feeling confident that UNHCR had
significantly increased our operational capacity within Kosovo. With
our staff numbering about seventy, we had markedly increased our
delivery capacity and were reaching areas that had not been accessible
before. The coordination with our partners was good on the ground,
with a key role played by agencies, such as the Mother Teresa Society,
that had the confidence of the beneficiaries. But the prospect for
political settlement was dismal. The consequences of Milosevic's
repressive approach not only affected the immediate humanitarian
situation but also had an adverse impact on the prospects for a just
and lasting political solution. The words of the presidents of Albania
and Montenegro stuck in my mind. In fact all the senior officials I
talked to commented that there was no hope for any solution that
relied on Milosevic. In different ways, and with varying degrees of
reluctance, they concluded that force would be necessary to bring an
end to the violence.

The international community began to consider taking firmer
action on the Kosovo crisis. On September 23, 1998, the UN Security
Council adopted Resolution 1199, demanding under Chapter VII
that "all parties, groups and individuals immediately cease hostilities
and maintain a ceasefire in Kosovo." It further demanded that the
Federal Republic of Yugoslavia "cease all action by the security forces
affecting the civilian population," "enable effective and continuous
international monitoring," and "facilitate, in agreement with the
UNHCR and the International Committee of the Red Cross

(ICRC), the safe return of refugees and displaced persons to their homes." The contact group that had successfully negotiated the end to the Bosnian War had been activated. It assigned Christopher Hill, U.S. ambassador to Macedonia, to concentrate on the political negotiations over Kosovo, and on October 6 Ambassador Richard Holbrooke was sent to Belgrade to enter direct talks with Milosevic. NATO was getting ready to issue an activation order for possible air strikes on October 12. Intense negotiations continued as the parties appeared to glide toward war, but in the end Holbrooke reached agreement with Milosevic to pull back Serb security forces and accept two verification regimes: one a cease-fire verification mission of two thousand members under the auspices of the OSCE and the other an aerial surveillance system conducted by NATO. An advance NATO base would be set up in Macedonia for logistics and, if necessary, security for the OSCE mission.

The pullback of Yugoslav forces from villages and highways beginning on October 27, combined with the worsening winter weather, led to a significant return of displaced persons. In particular, those who were living in the open returned to their villages or found temporary shelter with families or friends. UNHCR and humanitarian agencies made a quick shelter survey and started an emergency shelter repair operation for the people to survive the winter. The idea was to insulate with plastic sheeting one room for winter living. Though relieved by the return of a large number of the displaced population, we were aware that the underlying causes of displacement had not been reduced and that the return movements would remain fragile. The cease-fire agreement as concluded had to be followed by a negotiated political settlement. The international community, though committed to stop the repressive acts of the Serbs, was not willing to take action that might strengthen the KLA and thus the prospect of independence.

The international consensus rested on one point, that Kosovo should not be independent. The international actors were determined to contain the crisis within the region and prevent the further outflow of refugees and displaced persons. The need for an outside force to implement the cease-fire was recognized, but there was not the political will to impose such a force. The fact that Kosovo was a province of the Federal Republic of Yugoslavia limited diplomatic and political presence, including that of the United Nations, to Belgrade. Only the humanitarian agencies and NGOs operated in Kosovo. UNHCR found itself more than ever alone.

For the humanitarian agencies in Kosovo, the deployment of the OSCE Kosovo Verification Mission came as a promising first step. Its arrival was ardently awaited. The OSCE had never mounted contingents to conflict zones, although it had established monitoring stations along the Kosovo-Albanian border. The Kosovo Verification Mission (KVM) largely consisted of teams of the military in civilian clothes sponsored by OSCE member states. The OSCE regarded its mission as a "totally new adventure" that concerned "verification and not monitoring."[44] Would it, for example, be able to verify that UNHCR activities were progressing? What actions would it take against violations? What sense of security would it bring to the returning Kosovars? Would this new tool fill the gap between negotiating a political settlement and keeping the humanitarian crisis at bay?

Ambassador Holbrooke was determined to put into full effect the Serb withdrawal agreement with President Milosevic. But concerned, he pressed UNHCR to play the counterpart role to the OSCE verification mission and urged me to go to Kosovo. I made my third trip to Kosovo and Belgrade in 1998 from December 20 to 22. Ambassador William Walker, head of the KVM, welcomed and briefed me on the progress of the mission's deployment. We visited areas controlled by the government as well as by the KLA. Talking to the returnees, I gained the impression that the verifiers' presence did provide some sense of security to ethnic Albanians. However, they indicated that security would be assured only when the Serb forces and police departed. While emphasizing essential cooperation with the KVM, I also stressed the importance of UNHCR's holding a distinct and specific humanitarian role. I sensed that some confusion or tension might occur over demarcating responsibilities as the KVM reached its full strength of two thousand.

During my mission I was often accompanied by a government delegation led by Serbian Commissioner for Refugees Morina. The Serbian government took the attitude that UNHCR did not show enough concern for the fate of the Serb minority in Kosovo or for the Croatian Serb refugees. This criticism was voiced at every meeting. During a visit to a refugee center in Prizren, the building was mobbed by a mixed crowd of people from the Serb minority, who vociferously asked why I had not visited areas inhabited by affected Serbs. Commissioner Morina did not tell them of the sizable amount of assistance that UNHCR gave to the Serb refugees through her office but made statements that fueled their discontent. Serbs in Kosovo faced problems, but we later discovered that the authorities had bused in these Serbs to attend and agitate during meetings. Tension was rising between the Serb and Albanian populations. The government seemed determined to put up a strong resistance against any international pressure that favored the Kosovo Albanians.

During the lull in the fighting the KLA paramilitary units reestablished control over some villages and areas near urban centers. In turn the Yugoslav authorities positioned military units around the Kosovo borders. Before spring arrived, a series of incidents occurred between the KLA and the Yugoslav forces and worsened the situation. On January 15, 1999, the Yugoslav forces assaulted Recak village and, in the process, killed forty-five ethnic Albanians. The KVM team investigated the site and found evidence of "arbitrary detentions, extrajudicial killings, and mutilation of unarmed civilians." Ambassador Walker publicly condemned the massacre, causing a major diplomatic incident. The Serb government declared him persona non grata. The Security Council and the OSCE made strong protests, unequivocally condemning the massacre and called for an immediate cessation of hostilities and opening of dialogue.

Following up on the calls for dialogue, the Contact Group members organized peace negotiations to be held in Rambouillet, France, starting on February 6, 1999. Kosovar Albanian leaders from both the KLA and LDK, together with Serb community leaders, were invited. Representatives of the Federal Republic of Yugoslavia were also asked to attend. The Contact Group prepared documentation on the agreement on Kosovo to be presented to the parties. It stipulated the disarming of the KLA and the withdrawal of Serb forces. It provided for the restoration of Kosovo's autonomy and its independent institutions but left the question of the future status—i.e., independence—for consideration after three years. The OSCE in cooperation with the European Union was to constitute an implementation mission to supervise and direct the civilian aspects of the implementation that included coordination of international assistance, supervision of elections, and monitoring of law enforcement activities. NATO was to lead a multinational military implementation force (KFOR), demilitarize the international border, redeploy the Yugoslav Army within a specified time, and complete the final withdrawal within one year. NATO was also to be given the sole authority to establish rules governing the command and control over the airspace over Kosovo and freedom of movement throughout Yugoslavia.

UNHCR was to continue its lead role in humanitarian assistance and in the return and reintegration of refugees and displaced persons. We envisaged the process to be complex, requiring the parties to ensure those people's safe and dignified return, to uphold their rights, including reoccupation of their property, and to address the question of releasing those detained and tracing those unaccounted for. UNHCR was asked to make appropriate additions to the draft as well as plan for the return process, reflecting our experience of the Bosnian repatriation and concerns at some aspects of the Dayton Agreement. The draft military annex had almost identical language on KFOR's responsibilities for preventing violence against civilians as that in the Dayton Agreement. On March 19 the cochairs of the Rambouillet meeting declared the process effectively over. The Kosovar Albanian delegation signed the proposal on the table, but the Federal Republic and Serb delegation did not. The negotiations thus failed to materialize. That same day the OSCE chairman, Norwegian Foreign

Minister Knut Vollebek, decided to withdraw personnel from Kosovo, citing the deteriorating security situation on the ground. The next day the entire fourteen hundred KVM left Kosovo without facing any casualties. NATO Secretary-General Javier Solana noted a dramatic increase in the Yugoslav military activities following the pullout of the KVM contingent.

On March 22 Holbrooke and his negotiating team went to Belgrade to make what was to be the one last push on Milosevic. On the twenty-third Solana called to warn me that if Holbrooke were to leave Belgrade by 6:00 P.M., it would mean the breakup of negotiations. He had kept me informed of the developments during the preceding few days, and now he advised me to pull all my staff out of Kosovo. UN headquarters also announced the application of Phase 5 security to Kosovo—i.e., evacuation of all staff. We immediately notified our staff. It was a great relief when we were informed that they all had crossed the border and arrived in Macedonia. I learned later that they had made the last round of distributing humanitarian supplies and driven off in the emptied trucks. We suspended our assistance operation to four hundred thousand in Kosovo. It was with heavy heart that we left the people in need. The next night NATO started the air strikes.

We heard that the NATO member states had expected a few days', if not a few weeks', action to bring Yugoslavia back to Rambouillet. We had not foreseen the rapid refugee outflows to neighboring countries so soon after our withdrawal from Kosovo. People started to stream out, arriving in large numbers on the weekend of March 27–28. We strongly urged neighboring governments to keep their borders open. Tens of thousands entered northern Albania at Kukes, followed by similar moves a few days later into Macedonia to the Blace border point. In the first week some 156,000 people fled: 100,000 into Albania, 29,000 into Macedonia, and 27,000 into Montenegro. Most of them came by cars and tractors, but many of those who arrived at Blace, had been herded onto trains.

Interviews of the UNHCR staff members with the refugees confirmed that Serb forces were deliberately forcing Kosovar Albanians out of their homes. Masked men in uniforms knocked on doors and told people to leave or be killed. Their houses were then looted and burned. What we were seeing was not a normal refugee flight but mass expulsions and forced displacements of large segments of the population. Moreover, as European Commissioner Emma Bonino aptly observed, the current refugee outflow represented a new phase in an ongoing crisis in which Milosevic was not only the cause but also in complete control of deciding "when and where" refugees should go.

UNHCR's contingency planning within the region had covered up to a hundred thousand new arrivals in neighboring countries. We were now faced with two emergency fronts in Albania and Macedonia, where our reception capacity was still very limited. In Kukes, for example, there was one national staff member and three seconded technical staffers newly arrived from Bosnia. They made heroic efforts but needed the expert teams of emergency-trained people. They were on the ground a few days after the first arrival of refugees and brought the situation under control. Our serious problem was that we lacked sufficient and visible presence. The international media flocked to the border areas, and the European ministers descended in large numbers with their media entourage and emergency relief supplies. The news spread that UNHCR was not at the border when the refugee arrived, and we were branded for being slow and ineffective. It would have been good if we had foreseen or been warned that Yugoslavia would resort to mass deportation in response to the NATO air strikes. It would have been even better if we had developed a larger surge capacity that would have allowed us to switch overnight from a major operation inside Kosovo to several new catastrophic border fronts. Nicholas Morris, who had just returned to Sarajevo from meetings in Geneva, was on his way to Montenegro, Albania, and Macedonia. He had an impossible mandate to address both diplomatic and operational issues spread over a large area without even a helicopter at his disposal.

I was inundated with calls from Washington, Ottawa, Bonn, Rome, London, Athens, and Brussels. Most were genuine offers to help, while some were outright critical. On April 1, the EU president organized an urgent meeting at Petersburg, Germany, on the Kosovo-related humanitarian emergency in the southern Balkans. I briefed the meeting on the continuing expulsion of ethnic Albanians from Kosovo and UNHCR's new donor alert to cover the needs of 350,000 refugees, such as shelter, food, health, and sanitation. I was struck by the Albanian foreign minister's severe criticism of UNHCR's effectiveness, urging me to exercise my authority to improve our operation. Commissioners Günter Verheugen and Bonino, who had just returned from the field, reported on the need to bolster coordinated emergency response. They also referred to the necessity for UNHCR to improve relations with the refugee-hosting governments. I realized the seriousness of the situation.[45] I planned to go to the region on April 6 as soon as I convened the Humanitarian Issues Working Group meeting to inform governments and agencies of the situation and to mobilize resources to carry on the operations.

As I was duly warned at the EU Petersberg meeting, I knew full well the difficulties we faced with the refugee-hosting governments. Macedonia and Albania faced the common threat of massive refugee inflows, but they approached the problem in completely different ways. For the government of Macedonia, the refugee presence raised a fundamental question of national security. Historically, Macedonia consisted of a majority Slav population and an ethnic Albanian minority. The sudden influx of Kosovo Albanians that would represent over 10 percent of the country's entire population could tilt the delicate ethnopolitical balance, especially if their stay turned long. Local opinion was not in favor of NATO, or of air strikes, or of the growing presence of international aid workers. Macedonia took the attitude that the international community was responsible for creating the refugee problem and was obliged to solve it. Albania, on the other hand, was in support of the independence struggle in Kosovo and had allowed various Kosovo Albanian factions to base themselves in its north. The government declared the solidarity of all ethnic Albanians in the Balkans. Gaining entry and asylum in Albania was therefore not a problem for the refugees from Kosovo. The government was primarily interested in gaining international aid and security guarantees by its acceptance of refugees.

The positions of the two governments caused difficulties to UNHCR in different ways. The Macedonian government had generally admitted Kosovo Albanians so long as their numbers were limited. But when massive arrivals started on March 30–31 the Macedonian border guards slowed entry by meticulously checking each one. Refugees and vehicles accumulated on the other side of the border, at times stretching back ten kilometers. Then the trains packed with refugees arrived. Though a limited number was allowed in for processing, subsequent arrivals were bottled up at the no-man's-land at Blace between the border posts. The situation drew intense international attention. Our staff was among the refugees, attempting to ameliorate their needs. Together with NGOs, especially the local El Hillal, they did get food, some shelter, and health care to the refugees. At the same time, the UNHCR staff made clear statements against the government's reluctance to grant asylum and the treatment of those stuck at the border. We became subject to strong criticism by officials from U.S. and alliance member states, whose primary concern was to prop up the government and to ensure the maintenance of the NATO presence in Macedonia.

Two attempts were made to solve the impasse. One was to request NATO forces on an emergency basis to construct camps to accommodate the refugees. The other was to transfer refugees to other states in or outside the region in order to alleviate the Macedonian burden. The Macedonian government pressed for quick action but was not ready to provide campsites away from border areas. I was hesitant to ask NATO because UNHCR's preference was for civilians to be in charge of camp construction. We could have built the camps together with the NGOs and the Red Cross if we could have obtained the right political support. We relented because asking NATO's help with the refugees was clearly the key to unblocking Blace. Nicholas Morris, arriving in Skopje on the morning of April 3, entered immediate consultations with NATO/KFOR and requested the British and French forces deployed there to start constructing the camps. NATO was pleased to engage in a humanitarian mission.

The second attempt had serious protection implications. Norwegian Foreign Minister Knut Vollebek, who was visiting Macedonia at the time, made an unsolicited offer to take six thousand refugees from Macedonia. However, most Western European governments resisted the idea of spreading the refugees outside the region. The British foreign minister proposed setting up a security zone on the Kosovar-Macedonian border. The German government promoted plans to transfer refugees from Macedonia to Albania. Starting from the principled position of asking all states to keep their borders open, we had to explore the possibility of relocating refugees to neighboring countries, especially Greece and Bulgaria. We received no immediate offers from these countries. We decided to develop a regional evacuation program under the rubric of burden sharing. With the relocation decisions taken, the Blace crossing was unblocked. The government of Macedonia agreed to accommodate the refugees as transit camps became available. In the late evening of the fourth, five thousand refugees moved to the newly established transit camps. Gradually more followed.

In the meantime Secretary-General Solana invited me to enumerate the most critical requirements that UNHCR faced that could be supported by NATO. After serious examination with colleagues, we made a four-point request on April 3, explaining how the scale of the crisis had overwhelmed our capacity to respond in Albania and Macedonia. First was the "continued assistance with the management of the airlift operation that we had already established." Second was the "support in offloading and immediate storage of aid arriving by sea or air into Albania and FYROM (Macedonia)." Third was "logistical help in the setting up of refugee camp sites." Fourth was "support to UNHCR in obtaining the agreement of Alliance Member States primarily in the region—and most notably Greece—to accept some of the refugees currently in FYROM [Macedonia] on a temporary basis."[46]

The first two points were assistance that had started and had precedents. The third and fourth points were exceptional and had to be understood in the context of the Macedonian border crisis, where refugees were prevented from entering the country. Urgent measures had to be found to construct refugee camps virtually overnight, as well as to divert the refugees to other states in the region. Therefore, while accepting the offer of the secretary-general, I had to remind him of the importance of "retaining the civilian and humanitarian nature of the aid operation in order not to unnecessarily expose the front-line states, the relief workers on the ground and the refugees themselves." I suggested he obtain support from alliance member states through the Civil Emergency Planning Department at NATO headquarters. We also responded to the offer of help from the OSCE and asked for OSCE and KVM personnel to enhance the processing capacity urgently required at the border entry points.[47]

In contrast with Macedonia, the problems in Albania were not of receiving refugees across the border but of relations with the military. Because of the lack of resources, infrastructure, and organizational means, Albania wanted the international community to take over the management of refugee protection and assistance and had already called on NATO to help set up refugee camps and deal with emergencies. Several national military contingents from NATO countries, notably Italy and Greece, had concluded bilateral agreements with the Albanian government to provide military assistance programs. When the refugee emergency started, they switched their military operation to humanitarian aid. Other countries followed, building camps and offering various support work. The government favored a program of giving ownership to donors. The idea was to have refugee camps run by the donor governments.

This situation was problematic for UNHCR. The Albanian government had gone directly to NATO for humanitarian aid rather than through UNHCR. NATO had decided to engage in humanitarian assistance even before the NATO-UNHCR agreement of April 3 and had gone beyond the defined areas of cooperation. The lack of consultation and coordination between the military and the humanitarian operations resulted in refugee camps with little common standards of protection, security, or assistance management. Moreover, U.S. forces, such as Apache helicopters and the task force of sixty-two hundred troops to support the war, were in Albania for nonhumanitarian purposes. The Tiranë airport, which served the transport of humanitarian supplies, also served as the logistical base for military activities.

As had been planned, I visited Albania and Macedonia from April 7 to 10. It happened to take place during a relative lull in emergency. Yugoslavia kept its border closed until the ninth, and relatively few people were crossing to Albania and Macedonia. The humanitarian agencies had a window of opportunity to start reorganizing for longer-term measures. My purpose was to establish better working relations with the host governments and ensure a relationship of mutual trust and transparency in humanitarian and military relations. I stopped in Rome on my way to Albania. Italy had considered the UNHCR response inadequate and been very critical of us. Besides, being a neighboring country, which had faced waves of Albanian refugees, it had a genuine interest in containing the crisis. I was able to consult with the highest authorities, the prime minister, the foreign and interior ministers, and the chief of police. I was also given an audience by the pope, who flew back from his country residence to show his support for our humanitarian mission.

I started my field visit in Tiranë, where I met President Rexhep Meidani and Prime Minister Pandeli Majko. The meetings were cordial and showed that UNHCR's relations with the Albanian government were improving. The officials insisted that UNHCR take over more decisively its support role to the government. I expressed my readiness to collaborate but pointed out that some order had to be applied to coordinate donor contributions, especially the management of nationally contributed camps. We agreed that it was extremely important to expand and strengthen support to the vast number of families hosting the refugees. New modes of assistance had to be devised, whether in kind or in cash. I flew to Kukes, the Albanian border town in the north that had served as the entry point for tens of thousands of refugees. Relief goods were being flown into the town, still full of the international press. I called on the mayor and pledged continued UNHCR support. Our colleagues had survived the critical emergency phase and had set up their operational headquarters with the necessary staff. The town center was like a huge parking lot of tractors. People were beginning to move toward locations in the south. Kukes continued to be the reception point of incoming refugees.

By the time I went to Skopje, the Blace crisis had been defused, but its consequences lingered. I found myself trapped between the government position, supported by key governments, such as the United States and United Kingdom, not to protest the improper handling of refugees, and the pressure from the media and NGOs to raise the very same points critically. The authorities warned me that any large refugee influx would gravely destabilize the ethnic balance of Macedonia. President Kiro Gligorov was particularly adamant, stating that changing the ethnic balance in the southern Balkans would have catastrophic consequences for the rest of the region. My appeal to the authorities to keep the border open in case of another large influx from Kosovo met with a surprisingly positive response, although the president was somewhat noncommittal. The experience in Blace—the media attention, international aid, quick refugee camp construction, and offers for burden sharing—had certainly contributed to easing the government position.

I called on General Michel Jackson, the commander of KFOR, at his converted shoe factory headquarters. Always stoic in a combat mode, he gave us a concise briefing on the camp setup. I thanked him for the NATO contribution that had helped defuse the crisis at the Macedonian border. However, I proposed to take over as quickly as possible, within a week to ten days, the management of the main camps. We were ready, and all the NGOs were lined up. NATO's noted ability to construct camps and move refugees rapidly contrasted with UNHCR's real or perceived slowness. Besides, NATO's aggressive media campaign was overshadowing UNHCR's. I thought the time was ripe for UNHCR to take back the refugee operation and prove and maintain the civilian character of refugee camps. Visiting the campsite, I was pleased that camp life was already in better order. There were emergency clinics run by the Israeli, Taiwan, and other military medical units. The refugees followed me all over the place. Several recognized me from my Kosovo visits. One little boy, probably nine or ten years of age, ran to me and asked me directly, "Would you take us home?" I was very touched by his genuine faith in me, and promised, "Yes, as soon as I can."

One bit of information passed on by General Jackson that disturbed me was the deployment of a new NATO force (AFOR) to Albania with an exclusive humanitarian mandate. A sizable force of some eight thousand was to be sent to Albania in support of and in close coordination with the Albanian civil authorities and the humanitarian agencies, particularly UNHCR. We had been neither informed nor consulted on such a plan, although while in Albania we had heard rumors of a new NATO contingent, separate from KFOR. I was uncertain of its real mandate. I called Secretary-General Solana upon my return and requested clarifications about AFOR. It was only later, on April 14, when I met him, that some clearer explanations were given. AFOR had a host of missions, some of which seemed useful for humanitarian operations, but others were extraneous. The dividing line between military and humanitarian areas of responsibility might become further blurred. My challenge would be to define clearly and absorb NATO's logistical support, which we needed, without letting UNHCR's image and activities be swallowed by NATO's much larger operation. Besides, NATO's public information machinery was turning more and more expansive.

However separate and different, one issue linked the Macedonian and Albanian operations. It was the transfer of refugees. In line with Macedonia's position to prevent the large-scale arrival of refugees from Kosovo, the government attempted to make arrangements with Albania and Turkey to transfer refugees from the border directly to these two countries. Some transfers had been facilitated by the United States but reportedly carried out in an abusive manner. Albania had been irritated by the process, especially by President Gligorov's intention of sending all Kosovo refugees to it. Foreign Minister Aleksandar

Dimitrov of Macedonia came to Tirane to resolve the incident, and the Greek foreign minister, Andreas Papandreou, was there to mediate. Though it was unplanned, I facilitated the meeting of the two foreign ministers, who shared with me their concerns and looked for a solution. I was surprised to learn that nine thousand refugees had already been transferred. I reiterated that any transfer of refugees from Macedonia should be carried out in close consultation with UNHCR in a properly organized way and that the move had to be voluntary and family separation had to be avoided. The next day I was told that a deal had been made between Macedonia and Albania to move refugees from Macedonia to Korce and other camps to be constructed in Albania. In the end, however, the transfer program to Albania did not yield much of a result. The refugees were not willing to move to Albania, and the UNHCR staff was firmly against undermining the first asylum policy.

The NATO air campaign against Yugoslavia that started on March 24 continued on till June 10, 1999. Planned to last for several days or at most weeks, the bombing initially struck military targets, including air defense and communications installations. It succeeded in grounding the Yugoslav Air Force but not in destroying its air defense. NATO attacks in Kosovo did relatively little damage to Yugoslav ground forces, which attacked the KLA throughout Kosovo. NATO's air campaign could not stop the expulsion and killings of Kosovo civilians. The continuing escalation of displacement and expulsion was not the result of the air campaign but the consequence of the particular constellation of the Kosovo War. A quick estimate of refugee numbers in mid-May gave a total of almost 750,000. The largest group was in Albania, totaling 431,000, followed by Macedonia with 234,000, Bosnia and Herzegovina with 18,500, and 64,300 in Montenegro. Another 43,000 had left Macedonia under the humanitarian evacuation program. NATO believed that there were at least 590,000 internally displaced.

In humanitarian terms, notwithstanding its content, the Kosovo crisis was still essentially a refugee crisis. UNHCR had to take the lead to address the issue amid a war of uncertain duration. Our first and largest challenge was to make sure that the refugees were properly accommodated whether in homes, camps, or collective centers. Though improving, the objective could not be easily attained. In Albania the security problems persisted throughout the country, and site availability and construction or refurbishing of camps tended to lag behind the needs. In Macedonia the special problem of ethnic balance led to the need to resort to an innovative burden-sharing scheme of humanitarian evacuation. I had outlined the basic content of the program at the Humanitarian Issues Working Group meeting on April 6. However, precise guidelines for the program had to be developed and communicated to governments that would be contributing to the scheme. I requested that Anne-Willem Bijleveld, director of operations for Europe, be in charge since we assumed that evacuations should be attempted within reasonable geographical limits, mostly in Europe.

Although covering only a minority of refugees, the humanitarian evacuation program turned into a high-profile activity that provided visibility to governments. On April 8, the EU ministers of justice and home affairs met in Luxembourg to deal with the question of those displaced from Kosovo. They adopted the position that these people required protection and should be accommodated in the region in order to facilitate their earliest return. They did indicate, however, that depending on the rapid swell of displaced persons, it might become necessary to take them outside the region on a temporary basis. The targeted slot for Europe was put at seventy thousand. Several member states declared their readiness to admit displaced persons. Germany was willing to admit ten thousand. Austria and Sweden would receive five thousand each. Portugal stated its readiness to take two thousand, and Ireland, one thousand. Albania expressed its readiness to take in a further hundred thousand refugees, who were currently in Macedonia. European states were eager to assist Albania in strengthening its capacity to take in larger numbers. Germany was committed to help provide assistance for forty thousand within Albania.

UNHCR found implementation of the evacuation program hard.

The target figure of moving two thousand a day out of Macedonia did not materialize; the procedure took time, the displaced had preferences, and the planes were too small to transport large numbers. Many governments did not fulfill the quotas that they had indicated. There were countries that were popular and others that were unpopular with the evacuees. A large number of refugees preferred Germany, and its quota was quickly filled. In Germany's capacity as the chair of the European Union, its federal minister of the interior, Otto Schily, took it upon himself to support UNHCR's call for expediting the evacuation scheme. For a while I had daily telephone contacts with Minister Schily to solicit his help with his EU colleagues. I even turned to him to double the German slot for another ten thousand. He found the request hard to fill since he could not ask the Länder to take more when other countries were not delivering. He made personal efforts to accelerate the camp construction in Albania, but the NATO capacity to build camps proved much smaller than we had expected. Under the circumstances, we had to solicit evacuations outside Europe. The United States and Australia were ready to participate. The United States announced its offer of twenty thousand slots. UNHCR was in a dilemma. The influx of refugees into Macedonia continued unabated, but the evacuation from Skopje was stalled. Albania was willing to accept refugees, but there were not enough volunteers to move to Albania.

We had no choice but to save the situation incrementally. As I had stated at the initiation of the evacuation program, we would not accept "random, disorganized and—worst of all—forced evacuation." Those currently fleeing Kosovo were refugees within the definition of the 1951 convention and had to be treated with all attendant rights by the countries in the region.[48]

While concentrating on the protection and assistance of refugees in Albania and Macedonia, we could not overlook the situation inside the Federal Republic of Yugoslavia. UNHCR provided some seven hundred thousand dollars per month to the government for over half a million ethnic Serb refugees from Croatia and Bosnia and Herzegovina in collective centers. Demands for help and the return of the

UNHCR staff to Yugoslavia came from the Serb refugee commissioner Bratislava Morina. We had maintained an office in Belgrade but had withdrawn most of the international staff on the instruction of the UN security coordinator. I requested that Commissioner Morina guarantee the safety and security of our staff not only in the capital but also in Novi Sad and Kraljevo, where the field offices had been vandalized. I also demanded that she and other Yugoslav officials "desist from making accusations and hostile remarks against UNHCR staff," which proved "counterproductive in our efforts to assist refugees."[49] Besides, the donor community was not forthcoming in extending assistance to Serb refugees. The situation of the displaced population within Kosovo was also deeply worrying, but we were unable to operate while the fighting continued.

We foresaw, however, that pressure for UNHCR to prepare for the return of refugees would increase, even before peace was restored. I asked Dennis McNamara, the director of the Department of International Protection, to succeed Nicholas Morris as special envoy. He would have to deal with the planning and implementation of the return phase of the operation. I tried to emphasize to all my contacts that UNHCR-assisted repatriation would be possible only after Serb forces had withdrawn. We started to plan with other agencies, taking into consideration the pattern of return and the types of civil administration to be established. We recognized that the presence of an international military force would be an important condition for any kind of return, not only to establish a secure environment but also to provide logistics and infrastructure reconstruction. We had to deal with the enormous challenge of postconflict mobilization of resources.

On a more immediate note, we had to decide by the end of May whether to embark on a program of winterizing the camps in both Macedonia and Albania. Procuring large amounts of building materials needed lead time. Particularly in Albania, we would have to remove refugees from tented camps and rehouse them in heated accommodations. Heating and electricity would be a major infrastructure challenge, hard for humanitarian programs to meet. Should the refugees return to Kosovo, winterization would become part of the reconstruction undertaking, which in turn would be part of a larger economic aid package. Yet at the time we did not know when the war would end.

Diplomatic negotiations were moving through several channels. The EU held a summit on Kosovo in Brussels on April 14, inviting UN Secretary-General Kofi Annan to participate. Annan had made known his views on conditions to end hostilities in Kosovo. Upon acceptance of these conditions by Yugoslavia, he was ready to urge the North Atlantic Alliance to suspend air bombardments immediately and then to resume negotiations.[50] I was visiting Brussels that day to confer with NATO Secretary-General Solana. I had a private meeting with Annan, and we shared views on the prospects for a diplomatic settlement, the repatriation of refugees, and UNHCR's relations with NATO. I was pleased to note that the secretary-general thought that there might be a role for the United Nations, not just in the humanitarian response but also in the diplomatic peace efforts. The EU summit had indicated that it was prepared to play a central role in the interim administration of Kosovo, to be sanctioned by the Security Council. Annan assured me that throughout the meeting he had advocated respect for the role of UNHCR with regard to repatriation and that he would appoint a special envoy for the region to ensure and expand a UN presence.

The United States was also reengaged in diplomatic action. Deputy Secretary of State Strobe Talbott, who had helped resolve the crisis at Blace when he was in Skopje in early April, came to UNHCR in Geneva on April 28 while on a Kosovo-related European tour to update us on the diplomatic moves. He said that an extraordinary amount of diplomatic and political pressure was being put on Milosevic, in order to create a situation that would allow NATO military action to stop. The two main conditions were the withdrawal of all Serb military forces and the deployment of international force. The language involving the NATO presence was subject to complicated negotiations. Talbott carefully spelled out the latest version, which had been changed from "NATO-led force" as a precondition to an "international security presence with NATO at the core, for which a UN umbrella would be welcome." A very special role was expected of the Russian authorities, especially Special Envoy Viktor Chernomyrdin. The Russians had close contact with the Serbs and were in a position to exert influence. Talbott believed that the Russians were working very seriously on peace but did not want to be seen as moving on behalf of NATO. They were relatively low-key about their real achievements. I briefed Talbott about the refugee situation, the problems in Macedonia and Albania, and the difficulties of meeting new outflows and planning for returns. He appreciated our work and was ready to support it.[51]

The war continued, but diplomatic efforts were gaining momentum. The G8 foreign ministers adopted the general principles for political solution to the Kosovo crisis. Chernomyrdin shuttled to Belgrade and was later joined by President Martti Ahtisaari of Finland. The two emissaries together with Talbott worked out the proposed framework for ending the war, which was delivered to Milosevic on June 3. It called for the withdrawal of all Serb military, police, and paramilitary. It required an international security presence with a substantial NATO participation and under UN authority. Details for the withdrawal of the Serb forces and the suspension of military activity were to be worked out in a military technical agreement. The talks made progress. On June 5 General Jackson met with the Serb delegation at a border to work out the technical agreement. The Serbs agreed to start withdrawing, there would be a pause in the bombing, and a UN Security Council resolution would follow. General Wesley Clark, the supreme allied commander, directed the military negotiation process while developing the option to resort to a ground war in case of failure. The heavy involvement of the Russians was necessary for moving the peace talks. General Clark was concerned over how the Russians would participate in the Kosovo NATO mission.[52]

It was in Cologne during the June 10 ministerial meeting on the Stability Pact for Southeastern Europe that Secretary-General Solana conveyed the good news of peace. I had been invited by the German president of the EU to report on UNHCR activities and was very pleased to state that we stood prepared to coordinate the repatriation. I reminded the meeting that the Kosovo crisis had a very wide and deep impact in the region, that 1.7 million people from countries of the former Yugoslavia lived away from their homes, and that we must take this opportunity to refocus on the displacement of people in the region as a whole. I strongly warned that it was essential to ensure the protection of Serbian and other minorities in Kosovo. I wanted to emphasize that we should not "create refugees by returning refugees." I was getting very worried that "the repatriation of ethnic Albanians may prompt the Serbs to leave the province."

In the course of the meeting, an unexpected invitation came from Chancellor Gerhard Schröder to me to attend the upcoming G8 summit on June 19. He wished to dedicate the Cologne Symphony Orchestra event to UNHCR for its dedicated work for the Kosovo refugees. I was surprised and touched. In the past we had tried to draw the attention of the G8 to the fate of refugees and the displaced and had never succeeded. This time the summit would be honoring the refugees through us! Fortunately, I was able to adjust a scheduled trip to the Great Lakes region in Africa and returned to Cologne eight days later. The city was festive, full of displays to receive dignitaries from all over the world. For the evening event, the heads of state and governments all assembled for drinks at the Cologne museum, then lined up to enter the symphony hall. I was placed between President Jacques Chirac and Chancellor Schröder. After the beautiful music program, the chancellor escorted me up to the stage, expressed his appreciation for the work we had done, and turned to me to say a few words. I felt very honored and thanked him for the recognition and for the chance to bring the fate of the refugees to the attention of such an august assembly. Our Kosovo operation had undergone severe days of harsh criticism. Somehow we had come through, and I was happy to have UNHCR bask in a few minutes of glory. The next morning we rushed off to Nairobi. The proceeds of the evening came as a contribution from the German government for Kosovo refugees a few weeks later.

Returns to Kosovo moved rapidly. The refugees had fled because they had been expelled. People had streamed out in large numbers within a short period soon after the start of NATO air action on March 24, 1999. When diplomatic negotiations succeeded in bringing about the withdrawal of Serb forces from Kosovo on June 10, those expelled immediately took to the roads. NATO forcers entered Kosovo two days later on June 12. UNHCR was not ready to advise the refugees to return immediately, but KFOR's announcement that the Serb troops had withdrawn from Kosovo was enough to trigger a spontaneous return. The Kosovars seemed to have received the information that it was now safe to go home.

Between June 15 and 20 some hundred thousand were estimated to have gone back. More than sixty thousand went back from Albania, and some thirty-five thousand left from Macedonia. In the words of Jessen-Petersen, who witnessed the departure, it was a triumphant scene: "old couples walking back to Pristina; tractors carrying young children, smiling and waving good-bye; a young man looking up at the sky, lifting his arms and screaming of happiness as he crossed the border." The scene represented not just individuals returning but "a people reclaiming its collective right to live in Kosovo and, most importantly [sic], to exist as an ethnic group."[53]

After the initial rush of the spontaneous return, UNHCR had to engage in an organized return for all refugees. We set the starting date as July 1. NATO insisted on early action. It was natural that it should wish to see all the refugees go back quickly. The fast return of refugees was seen to crown the success of its mission. We were concerned over the extensive destruction and the mines problem, but we had no choice. Large numbers were returning on their own anyway. We again had to shift our operation back to Kosovo, away from Macedonia and Albania. Both governments were keen to see the refugees go, although they assured us that they would not force them to leave. It was fortunate that the refugees were returning during the summer; we no longer had to make heavy winterization investments in asylum countries. We would have to consider the small-scale rehabilitation of sites that had been used by refugees and the repair of roads and runways that had been heavily used for logistical support. Albanian and Macedonian authorities asked us to be catalyts and advise the international community to provide compensation for the economic and environmental damages they had borne.

The rapid return of refugees to Kosovo continued unabated. McNamara, my special envoy, asked me to accompany the refugees going back on UNHCR's organized return program. On July 5 we left the camp in Macedonia in a convoy of six buses and several jeeps, crossed the once-packed Blace crossing, and in two hours arrived in Pristina. It was good to see UNHCR's Kosovo staff and confirm their safety after several months of separation. By then some 547,500 ethnic Albanian refugees had returned to Kosovo from neighboring Albania, Macedonia, and Montenegro. There were still 209,000 refugees in the region and approximately 91,000 evacuated to countries in Europe, and to Australia, Canada, and the United States under the humanitarian evacuation program. There were hundreds of thousands who remained displaced inside Kosovo and in need of UNHCR assistance. Those who had fled to Albania had their own means of transportation, but many of those who had been in Macedonia had been forced to leave on crowded trains. On my trip I was accompanied mostly by those who had neither the means nor the resources to return on their own.

During the two-day stay in Kosovo, I called on the NATO/KFOR commander, General Jackson, and asked for his views on the security prospects. Although he was attempting to demilitarize the KLA, he had some reservations over any quick establishment of security in the province. In Prizren we visited the headquarters of the German forces and the Orthodox monastery that housed Serb displaced persons. It was painful to go through the large hall turned into a community bedroom and talk with elderly Serb couples who seemed no longer to know where to go. We went to the largely destroyed town of Pec, where, as if by a miracle, UNHCR's small field office stood in good shape. Throughout Kosovo everybody seemed busy at work, repairing, cleaning, and restoring what they could. The KLA delegation, headed by Hashim Thaci, came to see me. I urged on them the importance of restraining the violence that drove the minorities, Serbs and Romas, to flee. I had just gone to a settlement of Romas on the outskirts of Pristina. About five thousand had come from various villages fleeing intimidation and harassment. The poverty was appalling.

The repatriation of Kosovo Albanians moved rapidly with relatively little complication. But it was in the aftermath of their return that serious minority displacement problems grew in intensity. The harassment and discrimination against non-Albanian communities caused a new and dramatic crisis of forced displacement. More than two hundred thousand displaced persons, mostly of Serb and Roma ethnic origin, moved to Serbia and Montenegro. Inside Kosovo the Serbs were blocked from returning to their areas of origin. There were pockets of Serb villages where the people faced threats of expulsions constantly. In the areas where the Serbs maintained their majority status, the Albanians were prevented from coming back. Having worked hard to try to protect the Albanians from persecution and violence, we now had to help the Serbs and other minorities against threats from the Albanians. In fact the security situation inside Kosovo remained extremely fragile. The houses of minorities were set on fire, and security and criminal incidents were on the rise. The security problem was particularly acute, owing to the absence of effective national and international policing.

The Security Council had decided to deploy international civil and security units and requested that the secretary-general appoint a special representative to lead the implementation.[54] The structure of the UN Interim Administration Mission in Kosovo (UNMIK) was complex. It incorporated several separate institutions—namely, the OSCE, EU, and UNHCR—as integrated parts of the overall UN peacekeeping setup. Dennis McNamara was appointed to head the Humanitarian Pillar, to collaborate closely with the civil administration pillar, and the reconstruction pillar. It was good that UNHCR was able to contribute to the overall efforts of the UN as a constituent part of the administration.

UNHCR's focus was on coordinating humanitarian relief operations for the returnees and displaced persons. It assisted and protected the minorities and also had overall responsibility for antimine actions. It carried out the emergency winter shelter program, which was the main material concern of all the humanitarian agencies. We worried all through the winter and made sure that no one would freeze to death, even in remote areas. Aside from dispatching winter emergency teams of experienced mobile field staff, we identified more than a hundred community centers throughout the province that provided twenty thousand places for anyone who might need emergency accommodation during the winter.[55]

On March 14, 2000, almost a year after the beginning of the NATO air operation, I visited Kosovo as part of an extensive trip through southeastern Europe. The objective was to examine the continuing intercommunal tensions that marred successful repatriation and the efforts to avoid humanitarian catastrophe in the winter months. I went directly from Podgorica, the capital of Montenegro, to Mitrovica, a divided town in northern Kosovo. After crossing the heavily guarded bridge that divided Mitrovica geographically and ethnically in two, I visited several apartments where ethnic Albanians had returned but lived under heavy KFOR protection. These returnees had to be escorted by French soldiers to cross the bridge even to go for daily shopping. Elsewhere in western Kosovo, some Serb leaders pressed for a plan for organized return with support from KFOR, but given the high risk of backlash, UNHCR favored a more prudent and gradual approach to the return of minorities.

In the Gnjilane area, in southeastern Kosovo, there were pockets of Serb villages. I was shocked to learn that children were escorted to school by the American troops. UNHCR was assisting the refugee information center in the town, where the Serb staff had to receive security coverage to come to work, then again to visit the homes of Serb returnees. UNHCR staff members with a few NGOs were working very courageously to try to protect threatened minorities. It was ironic that despite the full support and cooperation of KFOR contingents, present and patrolling, minorities could not avoid having to flee. The contrast between the size and sophistication of the U.S. Bondsteel military camp and the ongoing harassment of ethnic Serbs in areas just a few miles away was staggering. I enjoyed a hospitable

welcome at the U.S. camp and a good briefing from the force commander. It was interesting to note that the camp employed six thousand locals, but there were no longer any Serbs on the staff. In
UNHCR's field offices in Kosovo, the few remaining Serb staffers
made brave efforts to continue their service.

The force commander at the Bondsteel camp warned me of the
possibility of a new refugee exodus, this time of the Albanian community in southern Serbia. For the time being only seventy-six hundred had crossed into Kosovo. Whether they were all refugees or part
of traditional cross-border population movements seemed hard to
distinguish. Very few had crossed over to Macedonia so far, but the
government in Skopje was very nervous and fearful of a repetition of
what had happened in 1999. There were clearly provocations by
Albanian guerrillas and retaliations by the Serb military units sta-
tioned in the Presevo Valley in substantial numbers. We were told
that the Albanian leaders had been requested to restrain armed
groups from operating in neighboring areas. NATO troops were not
authorized to intervene across the border into southern Serbia.

Clearly the situation in Kosovo involving minority return was
volatile. There were signals of ongoing ethnic cleansings—i.e., expulsions of minorities—which clouded the scene. UNHCR tried to take
action on two scores. The first was to concentrate on the slightly less
targeted minority, the Romas, and arrange go see visits for leaders to
their original villages. I encouraged holding a roundtable discussion
on Roma Day, April 7, and inviting some Albanian leaders to share in
the discussion. The second action was to carry out concentrated dialogue with the Kosovo Albanian leaders on the problems of minorities. When the three main Albanian leaders—Rugova, Thaci, and
Rexhep Qosja—came to meet me, I told them that I understood the
depth and gravity of past wounds, but that now that they were the vic-
torious majority, they had the responsibility to respect the rights of
other communities and should keep the interethnic dialogue as open
and constructive as possible. They agreed with me in principle, but
Thaci observed that there was ongoing collusion between the Serb
minority and the authorities in Belgrade. The Albanian leaders were

reluctant to endorse any plans for minority returns but were ready to engage in confidence-building measures. They were against setting up enclaves because these might lead to secession.

One repatriation issue that caused great concern was the forced return of rejected asylum seekers from Western European countries. At the height of the military action the European countries had refrained from sending them back. Neither the exact number nor the profile of these people was known, but they were estimated to range in numbers from one to two hundred thousand. I could not object to their forced return to Kosovo on grounds of their needing protection since they were not refugees, but they might well have become refugees *sur place*, as a result of events after their rejection. I recalled the enormous difficulties I had undergone with European countries in connection with returns to Bosnia and Herzegovina. Germany, which generously accepted refugees on a temporary protection basis, was particularly eager to send them back, at times even forcefully and to areas other than to their homes, as soon as the war ended. The major problem in Kosovo was one of absorption. UNMIK was worried that there was a shortage of housing, jobs, and security coverage. Couldn't the Western countries postpone departures? There were always differences between the priorities of interior ministries and foreign ministries. I appealed to Western authorities to proceed with forced returns in a gradual and humane manner and especially to exclude any minorities from the return operation.

Military action had subsided in Kosovo, but peace was hardly established. In fact building peace and normality proved to be a process that had to be developed gradually on many fronts. The repatriation of refugees was an important component of peace building. Joint efforts were required on several fronts: assurance of security, improvement in economic life, and, above all, reconciliation among the various components of society. When ethnic tension simmered and symptoms of "cleansing" still persisted, the danger of backlash was very real. The overall peace implementation within Kosovo depended largely on the continued presence of UNMIK and eventually on the political decision over the future status of Kosovo.

I called on the respective presidents of the neighboring counties of Macedonia and Albania to thank them for their hospitality to the refugees. In spite of all the difficulties, it was good that asylum had been given to the refugees during their short but critical periods of need. UNHCR pledged continued support to the limited number of remaining refugees and to the rehabilitation of areas they occupied. We would rapidly phase down our presence and work.

As we wound down our operation in the Balkans, the situation of refugees in Serbia remained catastrophic. The result of this last Balkan War was the presence of about seven hundred thousand Serbian refugees. They came from Croatia, Bosnia, and Kosovo. They symbolized not the goal of Greater Serbia but in fact its failure. Visiting Belgrade in the spring of 2000, I was struck by the mood of anger and frustration. The Serbs felt themselves repeatedly victimized by unjust international treatment. When they fought "terrorists," they were attacked by NATO, and when they hosted refugees, they were hardly assisted. I had to remind the difficult Serb refugee commissioner Bratesla Morina, with whom we had exchanged harsh words, that UNHCR's assistance budget for Serbia was very large and that it would continue to protect and speak on behalf of Serbs in Kosovo. She did recognize that UNHCR's was the only objective voice, but she stated that the Yugoslav government had no intention of keeping Serb refugees and urged UNHCR to speed up their repatriation.

I recalled the miserable faces of refugees, old and young, whom I saw in flight and in camps and collective centers. They were the pawns of the power feud among leaders. But since the Balkan wars were defined by ethnicity, all victims inevitably belonged to the parties in the conflict. Win or lose, they gained or suffered from the consequences of war. The solution rested on greater ethnic tolerance. Community rebuilding centered on recognition of coexistence would be a long but the only sure way to peace. UNHCR's approach to the solution of the refugee problems in the Balkans that centered on repatriation eventually had to head toward ethnic reconciliation.

Conclusion

UNHCR played a lead role in the Balkans, in a full cycle that started from the displacement of Croats and Serbs in Croatia to the spreading conflict in Bosnia and Herzegovina to the repatriation of refugees and displaced persons following the Dayton Peace Agreement to the Kosovo crisis, and again to the refugee returns. The cycle represented all aspects of humanitarian action, from emergency response, operational coordination, refugee protection, to repatriation and reintegration. The total number of refugees, displaced persons, and affected civilians was staggering. On the eve of the Dayton peace negotiations, there were estimated 1,297,000 displaced persons in Bosnia and Herzegovina, another 820,000 in other republics, and 700,000 refugees in Europe, half in Germany. In addition, 3 million affected civilians depended on international assistance. The Kosovo crisis produced 750,000 refugees and 590,000 displaced inside the province. The relief operation was unprecedented in scale and had to be carried out against the backdrop of a devastating war. The safety and the security of the victims as well as of workers were always of priority concern.

What, then, did the international involvement achieve? What were the contributions by UNHCR? To begin with, we must recall the two basic conditions that framed the international response: the breakup of the Federal Republic of Yugoslavia and the political fight over ethnicity. Croats and Serbs confronted each other over the control of Croatia; Muslims, Serbs, and Croats waged war against one another in order to expand their territorial bases in Bosnia and Herzegovina; Albanians waged a secessionist war against the Serbs in the province of Kosovo. Each group resorted to killings and expulsions to back up its political position in the emerging new republics. Ethnic cleansing was not just an expression of hate but the political weapon to ensure a dominant presence in the emerging postconflict republics. The displacement of people became the very objective of the war.

Each ethnic group fought against others with a vengeance. UNHCR and the humanitarian workers who were witness to the atrocities had limited choices to adopt: to intervene or to make public denunciations, as they did in Banja Luka, or to help evacuate the victimized, as happened in Srebrenica in March 1993. We also appealed to European governments for temporary protection, to take in without lengthy asylum procedures those who managed to flee the war fronts. In some instances, UNHCR was criticized for lending a hand to ethnic cleansing. However, when the alternative was death, our colleagues in the field had no choice but the course that saved lives.

To UNHCR, ethnic cleansing was an aberration that had to be corrected when war ended. Assigned to carry out Annex 7 of the Dayton Agreement, we understood our role was to implement "the right of all refugees and displaced persons to return freely to their homes of origin," to ensure conditions of safety and mobility, so that people could go back to where they had come from. We directed our efforts to realize the return of minorities by running interentity bus lines, and we promoted open cities. The outcome of the peace agreement was in reality the separation of Bosnia and Herzegovina along ethnic lines: Republika Srpska and the Federation. Croat refugees from Bosnia tended to stay on in Croatia, and Serbs from Croatia, Bosnia, eastern Slavonia, and Kosovo remained in the Federal Republic. Sarajevo became largely dominated by Muslims, in spite of the call for multiethnicity. In short, the wars in the Balkans resettled population groups along ethnic lines. So long as economic and political factors eventually provided individuals with choices over where to go, the outcome of the wars might not be assessed as totally negative. In fact, minority return has increased in recent years. Serbs who remain in Kosovo have to be better assured of their security. Then some Serbs might go back to Kosovo. The real lesson to be learned is that reconciliation after bitter ethnic conflict takes a long time to heal.

The war in the Balkans brought UNHCR new partnerships of

diplomats and soldiers. UNHCR made full use of my chairmanship of the Working Group on Humanitarian Issues of the ICFY. This role gave us ample opportunities to participate in the Vance-Owen negotiations as well as to keep humanitarian issues at the top of political and operational agendas. Since the international community was unable to solve the causes of the wars, it tended to focus on supporting the humanitarian operations. For our part, we took advantage of these openings to share our concerns, promote the refugee protection cause, and solicit necessary resources. My first address at the Security Council was prompted by our lead humanitarian role in the former Yugoslavia. I could take advantage of the occasion to speak on behalf of the refugees. I could also urge the council to expedite the deployment of peacekeeping forces when needed and to promote and consolidate political settlements.

The Security Council designation of Srebrenica and several Muslim pockets as safe areas, however, gave false hope to the besieged people and ultimately led to the debacle. The political division within the council was a reality that resulted in proclaiming objectives that were not backed up by adequate means. UNHCR had reservations over the concept of safe areas. We found it untenable to run what in reality were huge refugee camps without adequate security. Secretary-General Boutros-Ghali had clearly presented to the Security Council the force requirements to protect Srebrenica but, even when they were unmet, could not overrule the decision of the council. Moreover, to begin with, UNPROFOR could not operate freely in eastern Bosnia because of Serb restrictions.

UNHCR's cooperation with the military took different forms in different places. We found the UNPROFOR humanitarian assistance mission compatible with our objectives. Having overcome the initial hesitation to receive military cover of humanitarian relief activities, we recognized that we needed the military to travel active war zones in central Bosnia. With UNPROFOR assistance, we played a crucial role in controlling the Sarajevo airport and ran the Sarajevo airlift for more than three years, in spite of security threats. At times we solicited its support for airdrops to besieged towns and villages.

On strictly humanitarian missions, the partnership with the military proved generally positive.

When the military became engaged in combat missions, UNHCR faced serious difficulties. In Bosnia, when NATO resorted to close air support and air strikes, humanitarian operations had to be suspended for reasons of safety. Moreover, the neutrality of humanitarian operations became questioned when the United Nations resorted to NATO action while running humanitarian convoys. In Kosovo, NATO action was necessary to counteract the Serb military aggression. But confusion grew when NATO member states extended bilateral military assistance to the building and running of refugee camps. NATO tended to put on a humanitarian face to offset some of the negative consequences of its actions. Carrying out humanitarian operations in situations of ethnic conflict required constant scrutiny between the objective of protecting the victims and the permissible and appropriate means to be used.

Two points stand out that characterized UNHCR operations in the Balkan crisis. The first was the comprehensive coverage of all categories of people in need—refugees, internally displaced persons, and affected civilians. The second was the heavy involvement in the return and repatriation process. When the Yugoslav delegation requested UNHCR assistance for the displaced population in Croatia in 1991, we had to decide whether to respond to a situation involving internally displaced persons or not. Refugee protection is a mandated responsibility of UNHCR, and we have no choice whether to act or not, but for the internally displaced, there was a degree of flexibility in formulating our judgment. Predicting the breakup of the Federal Republic, we chose to act since today's state borders would be tomorrow's international borders, and today's internally displaced persons would be tomorrow's refugees. Moreover, in war zone operations, a humanitarian presence was the most important protection tool for all victims—refugees, internally displaced, and affected civilians. The Balkan crisis represented the largest and most complicated mix of forced human displacement. Those who fled to European countries were unmistakably refugees. Those who went to other independent republics were also refugees. But in the case of Kosovo, which was a province of the Federal Republic, the Albanians who fled to Montenegro, or the Serbs who went elsewhere in Serbia, legally were internally displaced.

The postconflict return and repatriation operation had protection and assistance implications as difficult as the wartime emergency work. The aftermath of ethnic cleansing conditioned the return process. People returned to areas where they belonged to the majority ethnic groups, but minorities hesitated to go back to areas that had become dominated by other ethnic groups. In spite of the vast variety of efforts made to encourage reconciliation, we had to wait for significant and lasting changes to remove the political and psychological obstacles. Traumatic memories took time to heal. We learned to devise reconciliation and community-building projects. The Imagine Coexistence program grew out of our search to find ways of overcoming memories of mass violence and leading to forgiveness and reconciliation.

Operating in war-torn countries in the Balkans for nearly a decade, we saved innumerable lives and mitigated human suffering. We strove and came up with new approaches and new hypotheses to address constantly evolving situations. We often had to deal with problems that were beyond what we could achieve. The humanitarian "fig leaf" filled the gap that political and military action failed for so long to address.

3.

CRISES IN THE
GREAT LAKES REGION
OF AFRICA

Burundi and Rwanda, two very small countries in central Africa surrounded by two large neighboring countries, Zaire and Tanzania, are landlocked and hilly with a high density of human settlement. Though linguistically and culturally homogeneous, the population consisted, among others, of two large groups, the Hutus and the Tutsis. During the colonial period they formed part of German East Africa and later of Belgian-ruled Ruanda-Urundi until they became respectively independent in 1962.

The colonial powers ruled indirectly through Tutsi chiefs. However, with independence approaching, the traditional rule became increasingly challenged by the more numerous Hutus, who demanded social and political position and power. The oppressive Hutu republic was established in 1961, and large numbers of Tutsis fled to neighboring countries. By early 1960s there were some 150,000 Rwandan refugees in Zaire, Burundi, Uganda, and Tanzania. To UNHCR, the Rwanda refugees in the Great Lakes region of Africa were the first group linked with the decolonization process south of the Sahara. In spite of serious warnings from UNHCR field representatives, no political solution was found for the Rwanda refugees. Gérard Prunier estimates that an approximate figure of refugees who left Rwanda because of political persecution between 1959 and 1973 and who still

Refugee Camps in the Great Lakes Region, as of 1995

identified themselves as refugees in 1990 would be six to seven hundred thousand.[1] In addition to refugees, a large number of Rwandans migrated to the adjacent Kivu region in Zaire.

The consolidation of Hutu power in Rwanda had a strong political impact on Burundi, where the Tutsis felt more and more challenged. A failed Hutu uprising in 1972 led Tutsi extremists to carry out a large massacre of Hutus, followed by an outflow of refugees to Tanzania. The Burundi government struggled to carry out political reform by developing a multiparty approach. Elections held in 1993 resulted in the victory of the Hutu-led Frodebu Party. President Pierre Buyoya handed over the government to Melchior Ndadaye, receiving much international acclaim. Internally, however, serious political confrontation continued along Hutu and Tutsi divisions. Though the Hutus won political power, the Tutsis maintained control over the military. With the Burundian Army coup on October 21, 1993, and the murder of President Ndadaye, violence spread across the country, resulting in the deaths of over 50,000 Hutus and the exodus of more than 700,000 refugees to Rwanda, Tanzania, and Zaire. These were mostly women and children in a hasty escape while another 250,000 became internally displaced. To UNHCR, the Burundi refugee outflow marked the beginning of the major humanitarian crisis of the 1990s, which engulfed Burundi, Rwanda, and the entire Great Lakes region.

In the meanwhile, the Rwanda government faced pressure on two fronts. The Rwandese refugees who had been in Uganda since the 1960s turned increasingly militant. Trained in the guerrilla fighting in Uganda, the Rwandan Patriotic Front (RPF) prepared for invasion into Rwanda and began attacking the country from the northeast. This group consisted mainly of Tutsi exiles, who had helped Yoweri Museveni's National Resistance Army come to power in Uganda. Within Rwanda, the political challenge to the dictatorial Juvenal Habyarimana regime grew in strength, setting up opposition parties and demanding greater power sharing in national politics. Confronted with mounting pressure, the government decided to open the way for coalition building with various opposition groups as well as to enter preliminary talks with the RPF. Peace talks started between the government and the RPF.

On August 4, 1993, a final peace agreement was signed in Arusha, Tanzania. It provided for the establishment of a broad-based transitional government until elections, the repatriation of refugees, and the integration of the military forces of the two sides. It called for the creation of the United Nations Assistance Mission for Rwanda (UNAMIR) to serve as a neutral monitoring force to ensure the fair application of the Arusha Agreement. The implementation of the agreement moved forward slowly under constant prodding from the UN and interested international parties. Extremists in both parties were loath to implement the peace. Tragic events that unfolded in the spring of 1994 blocked the agreement from ever taking effect.

On April 6, 1994, I woke up to the BBC morning news report that the plane carrying the presidents of Burundi and Rwanda from Arusha had been shot down just before landing in Kigali, the capital of Rwanda. To this day no one is sure who shot down the presidential plane. Within an hour of the crash the presidential guard set up the first of many roadblocks, and violence spread throughout the capital. Tutsis were killed because they were Tutsis, but Hutus considered to be in sympathy with the democratic opposition parties were also murdered. Many priests and nuns, as well as those socially better off, were also targeted. UNAMIR could not respond to calls for help, nor did it have the capacity to carry out any intervention. The slaughter that started in Kigali spread all over the country.

France, Belgium, Italy, and the United States sent several planes and hundreds of soldiers to evacuate all foreign nationals. Belgium decided to withdraw its UNAMIR units and notified the United Nations. Secretary-General Boutros Boutros-Ghali found it extremely difficult for UNAMIR to function effectively without replacement of well-equipped contingents. The Security Council was divided over the question of whether to expand UNAMIR's mandate and size. On April 21, 1994, the council adopted Resolution 912, which decided to reduce the UNAMIR number from the existing 2,539 to 270. The secretary-general sent a special mission to Kigali and tried to move the warring parties toward a cease-fire. He also urged governments to contribute troops to UNAMIR. A month later the council reversed its decision, took a more positive stand, and agreed to increase the troops to 5,500 military personnel.[2] It also imposed an arms embargo on Rwanda. While some African states expressed willingness to contribute troops, UNAMIR forces remained at 550 two months after the adoption of the resolution.

In the meantime, the number of civilians massacred in Rwanda rose; altogether, 800,000 became victims of the genocide. The UN was criticized for its inability to deal with an unprecedented political and security crisis. The absence of strong and rapid military input from member states undermined the UN capacity. Justifiably, the Rwandans were left with a profound sense of betrayal and mistrust toward the international community, which colored the relationship in the following years.

UNHCR's immediate concern was over the situation of the Burundi refugees who had come to Rwanda the year before. I also worried about the safety of our staff, particularly the locals who could not be evacuated out of the country. The turmoil within Rwanda was bound to cause a new exodus of refugees to neighboring countries. My primary responsibility was to prepare for it. We decided to dispatch three emergency teams to Ngara in Tanzania, Goma in Zaire, and Mbarara in Uganda. At the same time, I felt very much frustrated that the absence of security prevented us from operating inside Rwanda. I took the occasion of the Human Rights Commission meeting to express my concern over the slowness of the political and peacekeeping measures and strongly appealed for the expansion of UNAMIR, both in mandate and in size.

The genocide in Rwanda led to the flight of mostly Hutu refugees to neighboring countries. The first group crossed the border into Tanzania at the end of April. Three months later more than a million fled to Zaire. The scale of the refugee exodus was massive and challenged the capacity of humanitarian agencies. What tested UNHCR and the entire humanitarian community even more, however, was the composition of the exiled population. The refugees had been led by the leaders of the Hutu regime, determined to keep control over the people, use the refugee camps as their base, and eventually fight their way back. Militarization was the major problem in the refugee camps, and the continuing lack of security inside Rwanda limited the possibility of their return. Their leaders also prevented them from leaving the camps. Maintaining security and order, separating the political and military leaders from the general refugee population, and establishing the civilian character of refugee camps became UNHCR's immediate challenge. With no concrete support from the United Nations or from the international community, UNHCR had to resort to its own devices to deploy a Zairean contingent under international supervision. With a limited mandate and capacity to oversee security in the camps for refugees and international workers, the Zairean contingent did assist, at least temporarily, in carrying out its mission.

The large presence of Hutu refugees in the Kivu region of Zaire as well as the Tutsi prevalence in Rwanda had a profound impact on the political process in the Great Lakes region, in particular on Zaire. The complex ethnic composition of the Kivu population, the acute question of citizenship in the Zairean constitutional process, and the rising tension between Rwanda and Zaire altogether undermined the possibility for any solution to the Rwandan refugee problem. In the end Rwanda, in close alliance with Zairean rebel forces that organized themselves and formed the Alliance of Democratic Forces for the Liberation of Congo (AFDL), attacked the refugee camps in Kivu and forced the return of a large number of refugees in November 1996. The remaining refugees headed west to escape being attacked or forced back to Rwanda.

UNHCR and its humanitarian agency colleagues led the search and rescue operation through the Zairean rain forest. The refugees fled west, just ahead of the front line of the war between the Zairean government troops and the AFDL forces. Whenever refugee groups were identified and collected, UNHCR helped them return to Rwanda. The multinational forces that were deployed to Kivu by the Security Council at the end of November proved ineffective either in preventing the humanitarian disaster or in rescuing the fleeing refugees. UNHCR assisted the government to rehabilitate those returned to Rwanda back to their communities. With a quarter of the Rwanda population composed of refugees, repatriating and reintegrating them in their home countries had important humanitarian as well as security implications that the government was ready to pursue.

The refugee crisis in the Great Lakes region revealed serious international shortcomings in dealing with fundamental political and security issues. To begin with, the refugee issue in the Great Lakes region had remained unaddressed for three decades. While African countries intervened to defend what to them were strategic interests, the international community was reluctant to take any action, whether at the time of the genocide in Rwanda, or by confronting the militarization of the refugee camps in Kivu, or by protecting and saving Hutu refugees fleeing through Zaire. Humanitarian organizations were left to tackle political confrontations and military conflicts, involving violence and coercion. The human cost was extremely high. There are questions on why international input was so limited, whether in diplomatic or peacekeeping activities. What could UNHCR and the humanitarian community have done better to settle conflicts more quickly and more decisively for the suffering victims?

Refugee Outflow

GENOCIDE AND THE FLIGHT OF REFUGEES

The genocide in Rwanda led to the flight of mostly Hutu refugees to neighboring countries. The first group crossed the border into Tanzania at the end of April 1996. It numbered some 250,000, and UNHCR was able to cope with it. The emergency team was on the ground in the Ngara region when the outflow started, and prepositioned emergency relief items proved enough to meet immediate needs. With the support of the United States and France, airlifts were mounted, drawing on stockpiles from all over the world.

The refugees were mostly Hutu peasants from Kibungo Prefecture, who were not fleeing the massacres but who, having been involved in killing Tutsis in eastern Rwanda, were escaping before the arrival of the RPF troops. Mixed among them was a notorious burgo-

Sadako Ogata (left) meeting Salvadoran refugees repatriated from Honduras, 1991 (UNHCR/ M. de Almeida e Silva)

Right: With Somali refugees in Ethiopia, 1991 (UNHCR/A. Hollman)

Below: With Cambodian refugees in Thailand, 1992 (UNHCR/G. Ouellet)

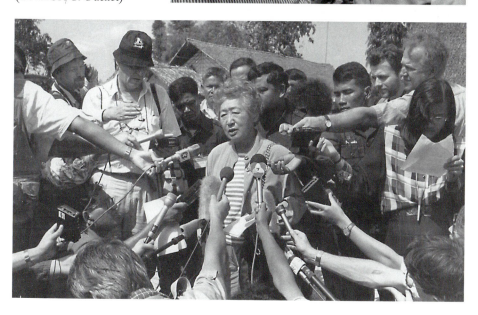

Left: With Iraqi Kurdish refugees in Iran, 1991 (UNHCR/J. Crisp)

Below: A UNHCR convoy in Bosnia (UNHCR/A. Hollman)

A Bosnian woman on a bullet-riddled balcony patched up with UNHCR plastic sheeting (UNHCR/L. Taylor)

Clockwise from top: Arriving in Sarajevo, 1992 (UNHCR/ S. Foa). Wreckage from an Italian UNHCR plane, shot down during the Sarajevo airlift (UNHCR/ A. Hollman). Exodus of Kosovo Albanians, walking toward Macedonia (UNHCR/R. LeMoyne)

With Rwandan refugees in Zaire (Alexander Joe/AFP/Getty Images)

At the Tingi Tingi feeding center, Zaire (UNHCR)

At Benaco refugee camp in Tanzania, Hutu refugees prepare for repatriation to Rwanda (Liba Taylor/Corbis)

In discussions with the Taliban Governor of Herat, Afghanistan, 2000 (UNHCR)

Afghan refugees in Pakistan learn mine detection techniques, in preparation for eventual return to their homes (Stephen Dupont/Baci/Corbis)

Returning Afghan refugees arriving in Kabul (UNHCR/P. Benetar)

Clockwise from top: Speaking to displaced Afghan women in Bamyan (UNHCR/ M. Shinohara). Farmers returning after the fall of the Taliban and easing of drought, 2003 (UNHCR/M. Shinohara). With Nelson Mandela at his home in Pretoria, South Africa, January 2000

Clockwise from top: With John Horekens, Sergio Vieira de Mello, and Boutros Boutros-Ghali, after the CIS Conference in 1996. The Ogata family. Mrs. Ogata receives a standing ovation at the opening of her last UNHCR Executive Committee Meeting in 2000 (UNHCR/S. Hopper)

master of Murambi, Jean Baptiste Gatete, who was responsible for mass killings in the country. UNHCR's attempt to move him from the Benaco refugee camp to Tanzanian police custody met enormous resistance. A crowd of some five thousand surrounded the camp, demanding his release. The riotous incident showed the complicated nature of the refugee population, mostly politically and criminally involved groups resisting the arrival of the RPF forces. The development also revealed the limited capacity of the Tanzanian police to control the activities of the refugees as well as to ensure the security of the humanitarian workers on the ground.

In the meantime the Security Council adopted Resolution 918 on May 17, authorizing the expansion of UNAMIR, but was unable to mobilize sufficient forces. Concerned over the spreading lack of security, Security-General Boutros Boutros-Ghali sent a letter to the president of the Council on June 16, requesting consideration of a French offer to set up a multinational force to ensure the security of displaced persons at risk in Rwanda. The French intervention, however, was fraught with complexities. The French involvement in Rwanda had been deep, and sympathy for the Hutu regime had been very real. Over the years, France had provided military training and equipment based on a military cooperation agreement with the Rwanda government in 1975, and arms deliveries to the Rwandese armed forces had continued until June 1994, despite the declaration of an embargo. During the international evacuation from Kigali in April and May, France had helped the departure not only of expatriates but also of a number of the country's ruling elite to Zaire, France, and other "friendly" countries. Security Council Resolution 929 of June 22, 1994, authorized a two-month French humanitarian relief operation. Gérard Prunier later provided an interesting background to the French return to Rwanda, based on their desire to maintain their influence in the country. The competition between the two political leaders of the French government, President Mitterrand and Prime Minister Balladur, accelerated the decision-making process to take action.[3] Together with the deployment of Senegalese troops, the French moved troops into the southwest of Rwanda. The Zairean government authorized the French troops to set up bases at Goma, Bukavu, and Kisangani.

As soon as the French established Operation Turquoise in the region, UNHCR's cooperation was requested. We immediately sent a senior staff member to Rwanda to make an initial survey of the situation and assess the needs of the internally displaced persons, refugees, and locally affected persons. He flew over the country on a French helicopter. On July 13, he reported on columns of people moving west. It was the first report on the human movement from conflict-torn Rwanda. As for the population assembled in the French-controlled area, UNHCR had serious reservations over the establishment of camps for the internally displaced persons or the provision of assistance within the country. We foresaw difficulties over the protection of these people. Besides, we were aware that we would have to undertake major relief operations in the neighboring countries of Burundi, Tanzania, Uganda, and Zaire.[4]

As a consequence of the French intervention, however, a humanitarian protection zone was developed in southwestern Rwanda. The RPF therefore focused on northwestern Rwanda, leading directly to the massive exodus of refugees across the border to Zaire. At the time we assumed that these people were fleeing in anticipation of the RPF advance. Very soon we learned that they had been directed by a well-organized movement orchestrated by the former Rwandan leadership and led to believe that "fleeing would be the only solution."[5]

The UNHCR field staff in eastern Zaire reported that the influx began on July 14 and that in no time the streets in Goma were filled with new refugees. Soon the movement became a "solid human river 25 kilometers long." By the seventeenth the estimated number of refugees ranged from eight hundred thousand to one million. The city had no capacity to absorb new arrivals, while the area around it was densely populated and intensively cultivated. There was an incalculable health risk in terms of sanitation and water. The city had to be emptied, and the refugees had to be directed to walk on for several more kilometers to campsites. The UNHCR field staff, along with the Zairean authorities, identified campsites and frantically set up camps. The first site, Kibumba, was packed in no time. Katale and Mugunga also filled up rapidly. The arriving refugees included several thousand members of the former Rwanda Army. Many of them were disarmed by the Zairean armed forces (FAZ) when they crossed the border, but others came across unofficial forest tracks and were not disarmed. The fittest of the former Rwandan forces settled on their own approximately twenty-five kilometers west of Goma in Virunga Park. The sick and the wounded were accommodated and treated at the sports center in Goma. On July 19 several thousand Rwandan refugees arrived farther south at Bukavu. There the soldiers gradually settled on separate sites, Panzi and Bulonge.

The emergency hit at the worst time for UNHCR. Our human and financial resources were already seriously strained by the outflow of Rwandese and Burundian refugees, while the challenges and demands of the Balkan crises continued to mount. In terms of management, the outgoing director for Africa, Nicholas Bwakira, a Tutsi from Burundi who had suffered heavy family losses the previous year, had just been reassigned to Pretoria. The incoming director, Kamel Morjane, had not yet assumed office. I asked Eric Morris, director of operational support, to proceed to Goma to deal with the situation. Additional emergency officers were assigned to the area. Foodstocks, blankets, water cans, plastic sheeting, and portable warehouses had to be redeployed from contingency stocks in the region. I called on the warring parties in Rwanda "to guarantee the safety of displaced people so they could remain where they are." I emphasized that "we must be allowed to help these terrified, traumatized and hungry people in their own country—otherwise their suffering will be compounded."[6]

There was a sense of doom in UNHCR, which had recognized that it did not have the capacity to cope with the impending demands. At 4:00 P.M. on July 15 we called for an emergency meeting of the Humanitarian Liaison Working Group, an informal consultative forum consisting of diplomatic missions in Geneva. It was a Friday afternoon, but we wanted to share our grave concerns before the ambassadors left for the summer weekend. I still remember how encouraged I was to find many ambassadors from major countries rushing over. We asked for extensive support of the kind that might cover services. My appeal was carefully noted. When I returned home at 7:30 P.M., I was surprised to find a call from U.S. Ambassador Daniel Spiegel conveying Washington's all-out readiness to help. I had rarely come across a government responding so fast.

All weekend my colleagues worked hard to prepare a package of services to present to governments. Normally UNHCR would have been appealing for money to pay for specific goods or services. But under these circumstances, we knew we would not have the time or capacity to put them into programs. We knew we had to be innovative and mobilize help primarily, though not exclusively, from military establishments. On the nineteenth we managed to present eight packages of services. They were airport services, logistics base services, road services and road security, site preparation for refugee camps, provision of domestic fuel for cooking, sanitation facilities, water management, and airhead management. Many of the packages were geared to the kinds of large-scale operations that could be best provided by the military. We also decided to extend the air cell that managed the airlift to Sarajevo to service Goma. We also asked UN agency colleagues to join in the operations.

All the humanitarian agency colleagues in the field—UNHCR, WFP, the ICRC, and NGOs—worked strenuously to contain the damage and continued to relay desperate pleas to Western capitals for speedy and coordinated substantial delivery packages. Humanitarian agencies were still handling the crisis alone after ten days, but they were overwhelmed by displacements, deaths, and suffering. Those in Goma thought that the American airdrops of humanitarian rations did not meet the real needs of the people. The French provided the only military presence and did support the humanitarian efforts.[7] Water tanks were badly needed but were slow to arrive.

On July 23 the United States announced its decision to take on four of the eight packages. In a letter from President Clinton to heads of states or governments, he called for a greatly enhanced international effort to deal with the Rwanda refugee tragedy, as "the overall relief task is more than the civilian relief organizations and the U.S.

and French military units can handle." As for the United States, he announced an immediate and additional contribution of seventy-five million dollars in cash and commodities. He also made known that he had "ordered the Defense Department to establish and manage an airlift hub in Uganda"; "to assist in expanding airlift operations near the refugee camps in Goma and Bukavu by providing personnel and equipment to enable airfields to operate on a 24 hour basis"; and to "establish a safe water supply and to distribute as much water as possible to those at risk." He stated as well that "the United States not only supports the efforts of the international community, but is and will continue to take a leading role in those efforts." Furthermore, he appealed to all Americans "to reach out with their own private contribution to relief organizations" and to "move us as a nation to take the practical actions that this crisis demands."

In the immediate short term, international efforts were focused on the human tragedy that unfolded in Zaire. The million refugees who had poured into the lakeside town of Goma and spread out into the surrounding volcanic land quickly began to die in massive numbers, victims of exhaustion, dehydration, and dysentery. An outbreak of cholera aggravated the situation. We estimated the death toll would reach forty thousand. Without an adequate supply of safe water, this acute infectious disease could not be brought under control. The United States installed a large purification unit at Lake Kivu from which water tanks would transport water to the refugees. It was the marvel of American military logistics capacity that a giant U.S. C-5 Galaxy transport aircraft could hold a water purification plant and two fire engines—contributions from the San Francisco Fire Department—and fly nonstop from California to Zaire, refueling in midair three times. At the same time, the large-scale U.S. approach proved not to meet the local demands, compared with the appropriate technology of NGOs bringing quick tanks and small delivery trucks.

Water supply efforts were central to bringing down the cholera epidemic and the alarming mortality rates of the first few weeks. The French contingent that had already been engaged in the region diverted troops from Operation Turquoise and actively contributed to the traffic control at the Goma airfield, handled cargo, repaired runways, and assisted in water transport and food distribution. A particularly gruesome task it undertook was collecting and burying the dead. Together with Caritas, the Zairean Boy Scouts, and other local service organizations, the French military rented heavy equipment to speed up the digging of graves to match the mounting dead. Hundreds of bodies were lying along all roads to and in the campsites. More than any other undertaking, I learned that burying the dead was torturous, exacting a heavy psychological toll on the soldiers and civilians involved. Troops from Sweden and Germany took part in the emergency humanitarian operation.

In order to assess and plan UNHCR's action with regard to the Rwandese refugee crisis, my colleagues urged me to go on a quick mission. I waited for the return of Peter Hansen, UN undersecretary-general for humanitarian affairs, to Geneva from the region on July 29 and solicited his views. Then I left for Nairobi and proceeded to Kigali immediately. The special representative of the secretary-general, Ambassador Shaharyar Khan, UNAMIR Force Commander General Romeo Dallaire, and representatives from the newly formed government were at the airport. We checked in at the Hôtel des Diplomats, which was barely standing, with broken windows and charred pillars. Wild dogs roamed the premises. There was some water kept in pails. Miraculously, at least the sheets in the hotel were clean and washed. We immediately proceeded to the UNAMIR headquarters for a briefing, then were invited to share a military ration lunch.

We called on the new government. The group that had been the primary victim of the genocide now held power. Many of the leaders had been refugees from the early 1960s. I called on Vice-President/Minister of Defense General Paul Kagame at his modest headquarters in the hills. He assured me of his collaboration and expressed his readiness to welcome back the refugees, but emphasized the importance of punishing the genocidaires. When I met with Prime Minister Faustin Twagiramungu and President Pasteur Bizimungu, they asked for particular attention to refugees who had been out of the country for many years. In fact they referred to the longtime association with UNHCR and said that the current outflow represented the fifth exodus of Rwanda refugees. These meetings marked the beginning of repeated encounters, at times strenuous, that eventually developed into mutual trust and collaboration. I drove around the city, badly destroyed everywhere. In UNHCR's office the safe had been looted, but all the files had been left on the shelf.

At the Kigali airport tarmac, we met the large delegation of U.S. Secretary of Defense William Perry flanked with State Department and NGO representatives. I was happy to note the presence of Phyllis Oakley, the assistant secretary of state in charge of refugees, and the president of InterAction, Julia Taft, all close collaborators of UNHCR. I thanked Perry for the generous and timely support given by his government. Then we started the 150-kilometer drive to Goma, in three jeeps with a UNAMIR escort. I was told that we were the first civilian group traveling by land across the war-torn country. The paved road was in surprisingly good condition. Yet we saw no one along the road until we approached the northwestern border town of Giseny. There we stopped at a tented clinic run by Médecins sans Frontières and a food distribution point run by the International Committee of the Red Cross. At the border crossing we saw a pile of confiscated weapons.

After crossing over to Goma, I immediately made courtesy calls on the Zairean authorities. I was eager to get direct briefings from Filippo Grandi and the emergency team colleagues, but formalities were considered important especially when the local authorities collaborated so closely with us and when Zaire was hosting huge numbers of refugees. Early the next morning I went around the lake. I was very moved to witness the San Francisco fire engines pumping the contaminated water from Lake Kivu into the huge caterpillarlike purification plant. This plant filled the water tanks that were critical for the camps. Although there were still bodies in plastic bags lying along the road, the city of Goma was gradually returning to normal.

The formalities completed, a French helicopter took us to the camps. We flew over the Katale camp, an enormous spread of refugees over black rocky volcanic terrain. We landed at the corner of the camp and visited the refugees. The tented hospital had water, and patients were lying all over the place. The death rate, fortunately, was beginning to fall. The most painful stop was at an orphanage where barely clothed infants and children simply lay around. Local Zairean women were volunteering their services. On the whole, however, order was beginning to be restored within the campsite, with food distribution starting and the burial of the dead mostly completed. After stopping over at the Kibumba camp, we returned to Goma and after a very full and charged day faced the eager press. At the time there was extraordinary media attention on Goma. There were more than three hundred reporters at the press conference. UNHCR gave two press briefings a day. Though exhausted after a physically and emotionally loaded day, I tried my best to respond to their questions, especially about the cholera outbreak. I was also asked how UNHCR could do better. I too kept asking the same questions. Could we have selected better campsites? Could we have stockpiled more water tankers? Could we have mobilized more emergency staff? I flew back that night to Geneva via Nairobi, to brief the UN Pledging Conference for Rwanda Refugees.

Heading toward Geneva, I felt at least that we had overcome the sense of doom of two weeks before. Emergency assistance was reaching the ground. The Goma airport was hustling and bustling with cargo planes. Relief workers were dashing in. The death rate was going down. Now coordination and traffic control were becoming the main issues. The Rwanda refugee tragedy had hit the international media, and the world was turning around to help. Yet I was fully aware of the deteriorating conditions in the camps. The dangers came not just from health hazards or a shortage of relief supplies. Former soldiers and militias were resorting to violence and to the intimidation of refugees who wanted to leave the camps and return home. Maintaining the security and civilian character of the camps was to become the overriding issue of camp management in Goma.

The military forces that were sent from several countries at the height of the humanitarian crisis were ready to bring massive assistance but not prepared to deal with the maintenance of law and order in the camps. It is important to note that the dramatic military Operation Support Hope was a political initiative launched by President Clinton and directed from the White House. While the military recognized its special capacity to cope with calamities, it believed that humanitarian or police work was not its primary mission. From the very beginning, it would set up an exit date and abide by it. On the other hand, UNHCR and humanitarian and civilian agencies focused on the needs of the people and expected adjustments to exit dates for missions. The Pentagon had set the end of September as the exit date.[8] The exit date for the French had been determined by the Security Council resolution. Prime Minister Edouard Balladur together with Foreign Minister Alain Juppe informed me on July 22 that their humanitarian objectives had been achieved and they did not intend to exceed the two-month mandate. The French government wanted UNHCR to take charge of the situation within the "humanitarian protection safety zone."[9] When the last French soldiers left the Turquoise zone, and when the U.S. contingent left Goma on August 25, I recall how uneasy I felt. Not only were relief assistance setups inadequate, but also serious security problems were spreading throughout the camps.

One good development was the arrival of the Japanese self-defense forces to the region to succeed the U.S. and French forces. The Japanese Peace Cooperation Law, which had been adopted in 1993, authorized the participation of Japanese personnel, civilian as well as military, in humanitarian relief operations and in response to the requests of international organizations, including UNHCR. I had taken note of this provision and begun working with the Japanese authorities to examine the possibility of making active use of the law. In Japan too the Rwanda crisis provoked public demand for Japanese contribution and participation. At the time the government was headed by Prime Minister Tomiichi Murayama, the chairman of the left-wing Social Democratic Party, which had traditionally blocked Japanese participation in UN peacekeeping operations. The government became persuaded by the cry for worldwide humanitarian efforts. It first sent an assessment mission to the region, then consulted with the United States and France to sound out their reaction. I was extremely satisfied when I succeeded in convincing the prime minister that Japan should contribute to international humanitarian crises not only by money and goods but also with people—especially with trained and well-equipped soldiers. In fact three hundred self-defense forces were dispatched to Goma in mid-September to engage in airlift, water, and sanitation activities. Sending soldiers aboard was certainly a breakthrough in Japanese modalities for international participation. The force commander who served in Goma later told me many heartwarming stories of contacts among Japanese soldiers, Zairean contingents, and international humanitarian workers.

With the departure of French and American forces in August 1994 and Japanese troops three months later, the Rwandan crisis faded from the international political horizon and was left to the devices of humanitarian workers. However, the Rwanda refugee problem could not be solved by UNHCR and its partners. The camps remained under the control of the former Rwandan leaders and became the source of growing insecurity throughout the Great Lakes region. Even more bloody tragedy was to unfold in the following years on the same plains and beyond.

PLANNING FOR RETURN

While coping with the emergency outflow of refugees, UNHCR foresaw that planning had to advance on the solution to the crisis on hand. From the outset it seemed obvious that return was the main solution. The refugee outflow was too massive for the people to be absorbed by the neighboring countries or to be resettled in third countries. The RPF forces had entered Kigali on July 4, 1994, and the new Rwanda government was formed on the nineteenth. My special envoy for Burundi and Rwanda, Michel Moussalli, who had been closely following the developments in the region, moved to Kigali on July 14. He quickly established contact with the new government. His mission was to impress on the Rwandese interlocutors the need "to create a climate of confidence and reconciliation among the

Rwandese population so as to stop the exodus, and to encourage and facilitate return of refugees and displaced persons." The new government's response was encouraging. The president of the republic, Pasteur Bizimungu, the vice-president/minister of defense/commander of the RPF, Paul Kagame, and others showed readiness to deal with international humanitarian agencies and encourage the safe return of refugees.[10] The stated priority of the authorities was the return of refugees. Daniel Bellamy, who had made the aerial survey over Rwanda on July 13, drove through the country from July 23 to 28 and witnessed the return of several thousand people. He estimated that there were some two million Hutus who had recently fled to Zaire, Tanzania, Burundi, and Uganda. In 1959 and 1960, between one and three hundred thousand Tutsi refugees had left for the same neighboring countries. The internally displaced persons within Rwanda might reach two million. Bellamy reported that the national infrastructure—roads, bridges, hospitals, government buildings, schools, etc.—had not been destroyed. No mines seemed to have been laid. However, looting that took place everywhere was catastrophic.

Bellamy predicted the spontaneous return of all groups. Many recent refugees were coming back by foot, because they either felt it was safe to go home or could not manage to survive in the camps. The new Rwanda government by radio broadcast invited the refugees to come back, but it did not proclaim an amnesty. Those who responded quickly to return were the Tutsis who had fled in 1959 and 1960. They were relatively well-off people and came from Burundi in private sedans with domestic goods to reestablish themselves in Kigali. Bellamy feared that animosity might grow, as their presence would increase the power of the dominating Tutsis in Rwanda, particularly in Kigali. He proposed that UNHCR persuade the government to proclaim amnesty officially for all illegal departures, while coupling it with the announcement that criminals would be prosecuted in accordance with the law. In the French-controlled zone he saw the troops controlling order. The extremists and military personnel were moving to Cyangugu and Bukavu. He predicted the eventual RPF takeover of this zone and unavoidable tensions with those who had collaborated with the French. In short, he concluded that coupled with the Burundi situation, "this region is a powder keg." He urged UNHCR to reestablish its presence swiftly throughout the region in a way that its service "will make a difference."[11]

Difficult as it might be, so long as massive repatriation was foreseen from the neighboring countries, UNHCR had to start preparing. I agreed with my colleagues to accept the U.S. government offer to commission Robert Gersony, a rural development and human rights specialist with relevant experience in Africa, to go to Rwanda and assess the conditions for repatriation and reintegration. He was well known to UNHCR for his expertise and close collaboration in a prior operation in Central America. We notified the Rwandan government of our plan to dispatch this mission and asked the government to provide full cooperation and to assure access. Gersony and his team arrived in Kigali on August 1, met at length with the minister of rehabilitation, and spent a few days explaining the overall objectives. It was necessary to establish confidence ahead of time so that problems that might occur could find ways to be solved. Gersony received a letter from the minister permitting the team unlimited access. It proved useful when the team got into areas that others so far could not enter and because it moved without any government accompaniment.

I assumed that the mission was moving smoothly. It was thus with great unease that I heard from Gersony that he wished to consult urgently on matters too delicate to speak by phone. On September 13 he came to my office and reported that he had found conditions "that are not conducive for return at the moment." UNHCR's challenge therefore was to use its good offices to improve the human rights environment and create conditions for return. To create such conditions was a very tall order. We had to decide how and with whom to share the information and to be prepared for dissent from those who should know. I also had to review the repatriation policy and related operations.

Gersony and his team visited 41 of 145 communes and collected materials from 10 additional communes. Altogether they covered 38 percent of the country. They also visited 9 refugee camps in Zaire,

Burundi, and Tanzania. They conducted more than 200 individual private interviews of about one hour each with local residents, former displaced persons, spontaneous returnees, and current refugees. Another 100 persons were interviewed in small groups in a less private manner.

Our group started the field trip from the Ruhengeri and Gisenyi prefectures, where people were already returning from Goma. To Gersony the issue was how to accelerate the process and assist in bringing about a first success out of the large relief problem on hand. As he moved from village to village in Ruhengeri, the general condition seemed secure, stable, and peaceful. A liberal border-crossing policy by local authorities permitted families to walk home for brief exploratory visits, confirm for themselves the security situation, and return to Zaire to bring back their families. However, the UNHCR Goma office had reported incidents involving returnees, specifically that a group of up to 150 refugee returnees had been questioned and killed by RPF soldiers.[12] In Gisenyi Prefecture, there was a systematic pattern of arbitrary arrests and disappearances of adult males, all of whom were suspected of being militia elements associated with the former government. Of an estimated 400 arrests, half might have been refugees or returnees.

In the southern and southeastern regions of Butare, Kibungo, and parts of Kigali prefectures, the situation was much more drastic. Gersony's team uncovered shocking evidence of new killings that had occurred in the spring and early summer immediately following the expulsion of former government and militia elements. Butare and Kibungo included vast deserted areas. Ten thousand Tutsi returnees from recent and older times armed with spears and bow and arrows were present. These RPF actions were consistently reported to be conducted in areas where opposition forces of any kind, other than attempts by victims of these actions to escape, were absent. Large-scale indiscriminate killings of men, women, and children, including the sick and the elderly, were consistently reported. Particularly random and violent were mass killings at meetings. Local residents, including whole families, were called to community meetings to

receive information on security, food distribution, etc., and once a
crowd assembled, they were assaulted with sudden sustained gunfire
or locked in buildings into which hand grenades were thrown. There
were also house-to-house killings, pursuits of hidden populations, and
disposals of large numbers of bodies by the RPF. The team estimated
that from late April and May through July, more than 5,000 and perhaps as many as 10,000 per month might have been killed. During
August the number might have been somewhat less, but it probably
was at least 5,000. The team did not visit reported sites of fresh bodies of Hutus but directly observed 150 bodies that appeared to have
been dead for about seven to ten days and included men, women, and
children. From the UNHCR offices in Tanzania there were reports
recording the arrivals of injured refugees and stories of killings and
discovery of bodies found in the river, but no reference to possible
RPF atrocities.[13] Gersony concluded his mission briefing by stating
that there was a prevalence of systematic and sustained killing and
persecution of civilian Hutus by the RPF.

Gersony's information had enormous political and humanitarian implications. I thought my office could not deal with it alone.
After serious debate among the senior colleagues involved in the
Great Lakes region operation, I decided to consult Kofi Annan,
undersecretary-general in charge of peacekeeping operations, who
was on his way to Rwanda. Gerald Walzer, the deputy high commissioner, accompanied Gersony to consult with Annan about the treatment of the information. They met in London on the fourteenth, and
decided that Gersony would go to New York and Washington to
inform a small group of interested parties, the task force on the Great
Lakes region in the UN Secretariat and the U.S. State Department
and AID officials in charge. I was told that to most people the content of Gersony's findings was not entirely foreign. However, the scale
and the systematic thoroughness of the undertaking caused great concern. One question we faced was how and whether to inform the
Rwandese government. Since his mission had been accepted by the
government, which provided him free access to wherever he wished to
go, I felt it important that we share his findings. Gersony accompa-

nied by Morjane managed to arrive in Kigali, brief Annan and the force commander on the twentieth, and present the information to government ministries that day. I was also concerned for the safety of the two men as they carried out their mission to Kigali.

The report caused an uproar. On September 25, UNAMIR Force Commander Tousignant was requested to attend a meeting with President Bizimungu. The UNHCR representative Roman Urasa and government staffers were also present. The president opened the meeting by expressing his dismay and anger that an investigation could be conducted within Rwanda without his knowledge or approval. He believed that he had been betrayed by UNAMIR and stated that this put in question the future of its presence in Rwanda. He demanded a copy of the report. The force commander stressed that UNAMIR had been unaware of UNHCR's investigation until September 20, and he invited UNHCR to comment. The UNHCR representative explained that there was no "report" as such, but possibly a verbal briefing from Gersony to the high commissioner. The president indicated strong dissatisfaction and demanded that the UN provide objective evidence to substantiate the allegations. The media became aware of the developments both in Geneva and in Kigali.

In response to inquiries, a UNHCR spokesman stated on September 23 that "it had reports of massacres by Rwanda Patriotic Army [renamed from the RPF after the government had been established] which are estimated to have claimed thousands of victims in the last two months" and that UNHCR "had stopped its support for voluntary, spontaneous repatriation to Rwanda some 10 days ago. It had transmitted the eyewitness accounts to the UN Secretariat in New York and to the Kigali government."[14] My office came under fire from the Rwanda government. President Bizimungu accused us "of a malicious campaign to stop refugees returning" and that we had "private motives," to protect our jobs by keeping refugees in the camps. Our UN colleagues in Kigali reacted none too kindly either.[15] The Rwandan government seemed to have taken the allegations seriously and tried to control the activities of the RPF. Thereafter the UNHCR offices reported fewer incidents.

The secretary-general, who was facing the General Assembly debates, was concerned about the political fallout. The political interest of the U.S. government was not to weaken the new government, although it did not condone the killings. UNAMIR was upset as it believed it had been undermined for not having uncovered the reported facts. I was exposed to a lot of criticism. The secretary-general believed that UNHCR had publicized the information and criticized me for giving away too much material. I explained the sequence of actions taken and tried to correct the confusion that seemed to have occurred. In response to a formal letter of protest from the president regarding the allegations of revenge killings by the Rwandese forces, the secretary-general wrote on October 5, sharing his "concern about the serious implications of these allegations for the efforts aimed at promoting stability and national reconciliation in Rwanda." He stated that he had "directed that they immediately be brought to the attention of your government." In order to address these allegations and to ensure that they were thoroughly investigated, he informed the president that "arrangements are being made for such an investigation to be carried out by the Commission of Experts established under Security Council resolution 935 (1994) and the Special Rapporteur."[16] This was the commission that was carrying out the investigation of the atrocities and acts of genocide perpetrated in Rwanda. Gersony formalized his report for presentation to the Commission of Experts on October 11.

The lessons we learned were somewhat bitter. I learned the difficulty of gaining overall support from various parts of the United Nations and from involved governments, although I had tried hard to follow a careful and judicious consultation process. I also realized the enormous sensitivity on the part of the Rwandan authorities, who believed that the United Nations was critically examining the Rwandese atrocities while it showed little remorse over its failure to act during the genocide. On the other hand, the Gersony report forced a necessary policy review for UNHCR. I had to revise our policy of repatriation. The report had some impact on containing the Rwandese action, but we felt obliged to suspend repatriation. The danger of

UNHCR's losing credibility with refugees was the basic issue at stake, for we would have to persuade them to return someday. I believe the decision under the circumstances was unavoidable, although the suspension might have had a discouraging effect on those who might have opted to return.

In the meanwhile, security conditions in the camps were rapidly deteriorating. The threat to refugees came first from former soldiers and militias acting on their own or on behalf of the political leaders. Violence was exercised upon refugees who indicated their willingness to return, and especially serious disruption took place during food distributions. UNHCR was facing some very complex and difficult protection problems. We had to walk a narrow line between two impediments: "coercion not to return (in camps) and no guarantees of a safe return (in Rwanda)."

An intense debate took place within UNHCR. The staff generally supported an early return but was divided between those who were ready to "promote" return and those who were prepared only to "facilitate." Promoting return represented a proactive approach that involved a series of activities: information campaigns on conditions in their places of origin and visits to ascertain the actual conditions and to organize and run convoys to help transport returnees back. The facilitation approach was a fairly passive provision of assistance to those who had decided to return. Transportation would be made available in response to their needs. The two approaches derived from differing assessments of the security conditions within Rwanda. The factor of security in the refugee camps further complicated the assessment.

The UNHCR office in Goma attempted to break the control of the military and militia elements in the camps that intimidated the refugees who opted to return. The staff was concerned over the destabilizing impact of the camps on the region and strongly advocated an early return. The position of UNHCR Kigali was complex. It followed the Rwanda government policy of insisting on return but stressed the need for well-organized and staggered returns since it recognized the danger of upsetting the fragile internal conditions.

The Division of International Protection at headquarters represented the cautious approach to return. UNHCR's protection activities traditionally focused on securing respect for the rights of asylum seekers and refugees in receiving countries. When it came to repatriation, it necessarily became somewhat ambivalent, as the situation in neither Rwanda nor the camps could be judged secure.[17] Of the humanitarian organizations, only the International Committee of the Red Cross considered that any return would be premature. The ICRC was always the closest and most reliable partner for UNHCR. However, its concentration on the protection of combatants, civilians in conflict situations, and prisoners largely influenced its perspective. In Rwanda the prisons were flooded with untried perpetrators of genocide with no prospects for solution in sight. UNHCR had to solve the displacement of over a million Rwandan refugees.

My position from the very beginning was to favor an early return of the refugees. Given the massiveness of the outflow, the camps could not be viable for long, and I was in search of early solutions. The fact that I supported the Gersony mission attests to my readiness for early preparation. The suspension resulting from Gersony's report was clearly a setback for the return of refugees. I opted to continue the search for solutions. In December, as we noted signs of improvement of security in Rwanda, we lifted the suspension and entered a phase of facilitation of those who volunteered to return. We began concentrating our efforts on building better security in the camps.

MILITARIZATION OF REFUGEE CAMPS

We had devoted the first critical weeks to improving the camp conditions for over a million refugees in the Kivu region. We had also examined the conditions in Rwanda to prepare for return. Now, in late summer, our attention turned more and more to confronting the effects of the militarized refugee camps. The presence of the Rwandese armed forces and the political and administrative leaders had strong intimidating effects on the camp population. I had to find ways to separate the armed elements from the refugees and tackle the general practice of intimidation.

Altogether, nearly fifty thousand soldiers and militias were estimated to have crossed over to Zaire from Rwanda. Roughly ten thousand former Forces Armées Rwandaises (Rwandan Armed Forces, FAR) took refuge in the French-controlled zone and later moved to South Kivu. About fifteen thousand soldiers from other areas crossed to North Kivu. In addition, men serving in the militias numbered between fifteen and twenty-five thousand. In Goma, the former FAR troops set up to the west of the Mugunga camp in Virunga Park. The military together with the government in exile took over the premises of a Protestant school also near the Mugunga camp. Later the former FAR headquarters was moved to a new location and became known as the Bananeraie, since access roads went through a banana plantation. In Bukavu the former FAR was installed in the Panzi and Bulonge camps. The military camps caused us great concern. Should we provide them with food, water, and medicine? If so, how should we distribute these? The militias were harder to identify and normally present in all camps. During border crossings, Zairean authorities seized large numbers of individual and collective weapons. But those who entered Zaire at unofficial crossings had not been disarmed. Violence and intimidation in the camps increased greatly.[18]

I had to concentrate more and more on the security problem in the refugee camps. On August 30, 1994, I reported the worsening camp situation to the secretary-general and asked for intervention. Stating that many of the soldiers, militias, and former government officials should be excluded from refugee status because of their involvement in atrocities in Rwanda, I proposed four action points in order to reduce risks of exploding circumstances. "1) Totally disarm the soldiers, collect all arms and military equipment, and gather them in secure place far from the border. 2) Isolate and neutralize civilian leaders. 3) Set up a mechanism for dealing with perpetrators of crimes. 4) Ensure maintenance of law and order in the camps through the deployment of police, etc." I asked for his views.

In principle, the implementation of security measures rests with the host government. Security had to be strengthened in Tanzania, to which Hutu refugees had fled in large numbers. For example, when the serious incident took place in the Benaco camp over the arrest of Jean Baptiste Gatete, the Tanzanian authorities took stern measures against his militias, which rose in his defense. The authorities persisted and eventually took Gatete out of the camp. UNHCR gave equipment and training to the Tanzanian police forces assigned to the camps. Their presence in refugee sites proved effective.

In the case of Zaire, the government was incapable of providing security. To begin with, the president and other officials had close links with the former Rwandan government. The capital city, Kinshasa, was a thousand miles away from Goma. The provincial governments were weak. The number of refugees, consisting of military and militia elements, was huge. The Zairean authorities, however, began to ask the international community for security assistance. Vice Prime Minister Kamanda wa Kamanda, who addressed the UNHCR Executive Committee in early October 1994, focused on the camp situation in the Goma area. He stated that former Rwandese military were harassing refugees and locals. He was not in favor of a full-scaled deployment of UN troops because Zaire was not a country at war, but he made it clear that his country would accept a limited security force or international police. He also said that Zaire was prepared to extradite those responsible for the genocide who had taken refuge on its soil.

The UN office in Kigali also felt the need to address the camp security issue. The United Nations was represented in Rwanda by the secretary-general's special representative, Ambassador Shaharyar Khan, and the UNMAMIR mission, but neither had operational responsibility in Zaire. The special representative, however, took the initiative to study ways of separating and relocating former Rwandan authorities and confirmed the need to remove the camps from the border. He thought that a UN force could be entrusted to handle the operational responsibility. A joint UNAMIR/UNHCR/UNDP technical mission was sent to Zaire in mid-October to assess the logistical, political, security, humanitarian, and financial implications for the repatriation and relocation of camps. The preliminary conclusion was to propose the establishment of an international force with the objective of restoring and ensuring order and security in the camps. Actual separation of the armed elements could be carried out on a voluntary basis.

While New York grappled with reaching a decision, the situation in the camps deteriorated further. The situation in the Goma area had been serious from the early days following the refugee arrival. There were frictions among the Zairean military and refugees, local people, and the police. The Zairean military harassed relief workers and confiscated their vehicles and equipment. The former Rwandan military used violence to control civilian refugees and local people. Groups of refugees fought one another for control of relief supplies.[19] The conditions worsened when drastic palliative measures were introduced, and the cases of refugees killed, harassed, and intimidated climbed. Within the camps the coercive activities of the Rwandan military, militias, and political leaders in the camps began to threaten the relief efforts.

The UNHCR Goma office had already asked headquarters for serious consideration to deploy an international armed force to protect its operation. The humanitarian workers in Goma agreed on the need to introduce "a credible international force, be it a police or military force, and this force is needed very urgently." They did not think that a contingent to back up a Zairean force would be desirable. They argued that "should this be the case, and notwithstanding the fact that an international force would need to liaise with the regional authorities, we strongly believe that such a structure would assist in ensuring security in the camps, entering into a dialogue with the refugee population, separating the 'wolves from the sheep' and facilitating, in due course a voluntary return movement."[20] The NGO community began seriously examining the security question.

It should be understood that the Rwandese refugee camps that spanned Kivu were like medium or large towns, requiring management. Supervised and assisted by authorities, whether the government or agencies appointed by UNHCR, the refugees played a part in organizing the camp structure. In the case of the Rwanda refugees, the political and military leaders among them re-created the administrative structures that had existed in Rwanda. They set up a liaison organ, the Social Commission, that dealt with such internal coordination as the day-to-day distribution of goods intended for them. As the camps became more organized and political factions emerged, the commission was superseded by a group known as Rwandan Civil Society in Exile. This became the umbrella body, with several hundred smaller associations with widely varying objectives. Both the Social Commission and the Rwandan Civil Society in Exile were headed by people who had been well known among the refugees. They came to play important roles in the camp community.

A second control mechanism was a security committee established within each camp. As security in the camps deteriorated with no international measures forthcoming, the agencies and NGOs in the camps sought a quick alternative. Numerous proposals were made to press for the early setup of security management. In the end, security committees consisting of young, educated men of "good moral standard," were organized. The committees patrolled the camps, resolved security problems, and maintained close links with various interested parties. Officially they reported to the Zairean camp administrators appointed by the Zairean governor or to NGOs responsible for managing the camps. In fact they reported directly to the refugee structures.

A third means that brought the refugee population firmly under the control of the former Rwandese officials was fund-raising. The entire refugee population was required to contribute financially to these officials for the overall objective of fighting back someday and returning home. Each family had to make a monthly payment. If necessary, families sold food and nonfood items distributed by relief agencies to make the payments. The same applied to a share of the revenue from commercial activities developed in the camps and the proceeds from illicit activities. Collections were also taken up by representatives of religious congregations, whether Catholic, Protestant, or Muslim. Contributions were also sought from Rwandan refugees in other countries and from Rwandans still in the country and those living abroad.

Indirectly and almost always unwittingly, however, the agencies and nongovernmental organizations operating in the camps provided important backup for the control mechanism. They employed those who tended to be better educated and came from the elite. In addition, for reasons of convenience as well as conviction, some religious NGOs preferred to hire members of their own congregations. In normal refugee camp management, it would be both welcome and desirable that the communities take charge of their daily affairs. In the context of the politically charged refugee situation in the Rwandese camps in Zaire, these structures consolidated the control of the leaders and strengthened the overriding objective of returning together and winning the war.[21]

On September 29 Médecins sans Frontières representatives called on me to express their concern about the undesirable situation of the camps controlled by the former Rwandese regime and to inform me that they were thinking of withdrawing. I shared their analysis, but my mandate would not allow us to leave the refugees. A nongovernmental organization was free to choose its course of action. Half the refugee population, after all, were women and children. In the end Médecins sans Frontières–France made public its decision to withdraw in a letter on December 1, addressed to me and to members of the Security Council. The group stated it had to take a definite stand that its "presence would continue to be used by the leaders to legitimize their past and future power." It feared "a coming offensive against Rwanda from the camps that would lead to another round of genocide by extremists of Hutu power," and it could not negotiate with such people.[22]

Care International had also decided to suspend its activities in the Katale camp in Goma in late October, following direct threats against its staff and facing increased violence. It wrote me that the camp was "in the hands of the elements of the Hutu militia, that they are attempting to use the camp as a base for military incursions into

Rwanda, and that they will brook no interference with their control." Care's grave concerns were the "continued existence of a military and political leadership which carried out a genocide" and the fact that "this leadership is now largely dependent on an economy based on humanitarian aid." Care did not publicize its withdrawal decision, as it intended to continue its work in other camps in Goma and in other places in Zaire and in Burundi and Tanzania.[23]

In the absence of the deployment of an alternative force, I had proposed to the secretary-general a security assistance package program. The heart of the package was the deployment of an international police contingent for an initial period of six months. This approach was to have the limited objective of "monitoring and reinforcement of overall security situation in camps; security of delivery of humanitarian assistance; security of voluntary repatriation operations; security of humanitarian personnel." It was not to encompass the separation or relocation of the military or the militias, because police could not do such work. The contingent was to assist the Zairean security forces and to be assigned to the Goma zone (six camps with estimated 850,000 refugees), the Bukavu zone (twenty-eight camps with 290,000 refugees); and the Uvira zone (twenty-five camps with 250,000 refugees). The deployment of personnel was to take place through bilateral agreements between Zaire and the contributing countries under UNHCR auspices.

I presented the package to interested member states and sounded out their reactions in Geneva. The European Union countries and Switzerland expressed interest. The Netherlands identified experts for training the Tanzanian police and assigned a police officer to go to Goma. The United States proposed an alternative so-called bubble project, which closed camps one by one after providing security and allowing refugees to exercise their free choice on return. Canada was not ready to associate with the Zairean government and its security forces. Japan recognized the need for an international police presence in the camps but thought the deployment would require support from the Security Council. UNHCR introduced the proposal to the general meeting of the African Group in Geneva. The representative of

Senegal insisted on close cooperation with the the Organization of African Unity and thought that with its secretary-general's support, the proposal would be received more positively. The Ivory Coast representative explained that it was not the tradition of his country to send military contingents abroad, but given the particular nature of the operation, it might consider an exception. I was advised to write to its highest authorities, underlining the humanitarian aspect of the mission in addition to whatever the secretary-general might decide to request.[24]

Secretary-General Boutros Boutros-Ghali met me on November 8. While asking UNHCR to continue studying its proposal, he decided to advocate officially the dispatch of a special force capable of putting an end to the activities of the former Rwandese military personnel and militias. Feeling that "you cannot cure cancer by an aspirin," he told me he wished to test the will of the member states. In a report on the situation of the refugee camps in Zaire to the Security Council on November 18, he stated that the former Rwandan Armed Forces (FAR) and the militias were in control of the camps and were prepared to use force to prevent the return of the refugees; that the security conditions and working conditions of the humanitarian workers were very bad; and that the UN mission that had visited the sites had reported that the separation and displacement of military personnel would be extremely costly, arduous, and lengthy. The choices left to the United Nations were to deploy peacekeeping forces of three to five thousand for a period of twenty-four to thirty months to ensure security in the camps and enable the continuance of the work of the humanitarian agencies or to plan for a UN force of ten to twelve thousand men for a period of six months under Chapter VII and under UN command to separate the former Rwandese leaders, the former FAR, and the militias from civilians. There was also the option to dispatch a multinational force under Chapter VII but not under UN command with identical tasks.[25] In response to the secretary-general's report, the Security Council president stated on November 30 concern over the situation and requested the secretary-general to continue the investigation and to submit detailed information on the operation, its implementation and cost. In the meantime, Annan informed me of a possible commercial option contracting the service of Defense Systems Limited (DSL), founded in 1981 by former members of SAS United Kingdom.

At a meeting in Geneva with the secretary-general on January 10, 1995, I was told that his contact with thirty-nine countries had resulted in only one positive response. He therefore thought that the only option left would be a commercial one. A preliminary examination of the cost proposed by the DSL firm was some $250 million over two years. I knew I could not raise such a large sum from donors. Nor could I figure out how commercial firms could account for operational failures of a political and humanitarian nature. The secretary-general then said that I should pursue the UNHCR proposal.

I decided to go back to the proposed security assistance package, my little "aspirin" operation, which involved Zairean security forces supervised by international observers. They were very limited in scale and certainly different from the peacekeeping forces authorized and managed by the United Nations. They might not prove fully satisfactory, as colleagues in Goma had earlier warned. Still, we started frantic bilateral negotiations with the Zairean authorities and bilateral donors. Since we had already been alerted of the difficulties that the secretary-general was facing, some preparation had been under way. One decision that had to be made ahead of time was the ordering of uniforms for the proposed Zairean contingents, an absolute necessity if the internationally sponsored Zairean forces were to be distinguished from those flooding the region.

By the time we had the decision for the deployment of the Zairean contingent, the uniforms were on the way. The first group of a hundred men from the elite Special Presidential Division arrived on February 11. I wrote to the governments of Senegal, the Ivory Coast, Cameroon, Morocco, Algeria, Tunisia, and Italy requesting that they make available military or police experts, all of whom had to be bilingual or at least French-speaking. The negotiating process was complicated, but in the end some thirty military and police officers from European and African states joined to supervise and train the Zairean contingents. The overall cost was relatively limited, especially in comparison with that of UN peacekeeping. The contingents were paid incentives by UNHCR directly and individually. On January 27 an agreement was signed between UNHCR and the government of

Rwandan and Burundian Refugee Movements, 1994–1999

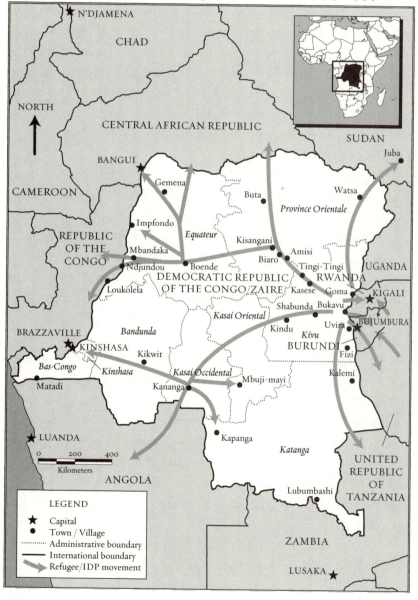

LEGEND

★ Capital
● Town / Village
┈┈┈ Administrative boundary
─── International boundary
➤ Refugee/IDP movement

Zaire concerning the creation of the Zairean Camp Security Contingent (CZSC). When I visited Goma on February 19, I had the unusual task of trooping Zairean contingents together with the minister of defense of Zaire. By the end of April the overall number had reached over fifteen hundred.

By mid-1995 the new arrangements had brought some security to the camps. The military contingents were retrained to carry out policing functions. They worked closely with the international advisers. Their mission was narrowly defined: improve law and order in the camps; prevent intimidation and violence against refugees wishing to return; escort refugees to the border; and protect humanitarian workers, infrastructure, equipment, and supplies. However, given the entrenched power structure and the militarized nature of the camps, problems were bound to emerge.

The establishment of the CZSC should be understood as a temporary measure to deal with the practical needs of introducing some law and order and security to refugee camps. Clearly, the international system lacked appropriate instruments to control an unusual volatile situation of a refugee population led by criminals, military personnel, and political leaders, who used their exile to reorganize, remobilize, and eventually return. Intimidation and control of the refugees were therefore an integral part of the exiles' policy of war and victory. The United Nations and the major powers were aware of much of the nature of the exiled population. Nevertheless, the secretary-general opted for a peacekeeping model, notwithstanding there was no peace to keep. He challenged the member states with a request for troop contributions, although he sensed that they would not respond. UNHCR recognized that the task was more of policing and of separating the refugees from their leaders. But the host government had no law and order function even for itself. Eventually a compromise arrangement, the CZSC, was devised after several months of no action.

Would an early implementation of a security arrangement have made a difference? I see much merit in a speedier action. Had the UN more resolutely turned to an international police force at an earlier stage, the camp control structure by the former Rwandese leaders might have been a bit less entrenched. Refugees might have felt freer to return. As for the particular choice of a Zairean contingent, it was the only available solution to UNHCR that had to deal with the critical situation on hand. The CZSC presence did produce stability and the return of refugees in the first year. However, given the local ethnic conflicts that grew in North and South Kivu between the local Zairean Tutsis and Zairean Hutus and other people, a government-sponsored contingent would not have been able to withstand for long. The Zairean Tutsis joined the Zairean rebel forces, supported by the Rwandan forces in an all-out war against the Zairean government. The CZSC forces fled west with the refugees.

The preferred solution clearly would have been the deployment of an international separation force that could have put an end to militarized camps by dividing the civilians from the military and protecting refugees. Closely keeping law and order, such a force could have demobilized the soldiers and handed over the genocide criminals to face justice in Rwanda. However, the international community was not in possession of such a force. Nor was there any political will to face and intervene for the protection of refugees and victims.

War over Refugees

RISING TENSION: RWANDA AND ZAIRE

The existence of large-scale militarized camps in eastern Zaire was a given against which UNHCR had to seek ways to protect refugees while preventing the aggravation of the situation. Our basic policy was threefold: to contain the intimidating impact of the former Rwanda military and militias in the camps, for which UNHCR deployed Zairean contingents, to develop conditions in the countries of origin of the refugees in order to ensure their safe return, and to mobilize international and regional backing in consultations and con-

ferences in order to arrive at a consensus on the solution to the problem of refugees.

The goal of the Rwanda government was to attain its security,
internally and externally. It was essential to close the camps and settlements of refugees and the internally displaced, which were viewed
as strongholds of the former regime intent on seeking opportunities
to restore its power. Zaire, on the other hand, held divergent interests.
Its government wished to push back the refugees to relieve the major
point of contention with Rwanda as well as the source of tension with
various minority tribes in Kivu. President Sese Seko Mobutu, on the
other hand, wanted to hold on to the refugees and use them as pawns
in his domestic and regional power relations.

In February 1995 I went to five countries in the Great Lakes
region to assess the situation on the ground. In the refugee camps in
Tanzania and Zaire, I was pleased to note that the presence of the
Tanzanian police and of the Zairean security contingents was making
some improvement. In Goma the entire refugee population was
counted and registered. In fact eight thousand Rwandese refugees had
been repatriated from the area. The security in the camps increased
the possibility of refugees' coming forward to opt for return. The
number of refugees returning from Zaire to northwestern Burundi
was also increasing. I thought that strengthening the security measures in the camps was absolutely linked to repatriation and could lead
to solving the enormous humanitarian catastrophe of the Great Lakes
region.

Another purpose of my mission was to prepare for the conference
that UNHCR was hosting together with the Organization of African
Unity. At Burundi's initiative the ordinary session of the OAU Council of Ministers in June 1994 had agreed to hold the Conference on
Assistance to Refugees, Returnees and Displaced Persons in the
Great Lakes Region. The UN General Assembly in the same year had
endorsed the initiative. The objective was to address the serious security and humanitarian concerns in the region.

I appealed to all five presidents in the region for their cooperation.
The strongest reservation came from the government of Rwanda, which

was not inclined to allow international scrutiny into developments within its country. I solicited intervention from President Museveni of Uganda. As a close collaborator of Vice President Kagame, who had enjoyed his patronage, Museveni had a strong influence over the RPF. He assured me that he would persuade Rwanda to participate.

Taking place in Bujumbura under curfew, this was the first international conference since the catastrophic displacement of some 3.8 million people in the Great Lakes region and after the genocide in Rwanda. Participation was open to OAU member states; countries of origin and asylum of refugees—i.e., Burundi, Rwanda, Tanzania, Zaire, Kenya, Uganda, and Zambia—donor governments; and members of the UNHCR Executive Committee and UN agencies as well as nongovernmental organizations. UNHCR put major efforts into preparing the documentation, particularly a draft plan of action.

In my opening statement, I recalled the violence and chaos of the past year and appealed to "all people in this region, and especially their political leaders, not to allow hatred and war to dominate, but to walk the path of national reconciliation." After five days of intensive discussions and negotiations, the laboriously prepared plan of action was adopted. It endorsed the repatriation and reintegration of refugees as the solution for the tragedies in the region and assigned measures to be taken by Burundi and Rwanda, the countries of origin of refugees, as well as by Zaire, Tanzania, and other countries of asylum and by the international community. Of particular importance was the agreement to set up a follow-up committee to monitor the implementation process. Through the working of the follow-up committee UNHCR and the OAU were to move toward better security and stability in the region.

Throughout the conference what caused strong opposition from the Rwanda delegation was the reference to internally displaced persons in the conference documentation. The Bujumbura Conference was taking place against the growing confrontation in the southwestern provinces in Rwanda—i.e., in what had been the French humanitarian zone Turquoise, where an estimated 380,000 people were left in thirty-seven camps after the last French soldiers had left on August

21. While UNAMIR, together with UN agencies and NGOs, were assisting the camps, they became scenes of violent clashes between the displaced population, which included Hutu genocidal elements, militias, and former government members, and the RPA, which came in to take control. The Rwandan government not only regarded the presence of the camps for the internally displaced as a security threat but also feared its use as a symbol of its inability to claim full sovereignty over its territory.

UNAMIR and UN agencies for months had carried on negotiations with the Rwanda government to work out a program for the humane and orderly closure of these camps. With a population of some 120,000 the camps of Kibeho became the rallying point of continued opposition to the government. Pressure mounted to force a closedown. On April 18 the government decided to resort to force. RPA surrounded the Kibeho camps with two battalions and cut off the food supply. Five days of intensive violence resulted in a large massacre of the population. The casualty figure added up to several thousand.

UNHCR had not been involved in the assistance operation in Kibeho but, in response to the request of Special Representative Ambassador Khan, assisted the emergency transport of the displaced population back to its communes. I was outraged by the methods the Rwandan military applied. I thought the brutality was disproportionate to the stated objectives of moving the displaced persons to their homes. What concerned me most were the wider implications of the military action. Unfortunately, my premonition proved right. The Kibeho incident became the single most serious case that brought the repatriation movement to Rwanda to a halt. The momentum created by the Bujumbura Conference was stalled.

Meanwhile, political pressure to demand the departure of Rwanda refugees mounted in Zaire. The prime minister was aggressive in criticizing the Hutu extremists for preventing the refugees from leaving the camps and in attacking UNHCR's inability to carry out the repatriation exercise. He repeatedly pointed out that the Rwandan government was the "greatest intimidator" of the refugees. Mutual accusations between the Rwandan and Zairean governments increased. Zaire alleged that Rwanda was not allowing the return of refugees and was preparing attacks against Zaire territory. Rwanda criticized Zaire for training and arming Rwandan soldiers with a view to overthrowing the Kigali government. There were widespread reports that Hutus were launching attacks from the Zairean camps into Rwanda. At the time Rwanda was serving as a nonpermanent member of the Security Council. The Rwanda delegation took advantage of its strategic position and rallied international support. In particular, it lobbied for the lifting of the 1994 arms embargo on Rwanda.

When the Security Council adopted Resolution 1011 on August 16, 1995, and lifted the arms embargo on Rwanda under certain restraining conditions,[26] Zaire reacted strongly. Prime Minister Leon Kengo wa Dondo wrote a letter to the secretary-general protesting that Zaire was left with no choice but to request the United Nations to indicate other countries to which the refugees could be relocated. Such steps failing, Zaire would proceed to "evacuate" the refugees back to Rwanda. Within a few days some twelve thousand refugees were expelled back to Rwanda by the Zairean Army.

To cope with the crisis, the secretary-general decided to send an emergency mission to the Great Lakes region and nominated me to head the delegation. I told him that inasmuch as the cause of this *refoulemont* was highly political—i.e., the council's resolution to lift the arms embargo—I was not certain if I could solve the problem. However, upon his insistence, I started negotiations with Prime Minister Kengo, who was on a European trip. He called on me on August 29. His position was firm. He agreed to suspend the expulsions on condition that UNHCR carried out the repatriation of all Rwandan refugees by December 31 of that year. At the time there were some one million refugees in Zaire. Repatriating one million refugees in less than four months!

I left for the Great Lakes region for the second time in 1995, only six months after my previous trip. I started my mission from Bujumbura, where I found the atmosphere less tense than in February. I stopped over at the Gatumba transit center, where I welcomed back refugees from Zaire. My message to the president, prime minister, and other government authorities was to insist on adequate security to allow repatriation to continue. From Bujumbura, I flew to Arusha in Tanzania to call on the prime minister at the statehouse in Moshi. Tanzania also pressed hard to accelerate repatriation, although the prime minister said that it would not enforce as "crude" a measure as did the Zaireans. In Kigali, I found the atmosphere surprisingly open. The city had had a major face-lift. The once-devastated Hôtel des Mille Collines was nicely refurbished. President Bizimungu, Vice-President Kagame, and the new cabinet ministers all expressed their willingness to cooperate in receiving back refugees. They had closed the large camps of the internally displaced persons in Kibeho. They had even managed to receive the twelve thousand refugees who had been forced back from Zaire. They seemed to have gained confidence. They agreed for the first time to put points of agreements with UNHCR in a statement in the presence of the diplomatic corps and international agencies.

In Zaire, we were invited to Gbadolite, the country palace of President Mobutu. I explained to him that Rwanda had agreed to receive back its refugees and that it was now up to Zaire to take the necessary hard measures. The CZSC was playing a useful role in maintaining security in the camps, but the hard-core intimidating elements that obstructed refugees from returning had to be arrested by the Zairean authorities. We agreed to plan urgently for repatriation with the foreign and defense ministers. I was pleased with the agreements I gained from the contending parties, although I was fully aware of the difficulties that still lay ahead in turning their words into deeds.

One concrete result of my mission was the calling of a ministerial meeting of the Tripartite Agreement on Repatriation of Rwandan Refugees from Zaire. Tripartite commission schemes are mechanisms that UNHCR developed to assist the governments from which the refugees originated and in which they took refuge to collaborate in solving the problem through consultation and action. The first ministerial meeting took place in Geneva on September 25, 1995. At its opening I explained that the commission served as a pragmatic framework to translate promises and intentions into concrete humanitarian action in a coordinated and orderly fashion and in full respect of international standards concerning the rights and obligations of refugee populations. My appeal to the participants indeed was "to concentrate on the humanitarian and organizational aspects of repatriation, and to be guided by a sense of pragmatism."[27] The day's debate was carried out in an atmosphere of businesslike consultation. I was very much impressed by the restraint exercised by the Rwandese Minister Patrick Mazimhaka, who announced his country's readiness to receive six to eight thousand people daily. The commission was able to adopt a joint communiqué at the end of the day. It was indeed a great achievement.

Following the agreements reached at the Tripartite Commission meeting, UNHCR decided to move on to a more proactive return policy of promotion, shifting from the facilitation policy that had been followed since December 1994. This was based not only on the agreements that had been reached but also on positive feedbacks about the reception of those who had been forcefully returned to Rwanda in August. UNHCR renewed its support through engaging in an intensified information campaign, fielding additional repatriation monitoring staffers, bringing in more convoys, and increasing logistical capacity. We reduced nonessential care and maintenance services in the camps. By the third week of October these efforts were starting to bear fruits. The daily average of returnees climbed to over 540, with 1,500 on a single day, October 16. I thought we might be finally coming closer to reaching solutions to this massive refugee situation in the heart of Africa.

My optimism was short-lived. This time it was the working of internal Zairean politics that reversed what seemed like the emerging positive trend. In an interview to *Le Libre Belgique* on October 20, 1995, President Mobutu stated his readiness to continue hosting the Rwandese refugees in Zaire. Reminding readers that the Rwandese refugees had been welcomed warmly in Zaire under his instructions, he was not inclined to chase them out even if they caused ecological damages or inconvenience to certain personalities. He stated in the interview that "in my soul and conscience, as the head of state of this country, I cannot accept that they be chased out. They should be able to return freely to their homes. For those who do not wish so, Zaire would have to agree with the international community either to settle them as far as 150 km from the border of their countries, or elsewhere. It is more noble."[28] His words had an immediate impact. There was rejoicing in the camps. In the Uvira camps to the south of Goma, refugees who had been gearing up for departure were reported to have suddenly decided to start planting seeds and mending their roofs.

The policy divergence within the Zairean government came out into the open. Although Mobutu had assured me during my visit to Gbadolite that he was in full accord with the government on repatriation, he had reversed his position at the subsequent press interview. It was known that he had a personal affinity with the Hutus and supported them. When I was at Gbadolite, he even pointed to the grave site near his residence that he had built for former President Habyarimana. There was a burgeoning alliance with the former Rwanda military leaders in exile that would become more evident in 1996. Besides, his current situation of hosting large numbers of refugees gave him an upper hand politically within the country and internationally vis-à-vis the donor community. Mobutu was not easily prepared to lose his advantageous position. Prime Minister Kengo, on the other hand, emphasized to my special envoy Faubert that though the president could have a personal opinion and express himself at press interviews, it was the government that defined and carried out policy. In short, repatriation was the goal, and the set deadline was the end of 1995. In the absence of progress, the prime minister added that "he would have no choice but to resume what had been started in mid-August"—namely, forceful expulsion—although he recognized the need to factor in the "goodwill" of the Rwandans. Faubert would not accept a deadline. He also noted that the army was under the authority of the president and that this fact limited the likelihood of any forceful action similar to that taken in mid-August by the government.

My position was very much along the line taken by Faubert. I made it clear that UNHCR would redouble its efforts toward promoting voluntary return without committing itself to any completion date. Such a date, however, had some useful operational impact on all parties concerned. It obliged Rwanda to welcome back the refugees. It pressed the Zairean government to start arresting the intimidators in the camps. It exerted pressure on those in the camps who prevented many refugees from deciding to return. It was against these conflicting demands that former President Jimmy Carter decided to discuss with African leaders the means to end the conflicts in Rwanda and Burundi. His initiative was welcomed by the OAU, as he visited with the presidents of Zaire, Uganda, Rwanda, and Burundi to prepare for a summit meeting in Cairo. Archbishop Desmond Tutu of South Africa was to join Carter to serve as facilitator.

I received a letter from President Carter, who informed me of the upcoming meeting in Cairo from November 27 to December 2 and who invited UNHCR to attend. He explained, however, that although his preference was for me to join, official observers from the United Nations and other organizations would not be invited to all the meetings, because "one of the governments involved has refused to attend unless participation is restricted."[29] The exclusion of UN participation had serious implications. The secretary-general reacted negatively to Carter's request for UNHCR representation, stating that "when States concerned had made their own participation conditional on non-participation by the United Nations and the OAU, he could not accept the United Nations be brought in through the back door."[30] The secretary-general even telephoned me to make sure that I understood his position. I had no desire to participate, but I was a bit uneasy that issues relevant to UNHCR would be discussed by heads of state of the region without any inputs from us and that decisions might be simply handed down to us for implementation.

We learned of the Cairo Declaration when it was proclaimed. It was more a pronouncement of goodwill than a precise action plan. It stated that President Mobutu "pledged soon to remove from the refugee camps the identified intimidators." The Rwandan head of state "declared unequivocally that his government wanted the refugees to return to Rwanda at an early date" and "will guarantee the safety of the returning refugees." Altogether, the heads of state and delegations were convinced that when conditions were safe to return, a large number would go home. They came up with an optimistic forecast that "the number of returning refugees who avail themselves of UNHCR assistance should rise progressively to ten thousand a day within a short time."[31]

The UNHCR office in Goma observed that the Carter initiative had actually had "a negative impact on the return of refugees." The declaration turned all action plans into statements of general goodwill intentions. Without the Cairo intervention, it might have been more difficult for President Mobutu to disregard the completion date for repatriation and continue to use the refugees as pawns in his regional power game. The stance of the former American president derived from a laudable perspective that combined morality, human rights advocacy, and conflict prevention, but the result of his approach created something very different.[32]

The fact of the matter was that to accelerate repatriation in the face of diverse opposition from both Zaire and Rwanda, some pressure was necessary. UNHCR's official position was not to commit itself to a deadline, but it had to count on some external pressure to move the return process. The December deadline served this purpose. As we faced the end of 1995, the situation was grim. Under the circumstances, UNHCR had to define clearly the terms under which it could effectively perform its functions. First, the issue of relocation of camps had to be placed on the international agenda. Relocating camps consisting of more than a million people would be costly, with large financial implications for donor governments. Yet UNHCR could not continue to provide assistance to border camps that were threatening regional security.

Second, the question of the eligibility of refugees had to be addressed. The probability of a sizable number of people's not repatriating had to be recognized, with many falling into the category of those to be "excluded" from refugee protection. But how do you go about deciding who should fall under "exclusion" clauses, and what do you do with them? The International Criminal Tribunal for Rwanda had been set up by the Security Council on November 8, 1994, to deal with genocide and crimes against humanity committed between January 1 and December 31, 1994. UNHCR had to explore ways to cooperate with the tribunal to identify persons to whom exclusion clauses should apply.

Thirdly, we had to recognize that in the absence of coercion, the voluntary repatriation of Rwandan refugees would not be rapid. Yet we had to uphold voluntary repatriation not only as a matter of principle but also as the least disruptive option with a self-regulating process built in. In other words, refugees themselves would decide on the most opportune moment to return after they had assessed for themselves the issues of security and viability. In the meantime, a comprehensive set of actions would have to be addressed to create overall conditions favorable for return.[33]

Not only did repatriation of Rwandese refugees become deadlocked, but armed incursions into Rwanda increased as well. The UNHCR staff from the field pressed for the temporary relocation of camps. It also began asking seriously for the deployment of international monitors along the border areas.

In parallel with the dismal developments in Zaire, the internal situation in Burundi took a drastic downturn. The number of displaced persons within the country as well as refugees fleeing to safety in Tanzania and Zaire rose rapidly. When security incidents erupted in northern Burundi, necessitating the withdrawal of international humanitarian agencies, the secretary-general asked me again to go to Burundi. He did not wish to see all UN humanitarian operations withdraw from the country when the needs were great. I had to try to negotiate assurances of security from the government. It was my third mission to the region in one year.

I arrived in Bujumbura on January 7, 1996, and immediately began consultations with my UN and NGO colleagues. The city was facing Hutu opposition attacks and barely surviving with limited water and electricity supplies. Local officials were describing Burundi as in a state of war. I called on the president, prime minister, and foreign and defense ministers, attempting to invoke their commitments to establishing reliable security coverage of UN and international agency staffs. That night my colleagues suddenly advised me to leave the capital. I followed their recommendation. Apparently they had learned of some security threat to my delegation. I flew to Nairobi and called the secretary-general to make a quick report on the situation. I prepared for him a "your eyes only" note in which I emphasized the urgent need to dispatch a rapid deployment force. As high commissioner for refugees with a humanitarian mandate, I believed that I could not call openly for troop deployment, but the reality of the situation required urgent military intervention.

The secretary-general called for a stand-by force for humanitarian intervention. He proposed that up to a maximum of twenty-five thousand troops would be trained, earmarked, and ready to deploy at short notice under Chapter VII of the UN Charter. At the Security Council meeting on June 28, I stressed that "the people of Burundi need help." I urged that "humanitarian contingencies must be readied as soon as possible" and that the international community should provide for "a military component to ensure the protection of civilians and the security of humanitarian assistance operations."[34]

The situation in the Great Lakes region was heading again to a crisis. Obviously the presence of large camps along the Zairean border had a destabilizing effect on the whole region. Moreover, the ethnic strife among the locals in the Kivu region was turning more and more volatile. The disintegration of Zaire, the largest and the most geographically central state, was adding fuel to the fire, already spreading throughout central Africa.

SPREADING WAR IN CONGO

In mid-1996 the situation in eastern Zaire, Kivu, had turned increasingly tense. To begin with, the ethnic composition in Kivu was complex with a large number of Rwandans who had migrated to the region. In the Masisi zone to the north of Goma, the Hutus became agriculturalists and the Tutsis reared cattle. In the south the Tutsi cattle owners were a minority amid many tribes. These persons of Rwandan origin, known as Banyarwanda, became embroiled in the local ethnic conflict.

The political transformation process in postindependence Zaire had intensified ethnic strife. In 1960 a law was passed that conferred nationality upon all those living within Zaire's borders. An amendment to this law in 1981, however, conferred nationality on an individual basis and on those who could prove to have lived in Zaire for three generations. As Zaire moved toward constitutional government with elections announced for 1995, the Banyarwanda became increasingly vocal in their demands for political representation, while the local population became fearful of winding up as a minority in their own territory.

It was against the volatile situation in Kivu that the developments in Rwanda had profound effects. In North Kivu the presence of a large number of Hutu refugees since the summer of 1994 had a direct bearing on the situation of the Tutsis in Masisi, who found themselves targeted as a minority. The Zairean military forces tended to be more closely allied with the Hutu group. With violence breaking out, fifteen thousand Tutsis fled from Masisi and sought safety and security in Rwanda. Initially, the Rwanda government was uncertain how to deal with the Tutsis from Masisi and pressed Zaire to protect its citizens even though they were of Rwandan origin. The government even reproached UNHCR and the international community for ignoring a "second genocide in the Masisi."[35] In the end the government of Rwanda recognized these people as Zairean citizens requiring international protection and asked UNHCR to assist. I faced a very delicate decision. The denial of citizenship by the governments of both Rwanda and Zaire to this group would turn them stateless. The sites proposed by the Rwandan government to receive the refugees were too close to the border with Zaire to ensure their security.

I wrote the secretary-general that I was taking steps about which I had serious concerns. With "the reported involvement of Rwandese refugees in north Kivu in the ongoing fighting in the Masisi," the situation was further complicated. I warned that "the humanitarian problem in the Masisi, the citizenship issue and the security problem along the border, require our attention and need to be addressed. Failing an appropriate political action that aims at resolving the crisis, I feared an escalation of violence in the region, with the all attendant consequences on the repatriation and the overall security in the area."[36]

Because of the central importance of the citizenship issue, I sought the opinion of the UN Office of Legal Affairs, which examined the issue and concluded that the "collective deprivation of Zairean nationality from the Banyarwanda is unlawful under both customary international law and the international conventions to which Zaire is a party, notably the Convention against Racial Discrimination and the African Charter."[37]

In the meanwhile, ethnic competition also sharpened in South Kivu, as political leadership fell into the hands of anti-Banyarwanda groups, which passed discriminatory laws. The Rwandan Tutsis in South Kivu, known as Banyamulenge, had started to look for military training and access to weapons, in preparation for fighting in the event the situation worsened. In the course of 1995 many Banyamulenge youth went to Rwanda and received training from the RPA. In late September 1996 two columns of armed Banyamulenge fighters entered South Kivu from Cyangugu in Rwanda and the border province of Cibitoke in Burundi. Each consisted of roughly nine hundred men and carried mortars and heavy machine guns. The Rwanda Army gave them artillery cover as they crossed the border, firing directly at Zairean Army positions.

UNHCR faced a serious security incident during the summer, when 190 Banyamulenge citizens arrived in the UNHCR compound in Uvira, seeking protection. UNHCR transferred them to the local camp of the CZSC. The Hutu refugees were infuriated by these measures and threw stones around the CZSC camp. The Zairean contingent fired into the air to disperse the crowd. The Banyamulenge group requested to go to Rwanda and were kept in the CZSC camp while UNHCR tried to negotiate with the Zairean authorities for their transfer. The problem was further complicated by the over-all situation in Uvira, where armed Banyamulenge rebels fortified themselves in the hills surrounding the city. The Zairean Army (FAZ) launched an offensive against these armed groups and declared the region a "military zone." The road from Uvira to Bukavu farther north was heavily patrolled by the Zairean Army, which set up check-points. Tension rose throughout South Kivu.

On September 13 I was surprised by a communiqué issued by the Zairean minister of the interior, Kamanda wa Kamanda, who offi-cially accused UNHCR of providing logistical support to armed Banyamulenge groups infiltrating Zaire from Rwanda and Burundi. He furthermore stated that UNHCR had "repatriated to Rwanda in 1994–1995 about three thousand young Banyamulenge, who were trained by the Rwandan Patriotic Army (RPA)." The secretary-general issued a statement rejecting the allegations,[38] but he thought that since the high commissioner had been accused, I could not enter discussions with Minister Kamanda. He asked Ibrahima Fall, assistant secretary-general in charge of human rights, to proceed to Kinshasa as his special envoy.

I briefed Fall fully before his departure. He made a quick trip and upon his return informed me that all allegations with regard to UNHCR and the United Nations had been dropped. Minister Kamanda accepted the explanations presented by Fall. At issue were vehicles used for transporting troops or goods on behalf of the Rwan-dan Army. Two hundred UN vehicles had been put at the disposal of the Rwanda government after UNAMIR departed from Rwanda in April 1996. The vehicles had still kept the UN marks while serving the Rwanda government. UNHCR was cleared of allegations that we were involved in transporting the fighters. The real issue was over the return of Rwanda-trained Banyamulenge fighters to South Kivu.

We received information from our staff in South Kivu that Tutsi armed groups were infiltrating into Uvira and other zones. Concen-tration of military forces continued along the borders of Zaire and Rwanda as well as Zaire and Burundi. Shootings and massacres were reportedly taking place daily in the hills surrounding Uvira.[39] The allegation of Minister Kamanda was in fact a warning for the impending war and for UNHCR to be on guard.

The Executive Committee meeting of UNHCR on October 7, 1996, reflected the grave tension that existed between Zaire and Rwanda. Kamanda, heading the Zairean delegation, and Ephraim Kabaija, leading the Rwanda delegation, argued their respective positions. I stated that "cross border raids, the targeting of survivors of the genocide and attacks on Tutsi residents in the Kivu region of Zaire resulting in armed resistance, are causing more deaths and are undermining prospects for reconciliation." Furthermore, I stressed that "never before has my Office found its humanitarian concerns in the midst of such a lethal quagmire of political and security interests. While our humanitarian assistance and protection serve an innocent silent majority of needy and anxious refugees, they also serve the militants who have an interest in maintaining the status quo."[40] I knew that I had to come up with a set of proposals that would be agreed to by both the affected and interested governments.

Kamanda, heading the Zairean delegation, and Kabaija, heading the Rwandans, engaged in long and acrimonious exchanges. Zaire condemned the infiltration groups from Rwanda, which, for its part, came up with a proposal to close the refugee camps in Kivu and move to a blanket application of the "cessation clause affecting all who fled due to the events of 1994." Pointing to the situation in the Kivu region, Kabaija characterized the activities as "continuation of the genocide against the Tutsi population" and insisted that "the international community should act, and action should not be too late."[41] I had to present a new strategy. I told the representatives at the Executive Committee meeting that I was planning a step-by-step gradual closure and consolidation of the refugee camps and that the implementation measures would be addressed subsequently.

Rwanda had obviously begun to test the grounds. It regarded the situation developing in the Kivu region as military in nature and was trying to anticipate the international reaction if the RPA was to enter the camps in hot pursuit.[42] In fact, Vice-President Kagame during a recent visit to Washington had made "a veiled warning" that if the international community failed to take action, Rwanda would move. I heard about these developments in the course of consultations at the State Department when I visited Washington in September. The State Department seemed uncertain about how to react.[43] Kagame found the U.S. nonresponse confusing but apparently was not disheartened.

A few days after the Executive Committee session, I received disturbing information on the possibility of an attack by Rwanda on Zaire. The attack could take place in the coming days or weeks, depending on the escalation of the conflict in Kivu and on current political and diplomatic negotiations to defuse the tension. Rwandans were not optimistic that these negotiations would bring results. Nor did they believe that the Zaireans had the political will to stop ethnic cleansing or persecution of the Banyamulenge in South Kivu. This warning indicated that unlike the existing military action undertaken primarily by Banyamulenge forces, the forthcoming attack would involve regular Rwanda government troops. A military assessment of the relative capabilities of the two armies predicted that the Zaireans would be completely overwhelmed. The area of the attack would be primarily around Bukavu and could also extend to North Kivu. Refugee camps would be a definite target, for the intention would be to reduce the threat they posed to Rwanda. There would be large population movements, particularly of refugees.[44]

Over the weekend of October 19 and 20, 1996, attacks on refugee camps started in Uvira. About 220,000 Rwandan and Burundi refugees left the twelve refugee camps in the area. An estimated 30,000 Zairean civilians also fled their villages. The CZSC contingents succeeded in evacuating UNHCR international staff out of Uvira to the north. They proceeded to Bukavu, to Goma, and farther on to Entebbe, Uganda, on October 22. In the meantime, I had left for New York on a series of consultation and reporting engagements. I immediately consulted with the secretary-general and his senior staff on steps to be taken on the Kivu situation. The secretary-general noted that there was practically a war going on and suggested taking the "classical action" of going through the Security Council, although he believed the council "would be unable to do anything." The United Nations faced a clear dilemma. Its intervention might bring results but not necessarily of a successful kind. On the other hand, it might also be blamed for doing nothing. The secretary-general expected that if he were to ask for the dispatch of troops, member states would say no. He advised me to brief the council, and then he planned to write to it to sound the alarm. I said I wanted at least to issue a strong appeal not to attack the civilians and refugee camps.[45] At the conclusion of the meeting with the secretary-general and the senior UN staff, I told them that I "felt very alone in the Great Lakes region." I had flashback images of the refugees, especially the children, who had greeted me so warmly at the camps along the roadside.

At the Security Council meeting on October 25, I stated that "sixty thousand refugees and ten thousand Zaireans are walking now towards Bukavu in the north while some others have run to neighboring hills and banana plantations. The latest unconfirmed reports say that Banyamulenge forces have taken Uvira airport and are closing in on the town, and that fighting is taking place about 35 kilometers south of Bukavu. Large numbers of refugees who had sought safety in Uvira town and Zaireans are now reportedly heading south to attempt to cross Lake Tanganyika to Kigoma." We were loosing track of thousands of refugees. I added: "Goma is also the scene of tension and fighting and there are reports of armed infiltration around Kibumba camp which hosts some 200,000 refugees. UNHCR is consequently unable to deliver life sustaining supplies to many camps." Eastern Zaire "has reached a critical point to which a solely humanitarian response is inadequate." I emphasized that "the mounting military tension along the Zaire-Rwanda border requires new political initiatives."[46]

That day I received a desperate call from the UNHCR representative in Bukavu, who reported on the heavy fighting going on in the city. The archbishop of Bukavu was in the UNHCR office and appealed to me for international cease-fire intervention. Again I immediately contacted the secretary-general, but I felt very helpless.

By the next day all international agencies and NGO staffs were evacuated from Bukavu to Nairobi. The Zairean security contingents also suffered heavy casualties. A few were able to escape. I decided to appeal directly to the refugees caught in the fighting to consider returning to Rwanda. My statement was repeatedly broadcast by international and local radio stations. I tried to make known to them how "deeply saddened" I was that Rwanda and Burundi refugees again had to flee for their lives. While pledging to "do everything possible," I asked them to "consider where you will be safer—in Zaire or in Rwanda." Though making it clear that "that is a decision for you to make," I tried to persuade them to return home, reminding them that "eighty thousand refugees have recently returned home to Rwanda from Burundi" and were now busy resuming normal lives.[47] On October 30 Bukavu fell to rebel hands, amid reports of heavy slaughter. Archbishop Monsignor Christophe Munzihirwa was assassinated.

The secretary-general decided to appoint the Canadian ambassador to Washington Jean Chretien his special envoy to visit Kinshasa and Kigali and to meet with other leaders in the Great Lakes region to bring about a cease-fire and solution to the problems in eastern Zaire. Ambassador Chretien asked Dessalegen Chefeke, the UNHCR special envoy, to join his mission and assist him with information and logistical support. I welcomed the political input that Chretien could bring and was more than willing to cooperate. I was, however, not very happy about the call for an appointment of a humanitarian coordinator that some units of the UN Secretariat and agencies started to make. UNHCR had been at the forefront of the Congo refugee crisis. It had not been easy, but I was ready to take full responsibility and maintain the lead role. Now that the Great Lakes region was turning into a political and military catastrophe, I was not about to place UNHCR under a host of those who, in the name of humanitarian coordination, were likely to bring more confusion and complication.

I held intensive consultations with Ambassador Madeleine Albright and teleconferenced with White House and State Department senior staffs. I asked, first of all, about the possibility of an

American intervention to get the parties to stop fighting and with-draw to their respective sides of the borders. The U.S. government seemed to have been making several démarches to Kigali, Kinshasa, and Bujumbura. I proposed three steps: cease-fire, lines of separation, and setting up of humanitarian return corridors, all of which required an international presence. Ambassador Albright wanted to make sure that I was in favor of sending refugees back to Rwanda and not to push them farther into Zaire. I affirmed both points and said that to push the refugees farther into Zaire would be dangerous not only for the refugees but also for the security and integrity of Zaire. She also believed that Rwanda had to "go an extra mile" and reinforce the security and judicial assurances inside the country.

As for the humanitarian corridor, my plan was to develop two types of protected route, one for food and goods and the other for the repatriation of refugees. The UNHCR staff would guide and accom-pany the refugees all the way to their places of origin, where protec-tion and assistance should be concentrated. The return corridors would have to be protected by international observers. Requests for assistance would have to be widely made to mobilize international support. I knew from my previous experiences that humanitarian cor-ridors or safe areas worked only when they were adequately protected by military forces. I finally pleaded with the U.S. government to make a public request that the Rwanda government forces not attack refugee camps in the region. By then everybody knew that Rwandan forces were fighting inside Zaire, but no one was officially acknowl-edging this fact.[48]

The situation in the Goma area worsened rapidly. The Kibumba camp, twenty-five kilometers north of Goma with a population of two hundred thousand refugees, was attacked on November 1 by a com-bined force of Rwandese and Congolese rebel forces that were organ-izing themselves to form what became the Alliance of Democratic Forces for the Liberation of Congo (AFDL). The AFDL consisted of four groups that were fighting against the government of Zaire with a total force of approximately ten thousand, including the Banyamu-lenge. Its objective was to topple the Zairean political structure, not necessarily to attack the refugees from Rwanda. The Rwandan military forces focused on the refugee camps that were the power base of the former Rwandan Hutu political and military leaders and were also supported by the government of Zaire.

Refugee camps in Goma were attacked one after another. Fleeing people from Kibumba crowded into the Mugunga camp. From the Kahindo camp, fifty kilometers north of Goma, some one hundred fifteen thousand refugees also headed toward the Mugunga and neighboring Lac Vert camps, each hosting one hundred fifty thousand and fifty thousand refugees. The refugees were joined by large groups of local Zaireans, also fleeing the fighting. Close to half a million people were packed into a very small volcanic area. UNHCR had seventy-four teams of 5 to 10 people, who dug latrines through volcanic rocks. Sanitation teams sprayed and disinfected the camps, and about one hundred eighty workers helped pump water from the lake. The memory of the cholera epidemic that had swept the Goma camps in 1994 was vivid. Food had to be brought in quickly too. Everyone was working to avert a humanitarian catastrophe at the same time there was imminent danger from a military onslaught.

I cut short my New York mission and returned to Geneva on November 2. I immediately called a senior management meeting on the Kivu crisis. I asked Sergio Vieira de Mello, the assistant high commissioner, to proceed to Rwanda and Zaire and to negotiate ways to open emergency lifelines to the refugees and the displaced. The next day I was relieved to learn that with UNHCR emergency security coverage, 114 expatriate workers had left Goma. They had been trapped for several days in their offices but took advantage of a lull in the fighting arranged by the Rwandans and dashed across the border to Gisenyi. I was also told that several members of the Zairean contingents had been killed in the crossfire surrounding the UNHCR premises. I spent the next few days responding to press inquiries, briefing and consulting governments, and holding meetings with the staff. The issue of setting up a humanitarian return corridor to reach the refugees was on the table, but no government offered personnel.

Some unexpected developments that brought hope for a breakthrough took place. On November 8, I received a telephone call from President Museveni of Uganda, who had seen television pictures of suffering refugees in Goma and urged me to act. I told him that to respond, I needed support on several fronts, but especially assurances of security from the rebels. I asked him if he knew the so-called rebels and could get those assurances from them. After a winding discussion, he promised to take the following steps. First, he would reiterate the advice he had given to President Bizimungu of Rwanda to convince the rebels near the border to declare a cease-fire so that aid could go into Goma. Secondly, he would tell the Rwandan authorities to expedite the issuance of visas for Rwanda to UNHCR staff members so that they could proceed to help with the repatriation of refugees. (Rwanda was refusing visas to staffers who had worked in eastern Zaire.) Thirdly, he would allow trucks to bring goods through Uganda in addition to those coming through Rwanda.[49]

Within a few hours President Bizimungu in Kigali telephoned me that he was able to get assurances from the rebel forces to guarantee security. He himself would get visas issued to UNHCR staffers and help expedite the movement of goods from the Rwandan side to Zaire. With assurances coming from the presidents of Uganda and Rwanda, we decided to resume humanitarian assistance and immediately started preparation. Vieira de Mello called from Zaire, however, to tell me that Zaire refused to allow humanitarian assistance entering from Rwanda. Though the Zairean refusal was a matter for serious concern, we decided to go ahead with the assistance at a more limited scale, in view of the dire need of the refugees.

A third important telephone call came from Gordon Smith, the Canadian vice-minister for foreign affairs, on November 11. With the first witness accounts of the suffering of refugees trickling into Gisenyi, the Security Council had finally asked the secretary-general on November 9 to lay the groundwork for a multinational force to help end the crisis and to report back by November 20. Pressure mounted on the UN to move with a greater sense of urgency. The Canadians were ready to take the lead to form a multinational force to be sent to eastern Zaire. They agreed to offer General Maurice

Baril, former military adviser to the UN Peacekeeping Department, to serve as the force commander. Rapid consultations were taking place in New York. It was reported that U.S. troops would secure the Goma airport with troops in and around it, but would not move outside the immediate airport confines, and that the French would play a similar role in the Bukavu airport.

The operations were envisaged in two phases. In the first, Canada would lead the operation to secure routes for provision of humanitarian assistance and for voluntary repatriation movements. However, it was made clear from the start that the Canadian forces would not get involved in disarming or neutralizing those who opposed the refugee returns. Their intention was to intervene to contain the immediate humanitarian crisis but not to move on to take such steps as setting up humanitarian corridors along areas that locked security in Zaire and in Rwanda for the return of refugees. A more robust UN follow-up force, charged with assisting the returns would be deployed in the second phase. I was certainly pleased that at long last a multinational force might be deployed in eastern Zaire. However, I was certainly not satisfied with what seemed like a fairly limited mandate given to the Canadian-led force, which "would leave the fundamental problems unresolved and the risks for frontlines being frozen once the multinational forces will leave."[50] There were other problems, such as the relationship between the multinational force and the humanitarian operation, particularly to solve the overriding problem of the safe and voluntary return of refugees.

On November 14 the Mugunga camp was attacked by rockets, mortar, and heavy artillery. The next day the refugees surged out of Mugunga and started moving toward Rwanda. They fled east from the camps because the Rwandan and Congolese rebel forces had attacked the Mugunga camp from the west, giving half a million people only one way out: to go to Rwanda. I had been aware of the Rwandan threat to attack the refugee camps, but it was a great shock to confront the bold measures. As soon as I heard that the refugees had begun to exit the camps, I rushed to the television and was stunned by the sight. Soon it became a torrential human move, featuring the somber faces of families walking straight toward Goma and on to Gisenyi. It continued the whole day. The rate of return was twelve thousand per hour. By nightfall on the fifteenth some two hundred thousand returned to Rwanda, and another three hundred thousand were reported on the road.

The Rwandan attack on Mugunga had two immediate and wide-ranging results: the dampening of the international commitment to intervene in the Kivu crisis and the sudden massive return of refugees to Rwanda. On November 15 the Security Council had adopted Resolution 1080 which approved the deployment of the Canadian-led multinational force to Zaire. To Rwanda, the deployment of an international intervention force for eastern Zaire would have been the worst impediment to their military design. Vice-President Kagame disclosed his strategy in an interview with the *Washington Post* a year later. To him, the Congolese rebel forces were moving successfully to the north when he faced what "he feared the most—talk of a U.S. backed international intervention force for eastern Congo." He had to "prepare a scheme to bury the plan." The attack on the Mugunga camp from the west was Rwanda's countermeasure against any decision by the Security Council to deploy forces.[51]

Massive repatriation or no repatriation, the mandate given by the Security Council Resolution 1080 still remained in place. The deployment of the multinational force had presumed the existence of a large number of refugees in Zaire. Many governments began to express reservations about the urgent deployment of the force. Yet the situation in the region remained volatile. Most refugees returned to Rwanda, but many remained in Zaire and fled farther west.

In addition to the massive return that the Rwandan government had to confront, it chose to negotiate with Tanzania to receive back the close to one-half million Rwanda refugees who had been hosted there. Tanzania had been keen to unburden itself of its heavy load of refugees. Following the developments in Zaire, it also wanted to put an end to the Rwanda refugee problem. Rwanda wanted to solve the refugee problems in one go. To the Rwandans the large sprawling refugee camp belt along the border had been a genuine security threat.

Bilateral negotiations advanced without involving UNHCR. The Tanzanian government informed us that the repatriation exercise would be "ideally voluntary" but that the refugees would be told that they had no choice.

As it turned out, the repatriation turned disastrous. The leaders led the refugees away from the Rwanda border and marched them in the direction of Kenya. Tanzanian troops intervened and forced them back to cross the border to Rwanda. UNHCR was severely criticized by refugees, governments, and human rights groups for allowing such a devastating repatriation. In fact, the Rwanda refugee repatriations whether from Zaire or Tanzania were clear cases of forced return, the kind of return that UNHCR had consistently opposed but failed to overcome. The fundamental shortcoming was that we could not separate the military elements from the civilian elements, nor could we obtain help from the United Nations or member states. The militarized camps undermined the safety of the refugees and threatened the security of the states in the entire region.

While dealing with the painful aftermath of the repatriation from Tanzania, we also had to contend with the search and rescue operation of the missing refugees in North and South Kivu. The multinational force had to decide how best to implement its given mission. Many governments began to express reservations on the urgent deployment of the force, believing that the situation on the ground should be further assessed before any decisions were taken. At the same time, the situation was clearly far from settled. No cease-fire had been established between the Zairean government and the rebels. There were some five hundred thousand refugees scattered through eastern Zaire. The issue of the number of refugees in eastern Zaire became more and more contentious, reflecting the varying intentions of concerned governments.[52]

The U.S. military became heavily involved in information gathering. It carried out aerial observations from November 15 to 21 of an area approximately 100 kilometers wide in Zaire west of the Rwandese border. The survey estimated that some 600,000 had returned to Rwanda and identified a number of groups spread out in the region. However, what the observers could find was necessarily limited because of the weather, the thickness of the rain forest, and the area of coverage. The U.S. and British planes flew farther over an area 150 kilometers deep. They were able to identify a group of some 165,000 but no other substantial presence.

UNHCR, on the other hand, based its estimates on the population that existed before the exodus, which totaled about 1.2 million. Accepting the sizable returns from the camps in North Kivu, we calculated that some 700,000 refugees were still in Zaire. We sent teams out to look for refugee groups where possible in the Kivu area to collect information, as well as to gather returnee figures from Rwanda. The discrepancy between the two attempts was large, reflecting not only the reality of limited access but also the efforts by the U.S. and U.K. governments, strong supporters of Kigali, to downplay the problem.

Since the number of unidentified refugees left in Zaire had implications involving the mandate and deployment of the multinational forces, the number game turned political. UNHCR's original refugee population figure was brought under scrutiny. I decided to stand on my 1.2 million figure. The first registration of all refugees in Kivu had been done in January 1995. A census verification of the refugee population of the camps for September 1996 did not take place, but a population figure was agreed to by UNHCR and the World Food Programme (WFP) pending official verification. The figure of 719,000 for North Kivu was confirmed in a UNHCR and WFP assessment mission in October 1996, in which the U.S. government and the European Union participated as observers.[53] By any basis for refugee population estimation, I thought I held a strong position. Besides, I was annoyed by the attempt to lower the estimated number of refugees still missing in Zaire. Excuses were being sought for terminating the mission of the multinational force.

On December 13 Gordon Smith called to inform me that General Baril had recommended the end of the multinational force by December 31 and asked for my reaction. I distinctly indicated that I did not think that the mandate entrusted by Resolution 1080 had been accomplished. I immediately called Kofi Annan to report on my reaction and solicit his support. The next day Baril announced Canada's recommendation. He recognized the humanitarian efforts of the agencies and the continued needs on the ground. He found, however, that the multinational force in its present configuration could not carry on its expected function. In other words, "Canada is alone, there are no takers and therefore no operation." Soren Jessen-Petersen, UNHCR's representative in New York, who attended the meetings, concluded, "a sad end to a sad experience—as frustrating and infuriating to the Canadians as it has been to us."[54]

Ironically, this was also a time of tense anxiety for the United Nations. Secretary-General Boutros Boutros-Ghali's candidacy for a second term had been vetoed on November 19, and he had withdrawn his candidacy on December 5. The Security Council had been undergoing intense negotiations. On December 13 Kofi Annan, undersecretary-general for peacekeeping, was chosen to be the incoming secretary-general. I was happy that Annan was elected. He was the closest supporter of UNHCR in all its field operations. I wished him, and peacekeeping, well. UNHCR still had to carry on a major rescue operation in Zaire, alone with only humanitarian partners.

CONGO RESCUE OPERATION

The multinational force wound up its aborted mission at the end of 1996. While governments fought over the issue of the numbers of refugees stranded in Zaire, UNHCR had to embark on an unprecedented search and rescue operation for the lost refugees. The reality was that after the attacks on the camps, those refugees who had not returned to Rwanda fled in all directions. Some fled north beyond Masisi and crossed into Uganda. Some others went south through Fizi toward Tanzania. The majority headed west, dispersed, and disappeared deep into Zaire. Many stayed with their military leaders either because they relied on their protection or were compelled to remain. Many more perished rapidly.

Faced with this new and extraordinarily difficult situation, UNHCR decided that its only option was to proceed as fast as possible to solve the refugee problem through repatriation. At a meeting of senior staff at headquarters, it was agreed to avoid the reestablishment of camps and to search, provide emergency assistance as necessary, and explore means to transport the refugees back to Rwanda. In the vast area normally under the control of the Zairean government, UNHCR was to carry out a search and rescue operation with UN and NGO collaborators. The means we had were exclusively humanitarian. Speed was considered essential, for the longer the refugees stayed, the bigger the risk of their becoming involved in the conflict. The issue of who might assist in separating the militants and in ensuring staff security was hotly debated. In the Kivu camps, CZSC troops had been assigned to these tasks and had contributed substantially. However, in the context of civil war between government troops and the rebels, the CZSC might be obliged to join a Zairean counteroffensive, and UNHCR's credibility might be seriously compromised. Still, there were no alternative countries or organizations to turn to for help. We agreed that all outstanding payments to the contingents should be made up to the end of December, when the contracts would end; then we should examine what new arrangements could be negotiated. As for the area controlled by the rebels, UNHCR should continue its presence, even if substantially reduced, to search and help the refugees repatriate. The abandoned campsites were in catastrophic condition, and cleanup operations had to begin quickly. Eventually environmental rehabilitation would have to be undertaken, but it would be addressed after the situation stabilized.[55]

The operation started from the vicinity of Goma. The UN team in Goma met Laurent D. Kabila, the chairman of the AFDL, on November 16, 1996. I assigned Filippo Grandi to be the incoming head of the reestablished UNHCR office in Goma. As a top trained emergency officer who had proved his leadership during the Goma crisis in 1994, he was to carry out the difficult task of negotiating with the rebel groups while rescuing the fleeing refugees. The list of other UN agency staffers was presented. The UN operational agencies in the alliance-controlled territory were to set up offices in Bukavu and later in Uvira. Kabila promised to designate liaison staff of the AFDL at these points. It was the UN's understanding that the representation by its humanitarian agencies had no implication for recognition of the official status of the AFDL. At this first meeting Grandi requested access to the thousands of refugees in the area. Kabila expressed his support of the work of the humanitarian agencies. He also stated in blunt terms that the situation had changed so that there was no more need for humanitarian corridors or intervention by international force.[56] The UNHCR search team reported the first discovery of some forty thousand refugees on November 26. The search had been carried out by jeep and by foot. Whenever refugees were identified, the team was to help prepare them for return.

In the meantime, the front line moved rapidly west. The refugees also fled westward in parallel with the war. Piecemeal information of the whereabouts of refugees started to come to UNHCR from NGOs and local Zaireans. One group seemed to have gone some eighty kilometers northwest from Goma to Amisi and Tingi Tingi. Another from Bukavu had gone equally far west to Shabunda. Between Tingi Tingi, Amisi, and Shabunda, more than two hundred thousand refugees were reported to have organized themselves into camp settlements. In late December, UN agencies, accompanied by Zairean government officials, carried out a mission from Kinshasa to Tingi Tingi and Shabunda. They were able to witness the refugee presence. They could prove to the world that the refugees actually existed! But then the challenge was to decide what assistance to bring in and how. Airstrips were small and even waterlogged on most days. There was hardly any food, and people were eating roots and vegetables. Even lifesaving needs for the most vulnerable refugees would be impossible to deliver without resorting to rail and/or air and onward delivery by trucks. The mission recommended several emergency assistance measures, but the key question of how to undertake repatriation was hard to solve. The possibility of airlifts was debated, but aside from being an extraordinary logistical proposition, for Shabunda alone it would require more than a thousand flights for the kind of small aircraft that could land at airstrips to take back the existing population. Transporting by land would require political agreements among the government of Zaire, the AFDL, and the government of Rwanda to set up something of a humanitarian corridor. Then a neutral international force would be needed to ensure safety and adherence to such agreements. And military conflict was bound to spread in the meantime.[57]

The humanitarian situation in eastern Zaire continued to deteriorate. More than two hundred thousand Rwandan refugees identified in Tingi Tingi, Amisi, and Shabunda remained difficult to reach and were reported to be in desperate condition. On February 1, 1997, Grandi met with Kabila and his senior staff to solicit further support for the repatriation of refugees and for the limited provision of relief. He also raised the issue of security for the relief operation. Kabila expressed his satisfaction with the cooperation with the UN and assured cooperation with the humanitarian operation. He stated his concern, however, over the reports of human rights abuses caused by the ADFL. As for the forecast on the military situation, he said that "international pressure" was holding him back from taking over Tingi Tingi and that he was "hoping to reach a negotiated solution of the conflict."[58]

Emma Bonino, the head of the European Union's humanitarian office, who went to Zaire, called me on February 2 to tell me that Tingi Tingi was "more than desperate." She believed that the humanitarian agencies were doing their very best but advised that we should "all be more aggressive and get the politicians in there."[59] The front line moving west was badly affecting the refugee population. A large part of the Amisi group joined the Tingi Tingi group while the Shabunda group dispersed and moved elsewhere. Many of them were no longer accounted for. On the Zairean side of the front, security was deteriorating, including that for humanitarian organizations. In an incident at Kisangani, UNHCR staff members were even threatened by Serb mercenaries, who held them responsible for UNHCR's role in the Balkans.

In order to assess the situation properly, negotiate with the leaders concerned, and assist in the repatriation of the refugees trapped in Zaire, I decided to undertake an extended mission to the region. From February 7 to 16 I traveled to Zaire, Kenya, Burundi, Rwanda, Uganda, and Tanzania, to the capitals and the refugee assembly points. It was one of the most grueling of all the missions that I had undertaken. I started from Kinshasa. The reception was positive, although the government on the whole seemed to feel abandoned by the United Nations and the international community at large. The termination of the multinational force had been a major setback for Zaire, since it had expected the intervention to prevent the advancing attack by Rwanda and the Zairean rebel forces. I asked for the removal of all obstacles to relief personnel and goods in order to reach Kisangani, the largest city between Kivu and Kinshasa, which served as the operational focal point for rescue operations for the Rwanda refugees. All the Zairean authorities stated that they wanted to see the refugees repatriated not moved farther into Zaire. Prime Minister Kengo showed some flexibility and invited me to formulate proposals for the safe passage of the refugees, so long as the plan respected Zaire's territorial integrity and sovereignty.

It was precisely to cope with the sensitivity over sovereignty that I had started my visit from Kinshasa. From there we flew east to Kisangani in order to reach Tingi Tingi, where many refugees had assembled. At the Kisangani airport, governors of Haut-Zaire and Maniema provinces received our mission. Both emphasized that the humanitarian situation in the provinces was disastrous, with starving refugees and internally displaced persons. They criticized the UN agencies and the NGOs for spreading wrong information without fully coordinating their efforts for an effective relief operation. The two governors and we, accompanied by a host of journalists, took a battered-looking DC-3, a cargo plane that the IATA would not have approved. We landed at an airstrip where refugees had assembled on both sides. I visited the health clinic and the therapeutic and feeding center for unaccompanied minors. There were an estimated fifty-five hundred children. They were in awful shape. There was also an unusual setup to provide supplementary feeding for adults. I went as well to the warehouse, which was reasonably well stocked. I noticed the presence of many young men. Whether they all were ex-FAR members or young males of fighting age pressed to participate in the war was hard to judge. There were several CZSC soldiers who had accompanied the refugees all the way in their flight. I was told that nonpayment of their salaries was causing problems. I told them that the question had been addressed in Kinshasa and that they would be paid in the next few weeks.

The refugees were lined up with handwritten banners, highly critical of UNHCR. One of them declared: UNHCR RESPONSIBLE DE GENOCIDE INTELLECTUEL. UNHCR staffers who had managed the Kivu camps were singled out as culprits. One woman read out a note in which she first accused us of having betrayed the Rwandan refugees, then said we were expected to protect them and publicize their plight. An atmosphere of angry resentment prevailed. What was even worse was the fact that we knew that the particular airstrip on which we had landed was being used to bring both relief goods and weapons. There was a large arms cache in one part of the field.[60]

This stockpile of arms and ammunitions at the eastern edge of the landing strip in the middle of the camp concerned us greatly. The UNHCR staff had observed arms, ammunitions, and uniforms being supplied daily by the same planes that the humanitarian agencies used to transport their workers and supplies. Refugees unloaded arms from the planes, and most of the arms were destined directly for the front line; they might also be used to defend the camps. Moreover, at the time refugees from the Amisi site were approaching Tingi Tingi, fleeing ahead of the alliance advance. We left Tingi Tingi with a heavy heart. We had witnessed the refugees in the midst of a militarized setting awaiting a military confrontation. We could neither halt the entry of arms nor evacuate the refugees from the camps. I sent a message through Grandi and appealed to Kabila and to the AFDL not to attack the camps. An unknown village, Tingi Tingi, was put on the war map as the world watched the moving front line.

While very worried about the course of events, we flew out of Kisangani to Nairobi and farther on to Burundi, Rwanda, Uganda, and Tanzania. I recognized that the security situation in some parts of Burundi had somewhat improved. However, the government had embarked on a policy of regrouping and forcibly moving people from their villages to areas it considered safe. International organizations were expected to feed the people away from their homes and fields. I expressed my disapproval of such a forced displacement practice, which was accompanied by arbitrary military action. President Buyoya defended the policy as necessary to keep rebel fighters from infiltrating the villages and emphasized that it would be only temporary.

In Rwanda, President Bizimungu, Vice-President Kagame, and all senior officials expressed appreciation for UNHCR's contribution to the massive repatriation of refugees from Zaire and Tanzania that they had just undertaken. We made field trips to the villages to which the refugees had returned. They were still in makeshift accommodations. Now reintegration of the returnees was becoming the main challenge. The government emphasized the importance of continued UNHCR support. The president repeatedly insisted that when one-quarter of the population consisted of returning refugees, UNHCR had to stay on and help for a long period. The Rwandan government had requested UNHCR to help with the reintegration of the 1959–1960 caseload of Tutsi refugees and appreciated our support. However, it had been bitter over the assistance UNHCR had given to the Hutu refugees of 1994 in the camps in Goma and in the neighboring countries. Now that the majority had returned, they hoped for UNHCR's all-out support for those who had returned.

I explained to them that UNHCR would shift its policy focus to reintegration and reconciliation. We would concentrate on shelter programs and initiate a special program for women. Aloysia Inyumba, the young and resourceful minister of women and women in development, had alerted me that more than half the households in Rwanda were headed by women, many of them aged only sixteen to twenty. A women's initiative program that had been launched in postconflict Bosnia had proved helpful, and we were ready to extend the scheme to Rwanda. However, I had to emphasize that we would have to hand over the long-term rehabilitation work to development agencies, because donor governments would not fund UNHCR forever. I also drew attention to the continued presence of Rwandans in Zaire and the need for their repatriation. An estimated two hundred thousand refugees in the Tingi Tingi area might be tracking their way back. The president reaffirmed his readiness to receive them back, while those who had committed crimes would be judged according to the law.

In Uganda we discussed the security concerns of the Sudanese refugees in the northern part of the country. The main discussion, however, centered on the political and military developments in Zaire. President Museveni was in favor of an eventual negotiated settlement between the government and rebel forces. In his usual casual way, he observed that since one part of the Rwandese population had lined up with one part of the Zairean population, while another had allied itself with yet another, there would be no solution but through negotiation. In other words, he was looking for a solution that would be short of the removal of Mobutu. I got the impression that he had been making diplomatic overtures.

In Tanzania we visited Kigoma, the western port town on Lake Kivu. Boatloads of refugees were arriving from Zaire, and the town was overwhelmed by the urgent need to accommodate them. A large warehouse had been converted to serve as temporary reception center. We flew to the capital, Dar es Saalam. I shared with President Benjamin Mkapa my concern over the mop-up of Rwandan refugees that was still continuing. I emphasized the need to carry out the screening of the remaining refugees, as had been agreed upon at the time of the massive repatriation a few months before.

As we rushed through so many countries, it was extremely difficult to link up with UNHCR offices. Finally, at the Entebbe airport, as we were leaving Uganda on February 14, our satellite phone succeeded in connecting with headquarters in Geneva. We were informed of the impending danger at Tingi Tingi. I called Secretary-General Kofi Annan in New York and asked for his help. He quickly informed the five permanent members of the Security Council and issued a statement in which he appealed to both parties to stop turning the refugee camps into battlefields. Two weeks later UNHCR and all humanitarian workers were advised by local military authorities that their safety could no longer be assured. They were forced to leave Tingi Tingi. On March 3 at a press conference Kabila confirmed the takeover of Tingi Tingi and asked humanitarian workers to come back to assist with the repatriation of those who remained. When they managed to return from Goma a week later, they found only two thousand refugees left behind. Some one hundred sixty thousand were thought to have fled again westward. Many others had disappeared from the vicinity of the campsites. In fact Tingi Tingi proved to be the last line of defense for the Zairean forces. The AFDL moved rapidly north and entered Kisangani on March 15. The Zairean soldiers, looting on their way out, abandoned the city.

The search operation entered an even more difficult phase. Small groups of refugees were attacked whenever they came out of their hiding in the forest. The fact was that UNHCR's relief operation from the east had to be carried out in parallel to the AFDL's running the war, while operations in government-held areas in the west also had to retreat in parallel to the withdrawal of the government forces. In early April, UNHCR for the first time reached a large group of some eighty thousand refugees fleeing ahead of the advancing AFDL. We gave them food and other necessary aid and helped them settle in two makeshift camps in Kasese and Biaro, twenty-five to forty kilometers south of Kisangani. Grandi started negotiating with Kabila to airlift them back to Rwanda. The AFDL seemed uncertain of the composition of the population. It did not have time to purge the elements that were undesirable to it and therefore blocked our access and delayed responding to our request. While the relief workers tried to reach the refugees, the rebels and the Rwanda forces, together with some local villagers, ravaged the refugee communities. The troops sealed off the region.

It was at this point that Grandi called me from Kisangani. Having lost all contact with the people, what should UNHCR do? "Should we withdraw and denounce to the world that maybe refugees are being killed, or should I continue to negotiate and try to have access, at least as much access as I can, to rescue as many as we can?" It was not an easy decision for me. What was unfolding in the field was really a story of terror, killing, and human suffering. My concern was for the victims, but I also worried about the safety of my colleagues as they engaged in the rescue operation against forces determined to wipe out the refugee population in the thick Zairean rain forest. There were of course pros and cons to either decision. After a long discussion, I advised Grandi to stay. I believed that our presence near the refugees when they are in danger is the most important service we can give. There might still be lives we could save.

For my part, I tried to do everything possible to mobilize international pressure on the AFDL. I issued a joint appeal with EU Commissioner Bonino and the heads of UNICEF and the WFP, calling for humanitarian access. I wrote to the secretary-general informing him of attacks on humanitarian operations that were "orchestrated by the Alliance." The overall dilemma we faced was the need to "take and encourage any action that might stop and prevent such killings" and the probability that vigorous protest might lead to further obstruction to rescuing the refugees and putting the lives of humanitarian workers at risk.[61] Ephriam Kabaija, the Rwanda official who had always been the leading manipulator on punishing the Hutu refugees, had apparently been in the Kisangani area. He strongly reacted to the international protest and refuted as unfounded the UN allegations of refugee presence and massacre in Kasese and Biaro. I solicited strong intervention from Ambassador Mohamed Sahnoun, the joint special representative of the UN and OAU secretary-generals, and Aldo Ajello, the EU's special envoy to the Great Lakes region. Both of them were actively negotiating with Kabila and local Zairean leaders and firmly supporting UNHCR in the field to help assuage the humanitarian situation.

Pressure on Kabila brought results. He felt that he had become a "man under watch" and did not enjoy it. On the other hand, the AFDL and the Rwandan troops had succeeded in attacking the refugee population and again dispersing the survivors into the forest. On April 27 Kabila, after a long meeting with international negotiators, agreed to the airlift repatriation plan presented by UNHCR. However, he attached two conditions: first, that it be conducted by air directly from Kisangani to Rwanda, and second, that it be completed within sixty days beginning May 1. These were very difficult conditions to fulfill, considering the vastly scattered situation of the refugees and the numerous obstacles expected from the alliance. At the meeting, Grandi handed over to Kabila the letter in which I wrote of my grave concern over the missing refugees and asked for his cooperation to establish their whereabouts. I added that "as High Commissioner I am responsible to the international community for the international protection and physical well being of the Rwandan and Burundi refugees, in Zaire." I gave a rough estimation of the number of Rwandan refugees with whom we had lost contact to be almost 170,000 and of Burundi refugees to be still around 45,000.[62] A few days later I reported these developments to the Security Council in New York and asked for its continuing commitment to keep the pressure on all parties so that we could carry out the repatriation operation.[63]

UN planes were able to airlift more than ninety-six hundred Rwandan refugees from Kisangani in the first week of the operation. A shocking incident occurred on May 5, when a stampede took place in the freight train transporting refugees from Biaro to Kisangani. Ninety-two persons were suffocated or crushed to death among more than two thousand refugees packed in by the AFDL troops. The deaths were reported to have been caused by a rush following rumors that a particular freight train would be the last one sent to the area to pick up refugees. I was really shaken by this event in light of the fact that more than enough refugees had died of the prolonged effects of malnutrition, disease, and exhaustion, and so many others had been brutally killed by machetes and gunshots. As far as this particular incident was concerned, the immediate cause was the lack of proper communication between the alliance and UNHCR concerning the train operation. I insisted on the need for more consistent and continuous operational cooperation with the alliance and the local authorities.

The alliance authorized UNHCR to accompany trains carrying refugees. However, the overall security situation in eastern Zaire remained tense and dangerous.

The killings and atrocities carried out after October 1996 were committed by three groups: the former Zairean government forces (FAZ) and mercenaries; the former Rwandan Armed Forces (ex-FAR) and militia from the camps; Kabila's troops (AFDL) and the Rwanda government forces (RPA). The nature and scale of the killings and atrocities by each group differed significantly. The ADFL troops and their Rwandan allies, however, carried out large-scale killings of civilians and refugees.[64] In mid-May 1997 I sent a mission led by Dennis McNamara, director of international protection, to the Great Lakes region to assess the protection situation. The humanitarian agency staff operating in the region had observed that the Alliance forces embarked on a systematic "search and destroy" operation for Hutu refugees remaining in the area. There were ex-FAR troops and militias mixed in with refugee groups, but many unarmed civilians, including women and children, were victimized. The heavy involvement of the Rwandan troops was widely noted inasmuch as the perpetrators of the killings spoke Kiswahili and Kinyarwanda, languages used by those who came from southern Uganda, eastern Congo, and Burundi. In addition, many commanding officers were fluent in English, proving a close affinity to the RPA. In fact, the Rwandan troops seemed to have led the attacks on the Kasese and Biaro camps.[65]

The atrocities by the AFDL in Zaire attracted international attention. On May 17 the AFDL entered Kinshasa with relative ease and renamed the state the Democratic Republic of Congo. The conditions in the country, however, continued to deteriorate. Strong criticism emerged particularly from two fronts, the human rights community and the U.S. government. For some time the international human rights community had made active inquiries into the reported massacres and other serious violations of human rights. In March the UN high commissioner for human rights had requested the UN special rapporteur, Roberto Garreton, to investigate the allegations. After a short mission Garreton issued a preliminary report that identified forty massacre sites and recommended further investigation. The UN Commission on Human Rights, the intergovernmental UN body dealing with human rights, sent several more teams, accompanied by forensic experts, to Zaire. Though the teams were denied full access to sites, they reported to the commission on July 2 that the alleged massacres might even have genocidal implications. The Congolese government continued to block the UN investigation, and the secretary-general kept exerting strong pressure. I welcomed the undertakings by the human rights investigation teams. I hoped that the exposures could restrain, if not stop, further atrocities. Being on the ground, UNHCR could help facilitate their work through providing logistical support and other necessary services. At the same time, our staff had to be careful not to be identified with the human rights missions. In order for us to carry on our work of search and rescue as well as negotiate with the de facto authorities, humanitarian activities had to remain discreet and as much as possible nonjudgmental.

As for the United States, the exposures of killings and atrocities by the AFDL with the involvement of Rwanda obliged the administration to reorient its position. It should be recalled that while providing humanitarian assistance to the largely Hutu refugees in the camps in Zaire, the United States also extended military training and support to the Tutsi Banyamulenge in South Kivu as well as to the RPA. It was widely believed among the humanitarian workers operating in Rwanda and in Zaire that the U.S. training had enhanced the military capability of the Rwandan and alliance forces and that it had gone much further than tacit political support and soft security assistance. More active military support was considered to have been extended under the humanitarian demining and training program. During the time that killings and atrocities spread throughout Zaire, both Rwanda and Uganda consistently denied that their soldiers were fighting with the AFDL. The United States never openly questioned these denials. In fact I faced considerable difficulties because of the "outspokenly critical" attitude of the U.S. ambassador and his staff in Kigali to the efforts of human rights and humanitarian groups and "particularly [to] the work of UNHCR."[66] In contrast, the U.S. Mission in Geneva supported UNHCR and the humanitarian agencies and upheld their positions and activities.

As the Rwandan involvement drew international scrutiny, political, economic, and military support became an issue. Was the U.S. support to Rwanda helping Kabila and the AFDL? In response to questions by U.S. Representative Christopher Smith and testimony by Physicians for Human Rights at congressional hearings, the administration tried to downplay the significance of U.S. military assistance to Rwanda. While not ready to confront the role of Kabila's allies in the massacres, it took a clearer critical position on the human rights responsibility of Kabila himself.[67] As the human rights investigation teams faced difficulties in carrying out their work because of blockages and conditions placed by Kabila, the United States began to take steps favoring the investigations and insisting on accountability for the massacres that had taken place.

An important move came from the two visits to Congo by Bill Richardson, the U.S. permanent representative to the UN and President Clinton's personal envoy. His mission was to intervene with Kabila to come up with an overall settlement of the Congolese situation. In particular, he tried to pressure Kabila to cooperate with the repatriation of refugees as well as make serious concessions on the human rights investigation. Nudging Kabila on was important for Richardson not only for the solution of the refugee problem but also for UN relations with Africa. He had come to realize that an "extensive healing" was necessary between the UN and the Great Lakes countries. The defining point had been the failure to respond to the genocide. In discussions with leaders in the region, Richardson noted a deep distrust of the UN, including UNHCR, and of the international community, including the U.S. government. The leaders observed that the international community had sent additional troops and resources when the situation had become difficult in Bosnia but had pulled out when Rwanda turned difficult.[68] Besides the human rights investigation issue, Richardson thought there was a need for an impartial evaluation by eminent Africans.

Operational conditions in Congo continued to deteriorate. A critical situation surfaced on September 4, 1997, when authorities in Kisangani blocked UNHCR from reaching a transit center that held more than six hundred Rwandans and Burundians in preparation for return. Many had been undergoing medical treatment. My colleagues in Kisangani found out that in the two days that they were denied all access, the refugees in the transit center had been flown back to Kigali. There was no one left in the center for UNHCR to protect. I decided to report on what had happened in Kisangani and to announce my decision to suspend operations for Rwanda refugees to the Security Council.

After briefly summarizing the humanitarian situation in the Great Lakes region to the Security Council on September 9, I reported on the Kisangani incident. I emphasized that this was not an isolated case but attested to the context in which thousands of Rwandan and Burundian refugees were being killed by military forces and in which respect for humanitarian principles by governments in the region was rapidly deteriorating. I explained that I had therefore come to the conclusion that "the most basic conditions for protecting Rwandan refugees in the Democratic Republic of Congo have ceased to exist. The total lack of even minimum conditions for delivering protection and assistance obliges us to suspend our operations related to Rwandan refugees, including rehabilitation activities in the eastern provinces." I also shared my concern over the "safety and security of our staff and of other humanitarian agencies." Moreover, unlike the situation during the previous Kisangani crisis in April, when I had seriously considered suspension, there were very limited numbers of refugees whom we could rescue. The reaction in the council was tense. Expressing respect and support for my work, the members also voiced their concerns about Rwandans left behind and asked what I planned to do about it. I still recall the emotional plea by the ambassador of Guinea-Bissau who said that "HCR was the 'last hope' for those whom all had abandoned."

Announcing the suspension decision to the Security Council, I had an ulterior objective: to pressure the council to carry out what to

me was its side of the responsibility. It could not leave the task of confronting atrocities to the humanitarian staff forever. It needed to
come out more decisively against acts of injustice and breaches of
principles as well as address the root causes of problems in the region,
the unfair and inadequate political and judiciary systems, the poverty,
and the inequality. As far as UNHCR was concerned, I stated my
readiness to monitor and assess the conditions under which the
returnees were living in Rwanda, particularly those who were impris-
oned or who had been deported from neighboring countries. For the
increasing number of Rwandans who refused to be repatriated, I presented a plan to examine their claims in order to distinguish those
with valid claims and those who should be excluded from international protection. I made a strong pitch that "UNHCR will be able to
carry out its mandate only if states fulfill their obligations. Considerations of political and economic interest must not prevent from firmly
condemning the lack of respect for humanitarian and human rights
principles and respect internationally approved standards contained
in the OAU Refugee Convention."[69]

I felt a bit drenched after finishing a two-hour-long intense discussion with the council. After the session I briefed the press. I was
accompanied by U.S. Ambassador Richardson, at the time serving as
president of the council. He had visited the region twice and knew
and supported the UNHCR operation. He did not want me to
announce a final suspension, lest it adversely affect the secretary-
general's efforts to urge Kabila to accept the investigations into
human rights abuses. I compromised and agreed that at least to the
press I would emphasize my hopes that through council pressure,
Congo would change its attitude and make UNHCR's suspension
unnecessary. I added that I expected "a flurry of activities" on the part
of the Security Council to follow up on its declarations.

As things turned out, Kabila proved unmoving. In October,
UNHCR and the other international agencies and NGOs working
with refugees were ordered to leave Goma. The government also
commanded local authorities to seal the border between Rwanda and
Congo. The UNHCR staff began leaving Goma on October 6. On

the same day, Rwandans who had recently arrived in Congo were expelled. UNHCR was forced to suspend all operations for Rwandan refugees in the Democratic Republic of Congo. It was a disappointing ending. Yet by then UNHCR had accomplished most of the rescue operation.

There was, however, another distinct group of Rwandans that required UNHCR's attention. These Rwandans had moved farther west beyond the Congo border and entered some ten neighboring countries. Many of them were presumed to have been the remnants of the FAR and the Hutu militias that the AFDL and its allies had tried to destroy. Serious debate took place within UNHCR on the measures needed to determine the status of these people. To begin with, a strong sense of discomfort had prevailed within the office that we could not manage to separate genuine refugees from genocidaires, soldiers, and militias. We wanted to cease being associated with the perpetuation of impunity.

UNHCR mobilized protection officers from various field offices and put them to the task of screening the refugees. The position of the Rwandan government was one of serious skepticism. Aside from its basic view that all Rwandans must return, it was seriously concerned that screening might give the false expectation that there were still chances to remain in the countries in which they had sought asylum. The government was also worried that such a process might give the impression that Rwanda was not safe for return. It therefore exerted strong pressure on host governments to remove those seeking to stay. The screening exercise, however, encountered practical problems. Many refugees were simply unwilling or unable to give accurate information. Once they were recognized as entitled to refugee status, it was difficult to find ways to ensure them protection through local integration or third country resettlement. Moreover, what do you do with those who have been rejected? For the host governments, they could pose a greater problem than unscreened refugees, whom UNHCR would continue to assist.

Several countries postponed decisions to take part in the screening or simply disagreed with it. Most of them did not necessarily support the new government of Rwanda under Tutsi domination. Only in the Central African Republic, which had suffered serious lapses of security caused by the Rwandans, was UNHCR able to participate in the screening of 1,455 asylum seekers conducted by the government. Of these, 837 cases were granted refugee status, while 244 others were excluded. UNHCR had to find a solution for those recognized as refugees. A transit arrangement was worked out with Cameroon, but resettlement to the Scandinavian countries had yet to be explored. In the case of Congo-Brazzaville, the large Rwandan caseload of approximately 11,000 was clearly of a mixed nature. Besides women and children, it included former military and some of the most extremist elements. It was later in the spring of 1998 when I visited the country that I finally reached agreement with President Denis Sassou-Nguesso that rather than engage in individual screening as such, UNHCR would establish the "profiles" of the people and concentrate on helping the women heads of families, vulnerable individuals, and unaccompanied minors. The government would undertake local integration, provided it received external support. I recall appealing to the French government to respond to the request for assistance. Although the screening ended in a somewhat inconclusive manner, UNHCR's operation centered on Rwanda refugees in the Congo was largely over, except for some who stayed undetected in Kivu.

Transition from War to Peace

REPATRIATION UNDER DURESS

In the kind of intermittent hostilities that engulfed the Great Lakes region, no clear postconflict phase that signaled the start of refugee repatriation emerged in the region. In fact winners emerged only after prolonged periods of fighting, and agreements for peace were never finalized. The transition remained complex and prolonged. UNHCR had to apply different approaches in different places to settle problems.

For Rwanda, UNHCR's main operation was to assist the repatriation of refugees and to ensure their reintegration. In the six years between 1994 and 1999, more than three million Rwandans returned home from exile. They included disparate groups of people, who had fled the country over various periods of time. The majority returned through organized channels, but many returned spontaneously. Many of the latter were ethnic Tutsis who had been in exile since 1959 and who returned en masse starting in 1994 after the victory of the RPF. Altogether they numbered more than eight hundred thousand and constituted the old caseload refugees. The government showed strong interest in the repatriation of the Tutsi refugees. By radio broadcast, it invited them to come back from the neighboring countries. From Burundi relatively well-to-do people drove back in their cars and established themselves in Kigali. Many others returned from Uganda and northern Zaire. When I visited Rwanda in February 1995, I was flown to Nyagatare, in the northeast, to witness returnees accompanied by large herds of cattle. The government had to find stretches of land to settle them and asked UNHCR for support.

The "new caseload" referred to those who had fled in 1994 during or following the genocide, primarily ethnic Hutus. They were mostly forced to return en masse in 1996 and 1997 from Zaire and Tanzania. UNHCR provided operational support to the government agencies that administered the repatriation process. From the very first months after the genocide and the massive outflow of refugees to the neighboring countries, UNHCR considered return the main solution to the enormous displacement on hand. As early as August 1994, we sent Robert Gersony to Rwanda to assess the conditions for repatriation and reintegration. After the expulsion of refugees by the Zairean government in August 1995 and its announcement of its policy to complete the repatriation by the end of the year, UNHCR assisted the Rwanda government to prepare for the reception by setting up transit centers to provide temporary accommodation, health care, and meals while they awaited transportation back to their communes of origin. In hindsight, these preparations proved helpful for the returnees who underwent great difficulties after the attacks on the Goma camps on November 14, 1996, that forced them to return.

The more we came to know the circumstances of the attacks by the joint Rwandan and Congolese rebel forces, the less sanguine we became about the connivance that led to the military action. Nevertheless, UNHCR had to help this repatriation. I issued a press statement stating our readiness to assist: "We have been planning and waiting for repatriation to happen for two years. Now that they are coming back in such numbers, we are putting additional resources on the ground. We are determined to help them resume their normal lives." The rate of return was twelve thousand per hour. By nightfall on November 15 some two hundred thousand reached Rwanda, and another three hundred thousand were reported to be on the road. UNHCR mobilized all available staff and resources to meet the needs of the returning refugees. President Bizimungu called me to thank UNHCR for its efforts to support and assist refugees returning to Rwanda.

There were undoubtedly rough handlings of refugees who were not walking with the crowd back to Rwanda. Some were picked up and forcibly trucked to Rwanda. For those who returned, the government, together with UNHCR and other international organizations, made major efforts to cope with their reception. Because of the large numbers, the government abandoned screening at the border and decided to conduct it at the communes. Emergency aid was provided upon arrival, but UNHCR's regular repatriation packages, consisting of two months' food and other items, were also to be given at the communes. Buses and trucks ran back and forth, moving refugees to their final destinations. For most of the arrivals coming by foot, way stations were quickly set up along the return routes, providing food, water, and emergency medical care. Also, stockpiles of goods were readily available. The Rwanda government took the position that since the vast majority of refugees had returned, all international aid should now be directed to Rwanda. It called for a Multinational Marshall Plan for Rwanda. It reinforced its opposition to the deployment of the multinational force and argued that the need no longer existed. In fact the attack had been designed to block such intervention.

The sudden massive return of refugees caused serious unrest in Rwandan society. A significant number of individuals who had participated in the genocide and military activities had returned mixed in with refugees. There was rejection of the returnees. Extrajudicial executions based on popular and public denunciations occurred. There was a significant increase in killings and other attacks against the survivors and old caseload of refugees who returned. In the months following the massive repatriation, several incidents took place against expatriate workers. The murder of four members of a UN Human Rights Commission observer mission shocked the international human rights and humanitarian community in Rwanda. The security situation inside the country became a source of serious worry.

Coping with the aftereffects of large-scale returns from Zaire to Rwanda had been a tremendous challenge. Then the Tanzanian government began pressing for the repatriation of Rwandan refugees. Having followed the developments in eastern Zaire, the Tanzanian government decided to put an end to its Rwandese refugee burden. The principal secretary of the Ministry of Home Affairs informed the UNHCR representative that the president had requested that the ministry carry out the repatriation of the refugees. Furthermore, he stated that the Rwandan authorities had just confirmed to the president that they were now ready to receive the returnees from Tanzania. The UNHCR representative's report from Dar es Salaam indicated that Tanzanian authorities had been in close contact with their Rwandese counterparts at central and local levels. The repatriation exercise was to be "ideally voluntary, but it would be made clear to the refugees that they do not have any choice."

The process foresaw three sequential steps. The first was to take the persuasive approach and pressure the intimidators to refrain from blocking the returns. The second step was to resort to more forceful means of separating intimidators from the refugee camps by police and soldiers. After the closedown of the camps, the third step was to escort the refugees back to Rwanda. All steps were to be completed within a month. The decision left to UNHCR was how far to cooperate with the proposed repatriation. Tanzania expected us to be closely associated with this operation.[70] We were very concerned about our participation in an operation that might involve nonvoluntary repatriation with actual use of force.

On December 2, 1996, the Tanzanian authorities decided that all Rwandan refugees should return to Rwanda before December 31. UNHCR advocated flexibility and voluntary as well as orderly returns. The government assured the UNHCR representative that those who feared return would be allowed to remain in Tanzania and go through screening—i.e., examination of the validity of their claim for persecution. However, the government also made known that if UNHCR refused to be associated with the operation, it would carry it out as a bilateral exercise with Rwanda. After objections from UNHCR, we were assured that the repatriation would be voluntary and orderly, and flexibility would be exercised with respect to the deadline. UNHCR agreed to issue a joint communiqué with the Tanzanian government on December 5 and called on the refugees to repatriate.

The statement explained that the responsibility of the repatriation operation would be assumed by the Tanzanian police and, if necessary, the army. UNHCR would closely cooperate, and it was reassured that "the repatriation process will be carried out in an orderly and humane manner." UNHCR explained that it had already "made arrangements for reception and transit facilities, for the provision of food and material assistance, and the reintegration of returnees in their communes of origin" in Rwanda. The Tanzanian government and UNHCR urged all refugees to make preparations to return.[71] The Tanzanian authorities gave assurances that no force would be used and that those who wished to remain could. However, these guarantees were not included in the final joint statement, presumably for fear that publicizing the option to remain would play into the hands of extremists.

When repatriation began on December 11, thousands of refugees started leaving the camps on foot, carrying their belongings with them. They first headed toward the Rwandan border, but on the second day they were diverted in the opposite direction, farther east inside Tanzania, and toward Kenya. It soon became apparent that the refugee leaders in defiance of orders were directing the refugees away from repatriation. The Tanzanian government immediately deployed troops to redirect the refugees. The repatriation became a messy forced operation. There were more and more incidents of misconduct by the military and violations of human rights. Eventually some 483,000 refugees were sent back to Rwanda.

UNHCR came under severe criticism by refugees, governments, and nongovernmental organizations. The protest from human rights organizations was particularly harsh. Amnesty International issued a report that accused UNHCR of "condoning the mass *refoulement* of refugees to Rwanda by neighboring countries." In the organization's judgment, "to a greater or lesser extent, UNHCR has cooperated in repatriation operations from Burundi, Zaire and Tanzania." Underlying its criticism was the assessment that UNHCR had considered it generally safe for refugees to return to Rwanda and had failed to recognize the serious level of human rights violations in the country.[72] I recognized that UNHCR had failed to ensure a voluntary and orderly repatriation of refugees from Tanzania to Rwanda. I should have come out more strongly in expressing my initial doubts. As of this day, I am not certain if UNHCR could have actually prevented the repatriation and especially the course from turning so disorderly and violent. We might have stood aside and condemned the rough handling by the military. We might have disassociated ourselves from the operation. Instead, what we did was compromise, to save what little there was to save.

UNHCR was fully aware that the situation of safety and human rights observance in Rwanda was far from adequate or ideal. But the situation in the camps had been equally inadequate and insecure. Forces of genocide controlled the camps and continued to intimidate refugees who opted to return. At the bottom of the problem were the existence of refugee camps militarily and politically dominated by ex-

FAR soldiers and militias and the new Rwanda government's attempt to establish its security internally and externally against the remnants of the former regime. The asylum country, whether Tanzania or Zaire, had to pay a heavy price. After the fiasco in Tanzania, I restarted negotiating with the Tanzanian authorities, to deal properly with those refugees who had stated their desire not to return. We had to insist that their claims to asylum be examined and that they should not be simply rounded up and sent back to Rwanda.

Tanzania had freed itself of Rwandan refugees by the end of 1996 through the forceful repatriation of 483,000 persons. With the large part of the Rwandan refugees having returned, the challenge of solving the refugee problems in the Great Lakes region became diversified. The largest concentration of refugees in the region was the 260,000 Hutus from Burundi who were at the Tanzanian-Burundian border. Negotiation between the two governments took place on and off, and repatriation from Tanzania remained stalled.

In the Congo UNHCR's efforts to search for and rescue thousands of Rwandan refugees continued until September 1997. There were others in Congo (Brazzaville) and neighboring states. By then UNHCR had evacuated 63,000 refugees by air, in addition to 215,000 who had returned overland. The repatriation of Hutu refugees from Kivu resumed the next year upon the request of President Bizimungu and the reestablishment of UNHCR presence in Kivu. Some 35,000 were repatriated in 1998. UNHCR's main involvement with Rwandan refugees became centered on their reintegration.

In Burundi the short-lived civilian administration led by the Hutu president Sylvestre Ntibantunganya had been overthrown by the Tutsi former president Major Pierre Buyoya on July 26, 1996. The neighboring countries declared an economic embargo against Burundi as it set up a government based on the coup d'état. The peace process stalled within the country. One positive development was the closing of Rwandan refugee camps in Burundi in August 1996. A combination of factors contributed to the return of Rwandan refugees from Burundi. The old caseload Rwandan refugees had returned quickly after the establishment of the Tutsi government in 1994. More than 250,000 who had fled in 1994 were prompted to return when the local environment turned hostile and the economic embargo created tension in Burundi. With encouragement from the Rwandan government, UNHCR could carry out a well-organized repatriation, closing all seven Rwandan refugee camps and transporting the refugees back to their home communes. The refugees were provided a full repatriation package: two months' food, plastic sheeting, blankets, and agricultural seeds. The 123 Rwandan refugees who chose not to return were allowed to stay pending appropriate solutions.

The internal situation in Burundi, however, continued problematic. The government forced Burundians to designated sites under the so-called regrouping policy, which was defended as a temporary security measure for the population from insurgents. The government was in fact creating groups of internally displaced population, which the military moved by arbitrary action and which became dependent on external aid. The regrouping policy caused complications for the humanitarian organizations, which had to assist the displaced populations caused by government action. The security situation improved in some parts of the country in the north but continued tense in the southern provinces. The outflow of refugees continued from Burundi to Tanzania.

The Burundian military ascribed the lack of security in the southern provinces to incursions from refugee camps in Tanzania. There was grave mistrust between Burundi and Tanzania. On the other hand, Tanzania pushed the Burundian peace process and advocated strong sanction measures against the Buyoya regime. In my repeated meetings with Buyoya, the president accused me of allowing the refugee camps to become the base for rebel attacks against Burundi. My position was that UNHCR would make all efforts to maintain the civilian character of refugee camps. In fact we increased the presence of Tanzanian police within the camps to make sure that no military recruitment or training would be carried out there. We also strengthened the police capacity by providing equipment and some incentive payments. While strengthening the camp security conditions, I insisted that UNHCR could not be held responsible for what happened outside the camps. In reality, the Burundian refugees were critical of the Buyoya regime and represented groups opposed, at least politically, to the government.

The Burundian peace process was reenergized when President Nelson Mandela was appointed the new mediator in December 1999. Some agreements on the ethnic balance of the military were reached. Some dismantling of camps for the internally displaced took place. UNHCR and UN agencies started preparing for repatriation of refugees, dividing the responsibilities according to sector and geographic areas. The Burundian government was interested in promoting a well-planned repatriation and held a repatriation conference at the occasion of my visit in June 2000. I made a field trip to Ruhigi, the western province adjacent to Tanzania, to open a new school wing that would be ready to receive refugees. I noted that the visit was made possible by a very large deployment of military forces, as violence in Burundi worsened with the expected conclusion of peace. The Hutu speaker of the Assembly, with whom I had had long-term contact, observed that with a peace agreement possibly becoming closer, antigovernment forces were trying to gain the maximum ground, especially in strategic areas near the capital.

The sobering fact was that refugees were caught in the political struggle among the government of Burundi, the opposition groups, and the governments in the region, particularly Tanzania. In the Arusha process, the refugees were becoming the pawns of the various interest groups. The Burundian government wanted them back and tried to demonstrate that the conditions for their return were ripe and preparations were advancing. The opposition resorted to violent action to prove the unsatisfactory state of internal security. Tanzania was not keen to become engaged in tripartite talks with Burundi and UNHCR over the repatriation of refugees. The Arusha process as well as the repatriation of Burundi refugees remained stalled at the end of my UNHCR tenure and beyond.

FROM REINTEGRATION TO RECONCILIATION

The repatriation of over three million exiles between 1994 and 1999, particularly of two million refugees in a very short period in 1996, generated enormous rehabilitation needs in Rwanda. There was immediate rehabilitation work that could not await contributions from long-term development sources. For example, two hundred thousand school-age children returned in a few months' time. While the education system itself had to be redeveloped, immediate solutions had to be found to meet the shortages of schools, equipment, teachers, and funds. UNHCR had to address the needs of shelters and such public service facilities as schools, health centers, and water supply systems. If we were to make repatriation sustainable, we would have to examine the issues underlying Rwandan society that had led to division and conflict. In short, our contributions had to aim at rebuilding Rwandan society and advancing national reconciliation. We decided to achieve these objectives through several distinct initiatives: first, establishment of a nationwide shelter program; second, the rebuilding of the judiciary system, and third, promotion of the progress of Rwandan women.

A nationwide shelter program met several basic needs. In the chaos after the genocide in 1994, around 40 percent of the houses in the rural areas were destroyed, while eight hundred thousand Rwandans who had been out of the country in exile for several decades returned and occupied the houses of those who had been killed or who were in refugee camps outside the country. Two years later hundreds of thousands streamed back into the country and often found their houses destroyed or illegally occupied. The country was in a very fragile state in 1996, with old caseload and new caseload returnees, survivors of genocide as well as genocidaires, finding themselves with no solutions in sight. UNHCR understood that the property and shelter issues were central to alleviating the growing tensions. It decided to act quickly by rehabilitating and building as many houses as possible and creating new villages throughout the country.

Over a five-year period between 1995 and 1999, UNHCR spent $183 million for reconstructing or rehabilitating almost a hundred thousand houses, to cover the shelter needs of half a million Rwandans. The program targeted returnee populations, paying special attention to woman- and child-headed households and war victims. About 27 percent of these houses were constructed in almost three hundred settlements. Settlement sites were dispersed widely in rural areas throughout the country. To be designated as a settlement site by UNHCR, over twenty houses had to be built in one location, and 73 percent of UNHCR-supported houses were built in scattered and clustered locations. Both in settlement sites and in clustered and scattered locations, the beneficiaries made adobe bricks, dug the earth for foundations and latrines, and constructed earthworks and embankments. Two wooden doors and four windows were included in UNHCR's shelter package, which consisted of corrugated iron roofing sheets, poles, nails, and metal straps and plastic sheeting.

The UNHCR shelter sites were expected to link up with existing social infrastructures, such as water supply, health, and education services. One controversial issue was the relationship between the UNHCR-supported shelter program and the government-promoted village building program. Grouped resettlements that consisted of housing, basic social services, and infrastructure had existed as a traditional strategy to deal equitably with land shortages and economic opportunities. In 1996 the Rwanda government made a renewed push toward establishing villages of returnees. The perceived involuntary nature of setting up these villages led some donor governments to withhold support from UNHCR's shelter projects. UNHCR made efforts to distinguish between cases of voluntary and coerced schemes of village settlements and supported the government program when it allowed for the consent of the beneficiaries.

In June 1999, when I made field trips to Umutara Province, I was both impressed and surprised by the extent of our rehabilitation work. UNHCR had built new communities consisting of housing units centered on schools and clinics. A UNHCR water engineer had installed a water supply system that drew water from lower-level underground sources. What crowned the success for me was the multiethnic selection of inhabitants. The nationwide shelter program brought two distinct additional advantages: the first was its effect on the prevention of conflicts over land and property possession; the second was the access it provided to monitor the local reintegration of returnees.[73]

Rebuilding the judiciary system was an exceptional effort that UNHCR undertook in Rwanda. Our assistance ranged from provision of the most basic office supplies and equipment to the rehabilitation of courthouses and the training of judicial personnel. UNHCR's mandate to ensure the protection of refugees covers the repatriation as well as the reintegration period. In an extraordinary situation, such as in Rwanda, in which the capacity of the national authorities to provide protection to returning citizens was limited, UNHCR had to maintain a field presence in order to gain and retain access to the returnees in need. It was also in our interest to accelerate the process of reestablishing the rule of law for the population in general as well as for those still out of the country who were contemplating return.

Rwanda's judiciary system needed to be rebuilt almost from scratch. UNHCR provided large quantities of office supplies and such equipment as desks, chairs, computers, and photocopiers, so that judicial personnel could carry out basic work. Moreover, we rehabilitated or built large numbers of tribunal buildings, courthouses, and prosecutors' offices in the prefectures. The former government had destroyed what it could as it fled the country. Ministry of Justice buildings had been stripped bare. In order to bolster the judicial system, UNHCR also financed the translation, publication, and distribution of numerous documents. These ranged from the Constitution of the republic of Rwanda (June 10, 1991) and fundamental Laws of the Rwandese Republic Until 26 May 1995 to the African Charter on Human Rights (June 27, 1981), the Universal Declaration on Human Rights (December 10, 1948), and the Covenant on Civil and Political

Rights (1966). Other publications were: *Procedures for Prosecuting Crimes of Genocide and Crimes Against Humanity, Procedures for Investigating Evidence Relative to Confessions and Pleadings, and Lessons on Inheritance and Guardianship of Minors in Rwanda.* These legal documents were relevant to a wide range of problems related to justice throughout the country.

The killings and flight into exile of judicial personnel in 1994 meant that there were few magistrates and defense attorneys after the genocide. In 1995 and 1996, UNHCR financed a Belgian-based judicial NGO to provide basic intensive training to 150 persons to become inspectors and officers of the Judicial Police. We supported further intensive training and seminars on judicial process, procedures, and Rwandan law. The seminar program targeted a wide range of judicial personnel, from judges, attorneys, local authorities, civil servants, and police officers to prison authorities. The rebuilding of the judiciary was taking place against the backdrop of overcrowded prisons, in which more than 130,000 genocide suspects awaiting trial were incarcerated. Substantial international assistance was directed toward the enlargement and improvement of the prisons. UNHCR did not target its assistance to the prisons but attempted to improve the overall judicial system, which was more directly linked with assuring the rights of the returning refugees.[74]

The Rwandan Women's Initiative, to address the unique problems women faced in the country, began in January 1997. The main objective was to empower women to be proactive in the country's development. In postconflict societies in general, families headed by women dominate the scene. In the case of Rwanda, many families were headed by girls looking after several younger brothers and sisters. I believed that the reintegration of women and their participation in the economic, social, and cultural activities of the country would be key to the country's development. We drew from our experience in the Bosnian Women's Initiative and decided to concentrate on bringing progress to women as one of our main recovery programs in Rwanda. The projects supported under the women's initiative were administered by UNHCR and channeled through funds given to the Ministry of Gender, Family, and Social Affairs. We were fortunate that it was headed by Aloysia Inyumba, who had worked closely with us as minister of women and women in development. She went all out in her determination to bring changes to women and through women to Rwanda. Projects supported under the initiative were self-help–oriented and multisectoral in approach.

A wide range of training activities aimed at the empowerment of women was introduced. To begin with, women had to be trained for a variety of income-generating activities. Proposals, such as training in brickmaking and brick selling in response to construction needs, arrived from prefectural offices and local and international NGOs. Other activities, such as coffee grinding, mushroom cultivation, and fuel-efficient stove production, represented areas close to daily family living. Training to engage in commercial activities, such as accounting, marketing, and profit management, was also introduced. Women were given opportunities to participate in basic vocational training, from literacy, agricultural skills, and pottery to tailoring.

Of particular significance was the effort to promote women's rights. UNHCR supported research in the area of women's rights, in particular to inheritance and property. Legal rights to land and property, marked by the return of several million people from exile, were complex in Rwandan society. Underlying the efforts to strengthen the rights of women was the recognition that the overall level of education, particularly of girls, had to be raised. Workshops were set up to train girls to become school administrators, government officials, religious leaders, and representatives of women's groups. Public information campaigns were launched to sensitize the public to the importance of girls' education. UNHCR supported schools that accommodated female students, including an experimental girls' boarding high school outside Kigali.[75]

A major objective of the women's initiative was the networking of women and women's organizations. The headquarters of a leading women's association, Club Mamans Sportives, was installed in 1997 with some UNHCR funding. I was visiting Kigali at the time and was invited to attend the opening event. Among the founders were well-educated refugee women who had returned from Burundi. They had taken the initiative to plan and implement the establishment of a women's center. The rambling one-story building was constructed to accommodate meetings, seminars, and recreational activities as well as to hold training courses on tailoring, cooking, hygiene, nutrition, and literacy. A surprise occurred while I was there. The leaders decided to honor me with a gift. It was a cow, a special present given to express highest form of appreciation in Rwandan society. I was perplexed but received it as gracefully as I could. I did, however, leave its custody to the center. Every time I returned to Kigali, I went through the motion of receiving a calf and then turned it over as well to the center.

Despite the substantial progress made since 1994, Rwanda still found itself in a fragile position. UNHCR and other agencies made concerted efforts to help the nation building process at both the government institution and community rebuilding levels. The international donors extended substantial resources through UNHCR. However, reconstructing a conflict-torn country, especially following a genocide, proved formidable. The challenge was not simply to rehabilitate the physical infrastructure and to restore the administrative capacity. It was also to tackle the issues of justice and reconciliation between groups and individuals with differing and dividing memories and experiences. UNHCR had to underline its repatriation operation by constant efforts to seek reintegration, in short to bring people together.

REFUGEE PROTECTION AND STATE SECURITY

Repatriation and reintegration of refugees advanced substantially in Rwanda, but not in the neighboring countries in the Great Lakes region. The Kabila-led AFDL forces supported by the Rwandan allies unseated the government in Kinshasa on May 17, 1997. Though fighting continued between the AFDL and the remnants of the former Zairean regime, these armed groups, which included the Hutu refugees, no longer seemed to pose a threat to Rwanda. The Rwandan and Ugandan armies moved deep into the heart of Congo and stayed there. The situation produced a large number of internal human displacements, but any acute humanitarian emergency seemed out of sight. I believed that the time had come for a Great Lakes region-wide initiative to heal the wounds of the past years and to move the entire region toward rehabilitation and reconciliation.

I dispatched several senior colleagues to several capitals in central Africa to examine this issue. I discussed the subject with the secretary-general of the OAU, Salim Ahmed Salim. He agreed that the time was ripe for some healing initiatives. At the meeting of the World Economic Forum in Davos in January 1998, I was able to hold private meetings with President Museveni of Uganda and President Thabo Mbeki of South Africa. Museveni had superb political sense, and Mbeki outstanding strategic insight. Both expressed support. The idea of a regional conference emerged out of these consultations. Museveni was prepared to host a meeting and gave me practical advice on the modalities. Mbeki pledged backup in case a conference proved infeasible in the Great Lakes region. Although there were many problems to be resolved, the overall humanitarian situation in the region had reached something of a lull. The moment seemed better than ever since 1993 for undertaking regional consultation.

On my side, I decided to tour East Africa and test the grounds from February 5 to 25, 1998. It was the most extensive trip that I undertook as high commissioner, covering nine countries in three weeks. As for the immediate problems that had to be addressed on this trip, three required particular policy attention: the Burundi-Tanzania tension, the political development in Rwanda, and the general stability in Zaire. One of the staff who accompanied me throughout this mission was Pierce Gerety, then UNHCR's coordinator for the Great Lakes region. His dedication to refugees and to the humanitarian cause was special and deep. He flew in all kinds of small planes and constantly exposed himself to a lot of danger. He survived all these hazards but died in the Swissair crash in September 1998, as he left New York for Geneva.

It was my very good luck that I could start my mission by visiting the former president of Tanzania, Mwalimu Nyerere, in his village in

Butiana. After a two-hour flight and a fifty-minute drive, my colleagues and I were warmly welcomed by Nyerere. I had had several occasions to consult him over the preceding few years, and I welcomed the chance to spend several hours with him in his modest rural house. He shared his concern over the growing impact of the Tutsi-Hutu conflict in the Great Lakes region, as it began to color domestic politics in ethnic terms throughout the region. He seemed to think that ethnic issues were complicating Tanzanian politics. Refugee problems were no longer purely humanitarian but political questions. He recalled that during his presidency he had been a dictator who could receive refugees to the country. Now, in a democratic setting the refugee issue had become politicized. He believed, however, that solving the ethnic problem within Burundi would be difficult but was possible with time. There were opposition parties and highly qualified individuals. He observed that Rwanda did not have the political institutions to deal with the problem. He thought the Burundian process might eventually have an impact on the political course in Rwanda.

Visiting Tanzania and Burundi, I realized the depth of distrust on both sides. The presence in Tanzania of 260,000 Hutu refugees from Burundi represented at the time the largest refugee concentration in the region. President Buyoya reiterated firmly to me that in his opinion, Tanzania was supporting the Hutu extremist rebels operating in southern Burundi. The Tanzanian government categorically denied this allegation. I spent two days visiting refugee camps in the border district. I was confident that no military activity was visible inside the camps, even though the refugees were undoubtedly very much politicized and highly critical of the Burundian regime. Obviously, I could not be held responsible for what went on outside the camps. To avoid the repetition of what had happened in Zaire, I promised to provide what might be termed security packages. In Tanzania, for example, UNHCR would develop more systematic support and training for the police operating in refugee camps.

What impressed me most in this mission was the change I noted in the political environment in Rwanda. My schedule was packed with field trips. I was taken to visit UNHCR projects: the shelter projects for returnees in Kibungo, the Congolese refugee camp in Buyumba, a training center for women. It was significant that Emanuel Gasana, a hard-line senior official who had represented Rwanda at the Bujumbura Conference and objected strongly to any reference to internal displacement in Rwanda, accompanied me throughout the field visits. I noted from the conversation that instead of the predominantly "justice"-based discussion in which the Rwandans had engaged in the past, they were now talking about "reconciliation" and even "healing the wounds." Now that Kivu had been brought under Rwandan control, the officials were much less worried about the security threats from across the border and seemed to have relaxed their tight grip within the country. The government was setting up a Commission on National Unity and Reconciliation, headed by my trusted friend Aloysia Inyumba. UNHCR was prepared to support this endeavor. I broached the subject of holding a regional meeting on state security and refugee protection. To my great relief, Gasana reacted positively. In the past Rwanda had consistently refused the idea of a conference on peace and reconstruction in the Great Lakes region.

A second issue that Rwanda pursued was UNHCR's continued presence in the country to carry on a rehabilitation program. Having largely completed the repatriation of refugees, UNHCR started planning to terminate its program and hand over the work to development agencies. Already some donors were criticizing us for what they perceived as overstepping our responsibility and moving into development work. I had pressed the development agencies to accelerate their assistance, but their entry remained slow. It was the difference in the speed and mode of operation that produced a gap between the work of humanitarian and development agencies.

UNHCR set up a joint unit with the UN Development Program in Kigali to coordinate and prepare joint projects. The Rwandan government accurately perceived the nature of the impending gap. One official stated that "we want roofs for the houses, and we want UNHCR to carry out this program, because you actually put roofs on the houses." I emphasized that UNHCR could not and would not withdraw before other agencies became active on the scene. I tended to look at rehabilitation not as a material assistance program but as a social program to encourage communities emerging from conflicts to live in peace again. To me, rehabilitation was not an unnecessary expansion of UNHCR's mandate but the essential accompaniment to consolidate the solutions for refugees. Ultimately, it was a way to prevent future crises, but the development agencies would have to be convinced of their expected role.

A big surprise came at the press conference outside the presidential house. In responding to international journalists, President Bizimungu stated that he did not hold UNHCR responsible for the daunting problem of not separating combatants from refugees in the Zairean camps. It was the international community that did not respond to UNHCR's cry for help. I was both startled and impressed by such a clear enunciation of the president's position. Partly it reflected his confidence that the threats from the refugee camps had been overcome. I took it also as his recognition that UNHCR had not shied from attempting to solve what seemed like an intractable problem for so long.

The February 1998 visit to Kinshasa concentrated on regaining access to Rwandan refugees with whom UNHCR had lost contact after we had suspended our operation in Kisangani and when we were ordered to leave Goma in October 1997. I was treated properly as a state guest since I was the first head of an international agency to visit the Democratic Republic of Congo, renamed from Zaire. I stressed the importance of repatriating the Rwandan refugees as well as bringing back the Congolese refugees from neighboring countries. I also stated my willingness to examine the rehabilitation needs of areas that had been damaged by the presence of refugees. On the way back from Kinshasa, we made a short stop in Bukavu. At one time, on both sides of the road from the airport to the city, blue refugee tents filled the horizon. Now no refugee camp was in sight. Green foliage covered the land. The refugees had disappeared: killed, returned, or still lost? Congo too seemed ready to talk things over with its neighbors.

All the leaders I consulted with in the course of the tour shared a strong sense of dissatisfaction. They criticized the international com-

munity for not playing a more decisive part in dealing with the genocide in Rwanda and its aftermath. The strongest words came from
Prime Minister Meles Zenawi of Ethiopia, who accused the Security
Council of what he called its criminal negligence. I admitted that
there were limits to humanitarian action, but I then stated that
regional leaders were also responsible for not acting more positively.
Zenawi had taken the initiative for the OAU to investigate the causes
and establish responsibilities for the Rwandan massacres. He represented a new generation of African leaders who had fought for and
won their positions and were ready to assert their views.

All the leaders with whom I talked agreed that the mixed nature
of refugee caseloads complicated the implementation of refugee protection. While insisting that the rights of refugees to asylum and to
the absence of *refoulement* were of paramount importance, I tried to
convince them that the issue had to be addressed jointly in new and
creative ways. By the time I completed the three-week mission, a conference on refugee issues in the Great Lakes region was clearly on.

In May 1998 a two-day conference took place in Kampala, the
capital of Uganda, which hosted the conference. The secretary-
general of the OAU, Dr. Salim, and I served as coconvenors. The
Japanese government financed the meeting. I took the occasion to
speak at one of the most prestigious universities in Africa, Makerere.
I chose the subject "Solidarity and Nation Building" and attempted to
defend the centrality of the refugee problem to a wide audience.

The conference marked one of the more positive points in the
years of strenuous struggle to save refugee lives in the Great Lakes
region. There were of course still problems throughout the region.
While refugees from Rwanda and Burundi returned to their countries, new arrivals continued from Burundi to Tanzania. But there
were also Congolese going back to Congo from Tanzania. Internal
security was far from adequate everywhere. In Rwanda, insurgency
characterized the situation in the northwestern provinces, and
UNHCR's access to returnees was at best hazardous. In Burundi,
security had deteriorated in the southeastern provinces, and the peace
process remained stalled. Congo hosted refugees not only from

Rwanda and Burundi but also from Uganda, Angola, and Sudan. While the country was somewhat recovering from the aftermath of rebellion, there were divisive undertones among local power holders. Yet it was significant that at least they agreed to meet with their regional ministerial counterparts in Kampala.

The meeting was structured around two issues: refugee protection and security and postconflict reintegration and reconstruction. In a reflection of bitter lessons of the armed refugees in the Great Lakes region, the question of how to ensure the civilian character of refugee camps was a priority. Every participant emphasized the importance of maintaining the civilian character of refugee camps. But by what means. In principle, the security of refugee camps was first and foremost the responsibility of the host government. However, in the kinds of massive refugee outflows that had taken place, the existing OAU Refugee Convention provisions with regard to situating camps away from borders and prohibiting the circulation of arms were impractical, if not inadequate. The need to deploy international police or military forces to separate and exclude those not qualified to receive refugee protection was recognized.

Comparing the limited achievement of UNAMIR in Rwanda and ECOMOG in West Africa with that of the multilateral forces in former Yugoslavia, President Museveni argued that regional forces were likely to prove more effective. Obviously, new mechanisms had to be explored to deal with armed elements if refugees were not to threaten the security of host states. In the end, UNHCR was left to explore the converging issues of refugee protection and state security. It was extremely fortunate that Secretary-General Annan joined the Kampala meeting on the second day and reinforced the commitment of the United Nations to the follow-up of the outcomes of the Kampala meeting. We were able to take up the peacekeeping issues with the Department of Peacekeeping and incorporate the major points raised in Kampala in the secretary-general's report to the Security Council.

The question of postconflict reintegration and reconstruction elicited active interest on the part of those present. They agreed that UNHCR had a vital role to play in the initial stage of reintegration following repatriation. They noted that many key donors would support UNHCR's reintegration efforts but for only a limited time. They were also aware that development organizations were rarely able to assume responsibility for UNHCR-initiated activities before the organizations were obliged to phase out. The gap issue was hotly debated, and the meeting concluded that further thought must be given to ways in which it might be closed. All delegations insisted that it would be wrong for UNHCR to impose any predetermined timetable on its integration activities. Some argued that UNHCR should prolong its reintegration activities until returnees had achieved a basic level of self-sufficiency. Those present argued that it was shortsighted for donors to devote large sums of money to refugee emergency programs but to withhold their resources when conflicts ended and peace might be stabilized. In this context, the meeting called for a reaffirmation of the principles of international solidarity and burden sharing. I understood and appreciated the rationale of their position, but I also knew the difficulty of raising funds for post-conflict activities.

The Kampala Conference restored a degree of confidence that had been damaged in the course of the crises in the Great Lakes region, confidence among the governments of the region and between UNHCR and the governments in the region. I recognized where things had gone wrong and agreed that we should proceed to correct them and recover. There was one dark spot on the horizon, the last-minute cancellation of the attendance of the Congolese delegation. UNHCR had provided logistical support, but the delegation did not arrive at the airport for the arranged flight. There were murmurs among the delegations, particularly the Ugandans and the Rwandans who had supported the rebellion in the war. They were saying that President Kabila had proved less than trustworthy.

In August 1998 a new phase in the conflict in the Great Lakes region broke out centered on the Democratic Republic of the Congo. The neighboring countries that had intervened to bring down President Mobutu and to establish President Kabila split into two opposing groups. Uganda and Rwanda now turned against Kabila, while

Angola and Zimbabwe advanced troops in his support. Underlying these developments were several notable factors. First of all, Rwanda and Uganda, which had originally fought to attain the security of areas adjacent to their borders, were determined to remain involved in Congo. They became involved in the struggle over the control of territory and resources, especially of the rich mineral resources. Kabila contracted out mineral rights in exchange for military assistance. Congo became the scene of conflict among the armies of six neighboring countries, several Congolese regional power holders, and numerous local and international armed groups. Among them were still the remnants of the FAR and the Hutu militias. The informal economy, which had sustained the population under a corrupt and inefficient state, virtually collapsed.

Conclusion

The crises in the Great Lakes region of Africa were caused by ethnic tensions and armed conflicts that had lasted for several decades. The lack of local as well as international commitment to seek solutions to the refugee problems led to a recurrence of violence on an ever-greater scale. The genocide in Rwanda in 1994 never received a strategic response either by the United Nations or by the major states, and it left a deep-seated mistrust in the Rwanda government and people. To UNHCR, the UN agency mandated to protect refugees, the genocide and the mass exodus of over two million from the country posed a massive challenge.

When refugees fled to eastern Zaire in 1994, the international community readily mounted a major rescue operation, even dispatching troops to deal with the immediate threat of the cholera epidemic and to distribute humanitarian relief. On the question of the management of the Kivu camps marked by the presence of the ex-FAR troops among the refugees, UNHCR requested international help to disarm the military and to bring law and order in the camps by the deployment of police. The UN secretary-general attempted to obtain international support, but virtually no member state was ready to provide forces to intervene in the separation of the refugees and the armed elements. As a last resort, UNHCR had to turn to the deployment of trained Zairean contingents, under international supervision. The Zairean option was never considered more than a temporary measure to contain the military action within the camps and to control the intimidation by the Rwandan soldiers and militias that blocked refugees from leaving the camps to return home.

The fifteen hundred Zaireans brought some order to the camps, but the militarization of the camps as such could never be overcome. The presence of the camps posed security threats to Rwanda and inflamed local ethnic tensions. In the end, the problems presented by the camps were not solved peacefully by the repatriation of refugees, as had been planned, nor by attacks by military elements in the camps, as had been feared. Solutions came by the military attacks against the camps of the joint Congo rebel AFDL forces and the Rwandan Army. Thereafter, while many of the refugees were forced back to Rwanda, fighting spread throughout Zaire between the joint AFDL and Rwanda forces and the Zairean government. UNHCR had to undertake a search and rescue operation deep into the country, sending back by land and air those refugees who were scattered throughout the war zone. Again there was very limited international assistance, as the multilateral forces authorized by the Security Council in November 1996 to deal with the Kivu crisis was dissolved once great many refugees were led back to Rwanda.

Under the circumstances of intermittent conflict and forced return, postconflict nation building could not succeed. Conflict dominated Zaire, and tensions persisted in Burundi, from which refugees continued to flee to Tanzania. It was only in Rwanda that some three million refugees returned and UNHCR could become engaged in a large-scale repatriation and reintegration operation. Those who had been in exile since 1959 returned spontaneously in response to the government call, while others who had left in 1994 and later were forced to return by military action or strong pressure. The return process was marked by difficulties. The returnees constituted one-quarter of the population, but the country lacked both the space for them to settle and the social infrastructure to cope with their integration. Upon the insistence of the government, but also in the interest of protecting the returning refugees, UNHCR and the international agencies made major postconflict efforts. Through massive shelter reconstruction and social rehabilitation programs, we aimed to prevent the recurrence of conflicts and to encourage steps toward reconciliation.

In the course of promoting assistance to nation building, several shortcomings in the international system became apparent. The first was the lack of mechanisms that could serve to intervene to protect both refugees and the refugee host states against armed forces. Having been exposed to the devastating consequences of militarized camps in the Kivu, UNHCR turned to the secretary-general and the UN Department of Peacekeeping to devise means that could respond to acute security threats. In the end UNHCR had to resort to a limited and temporary measure of recruiting the Zairean contingent. A second shortcoming was the absence of schemes that linked emergency humanitarian assistance with longer-term development assistance. In Rwanda, UNHCR set up with the United Nations Development Program (UNDP) a joint reintegration unit to establish better-structured links. However, we could not deal effectively with the gap between the two operations and later resorted to holding a gap forum at the Brookings Institution with the World Bank and other development organizations.

Indeed, one of the fundamental problems of the Great Lakes region was the scarcity of resources, but the fragility of governments and their limited capacities discouraged the arrival of development resources. Moreover, the intensity of interethnic conflicts inhibited the governments from moving on to power sharing and building democratic institutions. It took a long time for the Rwandan government to recognize the relevance of communal reconciliation to rehabilitation. It was in 1999 that the government established the Commission on National Unity and Reconciliation, which was headed by Aloysia Inyumba. UNHCR was ready to assist and introduced the Imagine Coexistence experiments that we had undertaken to confront the healing process in the Balkans.

The final expression of reconciliation came in a citation that President Kagame gave me when I made my last visit as high commissioner on June 17, 2000. He explained that a new country such as Rwanda had nothing like a decoration to present, but he handed me a framed citation that declared me a "Friend of Rwanda." I was very much touched. I had gone through grueling times with Rwanda. I remembered numerous tense moments when I was accused of assisting the genocidaires. When the government attacked the Kivu camps and forced the refugees to return, I insisted that it assure the safety of all Rwandans. Now the country was in a much more stable situation and ready to reconcile, particularly with the United Nations and the agency that had been in the forefront of contentious relations.

For UNHCR, the lessons learned from the crises in the Great Lakes region of Africa spanned both the emergency phases and the recovery process. It covered all humanitarian actions both in war and peace. My greatest regret is that peace has not been restored to the region, and people, both refugees and the population at large, have continued to suffer.

4.

THE
AFGHAN REFUGEES

From the late 1970s Afghanistan went through twenty-three years of war. It was only in the twenty-first century, in the aftermath of the terrorist attacks on the United States, that the international community turned to help ensure its peace and stability. During the long period of war Afghanistan produced the largest and the longest refugee exodus in the world. The challenge faced by UNHCR was to bring security and assistance to the refugees in times of war and to help repatriate and reintegrate them with the arrival of peace. When I became the United Nations high commissioner for refugees in 1991, there were over six million Afghan refugees, mostly in Pakistan and Iran. When I left the office at the end of 2000, there were still close to three million refugees and many more internally displaced persons within the country. In a sense, the problem of Afghan refugees was part of my biggest unfinished work as high commissioner.

For two reasons, I have decided to include in my book the situation of Afghan refugees not only during the war but also in the repatriation phase. First, I became once more engaged in Afghanistan in the end of 2001 when post–September 11 world attention turned to the country. I was asked by Japanese Prime Minister Junichiro Koizumi to serve as his special representative for Afghan reconstruction and became actively involved in mobilizing diplomatic and financial support. Second, in the course of several visits that I made to the country, I saw extraordinary opportunities for solving the problem of Afghan refugees and displaced persons, and I helped assist the return and reintegration of displaced persons as an integral part of the country's reconstruction. As such I believe that this chapter, which covers the repatriation and reconstruction phases, adds to the overall understanding of how much a mission to protect refugees and solve their problems can contribute to peace and nation building.

The conflicts that led to the refugee exodus from Afghanistan had local roots but were aggravated by external interventions. The superpower rivalry in the cold war ignited violent battles by mujahideen and Islamic resistance groups. When Soviet troops withdrew after intense resistance by the mujahideen, the United States lost interest in Afghanistan. The emergence of the Taliban forces, which brought security to some parts of the country, worsened the lives of the people by imposing harsh and repressive control. Taliban rule intensified the involvement of Afghanistan's neighbors.[1] Pakistan notably expanded its influence by supporting the Taliban.

The people were left to suffer the consequences of continuous wars and weakening international commitments to settle the Afghan quagmire. They started to leave the country when Communists seized power in 1978, and they left massively after Soviet troops invaded in late 1979. Within a year an estimated 6.3 million Afghans fled to the neighboring countries, 3.3 million to Pakistan and 3 million to Iran. Between the Soviet withdrawal in February 1989 and the end of 1991, some 300,000 to 400,000 refugees returned home. Then the collapse of the Communist Kabul regime in April 1992 led to one of the most rapid and massive repatriation of refugees, around 1.2 million from Pakistan and another 200,000 from Iran. Thereafter, however, return continued but at a reduced level. The fall of Kabul to the Taliban forces in September 1996 produced 50,000 new refugees, 80 percent of them from Kabul. Another 300,000 internally displaced persons fled the fighting in the northern and eastern regions of the country.

Reflecting the social and ethnic composition of those who fled, the situations of the Afghan refugees varied significantly in Pakistan and

Iran. In Pakistan the refugees were mostly Pashtuns, who sought refuge mainly in Pashtun-dominated parts of Pakistan. Three-quarters were women and children, who were given adequate health and educational services, extended by international agencies and a host of NGOs benefiting from ample donor resources to cover the victims of Soviet and Communist invasion. By contrast, the refugees in Iran were Tajiks, Uzbeks, and Persian-speaking Shia Hazaras. Sixty percent were adult males, who were integrated into the Iranian work force. International assistance extended to the refugees in Iran was very limited. The 1979 Islamic revolution had strained the relationship between the new Islamic government and Western states.

For UNHCR, the Afghan refugees represented the largest refugee caseload in the world. Since the Geneva Accords of 1988, repatriation had been considered the solution of choice for most Afghans. Although many of them had integrated in asylum countries, especially in Pakistan, local integration could not be officially promoted by the government. A limited number of people, notably Afghan women, were resettled in third countries, but the reception of asylum seekers in Western European countries was generally not favorable. As their stays lengthened and their resources dwindled, the living conditions of refugees in Pakistan and Iran deteriorated. Serious drought, which affected the entire region periodically, further undermined the economic lives of the people. After the Taliban achieved control in 1996, constructive dialogue between the Afghan regime and the international community became almost nonexistent. International attention no longer focused on the Afghan refugee crisis. UNHCR's attention was also diverted to more critical fronts in the Balkans and in Africa.

Under the circumstances, no secure and stable conditions were likely to emerge to enable the solution of refugee problems. I made my last visit as high commissioner to Afghanistan, Pakistan, and Iran in September 2000, to raise the public profile of the Afghan issue and to review the overall direction of UNHCR work. In spite of direct and cooperative discussions with senior Taliban representatives and Pakistani and Iranian officials, I failed to obtain either help or atten-

Main Afghan Refugee Flows, 1979–1990

tion from major donors. What the refugees required was additional assistance to obtain repatriation packages for those who were ready to return even to the Taliban-controlled home country. What the asylum countries needed was continued assistance to ease the burden of hosting such large numbers of refugees for so long. I renewed my strong impression that Afghanistan was a forgotten country, if not an abandoned one. UNHCR had to come up with new initiatives.

The September 11, 2001, terrorist attacks on the United States and the U.S.-led military action against the Taliban and Al Qaeda totally changed internal as well as international dynamics. Security and nation building in Afghanistan gained worldwide support ranging from the military to humanitarian and development agencies and international and bilateral donors.

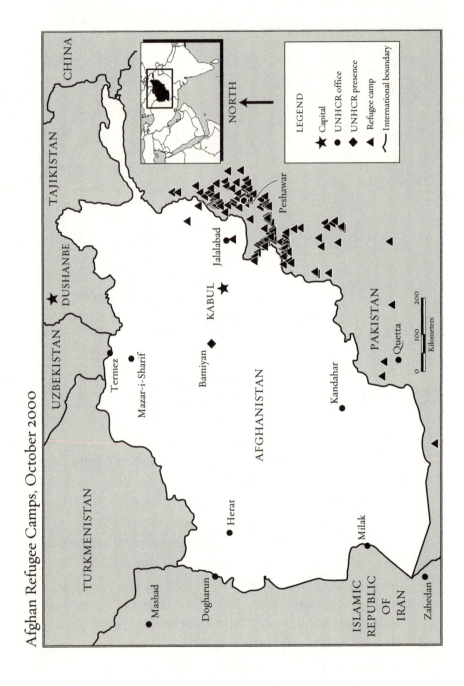

Afghan Refugee Camps, October 2000

LEGEND

★ Capital
● UNHCR office
◆ UNHCR presence
▲ Refugee camp
⌇ International boundary

NORTH

CHINA

TAJIKISTAN

DUSHANBE

UZBEKISTAN

TURKMENISTAN

Termez

Mazar-i-Sharif

Bamiyan

KABUL

Jalalabad

Peshawar

PAKISTAN

Quetta

Kandahar

Herat

Milak

ISLAMIC
REPUBLIC
OF
IRAN

Mashad

Dogharun

Zahedan

AFGHANISTAN

0   100   200
Kilometers

War and Refugee Exodus

PERIOD OF SUPERPOWER RIVALRY

Historically, Afghanistan has been a zone of conflict between great powers for centuries. It sits at the crossroads of strategic routes linking Central Asia, Southwest Asia, and the Indian subcontinent, and major wars have been fought among world powers to control this access route. Traditionally, Afghan rulers have guarded their independence by taking neutral stances and carefully maintaining the balance of power in the region. Domestically, the rulers oversaw the central government apparatus but left many local institutions and traditional structures alone. In short, the country was left with continuing diffusion of political power and perpetuation of old socioeconomic linkages.

During the forty-year reign of Zahir Shah (1933–1973), Afghanistan enjoyed relative peace and stability. The monarch survived through the Second World War and the cold war by following the traditional neutral policy lines. Zahir Shah was successful in exploiting Soviet-U.S. rivalry and obtained economic and military aid from both camps. A period of intense political instability began with Mohammad Daud, the king's cousin and former prime minister, who ousted Zahir in July 1973. Nearly thirty years later, when I had the honor of a personal audience with Zahir Shah in Kabul, he told me of the days when Daud toppled him from the throne while he was out of the country. He had then much appreciated the warm reception by Emperor Hirohito and the Japanese people and was happy to return home to Afghanistan so late in his life. Taking over power, Daud was supported by Soviet-trained army officers, Afghan Communists, the People's Democratic Party of Afghanistan, and the Soviet Union. He tried to mobilize the support of left-wing and nationalist factions, while suppressing the Islamists. The leaders of the main Islamist group, Jamiat-I-Islami (Islamic Society), fled to Pakistan, where they received assistance from the government and the U.S. Central Intelligence Agency.

Soviet leaders feared that these developments indicated that Afghanistan was descending into total chaos. They were particularly apprehensive of the prospect of Pakistan's moving to install an Islamist regime, with possible spillover effects on the Muslim Central Asian republics of the Soviet Union. They also worried that the United State might attempt to replace the Communist Afghan regime with a pro-Western one. The Soviets then carried out what they considered a "defensively motivated" military intervention to preserve Afghanistan as a neutral buffer state. From the Western point of view, Afghanistan had ceased to be a buffer state after April 1978 and had been in the Soviet sphere of influence. On December 24, 1979, a hundred thousand Soviet soldiers crossed the frontier and took control of the capital, Kabul. A devastating decade-long war erupted. Within weeks six hundred thousand Afghans fled to Iran and Pakistan, and massive outflows continued.

The Soviet invasion was a milestone that heightened cold war tensions in South Asia. Both superpowers intensified their rivalry and forged new partnerships to carry on the proxy wars. Nearly overnight, Pakistan, a linchpin of U.S. policy, began to exercise enormous influence in Afghanistan through radical Islamist and nationalist groups, waging low-intensity warfare. The legacy of the Soviet Afghan War had devastating effects not only on the lives of the Afghan people but also on the rudimentary social and political institutions for nationhood.

The superpowers poured in enormous quantities of weapons and resources. The Soviet Union had originally resorted to military intervention with the intention of stabilizing the situation in Afghanistan. But its presence had the opposite effect of causing nationwide mujahideen resistance. It pumped in five to ten billion dollars annually to finance the war and sent a military contingent of 115,000. To counteract the resistance, the Soviets embarked on a systematic destruction of agricultural crops and livestocks and saturation bombing against selective resistance strongholds. When Mikhail Gorbachev assumed power, he became aware of the difficulty of winning the Afghan War and was determined to extricate the Soviet forces from Afghanistan. To him the Afghan venture was an "exercise in futility."

The United States successfully coordinated military and financial assistance to the Islamist resistance groups in Afghanistan, which were supported by Pakistan and Saudi Arabia. These mujahideen fighters were able to counter the Soviet occupying forces, even leading to their eventual withdrawal. However, the Islamist groups that were mobilized belonged to radical and militant Islamic organizations. Gulbuddin Hikmatyar emerged as one of the main Pashtun party leaders, working closely with Pakistan's military intelligence service (ISI). Other regional mujahideen leaders came to power. They included Ismael Khan in Herat, the Uzbek warlord Rashid Dostum in Mazar-i-Sharif, and the Tajik warrior Ahmed Shah Masud in the Panjshir Valley. These local leaders resisted Taliban control and maintained their influence beyond the war period into the days when Afghanistan was brought under the control of the interim government of President Hamid Karzai.

The United Nations after six-year rounds of consultation succeeded in reaching the Geneva Accords on April 14, 1988, paving the way for the withdrawal of Soviet troops. As part of the terms of the accords the UN Good Offices Mission in Afghanistan and Pakistan (UNGOMAP) was established to monitor the implementation. President Mohammed Najibullah's power drastically eroded with the withdrawal of the Soviet military presence and the termination of assistance. The mujahideen fighters accelerated their fight. In addition to Hikmatyan-led Pashtun forces, thousands of Tajik Jamiat and Dostum's Uzbek militias poured into the capital. Najibullah, failing to leave Kabul, sought refuge in the UN compound, where he remained until he was hanged to death in 1996 by the Taliban forces. Even today, when we go by the UN compound, we recall Najibullah's death as the symbolic act of failure by the international community and the United Nations in the face of Taliban brutality. The factional fighting continued for months, destroying major parts of Kabul. A power-sharing arrangement emerged with Burhanuddin Rabbani as the ceremonial head of state and Hikmatyar as the prime minister with power to appoint cabinet ministers.

It was during this lull in the war that I made my first visit to Afghanistan and the region in September 1993. The collapse of the Communist Kabul regime in April 1992 had led to the rapid return of 1.7 million refugees. The time seemed ripe to plan for the further return of refugees. I started my mission from Tehran. With the reception of over 2 million Afghans, 100,000 Kurds, and the impending arrival of tens of thousands from neighboring Azerbaijan, Iran was turning into the largest refugee hosting country in the world. UNHCR had just worked out an agreement with Iran to establish a camp for internally displaced persons on the Azerbaijan side and to accelerate international assistance from both sides of the border. During the audience with President Hashemi Rafsanjani, I thanked him for Iran's generous reception of refugees. I promised to do my best to mobilize international support but was fully aware of the difficulties caused by the international standing of the postrevolutionary Iranian government.

We then left by military helicopter for the frontier town of Dogharoun, where the refugees were assembled to return to their country. Each refugee registered, and each was given twenty-five dollars to pay for transportation and three hundred kilograms of wheat to cover three months of food supply. The border area had turned into an enormous shopping center of household goods and farming tools. The refugees were excited to go back but worried about housing, jobs, and schools. We also visited the reception center in the old capital of Isfahan, where refugees were brought together from all over the country, processed, and put on buses to be driven to the border.

In Islamabad we held a series of consultations with government officials, after which we flew to Peshawar, the main center of Afghan concentration in Pakistan. At the time Peshawar was probably the city with the largest Afghan population after Kabul. The refugees were spread out in some three hundred villages. With the departure of more than one million refugees, a strange quiet prevailed over what looked like abandoned villages. I was asked to donate a few bulldozers to help flatten the land and start developing farmland. I visited health centers and high schools for girls. In general, schools for girls were exceptional, not only in Afghanistan but also in rural Pakistan, and the refugee girls had been given some privileged opportunities. Would they be able to gain better futures by the education they received? They seemed to think so. When I asked what plans they had for the future, they came back with immediate answers: "Doctors, engineers!" I visited several refugee homes. I was told that I was the first high commissioner allowed to visit the living quarters. In the traditional Afghan rural setting where women led secluded home lives, men, not even high commissioners for refugees, were not allowed to intrude into the homes.

We took a day trip to Kabul on a small UN plane. We visited the virtually bombed-out UNHCR office, where our local staff welcomed us cordially. We were received by President Rabbani, the repatriation minister, the deputy foreign minister, and other officials and invited to a lunch at the Foreign Ministry guesthouse. The large adjoining conference room was in shambles. Kabul was quiet that day with no sounds of shelling. Fruits and vegetables were sold in markets along bombed-out ruins. The UN agency staff members who had been evacuated to Pakistan were just returning. Obviously, repatriation was not just a question of logistics and repatriation packages. Refugees wanted to go back, but security had to be more firmly established throughout the country before we could promote or organize returns.

To judge from the uncertain political and military developments—the presence of mines, the lack of basic health and educational facilities, deteriorated or nonexistent roads and bridges, limited economic opportunities—the returnees were bound to face major hardships. Aside from providing the standard repatriation assistance packages that the refugees would take to their homes, we had to develop some new approaches, focusing on the specific needs of specific groups of people going back to specific locations.

UNDER TALIBAN RULE

The Taliban emerged in the fall of 1994. They started as a movement in the northern part of Pakistan and broke the stalemate in the Afghan civil war first by defeating the Hikmatyar forces in southern Afghanistan. Soon they controlled Kandahar. Their success in winning over the mujahideen in twelve southern provinces was said to have been made possible by Pakistani assistance. The Pakistan military had wanted to establish a pro-Pakistan regime in Kabul led by Islamic fundamentalists, most of them of Pashtun ethnic origin. The Taliban moved west and brought Herat under control in early September 1995, forcing the local warlord, Ismael Khan, to flee with his commanders and several hundred men to Iran. Then the Taliban turned east to attack the capital. After ten months' intense fighting and rocket attacks throughout the year, Kabul fell to the Taliban on September 26, 1996. The northern provinces remained in mujahideen hands.

The ideological origin of the Taliban did not derive from Afghanistan. The religious doctrine came from the Deoband branch of Sunni Hanafi Islam, which rose in British India in the middle of the nineteenth century as a forward-looking movement that aimed to reform and unite Muslim society as it struggled to live within a non-Muslim colonial state. The leaders saw education as the key to a new modern Muslim. They ran several thousand schools, or madrassas, all over India, and the Afghan government sought cooperation with Deobands to expand its own attempt to build modern state-controlled madrassas. Deoband madrassas developed fast in Pakistan, mainly for the Pashtun students in northern Pakistan. Since the madrassas did not demand any tuition fees, students from lower social strata as well as Afghan refugee children flocked to their schools. The preachers taught the students how to interpret the sharia and thus harmonize the classical texts with current realities. The Deobands took a restrictive view of the role of women, opposed all forms of hierarchy in the Muslim community, and rejected the Shias.

When the Taliban brought Afghan towns and cities under their control, they rigidly forced the application of their sharia-based edicts. As demonstrated in the bloody executions of Najibullah and his brother in the UN compound in Kabul, they enforced their rules with brutal force. They banned women from working. They closed girls' schools and colleges. They enforced strict dress codes for women. Television, videos, music, and games were forbidden. The Taliban religious police went about their business enforcing the sharia with cruel punishment.

The Taliban rule of Afghanistan resulted in two serious divisions in the country, hampering nation rebuilding: degradation of the status of women and ethnosectarian fragmentation. Traditionally in rural areas and especially in the Pashtun belt, women constituted a tiny percentage of the employment pool. Few had received any schooling. As a result, Taliban policies were resented less in these areas, and refugees continued to return there from Pakistan. However, in urban areas, where women were better educated and featured more prominently in the work force, such as Herat and Kabul, resentment grew against the Taliban. Educated Afghans and particularly women left the country, and no returns took place to these cities.

For the United Nations, the Taliban treatment of women caused problems. UNHCR, while concentrating on refugee assistance in the camps in Pakistan and Iran, tried to maintain contact with and extend support to those who returned to Afghanistan. We provided simple handicraft work and other kinds of services for women at their homes. To carry on this assistance, we needed female staffers to call on them. Female staff members from UN agencies and NGOs were constantly subjected to various kinds of harassment and obstructions. The Taliban tried to expel them from the country. The special representative of the secretary-general, Lakhdar Brahimi, tried to mobilize greater international support to influence the Taliban to exercise restraint. However, the Taliban cared little for a better international standing. Their main interest lay in expanding their domain farther north, to bring the entire country under their control.

The Taliban faced strong resistance by the military forces of the

Northern Alliance. As they attempted to fight their way north, they confronted the opposition comprised of Tajiks, Uzbeks, Hazaras, and Turkmens. In fact the front lines between the belligerents more or less coincided with the ethnic divide in the country. Although the ethnosectarian cleavage within Afghanistan was already notable in the post-1992 period, the rise of the Taliban accelerated it. In the meantime, the Pashtun minorities under pressure in the north tended to look to the Taliban for protection. The Uzbek-Hazara joint victory in Mazar-i-Sharif led to the massacre of Taliban prisoners. Other massacres were committed by the Taliban. Ethnic tensions and humanitarian catastrophes dominated the Afghan scene.

What further flamed the ethnosectarian division was the intervention of the regional powers. Pakistan gave its full support to the Taliban with weapons, equipment, military expertise, and intelligence. The ISI was reported to have been actively involved in directing Taliban operations. After all, the Taliban were largely Pakistani products, born and educated in Pakistan and in the refugee camps. Pakistan extended diplomatic recognition to the Taliban in May 1997. Saudi Arabia and the United Arab Emirates followed suit. As for the Northern Alliance, Iran became deeply involved through its support for the Shia Hazaras. In addition to the religious affinity, there were geopolitical reasons for Iran's backing of the alliance: Iran endeavored to maintain the encirclement of Afghanistan through the corridor that linked it through northern Afghanistan with Tajikistan. The Iranians gave military assistance to the Tajik commander, Ahmed Shah Masud, by air and by land. General Dostum had strong links with Uzbekistan. Russia no longer held any ambition to control Afghanistan, but because it was interested in preventing the spread of Islamic fundamentalism to Central Asia, Chechnya, and the Caucasus, it provided military assistance by air and by land.

The initial position of the United States toward the Taliban was one of sympathy, partly because of Pakistan. Moreover, after the Soviet withdrawal from Afghanistan, U.S. strategic interest in the region greatly decreased. However, the violent suppression of human rights, particularly of women's rights in Afghanistan, soon aroused the reaction of powerful feminist groups. In addition, the August 1998 terrorist attacks on the U.S. embassies in Kenya and Tanzania brought to the fore the presence of Osama bin Laden and his terrorist training centers in southeastern Afghanistan. Secretary of State Madeleine Albright publicly criticized the Taliban policies and backed the women's groups in their bid to mobilize support for Afghan women. Privately the State Department relayed its apprehension over the spread of militant extremism and Pakistan's unwillingness to constrain the Taliban. The presence of Arab Taliban became known as a threatening source of terrorism. The United States turned its attention to the capture of Osama bin Laden and started to tackle the danger of Afghanistan-based terrorist attacks.

With continuing fighting in the northern parts of Afghanistan and the negative impact of Taliban policies and practices, repatriation of refugees from Pakistan and Iran continued but on a limited scale. What made the situation particularly acute in 2000 was the severe drought in not only western but also northern Afghanistan and parts of the south. Displaced people were moving to cities inside Afghanistan. In the refugee camps in Baluchistan too, a severe water shortage was forcing many refugees to abandon the camps and move to urban slums. UNHCR undertook the consolidation of a large number of camps around available water points. However, with several million Afghans living in Pakistan and in Iran, some momentum to solve the problems of Afghan refugees, who were the largest groups of refugees in the world, had to be created. Assistance to Afghan refugees was declining. How could we deal with donor and asylum fatigue? How could we respond to the needs of the refugee? How could we overcome the military and political factors that exacerbated the humanitarian crises?

In September 2000 I went to Pakistan, Afghanistan, and Iran. My purpose was to assess the situation inside the three countries and to raise the public profile of the Afghan refugee crisis to cope with the prevailing donor and asylum fatigue that undermined UNHCR's operations. It was one of the most strenuous missions I ever took. I started from Islamabad, flew to Quetta, the capital of Baluchistan, took the plane to Herat, then drove on the bumpy road to Dogharoun to cross the border, flew to Mashhad and on to Tehran. This was the first visit of the most senior UN official to Afghanistan since the Taliban had taken over most cities. In preparing for the mission, we had to consult closely with the UN officials involved in Afghan negotiations to make clear that I was in no way going there to bless or to appease the regime. In fact I purposely decided not to go to Kabul to avoid having direct contact with the central government.

The Taliban regime had decided to welcome me, and to show a degree of openness and willingness to dialogue. It dispatched from Kabul to Herat the minister for martyrs and repatriation, the deputy foreign minister, and other officials. It recognized the presence of Western journalists in our mission. We met with the officials in Governor Khainullah Kharkwa's palace and held substantive discussions, each side represented by a delegation of seven persons. I opened the meeting by stating that I had not come to Herat to judge or criticize the Taliban, that my main purpose was to assess the situation of returnees and the viability of repatriation. I told them that some of the Taliban policies were discouraging the international community. Having held extensive talks with Afghan refugees, many of whom expressed their desire to return to Afghanistan, the international donors were particularly concerned about three issues: continued fighting in the country, which undermined security, violation of human rights, particularly the denial of rights of girls and women to education; the restrictive policy toward women's employment. I emphasized that these concerns had an adverse effect on repatriation. Educated women were reluctant to return to a country where they could not work or have their daughters educated.

The governor's response, predictably, focused on traditional practices and the lack of understanding by the West. He emphasized the Taliban's appreciation of the importance of education, including that for women and girls. He said that some steps had already been taken. I decided to take him up on his words and insisted on visiting the sites. We ended up changing our schedule and visited a nursing school attached to the university and so-called home schools, where young girls and boys were tutored privately. Only the female members of my delegation were allowed to go. When I insisted that the women journalists accompanying me should also benefit from the chance to make publicly known the changing Taliban practices, the reaction was very revealing. The governor said that he had no objection but that he had to be cautious lest such visits cause a backlash from the more conservative sectors of the Taliban movement.

In fact the next day all the female members of my delegation joined me in the visit. They were not supposed to take photos, but I am not certain how fully they obeyed this restriction. The chances were just so special. The students at the nursing school were as lively as any teenage female students I saw in other parts of the world. They responded actively to my questions. Their desire was to move from nursing to medicine and have the chance to become doctors. Considering that before the arrival of the Taliban, women accounted for some 40 percent of all medical doctors and 70 percent of all teachers in such cities as Kabul and Herat, their aspirations seemed not unfounded. The two home schools we visited were small-scale, run by women who had been teachers. They taught reading and writing and some English. Parents paid token tuitions. Later in January 2002, when I visited post-Taliban Herat, I came across the municipal education officer who had arranged my visits. He volunteered to tell me how complicated it had been for him to follow the governor's instructions and make those arrangements.

The Taliban administration was undergoing some change. In the course of the discussion we held, the governor solicited my support for changing the Afghan representation at the United Nations from the Rabbani government to the Taliban government, which controlled the country de facto. I explained to the governor that representation at the United Nations was determined by member states and that I was in no position to influence the course. I did, however, refer to the precedent of the issue of Chinese representation that year after year divided the General Assembly. I told him that it had taken more than twenty years after the establishment of the People's Republic of China in 1949 to have its representation recognized.

To claim that my visit with the Taliban was a breakthrough goes beyond what it actually achieved. However, it represented a major step in the ongoing communication between not only UNHCR but also the UN and the Taliban. I used the occasion of my visit to highlight the need to reinforce dialogue with moderate and pragmatic Taliban by a strengthened presence and increased activities inside Afghanistan. In my attempt to solve the situations of refugees all over the world, I had to deal with controversial leaders representing difficult regimes. Winning their concessions usually brought big gains to the solution of refugee problems. I had learned that historically major political concessions resulted from bringing to the negotiating table hard-line leaders belonging to bad regimes.

While focusing on the situation inside Afghanistan, my mission also addressed the problems of the Afghan refugees in the two asylum countries of Pakistan and Iran. There was a need to search for alternative approaches to the continuing repatriation impasse. The refugees were already in the third decade of displacement, and a marked change was taking place in the nature and composition of the caseload. The refugees were now mixed with inflows of migrant workers. For a good majority of the people, the reasons for their remaining in exile were becoming blurred. In Pakistan, where economic opportunities were limited, thousands were leaving the camps in the northwestern provinces and Baluchistan and moving to urban centers to try to find work. In Iran, Afghans had long provided a major labor force for construction work. Refugees and migrants were often singled out by the public as those who stole jobs from nationals. The Iranian authorities were reinforcing this perception by insisting on the need for an early and massive return to Afghanistan and were regrouping Afghans in camps. Pakistan had a less aggressive policy toward Afghans and was not likely to use forceful measures because of their close ethnic links. But for the refugees who had moved to urban areas, public attitudes were becoming more and more negative.

In Iran, Carrol Faubert, the UNHCR chief of mission, who had a proved record of innovative programming in the Balkans and the Great Lakes region in Africa, had launched what was called the Joint

Program with the Iranian authorities for a six-month experimental period. The program had the dual purpose of identifying unregistered Afghans who might be in need of protection and containing the deportations of refugees by the Iranian government. I visited a screening center in Mashhad where a joint team of UNHCR and Iranian legal officers was examining the claims of unregistered Afghans who had submitted to screenings. A good number among those examined were screened in—i.e., recognized as requiring protection—while others were given humanitarian consideration. UNHCR also stepped up assistance to voluntary repatriation. The returnees were allowed to take back their earnings simply by informing the authorities at the time of their departures. However, recently enacted Iranian laws on foreigners were unclear on the status of people in need of protection, and there was a large backlog of unscreened cases. The government was obviously interested in obtaining assistance to cover the long-term needs, such as health care, of those who were staying in Iran.

In Pakistan, UNHCR continued to concentrate its assistance in refugee camps. The threat of expulsion did not exist, but the refugees' situation had become tenuous as the result of the drought, especially in Baluchistan. Many had moved to the cities to gain work. My visit to the slums in Quetta brought to my attention the appalling conditions under which the refugees lived side by side with the urban poor. For those with definite protection problems, resettlement to third countries was a solution. But resettlement also required large resources for proper implementation. A thorough overview of UNHCR programs in Pakistan was called for. Camps in drought-affected areas had to be consolidated on the basis of access to water. While enlarging the repatriation activities, UNHCR had to strengthen its status-determining capacity to identify the protection-deserving cases.

One major objective that I had entertained for my mission was to raise public attention on the continuing Afghan refugee crisis so that donors would provide more resources for the repatriation as well as reception of refugees. Here I failed dismally. In spite of the press reports that covered the plight of Afghan refugees in the camps as well as the process of return, there was virtually no response. I thought that Taliban or not, Afghanistan was a forgotten country and that Afghan refugees were nearly abandoned by the international community.

An Afghan-related issue that drew attention, particularly in some of the industrialized countries, was asylum. Not only did Afghan refugees flock to neighboring countries, but individual Afghans traveled to Europe and North America. The only legal basis on which entry was granted was that of being recognized for asylum. After 1996 the number of individual asylum seekers from Afghanistan increased rapidly and together with those from Iraq recorded the top asylum-seeking population. The Netherlands and the United Kingdom drew the largest number. The United States and Canada also received considerable numbers.

By tradition and policy, Japan faced very few asylum seekers. The number of Afghans who were recognized as refugees or given long-term residence status on account of humanitarian considerations at the end of 2001 totaled sixty-two. For asylum seekers pursuing refugee status, final decisions were left to lawsuits at the district court level. In 2002, after I became actively engaged in the reconstruction of Afghanistan, I made an informal presentation to the Ministry of Justice over a rejected case. I asked it to refrain from expelling the applicant at a time when Japan was making a serious contribution to the rebuilding of Afghanistan and when I was personally involved in reconstruction efforts. Could the government not delay the action and let the applicant be returned when the country was much closer to achieving peace and stability? I could not make direct impact on court proceedings. The immigration authorities tended to press the failed asylum seekers to return voluntarily rather than resort to deportation.

There was, in fact, considerable popular feeling for Afghan people. I recall coming across two Afghan men in a subway in Tokyo. They recognized me, offered me a seat, and thanked me for all my endeavors. We entered into a conversation on recent conditions. Both were engaged in small businesses. One seemed to have proper legal status, but the other probably did not. I did not inquire. As the high commissioner for refugees I believed strongly in the importance of a legal base for asylum, but I also understood the reality of desperation for a citizen of a country that was so badly governed that there were no economic or professional opportunities for the future. These Afghan men seemed to have established some work base in Japan.

Afghanistan After September 11

SECURITY AND RECONSTRUCTION

The September 11 attacks on the World Trade Center buildings in New York and the Pentagon in Washington turned world attention to Afghanistan. American anger, fear, and uncertainty were very deep. At the time I was living in New York, and I personally witnessed the scenes of the disaster and understood the American response. Following the daily reports on television and noticing the discovery of Afghanistan on the global map, I worried that America's anger would turn against Afghanistan and its people. In fact, around the time of the September 11 attacks, as I have said, Afghanistan was a forgotten country, a country left to engage in conflict and oppression and to serve as the breeding ground for terrorism. Judging from the intensity of the feelings of the Americans, however, I thought it inevitable that the United States would resort to military action. It was a relief for me that about a week after the attacks, Secretary of State Colin Powell stated that the United States was not against the Afghan people but against the terrorists who had taken over the country.

The immediate military objective of defeating the Taliban and the Al Qaeda terrorists was achieved quickly. The Afghan Northern Alliance forces gave crucial ground support to the largely aerial American war action. However, conclusive victory proved hard to achieve. The Afghan terrain did not lend itself easily to capture a particular culprit, Osama bin Laden. Moreover, Afghan ethnic, cultural, and religious solidarity would not move the population readily to support external intervening forces. The key lay in how convincingly the international community could present the dividends of peace through reconstruction and reconciliation endeavors.

The UN secretary-general reassigned Lakhdar Brahimi to undertake the political preparation for the establishment of an interim Afghan administration. Brahimi shuttled among Afghan political groups and personalities and succeeded in opening the Bonn Peace Conference on November 27, 2001. It was a significant achievement that the United Nations took the political lead in the reestablishment of the Afghan government. UN humanitarian agencies and NGOs became reengaged in activities inside Afghanistan. The governments of the United States and Japan had cohosted the senior officials' meeting on Afghan reconstruction in Washington on November 20. At the time the Bonn process was at a start-up phase, and the political road map for the establishment of a legitimate government was still undetermined. The early convening of the Washington meeting was intended to send the political message that the international community would be providing significant assistance once the Afghans had agreed on peace. I considered the attempt to link military action more directly with reconstruction planning from an early phase to be positive. It would assure the immediate follow-up of post-conflict peace building.

For a long time Japan had entertained a special interest in the political stability and economic development of Central Asia. During the past two decades, while Afghanistan underwent numerous conflicts, Japan had tried several times to bring together the warring parties and even had had several groups come to Tokyo after the Taliban victory in 1996. Now with the prospect for peace on the horizon, Japan was ready to play an active part. In my new capacity as Prime Minister Koizumi's special representative on Afghan reconstruction, I led the Japanese delegation to the Washington meeting, where I formally stated that Japan was ready to host a conference in Tokyo for the peace and reconstruction of Afghanistan and to act as cochair.

In preparation for the Tokyo meeting, I visited Pakistan,

Afghanistan, and Iran in early January 2002, with a delegation composed of Japanese Foreign Ministry officials. The purpose in going to Afghanistan was to become acquainted with the new leaders of the Interim Administration, assure their participation in the Tokyo Reconstruction Conference, and get their views on reconstruction needs. I also went to Pakistan and Iran to assess their positions on the coming changes in Afghanistan.

It was with a genuine sense of keen anticipation that on January 9, 2002, I landed at the Bagram military airport. Many changes had taken place since my mission to the country in the fall of 2000. The Taliban were gone. American military action was gaining ground. A new interim government was being established. Upon arrival, we were met by Filippo Grandi, my last chef de cabinet at UNHCR, who was now serving as the head of mission in Afghanistan. From the airport my UN colleagues took us to the Shomali Plain, known as the fruit basket of the country, now destroyed but to which 109 displaced families, who had fled the fighting in the plain and taken refuge in former Soviet barracks, were returning. They must have believed that peace having arrived, they should go home no matter how cold the winter. I talked with the families and asked what they planned to do. They answered without hesitation that they wanted to go back to their original villages, rebuild their houses, start planting in time for the spring, and take up animal husbandry. In these words of returning displaced persons, I saw the first real signs of peace. UN humanitarian agencies and NGOs were on the scene, setting up way stations and providing donkeys to those who could not carry their household goods up the hill. We realized that short-term humanitarian assistance should be quickly complemented by rehabilitation and reconstruction efforts to build viable villages. There should be shelter, seeds, schools, health clinics, access to water. In short, there should be a seamless transition from emergency humanitarian assistance to reconstruction, a commitment I had constantly promoted while serving as high commissioner and now widely avowed at international conferences.

In the provincial capital of Herat, to which I flew three days later, I met Ismael Khan, who had retaken the governorship from the Taliban. The UNHCR office arranged meetings with the provincial government officials and a group of civil society leaders and also visits to schools. A girls' high school had just been opened, and UNICEF was running experimental classes to prepare for the new school year to begin in March. Rows of students welcomed me in the courtyard. Little girls in native costumes greeted me with flowers and songs. I went to classes. Since most girls had been prevented from going to school under the Taliban, there was a notable age variation in the student body. The girls were lively and obviously excited. I met with the teachers and asked them what they wanted most. There was a chorus of response: "Salaries!" They had not been paid for months and years. There was need for books, notebooks, pencils, in fact everything. My experienced UNHCR interpreter quietly commented at the end of the day, "This was a good day. Girls are going back to school."

"Back to home" and "back to school. These were small projects, but they represented enormous tasks that Afghanistan faced in order to return to normality after twenty-three years of war. The implied scale of the required challenge was huge. Out of a total Afghan population of 25 million there were 4 to 5 million refugees and internally displaced persons wanting to go home. There were 3 to 4 million children returning to school. From education to health, from towns and cities to rural areas, there was need to rebuild houses, restore arable land, and install electricity and water in order to restart normal communal life. Besides, how would people who suffered under the divisions of power, region, ethnicity, gender learn to live together again?

Afghan reconstruction had to be carried out on two fronts: state and society. At the state level, the most urgent task was to establish nationwide security and a functioning government. At the societal level, a range of measures—education, health care, and a host of infrastructure installments—had to be introduced to rebuild communities. The limited administrative capacity in Kabul had to be overhauled to run a government that provided basic services. I had an audience with Chairman Karzai and a range of ministers. I also met with Brahimi in his new capacity as the special representative of the secretary-general as well as with UN agency representatives, to listen to their plans and observations. While the United States carried on the War on Terrorism against the remnants of the Taliban and Al Qaeda in the south and southeast, the International Security Assistance Force (ISAF), authorized by the Security Council, looked after the security of Kabul. But there were worrying signs of security problems in many parts of Afghanistan. Most people I met, whether Afghan or United Nations official, urged extending and expanding ISAF's mission. Two other related endeavors were the establishment of the Afghan national defense and police forces and the demobilization and reintegration of combatants. Both required considerable time to put into effect, but the situation necessitated early results. Obviously, the establishment of security was the foundation which humanitarian and reconstruction work could proceed.

When I asked Chairman Karzai what he considered his priority needs, he gave me an interesting and frank response. He said that when he was not in the government, he had thought that his first priority would be education, followed by road repair and health. He was obviously thinking in terms of rebuilding at the societal level. Now that he was heading the administration, he said, he realized the absolute need for state building centered on a functioning government. He had to have money to pay the civil servants, buildings to house ministries, and telephones to communicate. He had to restore the supreme court, establish a central bank, issue currency, and build various governing institutions to strengthen the administrative capacity to work in accordance with the law. I have had some experience in helping to set up governing capacities in postconflict situations, but the Afghan needs seemed vast and substantial. Karzai emphasized the importance for the Security Council not only to extend but also to expand the presence of the ISAF to assure security throughout Afghanistan. He hoped that the Tokyo Conference would provide him opportunities to carry on bilateral consultations with all the attending states.

Positive responses to the Tokyo Conference came from both Pakistan and Iran. In Pakistan, we were received by Foreign Minister Abdul Sattar and States and Frontiers Minister Abbas Sarfraz Khan,

who expressed readiness to cooperate with the Afghanistan reconstruction efforts. Pakistan intended to pledge one hundred million
dollars, half in a line of credit. It considered the ISAF's presence
absolutely vital not only for Afghanistan but also for Pakistan. The
security situation in Afghanistan would remain risky, and the relationship between the Interim Administration leaders and the
warlords required continued nurturing and pressuring. Since reconstruction assistance would be the most effective tool to promote the
unification of Afghanistan, it should go directly to the Interim
Administration, not through the warlords. Recalling its support to the
Pashtun-led Taliban during the war, Pakistan was keen to make sure
that the Northern Alliance–led Interim Administration developed
into a genuinely neutral Afghan authority. Minister Khan reminded
the international community of the heavy refugee burden borne by
Pakistan and said he expected large-scale repatriation to start in the
spring.

Iran, on the other hand, had already started bilateral assistance for
the reconstruction of Afghanistan. President Mohammad Khatami,
Foreign Minister Kamal Kharrazi, and others exhibited a strong
desire to cooperate with Japan and reiterated their proposal for a joint
committee to consult about and implement reconstruction projects.
The defeat of the Taliban was a welcome development for Iran. Its
hope was to see Afghanistan reestablish its traditional neutral political position vis-à-vis its neighbors. Iran aspired to enhance its influence by strengthening its cultural and linguistic ties and the position
of Shia minorities and Hazaras. The foreign minister had already visited Kabul and entered specific project negotiations for rebuilding the
Herat–Mashhad road and payment of the salaries of the Kabul University faculty. To Iran, the repatriation of Afghan refugees was a priority. While the refugees provided the much-needed labor, they had
been resented as taking away jobs from the local people. UNHCR
would have to prepare for the repatriation of refugees from Iran.

The International Conference on Reconstruction Assistance to
Afghanistan was held in Tokyo January 20 to 22, 2002. Sixty-one
countries, many at the ministerial level, and twenty-one international

organizations participated. Its basic objective was to serve as a high-level intergovernmental pledging conference to demonstrate the commitment by the international community to support Afghanistan as it began its long journey to peace and stability. Altogether well over $4.5 billion were pledged for a five-year period, over $1.8 billion for 2002 alone. The United States, Saudi Arabia, the European Union, and Japan served as cochairs, and I represented the host government in this capacity. What impressed me strongly was not only the magnitude of the pledges and commitments but the fact that they came from a truly wide range of countries, surpassing the traditional notion of donor countries. The neighboring countries, such as Pakistan and Iran, made pledges demonstrating their preparedness to support the peace process. The Tokyo Conference represented a milestone in a series of meetings that had started in Washington and was followed by those in Berlin and in Brussels. It was closely linked with the implementation of the Bonn Agreement in that the cochairs' summary conclusions stated that "assistance will be conditional on all parties positively contributing to the process and goals agreed in Bonn with the aim of establishing peace, representative governance and stability in Afghanistan."[2]

Needless to say, the establishment of nationwide security was reiterated over and over as the overriding condition for the twin components of nation building, to advance the political and reconstruction processes. At the time an international presence was the only means available for the Interim Administration to count on for building security. Chairman Karzai requested the Security Council on January 30 to authorize the extension and expansion of the ISAF's mandate. The troop-contributing countries to the coalition forces remained reluctant, citing the unavailability of adequate forces, the security risk, the costs, and the Afghan people's sensitivity. The fact that the United States was fighting its own War on Terrorism in the south and southeast, with its own forces and tactics and with support from local warlords, meant that there was no unified international security operation throughout Afghanistan. While the Security Council authorized the deployment of the ISAF, it is important to recognize that the United Nations itself did not have a transitional administrative responsibility, as it had in Cambodia, Kosovo, and East Timor. The Afghan Interim Administration was the only responsible body, with the United Nations Assistance Mission in Afghanistan, (UNAMA), led by Brahimi, to assist. Several states volunteered to take lead roles over specific sectors. The United States and France were to train and rebuild the Afghan National Army. Germany was to train the national police. The United Kingdom was in charge of controlling the narcotics industry. Italy took responsibility for legal reform. Japan opted for working on the demobilization and reintegration of former combatants. Such a diversified provision of services was certainly novel, and the results were mixed. It took a long time for individual states to pursue reform activities in specific sectors, but the respective sectors were by their nature intersectoral. Given the fact that the overall security of the country greatly depended on the achievements in the various sectors, entrusting coordination to bilateral actors proved problematic. Judicial reform lagged, and drug control showed little progress.

To the Karzai administration, there were two sources of security threats that had to be dealt with. The first threat was from the remnants of the Taliban mixed with stragglers from Al Qaeda who suffered heavy losses in 2001. The second threat was from the mujahideen warlords who formally joined the Karzai administration while maintaining their military power bases. As far as the Taliban and Al Qaeda were concerned, their revival depended on the extent to which they could obtain arms, utilize the Pashtun community belt in the Afghan-Pakistani border regions, take advantage of the anti-Western fundamentalist sentiments, and mobilize a counterinsurgency campaign. The Northern Alliance, on the other hand, had benefited from U.S. military and financial support during the war against the Taliban but remained intent on maintaining its power base. Local warlords continued to count on resources gained from cross-border trade. Tensions persisted along ethnosectarian divisions.

The deployment of the ISAF only in Kabul was a serious shortcoming in establishing security throughout Afghanistan. Requests for expansion of its coverage were repeated at every Security Council meeting that debated Afghanistan by Karzai, the secretary-general, and several delegates, including me. However, no positive response came from troop-contributing states, which cited a shortage of troops. NATO took over the running of the ISAF, and finally the Security Council on October 13, 2003, authorized the expansion of the ISAF mandate to areas outside Kabul and its environs in Resolution 1510. Plans for disarmament, demobilization, and reintegration (DDR) started only in the fall of 2003, while the training of the Afghan forces would not reach the target figure of seventy thousand for several years.

Karzai's security challenge was to win the political battle by gaining the majority Pashtuns' confidence and by ensuring the loyalty of the warlords and disarming their militias. Dividends of peace and reconstruction were indispensable means of bringing the people away from the reemerging influence of the Taliban or transferring their allegiance from regional warlords to the central authority. In short, the issue of security was closely linked with achievements in the political and reconstruction realms.

On the reconstruction front, the World Bank, the Asian Development Bank, and the United Nations Development Program (UNDP) presented the assessment report on reconstruction requirements to the Tokyo Afghan reconstruction meeting. The report was to serve as the basis for the pledges and commitments expected from the participating governments. The long war years had deprived the Afghan people of all developmental benefits. In fact, according to any development indicators, whether GNP, GNP per capita, life expectancy, under-five mortality rate, or literacy, Afghanistan remained at the bottom. The needs therefore were total and comprehensive and could be broadly identified at three levels: urgent humanitarian assistance to reach the people immediately as they faced serious shortage of food, shelter, and medical attention; community development projects to respond to the widely held expectations and aspirations of the people for employment; large-scale infrastructure rebuilding, such as electricity, water, and road construction, to start the economy moving.

While the international financial institutions surveyed and assessed needs, the humanitarian agencies were mobilizing resources for the quick delivery of goods to the needy and vulnerable population. In fact, during the war period from 1979 to 2001, the Afghans had been aided largely through humanitarian interventions, the only kind allowed during the occupation, war, and rule of the Taliban. A wide range of NGOs was involved not only in refugee and returnee assistance but also in quick impact projects (QIP) types of rehabilitation work. The Swedish Committee was known for its educational work. The ICRC concentrated on hospitals, prisons, and general humanitarian needs. The NGOs more than the UN were the central actors during this period.

With the defeat of the Taliban, UN humanitarian agencies made a quick and active return. The World Food Program provided enormous food assistance to refugees and Afghan communities inside the country. UNICEF launched a back to school program, concentrating on the health and educational needs of children. UNHCR became engaged in the repatriation operations. One function that the United Nations persistently carried out was demining. A special factor that might affect not only reconstruction at all levels but also in security and political issues was the impending repatriation of refugees, possibly at a massive scale.

Repatriation, Reintegration, and Nation Building

One area of concern shared by a lot of donors was the transition from humanitarian to development operations. "A seamless transition from relief to development" had been the battle cry of Afghan reconstruction ever since the November 2001 meeting in Washington. In the actual situation in the country, it took a long time for the development agencies to become operational because they had been absent for some time. The Afghan government, coming out of war and poverty, expected grant aid to pour in and would not accept loans that would tie up its meager resources. But grants were not available for large-scale infrastructure programs. Consequently, projects involving electricity, water, and road reconstruction tended to get delayed.

At the Tokyo Reconstruction Conference, I found myself facing a peculiar problem concerning the treatment of humanitarian issues. Rumors circulated that the Japanese government had taken a position against including the UN joint humanitarian appeal on the conference agenda. Then I was told that the United States was against the inclusion. Coming from a humanitarian background, I would have been the last person to attempt to separate or sideline humanitarian problems. The Japanese approach had been more in line with promoting a seamless transition. In the end, in a compromise, the humanitarian agencies were invited to hold their own meeting the same premises immediately following the conference.

The episode, in itself not significant, symbolized the long-existing distance between the humanitarian and development communities. The treasury and finance ministries, which showed early commitments to Afghan reconstruction, were accustomed to dealing with international financial institutions but sparingly with humanitarian agencies. It was through working on the ground and addressing the needs in pragmatic and operational ways that little by little the development actors made inroads into Afghanistan, eventually producing a unique framework of nation building.

As for Afghan refugees no sooner were UNCHR staffers able to reinstall themselves in Kabul than a major planning exercise started in preparation for the refugees' return. The basic figures for refugees in Iran and Pakistan had to be adjusted upward from what UNHCR had officially used. Adopting the governments' figures, UNHCR had to plan on the basis of 2.3 million for Iran and 3.5 million for Pakistan. Depending on the security, socioeconomic conditions, and the messages that returnees would be sending back to those still in exile, the process was likely to snowball. In addition to refugees, there were two categories of internally displaced persons: those displaced by drought in the north and the west, concentrated near Herat and Mazar-i-

Sharif, and those displaced by conflict, especially from frontline areas in the central and northern parts of the country. The return of the displaced persons not only was a humanitarian issue but also had political implications for community reconciliation and peace building.

Since no international agencies are specifically charged with internally displaced persons in the UN system, the question of allocating responsibility for their protection and assistance became a delicate interagency question. Coordination of IDP assistance in Afghanistan had been the responsibility of the Office of the UN Coordinator for Humanitarian Affairs with implementing support by various agencies. With the likelihood of the large-scale return of refugees, some agreement with regard to aiding the returning IDPs had to be established. My position as high commissioner had been that UNHCR was requested to extend responsibility over IDPs by the General Assembly in many situations and had the necessary expertise. Therefore, UNHCR was best suited to deal with the repatriation of IDPs, lest they suffer discrimination or separate treatment.

Agencies working on the ground had already agreed in principle that returning IDPs should benefit from the same level of protection and assistance as returning refugees. The clear allocation of IDP responsibility to UNHCR dragged on a little longer until a decision was reached in the UNAMA context. Within the Afghan government, responsibility for IDPs was entrusted to the Ministry of Refugees and Repatriation. In the meantime, I actually came across a large group of IDPs, mostly drought victims, brought together at the Maslakh camp near Herat. Instead of being given the means to solve the displacement and to find ways to help them return to their villages of origin, they received assistance that only lured people to remain displaced. My own approach to refugees as well as to IDPs had very much been one of problem solving. Humanitarian agencies should not perpetuate displacement. There were, however, schools of thought that believed more strongly in humanitarian neutrality. They believed that staying away from solutions was important lest they inevitably be brought into contact with political or even military actors.

Refugees from neighboring countries started returning to Afghanistan at a scale far bigger than estimated. UNHCR had to readjust its original planning figure upward: for 2002, from Pakistan, from 400,000 to 1.2 million, while maintaining a 400,000 projection for Iran. In other words, the return for 2002 would be more than double what had been foreseen. Enormous adjustments had to be made in terms of revising the appeal for funds, procuring goods for assistance packages, and opening up suboffices and deploying staff. In the course of 2002 some 1.8 million returned to Afghanistan. The movement started with the urban refugees in Pakistan who had left under the Taliban persecution. They tended to flock back to the urban areas in Afghanistan. In fact, the ISAF's presence seemed to assure security and attracted a large number of returnees. It was estimated that some 500,000 came to the Kabul area, causing shortages of housing, water, social services, and jobs. Those from the rural areas in Afghanistan who had lived in refugee camps in Pakistan returned gradually by the end of 2003 more than 3 million refugees, together with the internally displaced persons, had returned to their places of origin.

At the central government level, the capacity to deal with the large-scale return of people was limited. Like many other ministries, the Afghan Ministry of Refugees and Repatriation, in charge of returning refugees and IDPs, was overwhelmed by the immensity of the task. Assisting returnees meant not only providing them with initial logistical support but also helping them reintegrate into their communities. However, the very communities to which they were returning also required major reconstruction assistance. UNHCR seconded several staff members to the ministries and sent a group of experienced Afghan staff members to train the refugee ministry personnel throughout the country. In fact several international agencies linked up with their respective counterpart ministries and served as what was referred to as the program secretariat. The arrangement was considered an innovative form of collaboration and capacity building that mutually benefited the Afghan government and the international organizations.

More reconstruction efforts, however, had to be concentrated at the provincial and communal levels. When I went to Afghanistan in June 2002 to observe the emergency loya jirga, the traditional people's assembly to elect and legitimize new rulers, I used the occasion to visit Kandahar to examine the repatriation challenges in the southern province. The expedition proved to be an eye-opener for the Japanese delegation and led us to initiate a comprehensive regional development program. Assisted by the advice and arrangements of Filippo Grandi, we flew by a small UN shuttle plane and then drove south to Spin Boldak.

We went farther and crossed the border to Chaman, on the Pakistan side. It was known as the no-man's-land, where Afghans who had been denied asylum by Pakistan were forced to stay. The camps in Chaman, spread out in a desertlike terrain, were flimsy and crowded. Altogether some four hundred thousand people were in this area, and all depended on international humanitarian assistance. Aside from refugees, there were victims of drought as well as Pashtuns from the north, who had fled persecution and violence from local warlords. Ashraf Ghani, the aid coordinator and troubleshooter of the administration, urged UNHCR to relocate the population and solve the highly political humanitarian problem. The refugees looked tired and forlorn. We tried to find out what they considered the solution to their fate. Some were willing to be relocated elsewhere in Afghanistan, even temporarily. Others insisted on returning to the northern part of the country, for which they wanted the presence of international security. Still others wanted to go to Pakistan. On return we stopped to visit camps in Spin Boldak run by Islamic NGOs. Schoolchildren had lined up for hours and waited for our visit. They recited poetry and sang beautifully in our welcome.

We learned much in the drive from Kandahar to Chaman of the terrible road conditions in Afghanistan. The traffic, however, was quite heavy because the road served as the main commercial connection from Pakistan to Afghanistan and beyond. I noticed truckloads of cattle coming from India on their way to Iran, a very hard trip to the slaughterhouse. We also encountered many trucks with returning refugees. Several families seemed to have gotten together, hired a truck, loaded it with all their belongings, and headed back. We talked with some of them at crossing points where the trucks stopped for refueling, and they sipped tea as they rested.

At the provincial capital, Kandahar, we spent hours consulting with the provincial government officials and UN agency representatives on how to solve the IDP problem in the area. Engineer Pashtun, an adviser to the provincial governor of Kandahar, who accompanied our delegation throughout the trip to the south, was a city planner trained at the American University in Beirut and returned from exile in Pakistan. He had a plan to relocate the IDPs to Zhare Dasht, an area near Kandahar. He emphasized that Afghanistan was an agricultural country and that rural reconstruction was the key to nation building. Refugees and IDPs should be led to return to the villages. The UN agency representatives were also interested in the rehabilitation of rural areas. UNHCR was ready to engage in the relocation of IDPs so long as they were willing to move. I believed that the international interest in extending educational and health care aid would be best served if the aid had a geographical context. I had learned through my UNHCR days that where a well or a school or a clinic was located made a big difference to community building. I also thought that the local population should share the benefits to be extended to returning refugees and IDPs. My Japanese delegation colleagues had been looking for opportunities to relaunch a regional development program that they had supported in Azra, Afghanistan, for returning refugees during the war. A comprehensive area development plan emerged among Afghan, UN, and Japanese officials. We all wanted to put into practice a quicker and more effective process of repatriation, reintegration, and reconstruction.

Following up further on the consultations, the Japanese government decided to finance a multisector reintegration program for Afghan refugees and IDPs in the three geographical areas of Kanda-

har, Jalalabad, and Mazar-i-Sharif. The first stage was to focus primarily on assisting refugees and returning IDPs to meet their needs,
transportation home, shelter, water, education, and health facilities.
The second stage was to enhance the household economies of these
people to make their returns sustainable. UNHCR was to identify
activities aimed at boosting the income-generating capacity of the
returnees. UNICEF would implement activities in education, immu-
nization, safe motherhood, water, and sanitation. The WFP would
promote food-for-work activities in village rehabilitations. Not only
humanitarian agencies but also development agencies such as
UNDP and Habitat joined in the program concentrating on urban
rehabilitation.

The comprehensive area development program became identified
as the Ogata Initiative. I was a bit uneasy as I was not certain whether
this particular approach to meet the huge needs of returning refugees
and IDPs would actually produce the desired results. In the two years
from the summer of 2002 to the spring of 2004, Japan provided
ninety-two million dollars to UN agencies under the Ogata Initiative.
The aim was to provide the resources to ensure the link between
humanitarian and development activities in the transition phase of
nation building. It also aimed at the expansion of reconstruction
endeavors from the capital to provincial centers. In the following
stages, transitional financing was to move on to longer-term infrastructure development projects, settlement site building, and land
restoration for agricultural use. Personally, I wanted to make sure that
some attention would continue for meeting the needs of returning
refugees, the internally displaced, demobilized soldiers, and other vulnerable groups that might still require humanitarian attention while
heading toward more self-reliance.[3]

Although it recognized the importance of advancing the return
and reintegration operations for vulnerable displaced people, the
Interim Administration wanted to be sure that the UN humanitarian
and development activities were integrated into the government's
national reconstruction plan. Leading the planning and financing
arms of the government, Ashraf Ghani insisted that the UN agencies

work closely within the framework of the National Area-Based Development Program (NABDP), National Solidarity Program (NSP), and National Emergency Employment Program (NEEP). To Ghani, a onetime World Bank development expert, humanitarian work might be at best useful in a transition phase but should be brought firmly under the national development plan. He presented the overview of the national budget that covered all development programs under twelve categories. The program relating to return of refugees and IDPs that covered the activities of UNHCR and the International Organization for Migration was included in the national budget. It was a new experience for UNHCR, by nature a humanitarian organization, to undertake a developmental role in the overall context of Afghan nation building. After all, the solution of refugee problems relied heavily on the kind of community and eventually nation to which the refugees would return. What the government programs attempted was to lead and coordinate all activities throughout the country and to ensure an equitable allocation of resources among the provinces. The difficulty with such a well-planned top-down approach was that it required taking into account the specific local situations and access to everyone in need at the receiving end. What the Ogata Initiative had provided was more of a bottom-up approach.

Also in the realm of establishing security assurance, attempts had to be made to spread the benefits of the Kabul-centered ISAF's influence outside the capital. In spite of the repeated requests by President Karzai, Secretary-General Annan, and member states at the Security Council, the ISAF's deployment remained concentrated in Kabul. Some initiatives had to be taken to spread security to the provinces. The United States took steps to deploy military security units together with small-scale reconstruction teams to selected areas. The establishment of provincial reconstruction teams by the U.S. Defense Department was a novel attempt to move out of the capital, Kabul, and fill the security gaps throughout the country.

Teams composed of small military units of up to about one hundred, together with a few civilian staffers from the State Department and the USAID, were deployed to the provinces to carry out small-scale public works activities. I was able to visit the PRT headquarters in Bamyan Province, where the team was busily reconstructing the local university. The plan was to dispatch PRTs to ten or more areas, each with a flexible reconstruction mandate, ranging from road repair and the restoration of community power stations to building police stations, schools, and local government offices. In principle, they were to work on projects that were outside regular reconstruction activities. Other coalition government forces began to join in on the PRT projects.

Under the limited security coverage by the coalition forces in Afghanistan, the PRT deployment might prove meaningful in spreading the message of peace and reconstruction throughout the country. Though some NGOs were reported to have been uneasy with any direct military engagement in reconstruction assistance activities, the modest military presence and patrolling gave some assurance of security. The introduction of the PRT to Bamiyan, together with the presence of the Afghan national army, was greatly appreciated by the local population and eased the tension between factions that existed in the region. President Karzai himself was positive.

There were similarities between the Ogata Initiative and the PRT. Both were attempts to spread the impact of reconstruction and security throughout Afghanistan with relatively modest resources. However, in order to enhance the effects of peace and a brighter future for the Afghan people, larger-scale reconstruction activities had to be introduced. A case in point was the rehabilitation of the major highway through Kabul, Kandahar, and Herat. At my very first meeting with President Karzai, he indicated his priority for having that road repaired. At the Tokyo Reconstruction Conference, I personally approached the presidents of the World Bank and the Asian Development Bank and pressed for top-priority consideration for road repair. I consulted the U.S. government, but the highway plan remained unaddressed. One of the obstacles was the financing modalities. The Afghan government would not accept loans to finance the project. Suddenly in the summer of 2002 the highway construction issue reached the highest level of the U.S. administration. The story ran that President Bush became aware of the issue, to him a simple question, and instructed the government to take the initiative. Calls came to Tokyo for U.S.-Japanese joint highway financing. At the UN General Assembly meeting in New York in September, President Bush and Prime Minister Koizumi announced the joint agreement to undertake the highway project. They committed a grant assistance totaling eighteen million dollars, with Saudi Arabia joining in. The European Union and other governments also began examining road construction projects.

At the end of 2003 the Kabul–Kandahar portion of the highway was finished. Would the ring road, the largest single investment in Afghan infrastructure building, symbolize the start of a major reconstruction phase in Afghan nation building? At least it would serve as a highly visible symbol of international cooperation that had to be carried further. There were many more roads still to be repaired. The reconstruction of the national ring road would have to move on to the repair of electric power stations and water supply plants. Nation building in Afghanistan has to move from the back to home and back to school communal endeavors to hard-core infrastructure reconstruction that will position the country on a developmental course.

In addition to physical infrastructure, building political institutions proved an indispensable component of nation building. The 2002 emergency loya irga had paved the way. I was pleased to be witness to the people's assembly of some 1,656 delegates from all over the country and abroad, including 200 women. The meetings were open, ceremonial, and emotional. In the end, by the democratic process of secret ballots, the loya jirga elected Hamid Karzai president. It also announced the names of all cabinet ministers, but the fact that it found it necessary to name twenty-seven ministers reflected the unresolved ethnic rivalries among Afghan political groups.

One year later the 502 delegates to the constitutional loya jirga examined and debated the draft constitution. The delegates represented every province and community. In the end they proved willing to reach compromises, and on January 4, 2004, they adopted the constitution by near unanimous acclamation. The political participation of women was greatly enhanced by this constitution, which established the Afghan Independent Human Rights Commission to protect and promote human rights.

The laboriously adopted political institutions continue to be challenged as the Afghans undergo a wide range of reforms. In the security sector the Afghan national army has to be established, and the training of the national police has to prove effective. The disarmament and demilitarization of existing armed forces have to advance, and the soldiers to be reintegrated into the developmental process. The Afghan economy has to shed itself from the opium production and drug trade through the introduction of counternarcotics institutions. Finally, the electoral processes, both presidential and parliamentary, foreseen in the course of 2004, must stand as the ultimate test of the effectiveness of the Afghan nation building.

Concluding Observation

The postconflict peace-building process in Afghanistan stood as a unique experience of following up military intervention with reconstruction efforts for the overall objective of ensuring peace. Due recognition should be given to the early linkage of military action with the Bonn political process led by the United Nations and the Tokyo Reconstruction Conference joined by sixty-one countries. Though the U.S. government formally denied its involvement in nation building, in fact it became heavily engaged in a wide range of activities that covered the assurance of security, the building of political institutions, and humanitarian and development assistance.

At issue was the question of who would take over what responsibility and produce how many results how soon. The security responsibilities were divided between the U.S.-led coalition forces continuing the war against the remnants of the Taliban and Al Qaeda in the south and the ISAF forces in charge of Kabul. In spite of repeated requests by President Karzai, the UN secretary-general, and many member states, the expansion of ISAF security coverage was not realized. Instead, two ongoing efforts were undertaken: the training and establishment of the Afghan defense and police forces and the expansion of the activities of the PRTs into the provinces. Both initiatives in themselves would undoubtedly enhance the security situation in the country. However, these programs were not coordinated between themselves or necessarily moved within clearly established time frames.

Similarly, the novel approach to divide sectoral reconstruction responsibilities among major states did not produce early results. Whether legal reform or drug control or demobilization, each sector required both mobilization and coordination of intersectoral resources, which often went beyond what individual states could manage. Needless to say, the Afghan government would clearly be the only responsible body to manage the wide range of reconstruction work, but UNAMA in the meantime expanded its range of assistance as the process was accelerated to keep up the nation building momentum.

One operational area that required a swift transition was between emergency humanitarian and longer-term assistance. Humanitarian operations had a head start in Afghanistan since they had been the only kind of international intervention allowed during the years of war and occupation. With the military action successfully expelling the Taliban and Al Qaeda forces, refugees and internally displace persons returned in large numbers. The back to home and back to school programs led by UNHCR, UNICEF, the WFP, and the international humanitarian agencies spearheaded the response to the demands of millions of Afghans to get back to normal life at the community level.

The government was particularly eager to solve the problem of the internally displaced persons. While many of them were victims of prolonged drought, quite a large number were victims of internal conflicts. They posed a challenge to governance. It was the convergence

of interest among the Afghan government, the international humanitarian agencies charged with the solution of refugee repatriation, and
the donor governments trying to bring forth a seamless transition
from humanitarian to development assistance that led to the innovative comprehensive area development program centered in Kandahar.
In addition, the Afghan government was determined to incorporate
the humanitarian programs within its national development framework and attempted to exercise control over the transition phase.

An active reconstruction process depends largely on input from
development agencies. In Afghanistan, however, those agencies,
which were not present during the twenty-three years of war, tended
to be late in their entry on the postconflict scene. Together with the
Afghan rejection of infrastructure rebuilding financed by loans, large-
scale reconstruction of roads and electric power stations resulted in
considerable delays.

Nation building in postconflict situations requires the spread of
both quick and visible dividends of peace. To be successful, the
Afghan exercise must bring together integrated results in security
assurance, political institution building, humanitarian coverage, and
reconstruction achievements. Serious international contributions
were made, but the final stage of nation building would depend on the
consolidation by the political and administrative leadership. The
weight of the past is still heavy. The division is real: regional, ethnic,
political, and historical. Action backed up by the emergence of equitable and rule-based political configuration will determine the final
outcome of the Afghan experience.[4]

5.

CONCLUSION: HUMANITARIAN ACTION IN WAR AND PEACE

———————

The ten years that I spent with refugees marked a period of continuous humanitarian crises. UNHCR worked like fire brigades through all the continents of the world. The nature of war had changed, and refugees fled internal conflicts and massive violations of human rights, caused by historic, ethnic, and separatist tensions and movements. Try as we might to protect the refugees and alleviate their suffering, humanitarian action alone could not lead to solving their problems. What was required was a convergence of interests covering humanitarian, political, and security action by major international and regional powers. Without backing by a comprehensive strategic approach, emergencies could not be contained in wartime, nor could solutions be found to bring peace. Reviewing the decade, I do not hesitate to claim that UNHCR contributed significantly during conflict by saving lives and protecting and assisting victims. It also played a substantial part in building peace through returning and reintegrating refugees to countries recovering from war. It could not, however, solve the underlying problems that had led to the conflicts.

This chapter assesses humanitarian action in situations of both war and peace. Reviewing the developments in the four case studies that were selected for the book, it first examines the strategic interests that underlay the policies and actions taken by the international community—namely, the United Nations and the major states involved. Second, it discusses the changing procedures of refugee protection that UNHCR had to adopt in order to provide protection and assistance required under the evolving circumstances. Third, it reviews and evaluates the expanding partnership with the military and the political bodies of the United Nations that helped solve the conflicts on hand. Last, it pursues the humanitarian contributions to postconflict peace-building efforts through repatriation and reintegration of refugees and internally displaced persons. Underlying humanitarian action throughout the decade and in diverse situations was the commitment to stay close to the victims and to find solutions to their plight.

STRATEGIC INTERESTS

The international response to humanitarian crisis situations is largely determined by the degree of strategic interests held by the major states. In contrast with the cold war the intervention by coalition governments stopped at the border. They acted to restore preconflict order but not to address the root causes that challenged the very order. The coalition forces shared a recognition of the strategic importance of the oil-rich gulf region and intervened to protect Kuwait from Iraqi invasion. The war, however, added humanitarian dimensions with the displacement of around four million people and the evacuation of more than a million migrant workers and foreign nationals from Iraq and Kuwait. It developed into a refugee crisis when Iraqi forces crushed an attempted Shia rebellion in the south and a Kurdish uprising in the north. The Iraqi society was characterized by a complex mix of multiple ethnic and religious groups. These people rose against the oppressive Saddam Hussein government, counting on the weakened position of the regime. They also expected protective intervention by the coalition forces, but the coalition governments remained ambivalent. They did not support the Shia rebellion lest it pave the way for the emergence of a pro-Iran Shia government in Baghdad, nor did they wish to promote Kurdish insurrections throughout the region. With NATO air bases located in Turkey, maintaining the internal political stability of Turkey was a matter of strategic concern for the coalition governments.

It was only with the devastating humanitarian situation developing at the Iraqi-Turkish border and broadly publicized by the media that the coalition forces, already present in the region following the Gulf War, decided to intervene to save the fleeing refugees. Their solution was to bring back the Kurds from the border mountain range to the plateau of northern Iraq and establish a safe haven of refugee camps inside their country. This plan had the advantage of preventing the aggravation of ethnic tension within Turkey. The principle of humanitarian intervention, lauded through the adoption of UN Security Council Resolution 688, was in fact a compromise formula that upheld the political and military objectives of the intervening states, while incorporating humanitarian concerns for the Kurdish victims.

UNHCR was pressed to take over the safe haven from the coalition forces and to provide safety and relief to the refugees. For us it represented a major deviation from the traditional practice of ensuring refugee protection in countries of asylum. My decision to accept and agree to help return the Kurds back home to safe areas was based more on realistic humanitarian grounds than on positive preference. I believed that we could not refrain from helping the Kurds who had been prevented from gaining asylum. We therefore had to adopt measures that would provide them with protection within their own country. The United Nations, for its part, negotiated with the Iraqi government and obtained an agreement to operate on Iraqi territory, including the deployment of UN security guard contingents. The Iraqi government acquiesced, preferring a UN presence to the prolonged stationing of coalition forces. The challenge for the United Nations was to give the returning refugees substantive security and assistance in the country from which they had tried to flee.

The solution to the Kurdish refugee crisis was attained through a combination of effective military intervention, humanitarian action, and political compromise. Underlining the success was a sense of realism shared by the contributing parties to find practical solutions that could meet all basic requirements. By contrast, in the humanitarian crisis situations that evolved in the Balkans and in the Great Lakes region of Africa, no comparable strategic action emerged on the basis of the convergence of interests among various contenders. Hence international intervention remained at the humanitarian level. The conflicts continued to expand, and refugees suffered with no solution in sight.

The wars in the Balkans resulted from the breakup of the Socialist Federal Republic of Yugoslavia, which had been held together by the Tito regime. Leading the non-aligned group of states, it had enjoyed a global political role during the cold war. In the five republics the major ethnic groups—Serbs, Croats, and Muslims—fought to ensure themselves majority dominance in the course of gaining independence. The process manifested itself in what became known as ethnic cleansing—i.e., expelling or eliminating individuals belonging to different ethnic groups through political extortion and armed force. It started in Croatia and spread throughout the republics.

The Europeans, with direct stakes in the Balkan conflicts that developed on their southern flank, attempted to lead the peace process. Fearing a deluge of arriving refugees, they shared the goal of preventing a massive outflow of displaced persons in the region. The United Nations became operationally involved in the Balkans in early 1992, through the deployment of UN troops (UNPROFOR) to designated protected areas in Croatia, and later expanded the coverage to Bosnia and Herzegovina, but no effective intervention force was ever deployed. The stakes were extremely high for European states to become actively involved in the Balkan quagmire. The major means to contain the situation were diplomatic negotiation and distribution of humanitarian assistance. UNHCR was virtually left to lead the massive humanitarian operation, serving as the "fig leaf" to cover the reality of strategic inaction.

The Security Council was divided over the action to be taken in Bosnia and Herzegovina. It debated and adopted numerous resolutions and statements by the council president but reached limited consensus. The nonaligned caucus in support of the Bosnian government pressed for the designation of five safe areas and the deployment of UNPROFOR to deter Serb attacks by its presence. The secretary-general requested additional troops to be deployed to the safe areas, but there was no response. By taking a stand without substantive backup, the council revealed its limit in both strength and authority. UNHCR and the humanitarian agencies were left to confront the growing Serb power. The safe area debate and the subsequent massacre in Srebrenica proved the limits of collective action in the face of diametrically opposed strategic interests. It was only after the debacle that NATO rose to meet the Serb offensive by the use of air power. The United States joined in the flurry of diplomatic negotiations that culminated in the conclusion of peace in Dayton. Four years lapsed with no decisive political decision backed up by military action, resulting in enormous human suffering throughout the Balkans.

Kosovo, which had been deliberately excluded from the Dayton negotiations, however, drew strategic attention once the situation deteriorated in 1998. The United States took the lead, supported by the Contact Group of states that had pursued the conclusion of the Dayton Agreement. Ambassador Richard Holbrooke actively carried out diplomatic negotiations, pressing Milosevic to pull back Serb security forces from Kosovo. NATO stood by firmly under an order of possible activation. The Kosovo situation was exceptional in that under the threat of international intervention, the Federal Republic of Yugoslavia was persuaded to withdraw its forces from its province of Kosovo, cease its repressive measures, and negotiate a political settlement. Teams of military personnel in civilian clothes sponsored by the OSCE member states were brought in to "verify" the compliance. Humanitarian agencies, notably UNHCR, the ICRC, and NGO teams, were permitted by the Serb government to continue humanitarian assistance inside Kosovo.

The diplomatic negotiations over Kosovo were closely coordinated by the Contact group countries, the OSCE, and NATO, in periods both preceding as well as following the NATO air action. Military action was tasked with the prescribed diplomatic objective of obtaining the withdrawal of forces and their termination of atrocities. However, in regard to the humanitarian consequences of its air action, NATO did not possess a clear view of the possible population displacement. Its air campaign not only could not stop the expulsions or killings of Kosovo civilians but in fact increased the number of people forced to flee across the borders to Albania and Macedonia.

In the political negotiations preceding and during the military action, the UN had a limited role. The Security Council played no substantial part in the authorization of NATO action. The fact that the UN was largely excluded from the Balkan settlement also undermined its influence over Kosovo. For the reconstruction phase, however, the United Nations was given the principal role in the interim civilian administration of Kosovo. UNMIK (United Nations Interim Administration Mission in Kosovo) was set up in June 1999, with peacekeeping responsibilities entrusted to the Kosovo force from NATO member states. Resolute international action backed up by military force ended the long-simmering Kosovo crisis but postponed the ultimate solution of statehood and ethnicity.

Unlike the conflicts in the Balkans, the genocide in Rwanda and the subsequent spread of fighting in the Great Lakes region of Africa were marked by the absence of any strategic approach by the major powers to the solution of the underlying problems. Since the 1960s UNHCR had been faced with refugee problems in the Great Lakes region rooted in the colonial rule that polarized traditional communal identities along ethnic lines. Large displacement of Tutsis from Rwanda to all neighboring countries remained unaddressed until 1990, when the Tutsis in Uganda created the Rwandan Patriotic Front (RPF) and achieved a military return. The power-sharing arrangement negotiated in Arusha between the returning Tutsis and the ruling Hutu regime had the backing of the United Nations. The Security Council created the UN Assistance Mission for Rwanda (UNAMIR) to serve as the neutral monitoring force to ensure the application of the agreement. However, the mission was limited both in mandate and in scale, and once the genocide erupted, the international community proved unwilling as well as incapable of intervening with political or military action. The Rwanda government interpreted the indecisive action by the Security Council as evidence of international betrayal. Its relations with the United Nations remained soured for years.

The international community responded actively to the millions of refugees who fled to Tanzania and particularly to Zaire in large and critical physical conditions. For UNHCR, once again at the forefront of the refugee crisis, the major powers mounted a rescue operation, unprecedented in scale and speed. However, they were not ready to deal with the basic security issue in the refugee camps—i.e., the domination of the refugees by the political and military perpetrators of the genocide. In fact the international military forces dispatched at the height of the humanitarian crisis would not get involved in police work, not to speak of attempting to separate the refugees from military or militia elements. The problem of militarized camps became the issue of paramount danger that UNHCR was left to attempt to solve alone.

To characterize the response of the international community as totally lacking in strategic interest might not be accurate. In fact the major Western powers had relationships of close alignment with various Rwandan regimes. The French support of the Hutu Habyarimana regime had been strong. It continued to provide military training and equipment on the basis of the Military Cooperation Agreement of 1975 despite the declaration of an arms embargo by the Security Council. At the height of the conflict, France mounted a humanitarian intervention, Operation Turquoise, to set up a protection zone in the southwest, authorized by the Security Council for two months.[1] This meant that the southwest was excluded from the RPF action. Many Hutus were protected in camps for internally displaced persons, while many ruling elites were assisted to depart to Zaire and France. The French forces left Rwanda in the end of August, but France's intention to maintain its influence over the Francophone African countries persisted. In particular, the French support of Zaire, led by Mobutu, greatly influenced the subsequent war in the Great Lakes region. Rwanda, on the other hand, moved militarily into Zaire in 1996 with the backing of the United States.

The spreading conflict over Congo, if not a war between France and the United States, had the character of a proxy rivalry, which adversely affected the settlement of peace in the Great Lakes region with prolonged humanitarian consequences. The U.S. State Department provided strong support to UNHCR and the refugee cause. The Department of Defense was known to have supported the RPF government by extending military training to its forces and the Zairean Tutsis in Kivu. The support under the cover of demining and other soft security assistance was substantially greater and considerably enhanced the military capacity of the combined Rwandese and rebel forces. In October 1996 the combined rebel forces started attacking the refugee camps in South Kivu, displacing refugees and Zairean locals.

With a major humanitarian crisis looming, the Security Council decided to dispatch a multinational force to eastern Zaire to intervene by containing the immediate disaster. In a bold move, the combined Rwanda and rebel forces bombarded the Goma refugee camps, opening one exit route for the refugees to return to Rwanda. Those left behind fled west throughout the Zairean forest. The Rwandan assault on the Goma camps was aimed at impeding the Security Council–mandated coalition force from intervening in what to the Rwandans was a successful military action. The massive refugee return to Rwanda certainly dampened the readiness of governments participating in the coalition force operation. To begin with, there was no interest among the troop-providing governments to move beyond any emergency humanitarian mission and become involved in disarming or separating the refugees from those who opposed their return. In short, no troop-contributing state wanted to become part of the Great Lakes conflict. While France advocated the reestablishment of refugee camps, the United States was in favor of concluding the refugee saga with a Rwandan victory.

The differences among the coalition states turned into an absurd

numbers game over the estimated figure of refugees who returned to
Rwanda or were left in Kivu. The U.S. and U.K. military engaged in
aerial observation to identify and estimate the numbers of those still
left in the forest. They were able to identify a group of some 165,000
but no other. UNHCR estimated that about 700,000 were still
missing. Even the original refugee population figure given by
UNHCR was questioned. The multinational force ended its mission
on December 31, 1996, leaving the humanitarian missions to continue
the search and rescue operation in Zaire.

The diverse political positions between France and the United
States undermined the possibility of forging a solution. Among the
neighboring states in the region too, there were severe divisions
between those who identified their security with a Tutsi-dominated
Rwanda and those who supported a Hutu-controlled Zaire. Above all,
however, the absence of a basic strategic commitment among the
major powers deprived the region from gaining a setting in which
political negotiations could proceed with or even without the necessary military backup. The dissolution of the multinational force without proving any achievement of its mission symbolized the realities of
the limited geopolitical commitment of the international community
to the Great Lakes region.

As for Afghanistan, the international community focused strategi-
cally at only two phases during the twenty-three years of war. One was
during the cold war superpower rivalry, and the other was after the
September 11 terrorist attacks on the United States. The Soviet
Union militarily intervened in the first phase while the United States
provided massive military support to the resisting Afghan muja-
hideens and to neighboring Pakistan, which served as their rear base
as well as hosted refugees. With the withdrawal of the Soviet forces,
the United States lost its strategic interest in Afghanistan but continued to pump in weapons under covert operations. In the following
years, Afghanistan was left to the fighting among local warlords,
closely linked with the regional powers that intervened according to
their interests. Assistance was left in the hands of humanitarian agencies and the NGOs. In the post–September 11 context, the United

States successfully carried out the military action against the Taliban and Al Qaeda fighters, together with the local resistance forces led by the Panjshir-centered Northern Alliance. The strategic setting now moved on to the fight against terrorism, an amorphous entity that could no longer be fought by solely traditional military means. Nation building, though initially rejected by the U.S. administration, increasingly came to bear strategic significance. War in Afghanistan had to be fought on military, political, and reconstructional grounds.

REFUGEE PROTECTION

As the nature of war in the 1990s shifted to ethnic and separatist communal conflicts, forced human displacement became an issue of primary strategic importance. Traditionally the protection of refugees had centered on the concept of international protection—in other words, of ensuring the safety of refugees once they crossed the border away from their persecuting political entities. On the other side of the border UNHCR awaited to provide protection and relief backed by the international community and supported by the asylum countries. In the ten years that I worked with refugees, the traditional modalities of refugee protection functioned effectively in only limited instances, while most situations required complementation, adjustments, or new initiatives.

In general, states avoided outright *refoulement*, or the rejection of refugee inflows at the borders, as happened with the Kurds who tried to cross over to Turkey or the Kosovo Albanians at the border with Macedonia. UNHCR pressed hard to keep the borders open, while the concerned states exercised major influence to find some compromise solutions. In northern Iraq, the coalition forces set up the safe area that brought the Iraqis back to their home. At the Macedonia border, UNHCR devised the humanitarian evacuation program, which added an international burden-sharing arrangement to ease the position of the refugee-receiving states. Increasingly, UNHCR gained experience, adapting to situational needs while adhering to the principle of refugee protection. Compromise formulas had been worked out, for example, over the Indochina refugees through the adoption of the comprehensive plan of action.

In most instances when the refugees were of close ethnic or religious origin, states accepted their arrival more readily, counting on the assistance to be brought in by UNHCR. The reception by Iran of the Iraqi Shiite refugees and the acceptance of Serb refugees by Serbia, the Hutus by Zaire, the Pashtuns by Pakistan are cases in point. However, the complicating factor was that many of these refugees were losers in the internal armed struggle and fled either to find a base from which to fight back or to seek alignment for better political settlement. Under the circumstances, refugee protection could no longer be addressed by the setting up of refugee camps even as far away as possible from the hazardous border areas. It became much more a hands-on physical protection of refugees and internally displaced persons, in the middle of war zones, as exemplified in Croatia and Bosnia or in the Great Lakes region of Africa, with serious implications for staff security.

Working in war zones for the protection of refugees meant for the staff on the ground daily hazards of negotiating with the local authorities, denouncing abuses, and finding the best available courses of action to save the lives of the victims. In the Balkans the main task of my colleagues was to respond to calls for help by those being forcefully expelled from their houses and villages. If we were to assist the victims to leave their houses or help them evacuate, we were accused of lending a hand to ethnic cleansing. In the Great Lakes region in Africa, when we tried to group together the fleeing Rwanda refugees in the Zairean forest to help them return home, rebel forces took advantage and rushed to the site to murder them to prevent their being rescued out. Yet to leave them unattended would have abandoned them more certainly to death. However limited and at times subject to abuses, being present in the war zones of the Balkans and the Great Lakes region in Africa was the only assured mode of protection.

But being close to the victims meant sharing their dangers. Staff security was a grave concern in the humanitarian operations, particularly in the Balkans and the Great Lakes region. We had fortified our

staff security coverage through training, equipment, and enhanced
insurance. However, the casualties in Bosnia, particularly in central
Bosnia, and in Rwanda, Burundi, and Zaire were heavy. We had to run
daily security reports, at times suspend operations and evacuate staff
out of imminent danger. In particular, repeated casualties in central
Bosnia in the summer of 1993; serious security incidents in Burundi
in 1996 that nearly brought down all humanitarian operations;
Rwanda during the genocide war; and Kosovo under NATO military
action: Security incidents were high, and death tolls were heavy, especially among our local colleagues. I had to take the position that we
should improve staff security coverage as close as possible to 100 percent. But the fact remained that there could never be a 100 percent
guarantee. If the staff were to engage in high-risk missions, the objectives of the humanitarian mission and assurance of the humanitarian
space should be clearly recognized by all concerned. The political
leaders in the world should be active in reaching out for solutions.
Whenever UNHCR was clearly targeted, we had to evacuate, if not
temporarily suspend our operations. What we had to do was to weigh
the significance of our mission against the impending security threats.

The security risk was not confined to the large emergency operations discussed in this book. It was everywhere. The brutal murder of
three staff members—Samson Aregahegn, Carlos Caceres, and Pero
Simundza—in Atambua, West Timor, Indonesia, on September 6,
2000, shook the world. The news arrived as I awaited the opening of
the UN General Assembly Millennium Summit. The previous year
more than 250,000 Timorese had fled from East Timor, the great
majority to West Timor. I had gone to West Timor and agreed with
the Indonesian government to carry out humanitarian assistance and
to organize a safe and voluntary return for those who wished. Many of
the refugees, however, were under the influence of the militia groups
that had opposed the independence. I witnessed the viciousness of
the domination of the militias when I visited the football stadium in
Kupang and they attempted to block us from even talking to the
refugees. They saw in UNHCR not an impartial humanitarian organization but one identified with the United Nations and the interna-

tional military force that had taken East Timor away from them. Our colleagues were targeted.

A few weeks later, while I was visiting Afghanistan, another incident took the life of Mensah Kpognon, the head of Suboffice Macenta in Guinea. I cut short my mission, postponed my audience with President Khatami of Iran, and rushed back to Geneva. The staff organized a memorial ceremony and a march expressing anger and frustration at the brutal killings of civilians and humanitarian workers. Other UN agencies and the staffs of humanitarian agencies joined in the rally. The physical hands-on protection of refugees and displaced persons faced heavy tolls. Yet it was clear that a meaningful protection of refugees and civilian victims could be carried out only in close proximity with them. The presence of humanitarian workers was an indispensable condition for protection work, but better security systems had to be devised to ensure the security of the staff itself. The staff security of the UN system itself had to be substantially strengthened. Together with colleagues from the WFP and UNICEF, humanitarian agencies operating in the front lines of areas of conflict, we pressed UN headquarters and member states for more funds and professional coverage to meet staff security needs. The response remained woefully inadequate.

Other proposals for refugee protection were presented to governments. A much more flexible asylum system had to be devised to respond to large-scale emergency refugee outflows. At the first humanitarian meeting for victims of the conflicts in the former Yugoslavia in July 1992, we requested governments to provide protection to all those in need without subjecting them to time-consuming and costly procedures to determine refugee status. European governments faced a flood of refugees from states in conflict situations. At the time, governments responded positively to those from Croatia and Bosnia. The more serious problem was over how to end their temporary status when situations improved. Some governments, particularly the Nordic states, treated those designated as needing temporary protection as refugees and provided them with permanent status after a certain period. Germany, with large numbers of Balkan asylum seekers, accepted them temporarily as war refugees but tended to press for their return as soon as it judged the war situation had ceased. I believed that UNHCR had to call for the end of temporary protection in order to maintain the credibility of the temporary protection formula. The challenge was to convince governments to maintain a humanitarian approach to solving refugee problems, even in the face of growing pressure by migrants asking European states for asylum.

Of all the existing tools for refugee protection, relief assistance played a central role. Following the experience in northern Iraq, UNHCR had improved its capacity to operate airlifts and convoys in the large-scale assistance operations in the Balkans and the Great Lakes region of Africa. In the Balkans, between July 3, 1992, and January 9, 1996, UNHCR led what became the longest-running humanitarian airlift in history with the participation of more than twenty countries. Altogether some 160,000 tons of food, medicine, and other life saving goods were delivered to Sarajevo in more than twelve thousand flights. During the same period we coordinated a massive logistical operation that delivered some 950,000 tons of relief supplies to various parts of Bosnia and Herzegovina for approximately 2.7 million beneficiaries. About 3,000 humanitarian personnel from over 250 organizations participated in the operation. All were subject to security problems, exposed to shelling and sniping, and at times even targeted. More than 50 of our personnel engaged in the operation lost their lives.

It should be emphasized that however impressive the statistics of sorties and tonnages, the assistance operation had its basic meaning in its close linkage with the protection objective. The Sarajevo airlift brought hope to the citizens that the international community stood behind them. The delivery of relief goods served as concrete proof that people's safety and survival would be assured. How humanitarian goods were distributed had serious implications in relation to the overall objective of the operation. UNHCR insisted that distribution had to be on the basis of needs of the victims, not on political expediency. In the three-party conflict in Bosnia, for example, there was constant procrastination over the delivery destination and the content of relief items. Muslims in the enclaves were surely in need of relief supplies. Serbs on the route blocked the convoys unless a substantial amount was allotted to them. Some Serb villagers required some assistance, but not necessarily on an equal basis. The Muslim government in Sarajevo boycotted the airlift in order to highlight the fate of the enclave population. I suspended the delivery operation in opposition to what seemed to be the politicization of humanitarian assistance. Nevertheless, we were careful in proving our impartiality, by selecting Muslim, Croat, and Serb organizations as local partners in the delivery of assistance. In Kosovo we entrusted the delivery to the local Albanian Mother Teresa Society to avoid contracting NGOs reputedly under the influence of government authorities. In addition to security considerations, assistance operations in internal conflict situations had to face daily political and military constraints derived from the ethnic and cultural mistrusts of the people.

In the refugee camps in Kivu along the Zairean border with Rwanda, UNHCR faced the formidable challenge of providing relief to refugees in camps known to include military elements. We had had to deal with militarized camps in Cambodia, Pakistan, Honduras, and elsewhere in the past. But the massive Kivu camps were under the influence of soldiers and militias as well as of political leaders from the Rwandan Hutu regime that had perpetrated genocide killings. They intimidated the refugees and prevented them from returning home. They dominated the relief efforts, harassed international relief workers, and even confiscated their vehicles and equipment. The humanitarian workers in the camps in Goma repeatedly asked for the deployment of an international force, police, or military. Initially, the Zairean government proposed to transfer the Rwandese armed forces to new sites and solicited the United Nations to provide security assistance for the camps. Two influential NGOs withdrew from the camps in protest of the militarized situation.

Unmanageable as the situation evolved, however, I believed that my task was to make all possible efforts to bring security to the camps. I solicited the secretary-general, who requested the member states to dispatch peacekeeping forces, but with no success. I worked out the Zairean security contingency arrangement under international supervision to bring law and order to the camps. Through 1995 the presence of the Zairean forces helped control the intimidations of the Rwanda military. The numbers of returnees increased. It was, however, not a long-term viable solution. Such options as stopping UNHCR assistance or disengaging altogether existed only in theory, not in reality. This did not mean that I saw the humanitarian operation in the camps as an end in itself or a humanitarian imperative. There were more than one million people in the camps, many of them women and children. Considerable numbers would have liked to return if they could. UNHCR's mission was not only to protect refugees in the critical phases of their flight but also to find solutions so that they would not have to remain refugees forever. UNHCR's efforts were directed toward minimizing the intimidating effects of the military elements in the camps, while improving the security and living conditions inside Rwanda for returning refugees. What we awaited most, together with the refugees, was the settlement of the conflict.

POLITICO-MILITARY RELATIONS

The decade of the 1990s exposed UNHCR to new partners. Civil and military collaboration broke fresh grounds in northern Iraq and grew in the course of the Balkan conflicts. Humanitarian organizations started working with the military through participation in Operation Provide Comfort, which was massive in scale and scope as over fifty international humanitarian organizations participated in the relief efforts run by twenty thousand military personnel using two hundred aircraft. Through this experience, UNHCR developed a cadre of professionals, logisticians, drivers, and radio operators, who could play the lead role in coordinating the complex Sarajevo airlift as well as run convoys throughout the region. At UNHCR headquarters, the airlift operations center was set up with seconded air force officers. Between the Sarajevo airport and the city, UNHCR staff ran convoys through the most dangerous route, "snipers' alley," protected by UNPROFOR forces. As UNHCR expanded its relief operation in Bosnia and Herzegovina, we had to seek the support of UNPRO-FOR for the protection of humanitarian workers and relief goods. Security Council Resolution 776 of September 14, 1992, recommended the deployment of six thousand soldiers to support UNHCR's humanitarian assistance operation. Efforts were made to improve civil and military collaboration through close consultation and mutual learning. UNHCR produced manuals for the military partners to explain the principles and procedures of humanitarian action, while the military reciprocated with manuals on its mode of operations. The UNHCR-UNPROFOR joint efforts brought better relief and support to the victims.

In the final analysis, however, the effectiveness of humanitarian and military collaboration depended on the outcome of the political negotiations, the decisions adopted by the UN Security Council, or the successful backing of military action in achieving the overall political goals. UNHCR together with UNPROFOR endured all security threats and operational blockages in the Balkans with the hope and trust that political negotiations under way would soon settle the conflict and move on to peace building. We worked closely with the ICFY negotiating teams and the contact group leaders. The results were long in coming. The fall of Srebrenica showed how inadequate political and military measures could lead to a debacle. To begin with, the member states of the Security Council could not agree on a course of action to deal with the Serb offensive over Srebrenica. It pronounced the designation of safe areas without providing adequate deterrent strength to the peacekeepers to protect the areas. Then it prolonged decisions on resorting to the use of air power.

Air action had serious operational implications for humanitarian agencies. I was aware that the use of air power would disrupt operations by unarmed civilians engaged in humanitarian relief activities. At the same time, it was clear that short of political action backed up by force, humanitarian action alone could not end the war in Bosnia. While I opposed the use of force to expedite the delivery of humanitarian assistance, I took no position on the use of force to back up a political settlement and thus end the war. If suspending humanitarian operation became necessary to enable action to end the war, I thought it had to be suspended. In the end, it was the NATO air strikes against the Serb military action over the safe area of Gorazde that led to the Dayton Peace Agreement.

In the Kosovo operation, NATO used air strikes with the clear objective of forcing the withdrawal of Serbian security forces. What NATO had not foreseen was the humanitarian consequences of its military action. Serb forces deliberately pushed Kosovo Albanians out of their houses. Nobody had foreseen the possibility of massive deportations and refugee outflows to Albania and Macedonia. In the beginning UNHCR could barely face the critical emergency situations at two border crossings. NATO was reported to have expected its campaign to last for several days, if not weeks. But the bombing continued for seventy-eight days. It succeeded in grounding the Yugoslav Air Force while failing to destroy the ground forces that resorted to the expulsions and killings of Kosovo civilians. Altogether some 750,000 refugees fled Kosovo, and at least 590,000 became internally displaced.

The fundamental shortcoming in the Western war strategy was the absence of any option to the air campaign in dealing with the kind of war that dominated the Balkans. As the ICFY negotiator Carl Bildt once remarked, with the kind of house-to-house communal conflict that was fought in the Balkans, the world needed crowd control systems, not missiles. Watching the bombs dropping from fifteen thousand feet while humanitarian agencies waited in vain for opportunities to come to the rescue of the people under bombardment, I began to question the effectiveness of high technology warfare. Air attacks were less risky than ground invasions in terms of soldiers' lives but could cause massive human suffering and outflows of refugees and internally displaced persons. The Kosovo air strikes brought to the fore the question of appropriateness of the available modes of military action, together with the worsening effect of collateral damages on vast numbers of civilian victims. General Wesley Clark, supreme commander of allied forces in Europe, recounted the political blockages he faced even to prepare for the ground force option, as the air campaign dragged on. "The American way of war: strategic heavy firepower"[2] was very slow to prove effective.

International political and military involvement in the Balkan conflicts was substantial, even if it failed for a long time to end the war. No such engagement was directed toward critical situations in Africa. When peace efforts to solve conflicts were insufficient or ineffective, the ability of humanitarian agencies to help refugees and other victims was greatly diminished. What proved particularly devastating was the absence of any effective conflict resolution mechanisms applicable to the African continent. In the course of the conflicts in the Great Lakes region, no response came to UNHCR's call for policing the militarized refugee camps or dispatching observer missions to border areas. Ultimately the Security Council authorized the Canadian-led multinational force to deal with the crisis in eastern Congo in November 1996. However, the forces were dissolved once large numbers of refugees had been led back to Rwanda even though many others were missing on their flight in the Congo rain forest.

The problems of refugees could not be settled without resolving the conflicts that drove people to flee. In turn, refugees and internally displaced people brought insecurity to communities that hosted them. The secretary-general identified the issue of forced population displacement in Africa as a serious threat to international peace and security and requested that UNHCR cooperate with the UN Department of Peacekeeping Operations to draw up proposals for the establishment of appropriate international mechanisms. UNHCR started the exercise with a focus on the problem of militarized refugee camps and settlements and then moved on to develop a ladder of options covering a range of security situations. At the primary level, security depended largely on the presence of humanitarian agencies in refugee camps and settlements. Training and support for developing the law enforcement capacities of host communities would have a preventive effect on maintaining local security. At the medium level, we foresaw alternatives such as deploying civilian or police monitors.

We proposed the installment of humanitarian security officers in camps and refugee settlements. UNHCR expected much from the implementation of the medium-level option, which included the introduction of subregional peacekeeping arrangements. A line of reports from UNHCR to the Department of Peacekeeping Operations was envisaged in cases of serious threats. Failing containment, the final-level alternative would lead to various intervening options by regional and international military forces. From experience, we were aware that UN peacekeeping operations, though indispensable, were too complex in the organizing process and too slow in constituting a viable response. Our proposals concentrated more on developing the medium option.[3]

The governments reacted favorably to UNHCR's ladder of options proposals. However, their responses remained mostly in the realm of interest and intention. I turned to the Security Council and repeatedly made strong appeals for support, because no other international organ had the authority to pronounce on threatening security situations or to direct and decide on peace operations. The Security Council invited me frequently, in fact twice every year after 1996, when the situations in the Balkans and of the Great Lakes region in Africa gained central attention in world politics. In my briefings, I had two objectives. One was to turn humanitarian problems into legitimate issues of peace and security, and the other was to bring internal conflicts to the domain of international peace and security. Some might argue that I should never have linked humanitarian with security and political issues. To start with, my mandate was to seek solutions to the problem of refugees. In the context of the decade of internal conflicts in which UNHCR operated, our protection mandate had to be exercised through hands-on physical protection of refugees. Humanitarian problems might be best addressed by humanitarian action, but it could not substitute for the necessary exercise of political will to solve the underlying causes of the conflicts. Working with the Security Council was my wishful attempt to move the political will of states as members of the UN organ specifically charged with the solution of issues related to peace and security. What I repeatedly tried was to convey the message of what refugees needed from the Security Council and what UNHCR "expected from the body responsible for addressing peace and security problems, in order to fulfill its core mission."[4]

To work in favor of winning the support of the Security Council and the member states did not necessarily bring satisfactory results. Whether coping with the horrifying feature of ethnic cleansing in the Balkans or genocide and rescue operations in the Great Lakes region of Africa, we did not wish to be left alone in facing intractable situations. What we needed was some predictable access to effective help to protect the security of victims. I recall insisting to Secretary Albright that what I wanted was an 800 telephone number that would respond immediately to requests for dealing with crises. The situation might be a large-scale emergency airlift, or stopping a sudden armed infiltration across borders, or separating militias from refugees in an armed camp. The donor countries were generally sympathetic to UNHCR's needs and provided relief resources to carry on humanitarian assistance. However, as for the vital political and military inputs to settle the conflicts, they would not overstep the boundaries of their geopolitical or domestic interests in determining their position in the Security Council or in resorting to bilateral action.

REPATRIATION AND NATION BUILDING

When conflicts are settled, refugees start moving back. Spontaneous returns are the first signs of trust in peace and the desire to go back to their places of origin. UNHCR's initial task is to plan for the return in terms of the number, destination, and needs. The challenges faced in the repatriation processes of the 1990s, however, reflected the very nature of the conflicts that had developed. These were mostly internal conflicts, with civilians being the target of violence and forced displacement. They frequently had no winner and did not end with a peace agreement. Even the Dayton Agreement, which prescribed a settlement between contending parties, depended on the presence of NATO-led forces to oversee the implementation and ensure security.

The transition from war to peace proved to be a complex and long-term process, depending on subsequent political and reconstruction developments.

Large-scale repatriation of refugees took place in northern Iraq, the Balkans, and in Afghanistan under the security of NATO or coalition military forces. UNHCR and the humanitarian agencies worked closely with the military forces particularly in the initial postconflict phases. The notable exception was in the Great Lakes region of Africa, where the conflicts dragged on with neither a clear peace nor a third-party military force to intervene and ensure security. In northern Iraq the repatriation operation of the U.S.-led coalition forces brought the Kurds back to their original homes, where security was assured in designated safe havens. Subsequent efforts were based on the memorandum of understanding concluded between the United Nations and the Iraqi government, stipulating joint cooperation to expedite voluntary repatriation. The coalition forces transferred the overall responsibility for repatriation and assistance to UNHCR, which, together with a large number of local and international NGOs, carried out major rehabilitation work. By early autumn 90 percent of all the Kurds who had sought refuge in Turkey and Iran had returned. In both speed and scale, the repatriation of Kurdish refugees was an unprecedented achievement, because of the early and decisive intervention by the coalition forces, the convergence of interests among the major players—the coalition countries, the UN, and the Iraqi government—to hand over the repatriation to UNHCR, and the effective rehabilitation work that UNHCR was able to undertake. Nation building in Iraqi Kurdistan, however, remained constrained as the result of the infighting between the two main Kurdish political parties and the reluctance of the Iraqi government and the international community to recognize the emergence of a Kurdish state.

By contrast, in Bosnia and Herzegovina NATO took over from the UN peacekeeping force, UNPROFOR, to organize IFOR, the international force to implement the Dayton Agreement. The postconflict peace operation proved larger in scale and even more daunting in the objectives than the wartime humanitarian operations.

IFOR consisted of sixty thousand troops, nearly twice the number of UNPROFOR. Its primary role was to put into effect the military provisions of the Dayton Agreement to oversee the military withdrawal of the respective parties and to establish the zones of separation between the two entities, Republika Srpska and the Muslim-Croat Federation. IFOR was also expected to increase its support for civilian implementation, including return, by stabilizing the security environment through its presence. In the first few months after the signing of the Dayton Agreement, the record of returns registered limited results, all to majority areas. Returnees felt confident going back to where the majority of the inhabitants had the same ethnicity. People would not go back even to their original homes if the ethnic composition of the area had changed in a way that made them the minority. For majority return, the challenge was reconstruction of the physical infrastructure. For minority return, the main obstacle was insecurity and fear. Returning minorities were frequently threatened, harassed, or even killed. So overbearing were the legacies of ethnic cleansing, that minority return remained minimal for nearly five years following Dayton.

Under the circumstances, UNHCR had to resort to new means to overcome the ethnic walls. It ran interentity bus lines, gave priority assistance to municipalities committed to open cities, promoted women's job training through the Women's Initiative, and launched the reconciliation program of Imagine Coexistence. Of particular importance was the search for remedial models to rebuild communities that had undergone mass atrocities. The search was for midpoint remedies that would fall between "vengeance and forgiveness"—i.e., between too much memory and too much forgetting. From job sharing to recreation sharing, the Imagine Coexistence pilot projects represented the most creative and constructive preliminary steps toward reconciliation. In bringing people back to communities to face those with whom they had fought bitter wars, the projects covered areas that represented the fundamental activities of community living and attempted to help the people regain the possibilities of living together again.[5]

In Kosovo, the repatriation of Kosovo Albanians went very fast. As soon as the Serb security forces agreed to withdraw, the refugees rushed back to claim their property and their right to live collectively. The return of Albanians, however, triggered the departure of the Serb and other minority populations, notably the Romas. Despite the presence of UNMIK and NATO forces, peace and security were hard to restore. The process of nation building in Kosovo moved gradually, in proportion to the slow progress gained in the establishment of security, the improvement in the economic life, and the process of reconciliation across ethnic lines.

The international community responded to the prevalence of ethnic strife and massive violation of human rights as an issue of impunity. While truth commissions were set up in South Africa and El Salvador to address the problems of atrocities and healing, the Security Council decided to establish the International Criminal Tribunal of the Former Yugoslavia in 1993 and the International Criminal Tribunal for Rwanda in 1994. The administration of international criminal justice was crucial to correcting the gross violations of human rights and forced displacements and restoring the rule of law. UNHCR cooperated closely with the tribunals by helping investigators access our records. Yet the slowness at which international criminal justice system proceeded limited the possibility of influencing the repatriation process, not to speak of finding ways to help people live together again. In the Balkans the courts brought justice to the violators of humanitarian laws but failed to arrest leading indicted war criminals and bring them to trial. From war crimes to property restitution, the rule of law was slow to establish justice and order to postconflict Balkan societies.

In the two situations of Rwanda and Afghanistan, the repatriation of refugees was at the forefront of the rehabilitation and reconstruction processes. UNHCR and the humanitarian agencies involved from the conflict phases contributed substantially to the rehabilitation and reconstruction of the two nations by reintegrating the returnees into their communities. In both cases, the scale of the repatriation was massive. An estimated 2 million people out of a total population of 7.5 million went back to Rwanda, and some 3 million refugees and displaced persons had returned to Afghanistan by the end of 2003, with possibly more to follow.

The Rwanda repatriation had to face the unprecedented challenge of reintegrating a population that consisted of victims of genocide, survivors of genocide, perpetrators of genocide, and other returnees from neighboring countries. The judicial system had virtually collapsed in the country and could not restore security or establish the rule of law. In fact more than one hundred thousand genocide suspects were held in overcrowded prisons. UNHCR responded to the repatriation challenge by massive reintegration efforts. It also assisted the physical rehabilitation of the judiciary system and intensive training of judicial personnel. Major components of the reintegration program consisted of providing shelter to returnees linked with the physical reconstruction of social service facilities, empowerment of women and local NGOs, and assistance to income-generating programs. The Rwanda government took the lead in the rehabilitation and reconstruction. UNHCR gave operational support to the government agencies and provided protection to returning refugees through the country-wide presence of staff. As the situation gradually stabilized, we focused our attention on programs that promoted reconciliation through supporting two commissions that the government set up, the National Unity and Reconciliation Commission and the National Human Rights Commission. Of the countries in the Great Lakes region of Africa, it was only in Rwanda that UNHCR could undertake rehabilitation operations. The government included substantial numbers of returning refugees in the nation building process. Elsewhere in the region, conflicts continued in Burundi and throughout Congo.

UNHCR's major contribution to Afghan refugees also spanned from their camp days in neighboring countries to repatriation and reintegration after the victory of the U.S.-led coalition forces over the Taliban and Al Quada in 2001. Reconstruction efforts involved multiple actors, both Afghan and international. The international community organized itself into several clusters of activities: the security operations run by the coalition forces led by the United States, state building efforts by the United Nations in support of the Afghan Interim Administration, and massive reconstruction work by a large range of international organizations, bilateral agencies, and NGOs. The return movements of refugees and internally displaced persons moved at a faster pace and larger scale than had been anticipated. UNHCR, UNICEF, the WFP, and humanitarian NGOs led the initial postconflict phase by quickly moving resources and personnel. They also seconded staffs to counterpart ministries in order to reinforce the government capacity to respond to rapid demands.

A major feature that characterized the return and reintegration process was the government's determination to bring all activities under its purview. Led by the finance minister Ashraf Ghani, the American-educated development economist with World Bank experience, the government insisted that all humanitarian and reconstruction operations be brought under the national development framework. The programs relating to repatriation and reintegration had to take on development roles in the overall context of Afghan nation building. Road and shelter reconstruction, irrigation and water supply, education of women and girls, health and sanitation—all activities that had to be implemented for the reintegration of returning refugees and displaced persons—were expected to move along with the improvement in the lives of the general public in view. Specifically there were protection- and security-related concerns for the returning refugees that had to be addressed. The effects of the continuing power feud among the warlords, the tension and violence among diverse ethnic groups, and, above all, the pervasive effects of poverty altogether undermined the early success of reconstruction. Repatriation and reintegration of refugees contributed to nation building but were also conditioned by the overall level of progress achieved by the state.

Nation building requires solid partnership among a wide range of actors. Of primary relevance in the consolidation of institutions and communities undergoing reconstruction is the state itself. Equally vital is the role of the military and police forces commissioned to bring and build secure postconflict environments. The humanitarian agencies provide immediate short-term relief to normalize the lives of people coming out of conflict. In the case of UNHCR, its role is to help return refugees and the internally displaced persons to their homes to be reintegrated into their communities. The development agencies are to join in at an early phase with plans and resources to carry on from early phases of reconstruction to solid medium- and long-term sustainable stages of development. As far as the humanitarian agencies are concerned, the efforts to coordinate a joint initiative with their development partners to fill the gap in the funding and operations remain to be realized.

In fact nation building needs more attention by the international community at large and especially by the main actors involved. In the ten years of continuous refugee crises, UNHCR established partnerships with a wide range of actors to meet the critical lifesaving challenges of conflicts and violence. In the early postconflict situations in which the possibilities of peace are still held in abeyance, the contributing elements are generally too slow to arrive and too limited in exerting responsibilities. The interface among the political, military, humanitarian, and developmental has to grow into a much more solid strategic partnership. Humanitarian action must bridge the war and peace. Refugees need it. Victims need it. Above all, the people need it.

Epilogue:
THE HIGH COMMISSIONER'S FAREWELL TO UNHCR

GENEVA, DECEMBER 20, 2000

Dear Friends: More and more frequently, as the time to leave approaches, I am asked—and I ask myself—what has been my vision of UNHCR over the past ten years?

When I came to UNHCR, I had to hit the ground running. The Kurdish refugee crisis happened a few weeks after my arrival. The war in Slovenia started when we had not yet finished repatriating the Kurds and soon spread to Croatia. After a few more months Somalia's disaster heralded a new series of African humanitarian tragedies. I realized that something crucial was going to happen to very key elements of the refugee equation—to borders, to wars, to the way people fled and the world responded. I had to think very quickly, and two main conclusions permeated my vision of the office in the years to come.

The first was that UNHCR would end if it remained a slow, static, conservative organization. If UNHCR was to stay relevant—and when I say relevant, I mean to *refugees*—then it had to be quick, smart, effective, and adaptable to a fast-changing environment.

The second conclusion was that just to speak from the high moral ground, on which—I was told very early on—stood the high commissioner, was not enough. Telling states to protect refugees was fine, but we had to help them do it and actively search for solutions while staying as much as possible close to the refugees themselves, so that our arguments would be credible.

Creating the most effective emergency mechanism in the United Nations was one of the responses to my first concern. Developing new ideas and tools, such as the concept of temporary protection, was an example of the second. Sure enough, we made mistakes. We also attracted much criticism—even from within the office. But we have kept a steady pace in adapting to a changing world, and we have had some resounding successes, of which we should be very proud.

In 1991 UNHCR was different from now—not just in size, which is not the most significant change. People did not use e-mail. Working with the military was a slightly suspicious activity. The high commissioner did not usually brief the Security Council, nor did staff speak freely to the press.

If I look back, the changes have been staggering. Yet we started expressing our view in political fora, made progress in technology and communication, and adopted a more open attitude toward the press, because it was *necessary*. Otherwise, we would have been marginalized. We may have had setbacks and hesitations, but I feel that we have maintained a central place in humanitarian and refugee matters.

If I look at the world, I see the future as rather unsettled—at least for a while. The long transition that started in the late eighties is not finished. Translated into UNHCR terms, this means that there will be more emergencies involving refugees and internally displaced people. I am *very* worried about West Africa—Guinea, in particular. The situation in Central Africa, especially in Congo, is far from a solution. And there are other flashpoints—Sri Lanka, Afghanistan and Central Asia, Colombia. Even previously stable regions like East Asia show signs of fragility. And we should not forget the immense destabilizing potential of one refugee crisis that we don't deal with directly, the Palestinians in the Middle East.

The risk of emergencies is further complicated by the fact that in many situations people on the move are targets, hostages and fighters at the same time—like in West Timor and Guinea. All this is very dangerous. The lessons of the Rwandan exodus in the former Zaire do not seem to have been learned.

Let's have another quick look at what I think are the crucial priorities.

It is essential that you keep refining UNHCR's ability to prepare for and respond to emergencies. We will continue to be judged and measured *primarily* in that area. I am very encouraged by the establishment of the Emergency and Security Services and by the approach that this unit is intending to take, dealing not only with the immediate emergency response but also with the security aspects of our work—security of refugees, security of staff. One important point is that more solid and predictable partnerships with governments must be established.

It is also important that you work on clarifying the relationship between refugees and migration. Globalization is changing the way people are moving across borders in search of safety or jobs, or both. Tragedies, such as in Dover, and recently in Indonesia, with hundreds of people dying while they are being trafficked, are likely to occur again. States are slow in responding to these challenges; the only people who are adapting quickly are those profiting from the new trends: the human traffickers, the drug dealers, the arms and diamond traders. These are problems beyond UNHCR's reach, of course, but can UNHCR really ignore them?

We cannot simply repeat that asylum and migration must be kept separate by governments and in the public opinion; we must propose something more concrete, examine where the points of difference and overlap are, and develop new approaches. I am pleased that the Department of International Protection is steering the so-called global consultation process, at the heart of which lies this very matter. It is a delicate issue—because it is so politicized—but I agree that the time has come to raise it, with due precautions, in international fora.

I think you should keep working on what we keep calling, for lack of a better term, the gap between emergency assistance and longer-term development. This is one of the most difficult challenges, but at least we have kept the issue alive on the international agenda; last week I participated in a video conference with the heads of the World Bank and UNDP to appeal for the discussion to be reinvigorated. As I have often said, I have raised the gap problem because we were very frustrated by lack of funding in the postemergency phase in places like Rwanda, Liberia, and Bosnia. Many of our current funding problems stem from lack of resources in this phase. We must improve our analysis of the causes of the gap and the quality of programs that we develop to address it.

Finally, don't be bureaucratic. Keep thinking. When I arrived at UNHCR, my greatest advantage was that I did not come from a bureaucracy. People have said that I have a tendency to be professorial. Maybe. But I also think that academic life has taught me to be free in my thinking, not to be constrained by schemes, categories, and—yes—red tape. Overly bureaucratic organizations are going to become irrelevant in a globalized world. Our contact with real people and situations has kept us alive. Maintain this approach. It is what makes us different from others—in a positive way.

I also know very well that during the past ten years UNHCR at times has been accused of expansionism. This is not correct. Yes, we have gone the extra mile to carry out our mission, and sometimes we had to do what others were not ready or not prepared to do. Of course we should always make sure that what we do is sustainable and coherent, but we should not give up on a project just because it does not fit into traditional schemes. I am very proud, for example, that we have decided to launch Imagine Coexistence. In order to be financed, in a highly competitive environment, UNHCR must develop new, *interesting* approaches to fulfill its core mission.

Dear friends: Being with UNHCR has been for me an immense learning experience. I must tell you that when I arrived in Geneva, I had a rather abstract image of the office: an organization with a noble cause but somehow aloof from reality. Year after year, however, I have had countless opportunities to observe and appreciate the courage, determination, creativity, and passion of UNHCR workers, especially in difficult field locations. I know how real, practical, and concrete our work can be and yet, at the same time, how it remains one of today's great causes.

And it is in this combination of very hard reality, and of powerful idealism, that lies the strength of UNHCR.

About two months ago, speaking in this atrium, the secretary-general of the United Nations told us that he would give UNHCR an able new leader. He has delivered on his promise. It is of great comfort to know that I am leaving UNHCR in good hands and after a smooth transition. Ruud Lubbers is an experienced political figure. I have met him several times in the last few weeks, and he has struck me as a humane and deeply committed person.

It is good for UNHCR to undergo a change in leadership. Mr. Lubbers's fresh approach and ideas will certainly open up new opportunities to resolve refugee problems. But I hope you don't mind if I tell you that I too see my departure as a fresh start! On Saturday I will fly to Tokyo, where I hope to spend a few months resting and going back to my roots. I have been away for ten years and must rediscover my country, there too lots of things have changed. More than anything, I want to spend time with my family, from whom I have been separated for far too long—just like many of you—while serving UNHCR.

But I wish to be in touch with refugee and humanitarian issues and of course with international politics. I plan to write a book, both a memoir and an analysis of the last decade seen from the perspective of my experience. The Ford Foundation has generously offered to support me in this endeavor. I also plan to remain involved in some of the broader issues I have touched upon in the past few years, particularly the concept of human security, which has raised much interest in Japan and which I feel needs to be better defined and developed.

But much as I am thrilled to start a new life, I also feel sad to leave UNHCR. In ten years I have made many friends, and as you know better than me, friends that you meet in difficult situations are friends for life. I look back to the past decade, and as in a long film, many different events unfold: fun, solemn, tragic.

Let me remember here in a very special way those of our colleagues who are not with us anymore and in particular those who died while carrying out their duty. This year has been *very* painful. The sense of fulfillment and satisfaction that I feel looking back to our hard and fruitful work is tainted by sorrow and anger at the thought of our colleagues murdered in Atambua and Macenta and of all the others—true heroes of our time—who have been killed traveling and working for the refugee cause. As I announced at ExCom [the Executive Committee], a memorial, the design of which has already been approved, will be placed very soon outside headquarters to remember all of them.

Sometimes in the past ten years the burden of suffering and death that our work entails has been difficult to carry, for all of us. Nothing can compensate the loss of our friends and of many refugees who have perished in spite of our efforts, but please, be *proud* of the courage of so many colleagues trying to help millions of people worldwide, and *rejoice* in the knowledge that you have indeed saved thousands of lives. This is an extraordinary achievement. And to signify that our work is also about life and hope, as I told you a few days ago, I decided that my simple parting present would be a small Japanese maple tree, which now stands in front of this office, waiting for spring to grow its leaves.

Dear friends: Before I say good-bye, let me add something important. People always ask me where I draw my energy from. And I think of all the refugees whom I have met in camps, in villages, in reception centers, in shantytowns. Well, I believe that what has kept me going is our collective effort to turn the terror and pain that I saw in too many eyes into the relief of safety and into the exhilarating joy of returning home. It has been a worthwhile effort.

Today, as I take leave from UNHCR, I feel happy, and privileged, to have gone down this long path together with all of you.

Thank you, and farewell.

APPENDIX 1

———————

Briefing to the Security Council by Sadako Ogata, United Nations High Commissioner for Refugees

NEW YORK, NOVEMBER 10, 2000

Mr. President: Thank you for inviting me, once more, to brief the Security Council. In six weeks, after ten years, I will leave office, so it is for the last time that I speak here today as the United Nations high commissioner for refugees. Therefore, rather than elaborating on specific regional crises, I will take this opportunity to give you some "food for thought," looking back at the experiences of the past turbulent decade; and reflecting on the future of refugee work—in particular, on its relationship with this body, the most important forum where issues of peace and security are discussed and addressed.

BETWEEN PEOPLE AND STATES

Mr. President: I briefed the Security Council for the first time eight years ago. Since then I have met with the council quite often; if my records are accurate, this is my twelfth briefing. Over the years, refugee issues have also appeared on the agenda of the council more regularly and frequently. This proves the obvious. The nature of contemporary wars, primarily internal and intercommunal, their intensity, and their objectives—especially the brutal expulsion of entire communities from specific areas—mean that conflicts today are *inevitably* the main cause of mass exodus. Internal conflicts and refugee flows in turn have become a threat to peace and security, across borders, in many areas.

More than ever, refugees and wars are inextricably linked. My first briefing to the council was in 1992, when the violent breakup of the former Yugoslavia was displacing millions of people. It was less usual than today that a humanitarian agency would be asked to speak before the Security Council, and it was the tragedy of ethnic cleansing which placed the United Nations refugee agency, whose mission is to serve people, at the center of the political debate on peace and security.

Over the years I have observed the interface between the political and humanitarian spheres grow and evolve. I have not ceased calling for political support for humanitarian crises. I have repeated, countless times, that humanitarian action can only address, not resolve, political problems. I have given much thought to the relationship of humanitarian and political bodies. Bridging the gap between the pressing, often dramatic interests of the most vulnerable and deprived people in the world and the legitimate concerns of states has been the crucial theme of my decade at UNHCR.

My central question to you today is therefore the following: What do refugees need from the Security Council? What does the UN refugee agency expect from the body responsible for addressing peace and security problems, in order to fulfill its core mission: to provide effective protection to refugees and find durable solutions to their problems?

I would like to elaborate on and make concrete proposals in two main areas: peace operations and peace building. Let me begin with peace operations.

PEACE OPERATIONS IN A CHANGING SECURITY ENVIRONMENT

As we have said many times, the nature of war has changed. But the concept of peace operations may still be based on the assumption that wars are fought across clear-cut front lines. And in spite of discussions on wider approaches, peace operations continue to be country-based and reflect neither the internal nor the regional nature of many of today's wars. You will appreciate that we at UNHCR ask ourselves such questions as an agency dealing, precisely, with forced population movements across blurred conflict lines and across borders.

We deploy our own staff, unarmed humanitarian workers, to dangerous and isolated duty stations. They are increasingly targeted and, as in the terrible September incidents of Atambua and Macenta, attacked and brutally killed. The gap in time between the beginning of humanitarian activities and that of peace operations continues to widen. Last, but certainly not least, in many places, like West Timor, Guinea, and Liberia, forced population movements have become the cause and conduit of grave insecurity and instability, and little is done to address the problem, as if we had learned nothing from the lessons of the former eastern Zaire.

Mr. President: This is a situation that worries me deeply. In most parts of the world where UNHCR and its humanitarian partners are called upon to operate, mechanisms to address security problems are slow-moving, unwieldy, and not adapted to the new type of conflicts. In many places they simply do not exist. Among my most vivid memories is the rescue operation that we set up in the former Zaire in 1996. When all deployment of international forces failed, our staff had to go and search for scattered, hungry, and terrified refugees in the rain forest of that vast country, sometimes even on foot.

I am aware of the difficulties—in political terms, in military terms, and in terms of resources. But there are a few points that I would like to raise and a few suggestions that I would like to make in this respect.

Let me insist, first of all, on the need to initiate and implement peace operations much more rapidly. The issue of timing, frankly speaking, is one that has not yet been satisfactorily addressed by governments. We know that peace operations will inevitably be slower than the humanitarian response. In refugee emergencies, UNHCR, other UN frontline agencies (especially UNICEF and WFP), the Red Cross movement, and NGOs will continue to be the first ones on the ground. But if there has to be complementarity in this endeavor, we must do all that we can to reduce the gap between the deployment of humanitarian personnel and the implementation of some security support measures. Otherwise, the cost is simply unbearable, as proven by the catastrophic consequences of inaction in the successive Great Lakes crises, for example, or by the recent murders in Indonesia and Guinea.

We at UNHCR have become used to being called to confront refugee emergencies literally at a few hours' notice. We have no choice; delays, in our work, inevitably mean that lives are lost. Since 1992 we have therefore progressively built systems to respond quickly to sudden, massive population movements. These systems are based, essentially, on the concept of standby resources that can be mobilized and sent to the field within seventy-two hours: staff, equipment, goods, money.

Since 1992, however, the environment has changed rapidly. Political pressure for quick solutions to refugee problems has increased, and there is a growing number of humanitarian actors, including sometimes government themselves. The Kosovo refugee crisis last year proved that we had to adapt our existing emergency response systems to a new and more crowded humanitarian space, and the area on which we are focusing in particular is to upgrade our surge capacity to address refugee emergencies at a very short notice.

But no matter how rapidly and effectively humanitarian agencies mobilize, their response will be inadequate unless the environment in which they operate is secure. I am speaking both of staff security and, from UNHCR's point of view, of the security of refugees and of the communities hosting them.

There is today an increased awareness that humanitarian agencies should not be left alone to confront difficult and dangerous situations. The question is, How do we ensure that? I have often spoken—also in this room—of the need to look at different options, not only full-fledged peacekeeping but also and especially measures intended to support local law enforcement capacity.

I insist on the word *support*. This is the key concept, and it implies working together, as opposed to straightforward intervention. I am also referring to very specific situations—especially insecure border areas in and around refugee sites. And I am thinking of relatively simple measures: assisting the judiciary; training the police and military; supporting the police with logistics and communication; deploying, if necessary, liaison officers to work as coordinators and advisers. We have some such programes—and they are working reasonably well— in western Tanzania, in the area hosting refugees from Burundi, Rwanda, and the Democratic Republic of the Congo. We need your support for similar programs in other critical spots—in Guinea, for example, whose government has requested international cooperation in addressing security problems in the areas bordering Liberia and Sierra Leone.

The response of governments to the concept of a ladder of options to improve local security in refugee-inhabited areas has been very positive but has remained—so far—in the realm of theory! It is urgent that we take steps to operationalize it and to implement concrete, predictable measures, for example, the deployment of humanitarian security staff. We need to know what contributions may be forthcoming—in human, material, and financial terms—and, again, how quickly they will be available.

Mr. President: I have insisted so far on intermediate security measures because I know that in most situations peacekeeping is simply an unrealistic option, but I also believe that the transition which has started with the end of the cold war has not yet ended, that new (or renewed) conflicts will flare up in different regions, and that the international community will have to maintain peace after very fragile cease-fire agreements are signed. Peacekeeping therefore will continue to remain necessary, but to remain relevant, it will have to adapt to the new environment and become much more effective.

We in the humanitarian community have welcomed the initiative of Secretary-General Kofi Annan of an in-depth review of peace operations. We have been among the most eager supporters of the Brahimi Panel report, and are participating very actively in the discussions on its implementation.

The report is very important and courageous in its attempt to discuss comprehensively and in a broader context how the United Nations can fulfill its key function to help maintain peace and security. But from a more specific, operational, humanitarian perspective, the report is also extremely relevant to UNHCR and its partners, particularly as it sets out a few objectives which, if achieved, would provide crucial support to humanitarian action: It stresses the need for quick decisions in responding to crises; it gives priority to quick fact-finding missions to the field; it underlines the importance of identifying, and pursuing, early solutions; and it places great emphasis on *presence* in the field. These are crucial aspects of the report, the importance of which UNHCR has advocated for years. They are also, by the way, basic elements of any humanitarian deployment. They clearly show the affinity—if I may call it so—between humanitarian action and peace operations and the need to refine their relationship and mutual support.

UNHCR and other humanitarian agencies have large programs in postconflict areas, where peacekeeping is vital. Think of Bosnia, Kosovo, East Timor, just to mention a few. Without peacekeepers, we could not have worked, nor continue to work, effectively in those areas. On the other hand, I am pleased that in discussing the concept of preliminary assessments, the role that is played (and can be played) by humanitarian, field-based agencies has been recognized. It is very important that these agencies are seen as complementary to peace operations and not just as other actors who happen to work in the same areas. In my 1992 briefing to the Security Council, I said that humanitarian action was becoming "dynamically linked to peacekeeping and peace-making." We were then learning important lessons from our close cooperation with UNPROFOR in Bosnia. I am pleased that now the United Nations are finally trying to make this concept a concrete reality.

But speaking not only from a humanitarian but also from a refugee perspective, I would like to take this opportunity to go beyond the conclusions of the Brahimi Panel report.

Look at West Africa, for example. There have been, as you know, cross-border attacks in both Guinea and Liberia, in areas hosting refugees and indeed *because* of the presence of refugees. Beyond Sierra Leone's borders, however, the only presence of the international community, amidst half a million refugees, is humanitarian, because UNAMSIL's mandate is of course limited to Sierra Leone. Yet not only are humanitarian workers seriously at risk in border areas of Liberia and Guinea, but there is also a very real danger that the Sierra Leone conflict will spread and that refugee flows will be one of the conduits of this propagation. The conflict, in simple words, may become regional, but the response, as I have said, continues to be country-based.

I understand of course that to expand peacekeeping beyond a country's borders presents many political hurdles and problems of resources. Sierra Leone is itself a good example of the difficulties encountered by a large operation in an area of relatively low strategic interest, with uncertain prospects, and high risks. The issue of insecurity spilling over across borders from countries in conflict and affecting in particular areas hosting refugees, however, should be examined and factored into strategies for such operations.

West Africa is a case in point, but the matter is broader and particularly serious in Africa; the Burundi, Congo, and Angola conflicts, for instance, pose similar problems. I would like to make a proposal. Could peacekeepers, in situations of refugee flows which may become carriers of instability be given a special, cross-border observatory mandate—in a word, monitor areas hosting refugees *beyond* the borders of the country in which those peacekeepers operate? Refugee-hosting countries, of course, would have to agree, but it would be in their interest, because this expanded concept of peacekeeping could address some of their own concerns in terms of security and stability.

Had we had this form of support, say, in West Timor, maybe the events of last September could have been avoided. Such an arrangement would have also been useful in the former eastern Zaire in 1994 to 1996, and perhaps some of the subsequent violence and instability could have been prevented.

PEACE BUILDING NEEDS MORE ATTENTION

Let me now turn to the second important area on which I want to focus, peace building. For years we have been saying that unless more attention is devoted to the consolidation of institutions and communities after conflict, peace will not hold. UNHCR of course has a very special interest in this process because of its mission to ensure that refugees return home and settle down in safety and dignity. And we have had very difficult experiences in countries emerging from conflict, with large numbers of people returning and resources rapidly dwindling after emergencies have subsided, as in Rwanda, Liberia, and Bosnia, just to mention a few examples.

Its focus on peace building truly makes the Brahimi Panel report very complete. Once more, however, we should shift into operational mode and look at how we can be as comprehensive in action as we are on paper. I will speak, again, from the perspective of the UN refugee agency. Our problem, as I have said many times, is that we do not have the resources, nor indeed the expertise, to run development programes, and yet development agencies are slow to come once emergencies have ended. There is a gap between emergency, short-term humanitarian activities and the implementation of medium to long-term development and reconstruction programs. During this gap, societies can unravel again very easily, and conflicts restart.

I have personally made efforts to coordinate a joint initiative with two key international development partners of UNHCR, the World Bank and UNDP. This initiative, which was launched in January 1999 under the auspices of the Brookings Institution, has become known as the Brookings process. We aimed in particular at filling the gap in funding and the gap in responsibilities and operations. In some countries we have initiated interesting and creative projects, for example, with the World Bank in war-affected areas of Sri Lanka. In others, such as Sierra Leone, we have made proposals for pilot projects involving all three agencies. We are now examining opportunities elsewhere; Burundi, if a peace agreement is eventually implemented, would be a possibility. On our side, we have made great efforts, yet the response by governments and organizations has been very timid, and raising funds for postconflict activities remains a very difficult and uncertain exercise. I must tell you that I am disappointed by the limited response to our work in this area.

For us at UNHCR, peace building is not an abstract concept. We see the concrete, sometimes desperate needs of returnees in devastated areas or in areas where communities continue to be deeply divided. We are doing our part to address these needs. In the eighties we initiated quick impact projects for emergency rehabilitation in areas of return. In some places we were criticized for having gone beyond our mission, but in countries like Rwanda, for example, could we have afforded to withdraw when returnees still lived under plastic sheeting? When schools had no roofs, no books, no teachers?

We are now going further and exploring new avenues—particularly in the promotion of community coexistence as a first step toward reconciliation. We have launched a pilot project, in returnee areas of Rwanda and Bosnia, called Imagine Coexistence, and consisting essentially of support to small, community based interethnic income-generating activities, around which we would like to build clusters of other activities branching off into the community—sports, theater, culture, dialogue. This is one of the innovative approaches that we are taking. But its impact once again will be limited, unless there are more rapid and comprehensive efforts toward peace building at various levels.

One crucial issue, which I would like to mention before concluding, is that of disarmament, demobilization, and reintegration. UNHCR is particularly anxious that effective DDR contributes to the creation of a safe environment for refugees returning home. Without any doubt, DDR is also one of the areas in which UNHCR expects more decisive action by the Security Council. In their great potential, and in the obstacles which undermine them, DDR programes reflect all the contradictions of peace building.

I see two problems which need to be addressed in particular: first, the roles and responsibilities of all actors involved in DDR-related activities must be clarified; second, there must be stronger focus on reintegration, because disarmed and demobilized soldiers, if they are not given opportunities for a future, will go back to more lucrative military activities. These are not small matters, and unless they are addressed seriously, little progress will be achieved in this important area.

ESTABLISHING SECURITY PARTNERSHIPS FOR REFUGEES

Mr. President: The last ten years have proven that if they are not part of a comprehensive political and security approach, humanitarian workers face dangers, are less effective, and even risk aggravating humanitarian crises. What we must establish, at different levels, are what we could call security partnerships for refugees, joint ventures between states hosting refugees, those ready to provide resources, and humanitarian organizations like UNHCR. In my briefing today, I have spoken of practical ways on how to promote such partnerships: by containing insecurity linked to refugee crises; improving peace operations; and focusing more decisively on peace building.

Through security partnerships, together we can create a better security environment, in which refugee protection and solutions can be more effective. This is an essential, if very complex, task. My successor, High Commissioner-elect Ruud Lubbers, has the experience and the stature to carry it out with energy, courage, and creativity.

I trust that the Security Council will give him the same strong and constant support that I have enjoyed in this chamber for the past ten years, support for which I would like to express once more my deep personal gratitude.

I do so, Mr. President, also on behalf of my colleagues and of all the uprooted people they so bravely work with in some of the most dangerous areas in the world.

Please continue to help them.

APPENDIX 2

The Mansfield Lecture, by Sadako Ogata,
United Nations High Commissioner for Refugees,
at the Mansfield Center for Pacific Affairs

Japan, the United States, and Myself:
Global Challenges and Responsibilities

WASHINGTON D.C., MARCH 10, 1999

Friends of the Mansfield Center, distinguished guests, ladies and gentlemen: It is a pleasure and a great privilege to be invited to give the Mansfield lecture, and I wish to warmly thank the Mansfield Center for Pacific Affairs and the Library of Congress for this opportunity. I am especially honored that speaking here tonight allows me to be associated with one of the persons I cherish and respect most, an individual who deserves grateful credit for having effectively highlighted the global importance of U.S.-Japan relations. I am thinking of course of Mike Mansfield.

By the way, I shall start from U.S.-Japan relations. This may surprise you, and perhaps you have been puzzled by the title I gave to my lecture, referring to the United States, Japan, and "myself." I realize that to add *myself* to such a central element of this century's interna-

363

tional relations may sound terribly out of place. Let me therefore spend a few moments clarifying it.

Since the mid-nineteenth century the relationship between the United States and Japan has been of course an important element of the international geopolitical scene on its own merit. Perhaps its most defining feature has been the dramatic shift it underwent fifty-four years ago. Two nations who fought each other in a colossal war have now been close allies for well over half a century. But there is another aspect to it, which is too seldom spoken about. One always refers to U.S.-Japan relations. I would like to talk about U.S.-Japan commitments. We are so focused on their political, economic, financial, and cultural differences and affinities that we tend to forget how together the United States and Japan can and should be essential to the world's wealth and stability. Let me even go further: They should be the driving force behind the achievement of global peace and prosperity.

Naturally, as a Japanese with a family tradition and a lifelong involvement in international relations, and having spent many of my formative years in the United States, I have a keen interest in relations across the Pacific. But as high commissioner for refugees, I feel even more urgently concerned by this relationship, by how it is of support to refugee protection, to humanitarian ideals, and to the concept of global solidarity in general. Much of the work of my office to protect and assist twenty-three million refugees, returnees, and internally displaced people worldwide depends on commitments from the United States and Japan—in terms of political backing, moral support, and financial contributions but, above all, in terms of global leadership.

When I look to the future of U.S.-Japan relations, however, I find many reasons for concern. In both countries, inward-looking trends are prevailing. The sense of international commitment is receding. Foreign policy is increasingly based on populist politics; quick fixes and tactics are substituting for long-term vision and comprehensive strategies. This has an impact on the relationship between the two countries. Has their importance to each other actually diminished? Is Japan not a priority for the United States anymore, and vice versa?

Building a strong economy was the cornerstone of Japan's ethos in the postwar years. This allowed the country to emerge from the ruins of war, to achieve a dominant economic role in Asia and to eventually contribute to the so-called Asian miracle. This very strong focus on economic recovery and the spectacular growth that it produced also partly explains the way the country has responded—or rather, insufficiently responded—to its recent economic problems. The crisis has hit and seriously undermined Japan's very source of strength, the economy. Its reaction can be described almost as a paralysis. This has drawn harsh criticism from the United States and calls for action from Japan's Asian neighbors. At the same time, the crisis seems to have revealed Japan's deeper incapacity to act and lead.

I believe that it is important for all of us to try to understand what has gone wrong in Japan's evolution since the postwar period. Not being an expert, but having been privileged enough to observe this evolution from different and interesting vantage points, I will examine this from a personal perspective.

Of the early postwar years in Japan, I recall, above all, a tremendous determination and desire to learn, to make progress. More broadly, the country was eager to regain an honorable place in the world. These attitudes had a very idealistic and strongly internationalist basis. Japan believed in the value of the international community; it believed in the United Nations. As an example, let me quote Foreign Minister [Mamoru] Shigemitsu, who led the first Japanese delegation to the United Nations in 1956: "We have determined to preserve our security and existence, trusting in the justice and faith of peace-loving peoples of the world. We desire to occupy an honored place in an international society striving for the preservation of peace. Japan is gratified that, together with the maintenance of peace, the United Nations places great importance on humanitarianism."

Pacifism prevailed too. You all know how deeply military defeat affected Japan. The country was in shock in the postwar years. Anti-military, antiwar feelings were extremely strong, and of course there was the protective shield of the U.S. security umbrella. It was from this environment—that of a country where tireless efforts to rebuild the

economy mingled with strong internationalist and pacifist ideals—
that I came when I arrived in the United States, in the fifties, to continue my studies at Georgetown University and then at the University
of California in Berkeley.

Coming to America from Japan, I found an open environment,
tolerant people, liberal academic circles. You could almost breathe
America's growing confidence in its ability, and indeed its duty, to lead
the world. There was an extraordinary openness, a true international
spirit. Many professors and students were migrants and even refugees
(I remember the huge impact of the Hungarian 1956 uprising on
American campuses). For Japanese students like me, it was a heady
experience, being at the sources of American power, democracy, and
technological progress, and being able to learn from them.

As a child I had lived for eight years in the United States and in
China, following my father's diplomatic postings. I was also very
much influenced by my family's critical attitude toward the militarization of Japan between the two wars—particularly after my great-
grandfather Prime Minister [Tsuyoshi] Inukai was assassinated by the
military in 1932. And of course I belonged to the postwar generation
of Japanese scholars of history and political science whose primary
motivation was to examine the causes of World War II. I was particularly interested in studying the causes that had led Japan to an
expansionist policy in Asia and to war and defeat. When I returned to
Japan, therefore, I concentrated on the study of Japanese political and
diplomatic history at the University of Tokyo and soon published my
doctoral dissertation on the making of Japanese foreign policy in
Manchuria in the early thirties. My interest in Asian international
politics, and particularly in U.S.-Japan-China relations, continued
through the eighties. Of my academic period, I remember most
vividly the extraordinary cooperation between Japanese and American scholars. Doing research and writing books together were not
only an intellectual exchange—which produced masterpieces like *Pearl
Harbor as History*, by Dorothy Borg and Shumpei Okamoto—but also a
way to build strong friendship and a vehicle to bring the two countries
together.

The alliance with Japan was a key element of the American security architecture during the cold war. Therefore, U.S.-Japan relations remained extremely close during most of that period. True, the Vietnam War and later rapprochement with China were two major political issues between the two countries, and the Japanese left often opposed the alliance with America. U.S.-Japan government relations, however, remained solid. For Japan, that was a time of very rapid, "miracle" economic growth, twice as rapid as France and Germany and three times the United States. Standards of living in the country improved. Japanese management became an admired, studied, and imitated model.

While Japan's economy boomed, its governments continued to base their foreign policy on the internationalist, pacifist attitudes of the postwar period. The call for international contribution by Prime Ministers [Takeo] Fukuda and [Yasuhiro] Nakasone and their successors was reflected in a substantial increase of overseas development aid. And in an area closer to my current responsibilities, Japan accepted over ten thousand Indochinese refugees starting in 1979, an unprecedented event in its history.

By the late eighties Japan had become the largest creditor nation of the United States. This marked a turn in the tide of U.S.-Japan relations. When Japan started purchasing U.S. government bonds, substantial portions of real estate in Hawaii, and even American landmarks such as the Rockefeller Center in New York, it began to be perceived as a threat to America, for the first time since World War II. A number of books published in the United States during those years—for example, *Japan as Number One*, by Ezra F. Vogel comes to mind—witness to this attitude. Admiring and imitating the Japanese model fell out of fashion. Praise for the industrious, savings-oriented Japanese became scorn for narrow and inflexible economic management methods. The United States started criticizing Japan for not sharing enough of the world economic and financial burden.

This provoked a backlash in Japan. A nationalistic, arrogant mood resurfaced. The crisis point was the gulf crisis in 1990 to 1991.

Although 70 percent of Japan's oil imports were from the gulf region, the country was not ready to send its military in support of Operation Desert Storm. The perception abroad, and in particular in the United States, was that Japan once again did not want to shoulder its fair share of the burden. There was much debate in Japan, including on constitutional matters, and the response was certainly slow, but in the end taxes were raised and Tokyo contributed thirteen billion US dollars (more than its annual development aid budget) to Desert Storm. This was very substantial, indeed, but much as there had been pressure on Japan to contribute, there was, at least from the Japanese point of view, very little international appreciation for a major effort.

After the gulf experience, Japan made another "internationalist" gesture by passing the so-called UN Peacekeeping Cooperation Law in June 1992. Its immediate consequences were the dispatch of observers to monitor elections, starting with Angola, and the deployment of self-defense forces to support the United Nations Transitional Authority in Cambodia and UNIFIL in the Golan Heights. In 1994, self-defense forces were also sent to Goma, in the former Zaire, to assist UNHCR and other humanitarian agencies with the response to the huge Rwandan refugee emergency. All these interventions, including unprecedented military interventions, certainly represented a breakthrough in Japanese foreign policy. It should be noted, however, that their mandate was carefully limited and defined, reflecting the prevalence—still—of a nonmilitary, largely pacifist consensus in national priorities.

Let me now go back to my own changing perspective. Starting in 1968, I served on the Japanese delegation to the United Nations General Assembly and in other fora, including three and a half years as minister at the Permanent Mission of Japan to the United Nations in New York. I therefore witnessed at first hand the increasing international involvement of my own country. In those times American and Japanese positions in the United Nations were close, but colored by different interests; the Middle East and Palestinian issues were a case in point. As the cold war drew to a close, international relations entered a more confused, less rigidly structured period. UN politics became determined by shifting alignments reflecting diverse national and bilateral interests, with multilateralism frequently losing ground and failing to resolve global challenges.

In 1991, at the height of the gulf crisis, I was elected United Nations high commissioner for refugees. The prediction that the end of the cold war would put an end to, or at least greatly reduce, the refugee problem proved wrong.

My first field mission, in April, was a helicopter reconnaissance of the mountains between Turkey, Iran, and northern Iraq, where over one million Kurds had taken refuge in the fastest mass exodus in contemporary history. The gulf crisis was a major turning point for humanitarian and refugee work. It gave a new dimension not only to material assistance to victims of conflict and mass displacement but also to the manner in which political action and humanitarian aid interact with each other. The Kurdish exodus was followed closely by other crises of major proportions; let me just mention the conflict in the former Yugoslavia, which displaced millions of civilians; a new explosion of genocidal violence in the Great Lakes region of Central Africa, which caused the flight of millions of people from Burundi and Rwanda. More recently, conflicts in Kosovo and Sierra Leone dashed the hopes that the post–cold war turmoil would just be a transient adjustment period. Something had fundamentally changed. Humanitarian action was not anymore confined to the rear lines of political and military conflict, as it had been, mostly, during the cold war. In northern Iraq, Somalia, Rwanda, former Zaire, and Bosnia—and still today in Kosovo, Sierra Leone, and Afghanistan—humanitarian action has moved to the heart of wars, to their geographical center, thus exposing humanitarian workers to the same kind of dangers to which are exposed civilian victims of conflict, and to their political core, often becoming, unwittingly, an instrument to prolong fighting and an unarmed pawn in the hands of the armed parties.

To be effective, humanitarian action has always required political solutions. In the post–cold war context, in which crisscrossing national interests have substituted for the ideological divide which predominated before, political support is even more essential to the solution of conflicts. And yet it has become harder to mobilize.

Most crises today are not addressed through the exercise of global leadership mobilizing international commitment, but through an ad hoc convergence of interests and makeshift ideals. Take the work of my office, for example. It protects and assists millions of civilians fleeing violence and conflict or trying to rebuild their homes and lives in situations of very fragile peace. But its action depends on creating an environment in which people stop being refugees, can return home safely, and live again in peace within their communities. In many cases efforts to create this environment are considerable. They include, most of all, political support and also material and financial resources, sometimes with military backup. They must be based on a comprehensive and well-planned political solution. Bosnia and Kosovo are examples of crises which are being addressed through such efforts, mostly thanks to the leadership of the United States. However, since the abortive Somalia operation in 1993, the U.S. has become cautious in dispatching ground troops or approving UN peacekeeping forces to prepare the ground for political settlements. In many crisis situations, like Afghanistan, Angola, southern Sudan, Sierra Leone, no such leadership has been exercised, and innocent people continue to suffer and die.

As I said earlier, Japan in the past fifty-four years has made significant efforts to become a meaningful part of the international community. This may appear normal to many in Europe or the United States. But it is less obvious if you are familiar with Japan—its insular mentality, its loneliness, one should almost say—and of course if you remember that the starting point of this internationalist trend was a devastating defeat.

I believe that at this delicate juncture in history, it is indispensable that Japan continues on this path. Its international commitment must be reinforced, and "internationalism" must be one of its leading policy goals. Before it is too late, Japan must move away from inward-looking and nationalist trends and its depression diplomacy, as referred to by Yoichi Funabashi. The temptation of such trends will remain strong as long as the current economic crisis persists, but the Japanese must not forget that not only their economy but also their political and security interests have a global base. Japan has benefited for decades from a favorable open international environment. It must now continue to endorse an internationalist approach. Policy guidance must be based on the reaffirmation of a globalist stance and actively seek public consensus in the same direction.

I am also very worried that the public commitment of the United States to provide international leadership is receding. Look at its elected representatives, its administration, its media, its civil society associations. With many notable exceptions, which must be recognized, their focus and attitudes are generally becoming inward-looking. They are often based on an internal political agenda, and often an electoral one, rather than on a broader commitment to international leadership. In this context, the unpaid American assessed contributions to the United Nations are a very serious problem. They cast a heavy shadow on the organizational viability of the United Nations. More important, they are perceived as reflecting a diminished interest in the international organization.

I do not wish to underestimate the deep causes that are at the root of this problem, and in particular the very fundamental frustration, in certain sectors of American leadership and society, over the impossibility to fully exercise a controlling influence in the United Nations. But America today must choose once more to be internationalist. Let us not forget that at all other critical junctures of its history, the United States opted for internationalism. In doing so, it provided global leadership in the true sense of the word, leadership that allowed millions of people in the entire world to live in peace, freedom, and relative prosperity. If America's choice today is once more in favor of internationalism—and I hope it will be—it will be difficult to seek public support for it, without, at the same time, providing a significant proof of commitment to the United Nations.

The direction which the United States will take is likely to have an impact on its major allies, including of course Japan. It is of grave concern to me that the United States' interest in Japan seems to be decreasing. The very importance of Japan in the Asian geopolitical context is seen as diminishing. President Clinton's nine-day visit to China last year was perceived as if America were focusing on China and bypassing Japan. This impression was reinforced by the criticism, expressed together by the United States and China, of Japan's financial policies. Indeed, Japan today is increasingly being seen as contributing to the risk of a major world recession.

Let me therefore go back to my starting point. We always speak of U.S.-Japan relations, but we should think of U.S.-Japan commitments. We should reflect on the broad economic, social, and democratic roots of our relationship that were carefully cultivated in the postwar years. As I said, when many of us came to study in the United States, we left behind a country recovering from war but full of the energy of a newly discovered openness to the world, and we had in front of us what we considered both the cradle and the realization of universal values upon which a free, democratic, and just global leadership had been achieved and had triumphed. In spite of all differences, there was a profound affinity between Japan's aspiration and potential, and America's achievements and strength. That affinity was rooted in an outward-looking, internationalist approach, in all fields—political, economic, social, and cultural.

I am deeply concerned that such an approach may be weakening—in bilateral U.S.-Japan relations and in the relations of the two countries with the rest of the world. This is most worrying to all of us, whose efforts will be in vain if nationalist or isolationist tendencies prevail. Internationalism today must be based on a keener recognition of the diverse development needs and cultural values in the world. This commitment to inclusiveness has two complementary facets: It must be turned externally toward less developed countries and internally toward the most vulnerable elements of societies and especially minorities, migrants, and refugees. It must be directed toward working for the realization of an inclusive international community, prosperous and secure, based on democratic values.

In conclusion, the United States and Japan must restore the sense of shared engagement that prevailed in the postwar years. Their commitment to bilateral relations can and must continue to be the cornerstone of an international system based on the mutual respect and enrichment of different societies and cultures, on democratic values and on peace and prosperity for all, the international system which the founding fathers of the United Nations wanted the global organization to uphold.

This in turn could lead to some clear initiative to rekindle internationalism in the next century. Let me therefore conclude my reflections with a proposal. Humanitarianism may offer a well-defined ground for America and Japan to launch such initiative. Why not together set a common humanitarian agenda based on a joint commitment to global solidarity toward refugees and other deprived people?

On our part, we stand ready to respond:

Thank you, ladies and gentlemen.

NOTES

INTRODUCTION

1. United Nations Convention Relating to the Status of Refugees: "Article 1 (2) . . . any person who . . . owing to well-founded fear of being persecuted for reasons of race, religion, nationality, membership of a particular social group or political opinion, is outside the country of his nationality and is unable or, owing to such fear, is unwilling to avail himself of the protection of that country; or who, not having a nationality and being outside the country of his former habitual residence . . . is unable or, owing to such fear, is unwilling to return to it. . . ." "Article 33 (1) No Contracting State shall expel or return ('refouler') a refugee in any manner whatsoever to the frontiers of territories where his life or freedom would be threatened on account of his race, religion, nationality, membership of a particular social group or political opinion."

I. THE KURDISH REFUGEE CRISIS: SETTING THE STAGE

1. UN Security Council Resolution 688 of April 5, 1991:
   1. Condemns the repression of the Iraqi civilian population in many parts of Iraq, including most recently in Kurdish populated areas, the consequences of which threaten international peace and security in the region;
   2. Demands that Iraq, as a contribution to removing the threat to international peace and security in the region, immediately end this repression, and in the same context expresses the hope that an open dialogue will take place to ensure that the human and political rights of all Iraqi citizens are respected;
   3. Insists that Iraq allow immediate access by international humanitarian organizations to all those in need of assistance in all parts of Iraq and make available all necessary facilities for their operations;
   4. Requests the Secretary-General to pursue his humanitarian efforts in Iraq and to report forthwith, if appropriate on the basis of a further mission to the region, on the plight of the Iraqi civilian population, and in particular the Kurdish population, suffering from the repression in all its forms inflicted by the Iraqi authorities;
   5. Also requests the Secretary-General to use all the resources at his disposal, including those of the relevant United Nations agencies, to address urgently the critical needs of the refugees and displaced Iraqi population;
   6. Appeals to all Member States and to all humanitarian organizations to contribute to these humanitarian relief efforts;

7. Demands that Iraq cooperate with the Secretary-General to these ends;

8. Decides to remain seized of the matter.

2. Letter from the high commissioner to Turgut Ozal, president of the Republic of Turkey, April 3, 1991.

3. Report from John Telford, Uludere/Turkey, to UNHCR, Geneva and Ankara, April 16, 1991.

4. Aide-Mémoire, Tugay Ozceri, undersecretary of the Ministry of Foreign Affairs, Turkey, and the high commissioner, April 17, 1991.

5. UNHCR, note for the file, meeting of secretary-general with U.S. delegation, April 24, 1991.

6. Ibid.

7. UN appeal for UN guard contingent and annex to UN-Iraq memorandum of understanding of April 18, 1991.

8. Note on UNHCR's emergency response capacity, Executive Committee of the High Commissioners' Program, EC/1992/SC2./CRP. 15, September 14, 1992.

9. "Britain to Push for Umbrella UN Relief Agency," *Guardian*, May 14, 1991.

10. "Strengthening the International Order," political declaration of the London Economic Summit 1991, July 16, 1991.

2. PROTECTING REFUGEES IN THE BALKAN WARS

1. Letter from Secretary-General Javiar Pérez de Cuéllar to the HC, November 14, 1991.

2. Personal and confidential note to HC from Eric Morris, director, Division of Programs and Operational Support, later compiled and presented on October 20, 1993.

3. UNHCR, update on the former Yugoslavia, September 6, 1992.

4. Report from Jose Maria Mendiluce, special envoy of the high commissioner for the former Yugoslavia, January 4, 1993.

5. UNHCR, statement of the HC to the International Meeting on Humanitarian Aid for Victims of Conflict in the former Yugoslavia, Geneva, July 29, 1992.

6. UNHCR, summary of principal themes raised during the International Meeting on Humanitarian Aid for Victims of the Conflict in the Former Yugoslavia, Geneva, July 29, 1992.

7. The six groups were: the Bosnia and Herzegovina Working Group, to promote a cessation of hostilities and develop a constitutional setup; the Ethnic and National Communities and Minorities Working Group, to recommend measures to solve ethnic problems with a special group on the former autonomous province of Kosovo; the Succession Issues Working Group, to solve issues emerging from the establishment of six new states; the Economic Issues Working Group, to deal with arising economic issues; the Confidence and Security Building and Verification Measures Working Group, to develop measures covering military movements, arms control, and arms transfers and limitations; and the Humanitarian Issues Working Group to promote humanitarian relief in all its aspects, including refugees.

8. For complete documentation of the International Conference on the Former Yugoslavia and the documents of the working groups, see *The International Conference*

on the Former Yugoslavia: Official Papers, vols. 1 and 2, ed. B. G. Ramcharan (Boston: Kluwer Law International, 1997). For a personal account of the political negotiations by the ICFY cochairmen, refer to David Owen, *Balkan Odyssey* (London, Victor Gollancz, 1995).

9. HC's statement to the 3134th meeting of the Security Council, November 3, 1992.
10. HC's statement to the Humanitarian Issues Working Group meeting, July 16, 1993, included in *International Conference on the Former Yugoslavia: Official Papers*, vol. 2, pp. 1419–24.
11. HC's letter to Secretary-General Boutros Boutros-Ghali, January 15, 1993.
12. UNHCR, update on former Yugoslavia, February 17, 1993.
13. Letter of HC to Secretary-General Boutros Boutros-Ghali, February 17, 1993.
14. Cable to Sadako Ogata, high commissioner for refugees, UNHCR Geneva, from Jean-Claude Aime, chief of staff, EOSG UNATIONS, New York, February 18, 1993.
15. UNHCR, Francois Fouinat, note for the file, visit to UNHCR office by Bosnian Vice-President Dr. Ejup Ganic, February 21, 1993.
16. *Times* of London, February 20, 1993. *Independent*, February 20, 1993.
17. Re: Decision to partially suspend aid to Bosnia-Herzegovina. Strictly confidential report from Irene Khan to HC.
18. UNHCR, Bosnia and Herzegovina, Laurens Jolles, report on situation in Srebrenica, March 15, 1993.
19. Letter from HC to Secretary-General Boutros Boutros-Ghali, April 2, 1993.
20. UN Security Council Resolution 713 of 1992 stated that all states should, for purpose of establishing peace and stability in Yugoslavia, immediately implement a general and complete embargo on all deliveries of weapons and military equipment to Yugoslavia until the Council decided otherwise.
21. Fax transmission from Jose Maria Mendiluce, special envoy, to HC, April 13, 1993.
22. Report by Tadeusz Mazowiecki, special rapporteur, on the situation of human rights in the former Yugoslavia, E/CN.4/1992/2-1/10.
23. UNHCR, "Safe Areas for Humanitarian Assistance—Position of UNHCR," December 14, 1992.
24. Dispatch from Jose Maria Mendiluce, Sarajevo, April 19, 1993.
25. UN Security Council Resolution 836, June 4, 1993.
26. UNPROFOR, interoffice memorandum, brainstorming discussion papers, February 4, 1994.
27. Letter from HC to T. Stoltenberg, special representative of the secretary-general, June 5, 1993.
28. Report from Kumin and Garlock, Srebrenica and the safe area concept, UNHCR Belgrade, May 22, 1993.
29. Memorandum from Nicholas Morris, UNHCR special envoy for the former Yugoslavia, to Yasushi Akashi, special representative of the secretary-general, "The Implications for UNHCR of Developments in Bosnia," May 6, 1994.
30. Report of the secretary-general, S/1995/444, May 30, 1995.
31. Statement by President Bill Clinton regarding Bosnia cease-fire agreement, White House briefing room, Washington, D.C., October 5, 1995.
32. Statement by the HC to the Humanitarian Issues Working Group of the International Conference on the Former Yugoslavia, Geneva, October 10, 1995.

33. UNHCR, note for the file, HC's meetings with Izetbegovic, Silajdzic, Cero, and Vladusic, December 7, 1995.

34. UNHCR, note for the file, HC's meetings with President Tudjman and Foreign Minister Granic, December 6, 1995.

35. UNHCR, note for the file, HC's meeting with President Milosevic, December 6, 1995.

36. UNHCR, Sitrep 27, Sarajevo, March 16-17, 1996.

37. UNHCR, note for the file on meeting with Serb residents in Vogosca, February 24, 1996.

38. HC's statement to the Humanitarian Issues Working Group of the Peace Implementation Council, Geneva, December 16, 1996.

39. UNHCR, note for the file, HC's meeting with President Milosevic, April 9, 1998.

40. Martha Minow, *Between Vengeance and Forgiveness* (Boston: Beacon Press, 1998).

41. UNHCR, note for the file on meeting between HC and Ibrahim Rugova and Veliko Odalovic, April 10, 1998.

42. HC's briefing to the UN Security Council, April 21, 1998.

43. Letter from HC to President Milosevic, September 26, 1998.

44. UNHCR, note for the file, on HC meeting with OSCE Secretary-General Giancarlo Aragona, Vienna, October 15, 1998.

45. UNHCR, note on EU Petersberg meeting on the situation in the southern Balkans, April 1, 1999.

46. Letter from HC to NATO Secretary-General Javier Solana, April 3, 1999.

47. Letter from HC to OSCE Secretary-General Giancarlo Aragona, April 3, 1999.

48. HC's statement to the Humanitarian Issues Working Group of the Peace Implementation Council, April 6, 1999.

49. Letter from HC to Bratislava Morina, Serbian commissioner for refugees, April 29, 1999.

50. UN press release, statement on Kosovo by the secretary-general, April 9, 1999.

51. UNHCR, confidential note for the file on the high commissioner's meeting with U.S. Deputy Secretary of State Strobe Talbott, April 28, 1999.

52. For the negotiation process, see Wesley K. Clark, *Waging Modern War* (New York: Public Affairs Press, 2001), ch. 14.

53. UNHCR, report from Soren Jessen-Petersen on mission to the former Yugoslav Republic of Macedonia and Albania, June 13-17, 1999.

54. UN Security Council Resolution 1244, June 10, 1999.

55. UNHCR, end of mission report by Dennis McNamara, "Humanitarian Activities in Kosovo," August 2000.

3. CRISES IN THE GREAT LAKES REGION OF AFRICA

1. Gérard Prunier, *The Rwanda Crisis: History of a Genocide* (New York, Columbia University Press, 1995), pp. 61-67.

2. UN Security Council Resolution 918 of May 17, 1994.

3. Prunier, op. cit., pp. 281-99.

4. Note from Gerald Walzer, deputy high commissioner, to Peter Hansen, undersecretary-general for humanitarian affairs, Department of Humanitarian Affairs, New York, July 11, 1994.

5. UNHCR, mission report from Eric Morris on Rwanda/Zaire emergency, ops room, July 24, 1994.
6. UNHCR, Update on Rwanda, July 14 and 17, 1994.
7. UNHCR Goma, sitrep from Filippo Grandi, senior emergency officer, July 24, 1994.
8. John Lange, "Civil Military Cooperation and Humanitarian Assistance: Lessons from Rwanda," *Parameters*, U.S. War College quarterly (Summer 1998).
9. UNHCR, note for the file on HC's visit with the prime minister of France, July 22, 1994.
10. UNHCR, report from Michel Moussalli, "Humanitarian Action in Rwanda," July 21, 1994.
11. UNHCR, report from Daniel Bellamy, special unit for Burundi and Rwanda, July 29, 1994.
12. UNHCR Goma, Filippo Grandi, reports on incidents involving returnees, August 12, 1994.
13. UNHCR Tanzania, protection reports from border-crossing points, May 14–15, 1994.
14. Reuters, September 23, 1994, Geneva.
15. Reuters, September 26, 1994, Kigali.
16. Letter from Secretary-General Boutros Boutros-Ghali to Pasteur Bizimungu, president of the Republic of Rwanda, October 5, 1994.
17. For comparative analysis of various positions with regard to repatriation, see Joel Boutroue, *Missed Opportunities: The Role of the International Community in the Return of the Rwandan Refugees from Eastern Zaire*, Rosemary Rogers Working Paper Series, Inter-University Committee on International Migration, Massachusetts Institute of Technology, June 1998.
18. UNHCR, Yvan Sturm, confidential report commissioned by HC and headed "Power Systems and the Means of Controlling Refugee Population, Militarization, Arms Dealing and Fund-raising Mechanisms in the North and South Kivu Refugee Camps," Geneva, December 1997.
19. UNHCR Goma, Filippo Grandi, "Deterioration of Security Situation in North Kivu," August 26, 1994.
20. UNHCR Goma, sitrep 13 from Joel Boutroue, October 28, 1994.
21. Yvan Sturm, confidential report. See note 18.
22. Letter from Dr. Philippe Biberson, president, Médecins sans Frontières France, to HC, December 1, 1994.
23. Letter from A. John Watson, executive director, Care International, to HC, October 21, 1994.
24. UNHCR, HC's proposal presented at the donors' meeting in Geneva, October 31, 1994.
25. Report of the secretary-general to the Security Council, S/1994/1308, November 18, 1984.
26. UN Security Council Resolution 1011, August 16, 1995.
27. UNHCR, opening statement by HC at the Tripartite Commission, Rwanda/Zaire/UNHCR, Geneva, September 25, 1995.
28. "Chasser les Refugies Rwandais? Je Ne Suis Pas d'Accord," *Le Libre Belgique*, October 20, 1995.
29. Letter from Jimmy Carter to HC, November 26, 1995.

30. Cable from Marrack Goulding, undersecretary-general for political affairs, to HC, subject: Cairo Conference on the Great Lakes region, November 27, 1995.
31. Cairo Declaration on the Great Lakes Region, November 29, 1995.
32. Boutroue, op. cit. p. 54.
33. UNHCR, report by Carrol Faubert, subject: Headquarters consultations on Great Lakes, December 18, 1995.
34. Statement by HC to the Security Council, June 28, 1996.
35. UNHCR Kigali, note for the file, report from W. R. Urasa, "Returnees and Refugees from Masisi," March 16, 1996.
36. Letter from HC to Secretary-General Boutros-Ghali, April 20, 1996
37. Communication from Marrack Goulding to HC, subject: Masisi refugees, New York, May 24, 1996.
38. Statement attributable to a spokesman for the secretary-general, Monday, September 16, 1996.
39. UNHCR Uvira, Alphonse Malanda, report of emergency mission to Uvira, August 7–October 8, 1996.
40. Statement by the HC to the forty-seventh session of the Executive Committee of the High Commissioner's Program, October 7, 1996.
41. Statement of the Rwandese delegation to the forty-seventh session of the Executive Committee of the High Commissioner's Program, October 7–11, 1996.
42. UNHCR Kigali, report from W. R. Urasa on the meeting with Vice-President Paul Kagame, July 12, 1996.
43. "Why Rwanda Admitted to Its Role in Zaire," *Johannesburg Mail and Guardian*, August 8, 1997.
44. UNHCR, confidential note from Augustine Mahiga, coordinator, Special Unit for Rwanda and Burundi (SURB), subject: Military situation in Kivu—possible attack on Zaire by Rwanda, October 16, 1996.
45. UNHCR, confidential note for the file, HC's meeting with Secretary-General Boutros Boutros-Ghali, October 23, 1996.
46. Statement by HC to the Security Council, October 25, 1996.
47. UNHCR, Update, "Ogata Urges Rwandan Refugees to Consider Repatriation," October 25, 1996.
48. UNHCR, notes for the file on HC's New York meetings, October 31–November 1, 1996.
49. UNHCR, note for the file, HC telecom with President Museveni, November 8, 1996.
50. UNHCR, report from Soren Jessen-Petersen to HC on the implementation of Security Council Resolution 1078, November 12, 1996. UN Security Council Resolution 1080, November 15, 1996.
51. John Pomfret, "Rwandans Led Revolt in Congo," *Washington Post*, July 9, 1997.
52. UNHCR, report from Soren Jessen-Petersen to HC on troop contributors' meeting, November 20, 1996.
53. UNHCR, Augustine Mahiga, coordinator, SURB, "Refugees in Eastern Zaire—Population Numbers," November 20, 1996.
54. UNHCR New York, from Petersen.unhcr@un.org, eastern Zaire, December 14, 1996.

55. UNHCR, Geneva, note for the file, policy meeting on the Great Lakes region, December 21, 1996.

56. UNHCR Goma, confidential note for the file, Filippo Grandi meeting with Laurent Kabila, November 16, 1996.

57. Report by Martin Griffis on the mission of UN agencies to eastern Zaire, December 18–20, 1996.

58. UNHCR Goma, note for the file, Filippo Grandi meeting with Laurent D. Kabila, chairman of the AFDL, February 1, 1997.

59. UNHCR, note for the file, HC telecom with Emma Bonino, February 3, 1997.

60. UNHCR Nairobi, note for the file, W. van Hovell, HC's missions to Zaire, February 9, 1997.

61. Letter from HC to Secretary-General Kofi Annan, April 23, 1997.

62. Letter from HC to Laurent Kabila, president of AFDL, April 25, 1997.

63. Statement by HC to the Security Council, April 28, 1997.

64. Human Rights Watch, Democratic Republic of the Congo, "Civilian Killings and Impunity in Congo, Human Rights Abuses Committed by the ADFL," October 1997.

65. UNHCR, report from Dennis McNamara to HC, "Protection Mission to Great Lakes Region," May 26, 1997.

66. Letter to U.S. Secretary of State Madeleine Albright from Leonard S. Rubenstein, Physicians for Human Rights, September 17, 1997.

67. Letter from Christopher H. Smith, chairman, Subcommittee on International Operations and Human Rights, to President Bill Clinton, August 28, 1997, "Investigations in Eastern Congo and Western Rwanda—A Report by Physicians for Human Rights, July 16, 1997; John Pomfret, "Massacres Were a Weapon in Congo's Civil War," *Washington Post*, June 11, 1997.

68. UNHCR, note for the file, HC's meeting with U.S. Ambassador Bill Richardson, Geneva, October 29, 1997.

69. Statement by the HC to the Security Council, September 9, 1997.

70. UNHCR Tanzania, report from Andrew Sokiri, "Return of Refugees from Tanzania," November 27, 1996.

71. UNHCR Tanzania, message to all refugees in Tanzania from the government of the United Republic of Tanzania and the Office of the United Nations High Commissioner for Refugees, transmitted by L. Kostalainen to UNHCR, December 5, 1996.

72. Amnesty International, "Rwanda Human Rights Overlooked in Mass Repatriation," January 14, 1997.

73. UNHCR Rwanda, *Rwanda Recovery: UNHCR's Repatriation and Reintegration Activities in Rwanda from 1994–1999* (Cape Town: CTP Book Printers, 2000), pp. 40–50.

74. Ibid., pp. 53–58.

75. Ibid., pp. 87–92. For evaluation of the women's initiative, refer to the report of the Women's Commission for Refugee Women and Children, "You Cannot Dance If You Cannot Stand: A Review of the Rwanda Women's Initiative and the United Nations High Commissioner for Refugee's Commitment to Gender Equality in Post-conflict Societies," April 2001.

4. THE AFGHAN REFUGEES

1. For the recent history of Afghanistan leading to the rise of the Taliban see Ahmed Rashid, *Taliban: Islam, Oil and the New Great Game in Central Asia* (London: I. B. Tauris Publishers, 2000).

2. Cochairs' summary of conclusions, the Tokyo International Conference on Reconstruction Assistance to Afghanistan, Ministry of Foreign Affairs, Tokyo, January 21–22, 2002.

3. Refer to Afghan Ministry of Rural Reconstruction and Development, "Background Note on the Ogata Initiative (OI)," April 21, 2004.

Background and Concept

1. The Government of Japan launched the OI in August 2002 to assist the smooth reintegration of IDPs and returnees to a secure living environment, to support regional comprehensive development in Afghanistan, and to achieve a seamless transition from humanitarian assistance to recovery and reconstruction, and eventually to longer-term development. To this end, the UN and other agencies, under the ownership of the Afghan Government, would implement projects focusing on regional recovery. Inherent to this concept is developing the capacity of the Afghan Government and enhancing cooperation between the national and sub-national levels. Interventions funded under the OI should converge into multi-sectoral appropriate assistance "packages" tailored to cater to the specific needs of each region in order to meet the OI objectives. To achieve this, implementing agencies must engage in joint planning prior to submitting proposals.

2. Three priority regions for comprehensive development under the OI were selected—Nangarhar, Kandahar and Balkh provinces and their surroundings. Under the fourth funding phase of the Ogata Initiative, Afghanistan's Central region was added through an expression of interest of the donor to possibly fund the interagency "Kapisa Initiative," a project submitted for funding by UNDP as administrative agent on behalf of ten UN agencies.

Funding phases

3. The OI is currently at the beginning of its fourth funding phase, both time-wise and programmatically, with each new phase building on the previous one(s).

PHASE I, starting in August 2002, totaled approximately US $27 million. It focused on assistance for the reintegration of returnees and IDPs to meet their needs in terms of transportation, shelter, food and water, education, and health facilities etc.

	Aug. 02–July 03	Agency	UNHCR	UNICEF	ICRC
PHASE 1		Project activities	1. Shelter 2. Supply of drinking water 3. IDP assistance 4. Distribution of seeds and agricultural tool kits 5. Mobile clinic unit; rehabilitation of a clinic	1. Shelter 2. Supply of drinking water 3. IDP assistance 4. Distribution of seeds and agricultural tool kits 5. Mobile clinic unit; rehabilitation of a clinic	1. Food distribution for returnees
	U.S. $26.7 million	Timeframe	Aug. 02–Dec. 02	Aug. 02–Aug. 03	Aug. 02–Aug. 03
		Budget (U.S. dollars)	12.8 million	10.8 million	4.6 million

PHASE 2, starting in October 2002, totaled approximately US $41 million. It focused on the sustainable return of refugees and IDPs, and also targeted local communities in areas of return. Activities in the fields of rehabilitation of technical and social infrastructure, capacity building and income generation were added.

	Oct. 02–Sept. 03	Agency	UNHCR	UNICEF	ICRC	WFP	MACA/UNOPS	UN-HABITAT
PHASE 2		Project activities	1. Shelter 2. Infrastructure rehabilitation (roads, irrigation, clinics) 3. Quick impact income generation 4. Winterization	1. Immunization 2. Safe motherhood 3. Nutrition 4. Water and sanitation in schools 5. Teacher training	Health assistance	FFW for returnees (road rehabilitation, irrigation infrastructure etc.)	1. Mine risk education 2. Mine clearance 3. Aid for mine victims	1. Shelter 2. Water supply
	U.S. $41.2 million	Timeframe	Oct. 02–Sept. 03	Oct. 02–Sept. 03	May 02–Dec. 02	Nov. 02–June 03	Nov. 02–Oct. 03	Nov. 02–Apr. 03
		Budget (U.S. $)	11.5 million	9.2 million	4.5 million	12.6 million	4.9 million	2.6 million

Coordination

4. In its original concept paper, the Ogata Initiative stipulated a coordination role for UNAMA. The aid coordination set-up was initially described as follows: "(1) UNAMA [. . .] will supervise the related agencies and coordinate the overall programs. Following up the regional situation, UNAMA will provide guidance to all related agencies. UNAMA will also coordinate the implementation with [the] Afghanistan Transitional Authority and local authorities. (2) Practical aid coordination will be ensured by mainly UNHCR, UNICEF and WFP. Coordination meeting[s] will be held in Kabul as well as in each region. Implementing agencies will share information and cooperate for aid coordination, thus achieving effective and strategic partnership. (3) Regular consultation meetings at the Embassy of Japan. [. . .] [R]egular consultation meeting[s] will be held to follow up the progress of activities by each agency. In addition, all stakeholders will exchange information and views on regional situations, thus pursuing more effective assistance."

5. In Phases 1 and 2, UNAMA was present at OI meetings at central level. During Phase 3, UNAMA regularly met with the donor, was actively involved in recommending proposals for funding and facilitated a number of Japanese missions to the OI target areas. Phase 4 marks the strongest UNAMA coordination role thus far, with proactive involvement in framework setting at the central level and coordination of joint planning at the regional level. UNAMA has also attempted to provide the link between the central and the regional levels, and to ensure a two-way information flow.

6. UNAMA coordination in the field was virtually inexistent during Phases 1 and 2. In Phase 3, it gained pace, but varied between the target regions with respect to its set-up and level of intensity. A major constraint for coordination was the sometimes-weak capacity and the high staff-turnover of UNAMA and the UN agencies, as well as—in the case of Jalalabad—the limited presence of agencies.

7. The UNAMA offices agreed in April 2004 to suggest to the agencies the streamlining of regional and provincial coordination structures into one "Ogata

Initiative Programme Committee" at provincial level, involving the provincial governments and including a capacity building component, and an "Ogata Partners Coordination Group" at regional level.

8. The Central Government, through MoRR. MUDH and MRRD, was less involved in Phases 1 and 2, but participated in the project selection process for Phase 3, and took up a much stronger role, especially through MRRD, in the planning of Phase 4. MRRD cosponsored the October 2003 workshop and took an active part in the development of a program framework for Phase 4. The provincial governments in the target regions (mainly the Governor's Offices and DRRD-PMAs) were also strongly involved in Phase 4 planning. They have, together with the UN, decided on target regions and priority types of interventions from a field perspective.

Capacity building of provincial government

9. A first structured approach to government capacity building was taken in Mazar-i-Sharif in Phase 3. In terms of concrete activities, WFP, UNICEF, and UNHCR jointly assessed how they could complement their activities in three districts of Balkh province that they commonly identified for implementation under Phase 3. UNHCR was designated as lead agency for planning and implementation of activities, and UNAMA plays the lead coordination role in the agencies' collective engagement toward government capacity development through the so-called Balkh Province Program Cell or Ogata Cell. The cell is located in the governor's office and brings together the different (deputy) department heads. Through a capacity development program that was elaborated together by the three agencies and UNAMA and sessions facilitated by UN staff, the members of the cell were first trained in developing and implementing a monitoring framework for Phase 3 of the Ogata Initiative, and have progressively been enabled to actively participate in needs assessments and planning for Phase 4. The Balkh Programme Cell will be renamed Ogata Initiative Programme Committee in Phase 4.

10. Through setting up Ogata Initiative Program Committees, which are modeled after the Balkh Ogata Cell, in Kandahar and Jalalabad, too, structured approached to government capacity building will take place on a larger scale in Phase 4.

Integrated approach of UN agencies

11. Integration of agency interventions took place for the first time in Phase 3 in Mazar-i-Sharif, where UNICEF, UNHCR, and WFP implemented their (separately planned) Phase 3 projects in the same three districts in a coordinated manner, and used a common implementing partner.

12. Planning for Phase 4 provided for much stronger inter-linkages of agencies' interventions than the previous phases, with a total absence of an integrated approach in Phases 1 and 2. UNAMA and the agencies have, at regional level, agreed upon a number of target districts in each Ogata province in January 2004. While funding for UNHCR, UNICEF, and UNMACA is confirmed already, and while the other agencies are awaiting a decision from the donor, the UN regional teams have started to jointly define a village (cluster) targeting process as well as a process for the identification of implementing partners.

PHASE 3, starting in March 2003 and still ongoing, totalled approximately US$ 22 million. It goes further in the direction of recovery, rehabilitation and (very moderately) development.

	Apr. 03– Dec. 03	Agency	UNHCR	UNICEF	UNDP	MACA	UN- HABITAT
PHASE 3		Project activities	1. Shelter 2. Supply of drinking water	1.Water and sanitation in schools 2. Teacher training	NABDP: 1. Housing reconstruction 2. Canal rehabilitation 3. Capacity-building of provincial administration	1. Mine clearance 2. Provision of a technical advisor in the South to oversee major ongoing reconstruction initiatives 3. Mine awareness	1. Shelter 2. Supply of drinking water 3. Road rehabilitation 4. Income generation
	U.S. $21.8 million	Timeframe	Apr. 03– Dec. 03	Apr. 03– Mar. 04	Apr. 03– Mar. 04	Apr. 03– Mar. 04	Apr. 03– Mar. 04
		Budget (U.S. $)	8.8 million	4.5 million	1.9 million	3.8 million	2.9 million

PHASE 4, which is starting in April/May 2004, is expected to total some US $22–24 million. To launch the planning process for Phase 4, the Embassy of Japan brought together all stakeholders in a workshop in Kabul in October 2003. A set of framework criteria for funding was finalized in the aftermath of this workshop and shared with all interested parties. Joint planning at regional level was done through workshops in the Ogata target regions. The three main themes of Phase 4 are employment creation, capacity building and community empowerment, with interventions expected to be more developmental in character. It was decided that the Phase 4 target regions include the provinces of Kandahar and Helmand in the South, Nangarhar in the East, Balkh and Faryab in the North, and Kapisa in Central region.

	Apr. / May 04– Mar. / Apr. 05	Agency	UNHCR	UNICEF	WFP	MACA	UN- HABITAT
PHASE 4		Project activities	1. Well construction 2. Road rehabilitation (FFW/CFW) 3. Income generation / skills development	1. School water supply & hand-washing facilities 2. Construction of latrines in schools 3. Hygiene education for teachers and community health promoters 4. Training of hand pump mechanics 5. Teacher training 6. Education, skills training, psycho-social support and employment provision for child soldiers 7. Establishment of community-based schools 8. Construction of four BHC	1. Construction of classrooms and teacher housing units; provision of furniture 2. Provision of water and sanitation facilities for teachers and students 3. Community & counterparts' empowerment through training	1. Survey, clearance, and certification of Ogata project sites 2. Training of new demining teams	1. Solid waste collection and environmental awareness for communities 2. City-level solid waste collection & disposal 3. Water supply and sanitation 4. Improvement of drains and culverts
	U.S. $22–24 million (exp.)	Budget ($) requested	2.2 million	3.9 million	3.2 million	3.9 million	2.7 million
		Budget ($) received	2.3 million	3.2 million	Not yet decided	3.2 million	Not yet decided

	Apr. / May 04– Mar. / Apr. 05	Agency	UNOPS	UNDP	UNDP on behalf of 10 agencies	FAO	WHO
PHASE 4		Project activities	1. Construction of classrooms and teacher housing units 2. Water and sanitation **UNODC** Drug awareness and community mobilization	1. REAP II: Construction of mini dairies; construction of cool & cold storage facilities; establishment of packaging/bottling facilities for mushrooms, honey, vegetables, crops, and fish 2. NABDP: diverse activities corresponding to PPE priorities 3. Capacity Building through Joint Monitoring Cells	Kapisa Initiative: 1. Creation of fish farms 2. Poultry production 3. Improvement of irrigation infrastructure 4. Establishment of a cold storage facility 5. Vocational training 6. Provision of business development services 7. Rehabilitation and construction of a market place and shop stalls 8. Provision of safe drinking water and sanitation facilities in schools 9. Mine surveys, clearance and certification of project sites 10. Assessments of rural economy subsectors and business skills training needs 11. Survey and rehabilitation study of Gulbahar textile factory	1. Establishment of sustainable animal health services 2. Establishment of an artificial insemination program 3. Honey production 4. Dairy production and marketing	1. Training of health workers 2. Health and hygiene education for women 3. Construction of training centers for MoH 4. Provision of drugs and equipment 5. Upgrading of nursery schools
	U.S. $22–24 million (exp.)	Budget ($) requested	UNOPS: 680,000 UNODC: 33,000	6.4 million	2.2 million	3.3 million	940,000
		Budget ($) received	Not yet decided	Not yet decided	Not yet decided	Not yet decided	Not yet decided

4. Statement of Lakhdar Brahimi, former special representative of the secretary-general for Afghanistan, to the UN Security Council, New York, January 15, 2003.

5. CONCLUSION: HUMANITARIAN ACTION IN WAR AND PEACE

1. UN Security Council Resolution 929, June 22, 1994.
2. Wesley Clark, *Waging Modern War* (Washington, D.C.: Public Affairs, 2001), p. 109.
3. UNHCR, "Security, Civilian and Humanitarian Character of Refugee Camps and Settlements: Operationalizing the 'Ladder of Options,'" EC/50/SC/INF 4, June 27, 2000.
4. HC's briefing to the UN Security Council, November 10, 2000.
5. Refer to Martha Minow, and Antonia Chayes and Martha Minow, eds. *Between Vengeance and Beginning* (Boston: Beacon Press, 1998), *Imagine Coexistence*, Publication of the Program on Negotiation at Harvard Law School (San Francisco, Josse-Bass, 2003).

INDEX

Page numbers in *italics* refer to maps and tables.